80386

A Programming and Design Handbook

Penn Brumm
Consultant/Development
Project Leader
Control Data Corporation

Don Brumm
Staff Systems Programmer
Operating Systems Development
Amdahl Corporation

TAB Professional and Reference Books

Division of TAB BOOKS Inc.
P.O. Box 40, Blue Ridge Summit, PA 17214

Trademarks

MS-DOS is a trademark of Microsoft Corporation.
UNIX is a trademark of Bell Laboratories.
MULTIBUS is a trademark of Intel Corporation.
The Instruction mnemonics in Section 2 are copyright of Intel Corporation.

FIRST EDITION

FIRST PRINTING

Library of Congress Cataloging in Publication Data

Brumm, Penn.
    80386—a programming and design handbook.

    Bibliography: p.
    Includes index.
    1. Intel 80386 (Microprocessor)—Programming.
2. Electronic digital computers—Design and construction.
I. Brumm, Don. II. Title.
QA76.8.I2684B78   1987   004.165   87-14008

ISBN 0-8306-0937-7
ISBN 0-8306-2937-8 (pbk.)

Questions regarding the content of this book should be addressed to:

    Reader Inquiry Branch
    Editorial Department
    TAB BOOKS Inc.
    P.O. Box 40
    Blue Ridge Summit, PA 17214

Front cover photograph courtesy of Intel Corporation.

Table of Contents

iPSB Parallel System Bus • iLBX II Local Bus Extension • iSSB Serial
Bus

Introduction

The most significant advance of Intel Corporation's 80386 32-bit processor is that it brings microprocessors to the world of virtual systems, opening the door to commercial and scientific uses once excluded from desktop systems.

A second major breakthrough is that the 80386 removes the barriers that operating systems and applications developers found in previous generations of microprocessor chips. Additional improvements include 32-bit instruction enhancements, large linear address programming model, and memory paging functions. Most important to businesspeople, these advances are incorporated in a superset manner to maintain full compatibility with software products developed for the 8086/8088 and 80286.

Generally, four types of people pick up a book like this. The first is a generalist who wishes to understand the history and architecture of a process or a physical entity such as the 80386 chip. The second is the programmer who, given a system by an original equipment manufacturer (OEM) designer, needs to program that system to function in the user world. Included in this second group are all those programmers who work for software houses that must keep up to date with the latest hardware revolution.

The third kind of person who reads a book like this is the OEM designer who has been given an assignment to take the chip and build a system. That designer first needs a good overview of the new chip's architecture. Finally, there are the managers who must oversee one or all of the first three.

It is difficult to structure material when writing about such an involved and interrelated subject as the 80386; what comes first, second, and so on? We finally decided to begin with basic building blocks (such as registers and data types) and go from there.

One additional factor was taken into consideration when planning the book. Often people are experts in one area and novices in another. In the areas of least knowledge, a quick refresher makes all the difference between a fast start-up and weeks of confusion.

Overall, this book is divided into sections to help each of its potential readers immediately identify where to go first. Chapters 1 through 5, the first section of the book, give the architectural overview of the 80386 to lead the reader from the internals of the chip outward to the associated subsystems that must work with the 80386. In addition, some basic concepts are explored.

Chapters 6 through 10, the second section of the book, are directed to the system-level programmer and/or programming manager, and go into the instruction set provided for the 80386 chip. Each instruction of the full instruction set is described and most are demonstrated so you can understand in detail how the instruction interacts with the various registers and system flags. The demonstrations are written to exercise flag settings and register changes. The code does not represent the most efficient or complete way to perform a function and is not intended to be a tutorial on how to program.

Chapters 11 through 14, the third book section, are where the general overview comes in. This is where you go if you need that quick refresher to some topic such as pipelining, interfacing concepts, and memory organization.

The appendices provide additional information that brings you up to date with this versatile and exciting new chip. Appendix 1 reviews background information about Intel Corporation and the design strategies that led to the 80386. Appendix 2 summarizes the various registers, bits, and flags that the 80386 uses. Appendix 3 assists when you run into a bit of jargon that is stated as letters you may not be familiar with. Appendix 4 reviews how the 80386 interacts with MULTIBUS® I and II. Appendix 5 lists an assembly language program that demonstrates several of the instructions that are available in protected mode only (more on protected mode in Section 1). The code was written using 80386 adapter board plugged into the processor slots of an 80286-based system. Microsoft Corporation's Macro Assembler was used as the assembler; it recognizes opcodes from the 8086 through 80286; the 80386 opcodes were input in hexadecimal form.

The 80386 provides unprecedented power at a microcomputer level along with upward compatibility from earlier chips. Users can gain immediate performance improvements from current software without the expense of converting to a new system. Future software development will unlock the total power of the 80386.

It would have been difficult to write a book like this, with its internal details of a new microprocessor, without the cooperative support of Intel Corporation, which loaned us 80386 documentation and an 80386 Adapter Board. A special thanks goes to Rod Skinner who generously gave of his time and technical support. Also, from Intel, Jenny Marquez was extremely helpful.

Qualified technical reviewers are difficult to find, especially those who willingly give of their closely scheduled time. We appreciate the efforts of Dave Birdsall and Gary Lewis for their reviews and technical comments.

Also helpful were Hank Ta and Tim Luong, engineers at Cassidy Computers, who built and tested our 80286 system and who installed and tested the 80386 Adapter Board.

Last, a sincere thanks to Bess Clayton for her continued support and assistance, without whom a lot of things could never happen.

1

Introduction to The 80386

Intel Corporation's 80836 Microprocessor enters the market with a unique advantage. It is the only 32-bit processor that taps into the existing $6.5 billion base of application software written for the previous generations of 8086/88 through the 80286 (the IBM PC and its clones).

Systems are said to be compatible if programs written on one will execute successfully on the other. If the compatibility extends in only one direction, from old to new, it is said to be "upward." Upward compatibility at the object level supports an end-user's software investment as new systems replace older and slower ones. The 80386 is upwardly compatible with older generations of Intel microprocessors. That is, software written specifically for the 80386 and using 80386 features generally will not run on the older systems. However, since the 80386 instruction set and processing modules are a superset of the previous instructions sets, the older code is upwardly compatible to the 80386.

The 80386 features multitasking, on-chip memory management, virtual memory with paging, software protection, and large address space. Hardware compatibility with earlier chips is preserved through the dynamic bus-sizing feature.

Intel implemented the 80386 using their CHMOS III technology, which is a semiconductor process that combines the high frequency of HMOS (*High Density Metal-Oxide Semiconductor*) with the modest power consumption of CMOS (*Complementary Metal-Oxide Semiconductor*). The 80386 can switch between programs running under different operating systems, such as MS-DOS and UNIX. This switching allows software designers to incorporate standard 16-bit applications directly onto the 32-bit system.

The processor defines an address space as one or more segments, any size from 1 byte to 4 gigabytes (four billion bytes). The segments can be individually protected by privilege levels and thus selectively shared between tasks. The protection mechanism is based on the notion of a privilege hierarchy, a graded or ranked series. That

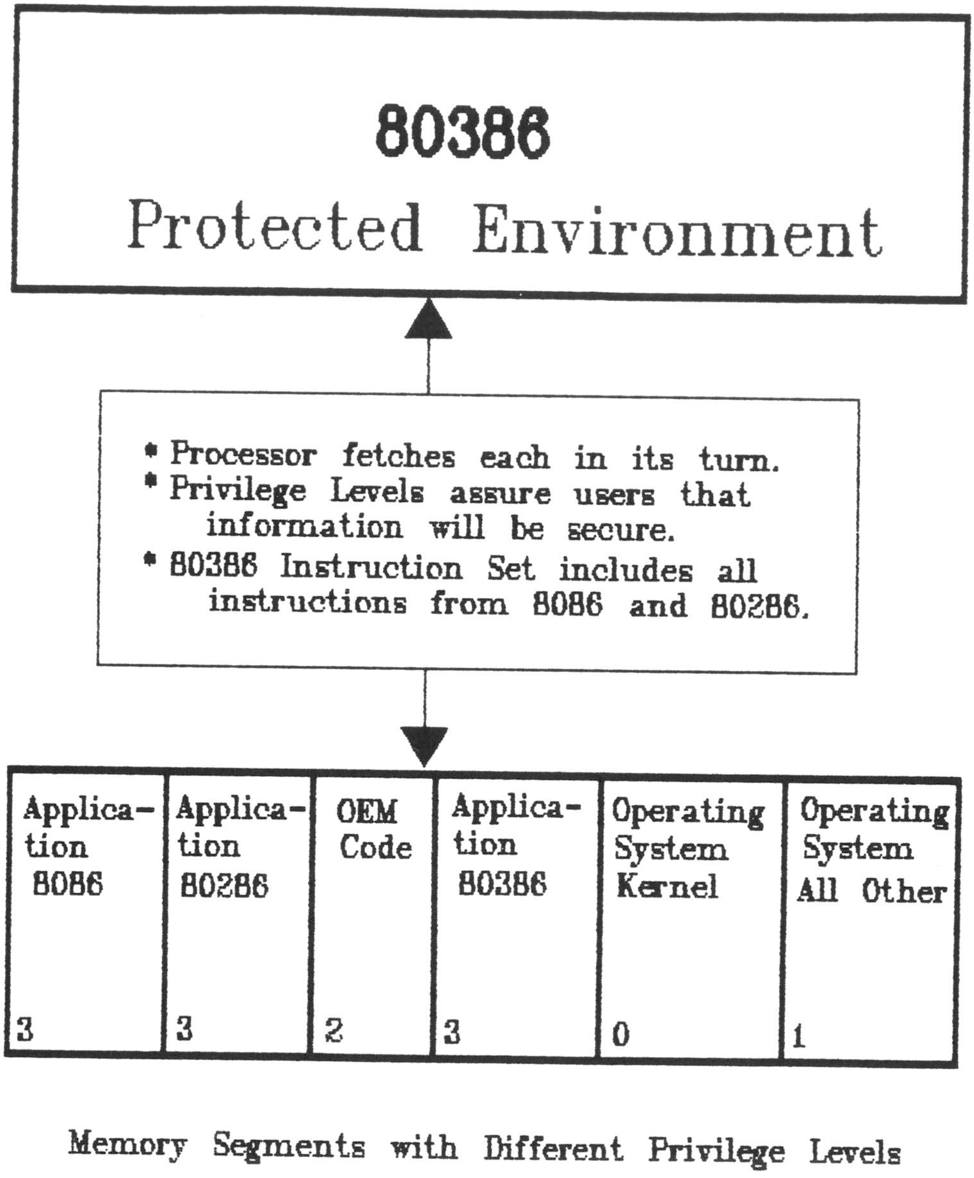

80386
Protected Environment

* Processor fetches each in its turn.
* Privilege Levels assure users that information will be secure.
* 80386 Instruction Set includes all instructions from 8086 and 80286.

Applica-tion 8086	Applica-tion 80286	OEM Code	Applica-tion 80386	Operating System Kernel	Operating System All Other
3	3	2	3	0	1

Memory Segments with Different Privilege Levels

Fig. 1-1. 80386 support.

is, various tasks or programs can be assigned certain levels that are used exclusively for that task.

In the illustrations in this book, note that certain register bits are undefined, or shown as reserved for future Intel use. Treat these bits as undefined since future processors may change them—without notice. Do not depend on the states of any of these *un*defined bits when testing the values of defined register bits. Mask them out when testing. Also, do not depend on the ability to retain information written into any of the undefined or reserved bits. When loading registers, always load these bits as zero or as unchanged from their stored values.

BASIC DEFINITIONS

Before proceeding, a few basic terms need defining. These concepts are often referred to both in this book and in articles about the 80386. Many of the terms have Intel and/or 80386-based specific meanings.

SEGMENT—Beginning with the 8086, Intel introduced the concept of segments, which are defined as units of contiguous (adjacent) address space. In the 8086, a segment has a maximum of 64K or 65536 bytes. In the 80386, that limitation no longer applies. Programmers can now view segments as one-dimensional subspaces, each having a length of up to 4 gigabytes.

GATES—A gate is a logic element that allows only certain processes to pass through it. The 80386 provides protection for control transfers among executable segments at differing privilege levels by use of gate descriptors. There are four kinds of gates (Call, Trap, Interrupt, and Task), all described in Chapter 6.

DESCRIPTOR—A descriptor is a data structure used to define the characteristics of a program element. For example, descriptors describe a data record, a segment, or a task.

TABLE—A table is a collection of data laid out in rows and columns for reference or stored as an array. Elements of a table can be obtained by direct calculation from a known selector or base address.

LINEAR ADDRESS SPACE—An address indicates the location of a register, a particular place in storage, or some other data source or destination. In the 80386, linear address space runs from byte 0 to 4 gigabytes. A linear address points to a particular byte within this space.

LOGICAL ADDRESS—First, there is no conceptual parallel from Linear address space to the space used by logical addressing. A logical address consists of a selector and offset. The selector points to some segment descriptor (part of which is that segment's linear base address). The offset tells how far into the segment the required byte is. The various terms used in this preliminary description are all described in detail within the first section of this book. Logical Address is mentioned here to introduce the concept and its difference from the other types of addresses.

PHYSICAL ADDRESS—The address which actually selects the memory where a required byte is located. In the 80386, linear and physical addresses differ only when paging is in effect.

TASK—A task is a basic, unique function of a program or system. It can be one instance of the execution of a program. Tasks are also referred to as processes.

TASK STATE SEGMENT—TSS. A TSS is a data structure delineated and pointed to by a descriptor, wherein the (interrupted) state of a task is stored. Systems software creates the TSSs and places the initial information in them, such as correct stack pointers for interrupt handlers.

MICROCODE—A list of small program steps, also a set of control functions performed by the instruction decoding and executing logic of a computer system. It's code that is "below" the level of assembly language.

PAGING—Paging refers to a procedure that transmits the consecutive bytes called

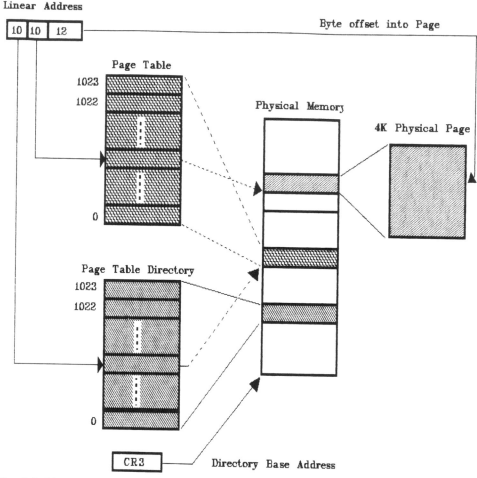

Fig. 1-2. Linear to physical address mapping.

a page between locations, such as between main storage and memory. Paging simplifies the operating system swapping algorithms because it provides a uniform mechanism for managing the physical structure of memory.

FLAG—A flag is an indicator whose set/not set state is used to inform a later section of a program whether or not a condition has occurred.

32-BIT PROCESSOR OVERVIEW

Integration of functions links elements into a single structure that cannot be divided without destroying the stated functions. The 80386 chip has an integrated memory management and protection architecture that includes address translation registers, multitasking hardware and a protection mechanism to support a number of operating systems. This memory management and protection mechanism translates logical addresses to physical addresses and enforces the protection necessary for maintaining task integrity in a multitasking environment.

Basic Units

Basically, the 80386 consists of six units that operate in parallel. Those units are: the Bus Interface Unit (BIU), the Code Prefetch Unit, the Instruction Decode Unit, the Execution Unit (EU), the Segmentation Unit, and the Paging Unit.

An interface is a device (physical or logical) that connects adjacent components, circuits, equipment, or system elements. The BIU provides the interface between the 80386 and its environment. It accepts internal requests for code fetches (from the Code Prefetch Unit) and data transfers (from the Execution Unit), and prioritizes the requests. At the same time, it generates or processes signals to perform the current bus cycle. These signals include the address, data, and control outputs for accessing external memory and I/O. The BIU also controls the interface to external bus masters and coprocessors.

Lookahead is a feature that permits a system to obtain code or data prior to actually using it. The Code Prefetch Unit performs the program lookahead function of the 80386. When the BIU is not performing bus cycles to execute an instruction, the Code Prefetch Unit uses the BIU to fetch sequentially along the instruction byte stream. These prefetched instructions are stored in the 16-byte Code Queue to wait processing by the Instruction Decode Unit.

The Instruction Decode Unit takes instruction bytes from the Prefetch Queue and translates them into microcode. The decoded instructions are then stored in a three-deep Instruction Queue, on a FIFO (First-In-First-Out) basis, to await processing by the Execution Unit. Immediate data and opcode offsets are also taken from the Prefetch Queue.

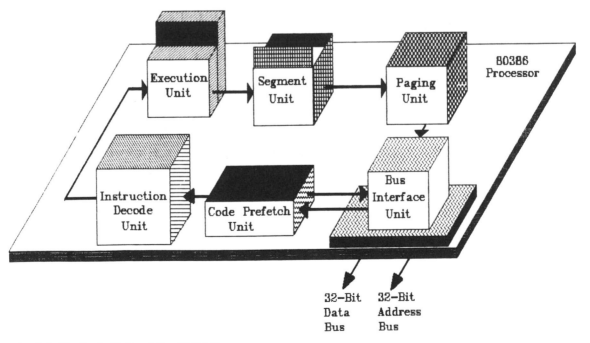

Fig. 1-3. Six Basic Units of the 80386 Processor.

The EU executes the instructions from the Instruction Queue, and communicates with all other units required to complete the instruction. To speed up the execution of memory reference instructions, the EU starts executing any memory reference instruction while the previous instruction is still executing. Because memory reference instructions are frequent, a performance gain of about nine percent is achieved by the overlap.

General registers are on-chip (internal) locations used for operations, such as binary addition, or to compute and modify addresses. They have found increasing use as replacements for special registers such as accumulators. The EU contains eight 32-bit general registers used for both address calculation and data operations. The EU also contains a 64-bit barrel shifter used to speed the shift, rotate, multiply, and divide operations.

The Segmentation Unit translates logical addresses into linear addresses at the request of the EU. The on-chip Segment Descriptor Cache stores the currently-used segment descriptors to speed this translation. While it translates, the Segmentation Unit checks for segmentation violations. These checks are separate from the static segmentation violation checks performed by the Protection Test Unit. The translated linear address is forwarded to the Paging Unit.

When the Paging Unit's paging mechanism is enabled, the Unit translates linear addresses into physical addresses. If paging is *not* enabled, the physical address is the same as the linear address, and no translation is necessary. The Page Descriptor Cache stores recently used Page Directory and Page Table entries in its Translation Lookaside Buffer (TLB) to speed this address translation. The Paging Unit then forwards physical addresses to the BIU to perform the memory and I/O accesses.

The 80386 is a 32-bit processor that uses separate 32-bit registers and data paths to support 32-bit addresses and data types. In fact, a 32-bit memory access can be completed in only two clock cycles, enabling the bus to maintain a throughput of 32 megabytes per second at 16 MHz. The processor addresses up to four gigabytes (4 billion bytes) of physical memory and 64 terabytes (64 trillion) of virtual memory.

Memory Management Unit (MMU)

To handle segmentation, the memory management unit (MMU) consists of a segmentation unit and a paging unit. The *segmentation unit* provides four levels of protection (zero through three) to both isolate and protect applications and the operating system from each other. This component also allows easy code and data relocatability and efficient sharing.

The MMU's *paging unit* operates beneath (and transparent to) the segmentation process. This transparency allows the physical address space to be managed separate and independent from the segment management. Each segment is mapped into a linear address space which, in turn, is mapped onto one or more 4K-byte pages. To implement an efficient virtual memory system, the 80386 supports full restartability for all page and segment faults.

Real and Protected Mode Architecture

The 80386 has two modes of operation: real address mode (called real mode)

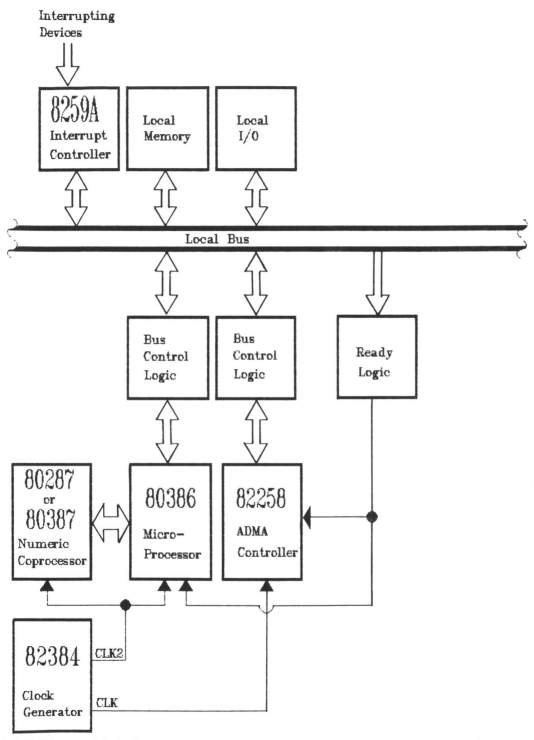

Fig. 1-4. 80386 system block diagram.

and Protected Mode. *Real mode* is required primarily to set up the processor for the protected mode operation and to allow execution of previous chip generation software. *Protected mode* provides access to the advanced paging, memory management, and privilege capabilities of the 80386. These design features allow object-code compatibility with previous Intel chips. Real mode, protected-mode, and virtual 8086 environment are overviewed here and discussed in detail in Chapter 8.

Real Mode. When the processor is reset or powered up, it starts in real mode. Here, the 80386 operates as a very fast 8086, but with 32-bit extensions if the programmer desires. Real mode has the same base architecture as the 8086 (see Appendix 1 for more information on the 8086), but also allows access to the 32-bit register set of the 80386. The 8086 addressing mechanism, memory size, and interrupt handling (and their consequent limitations) are all identical to the real mode on the 80386.

Real mode uses two components to form the logical address. A 16-bit selector is used to determine the linear base address of a segment. The base address is then used as the 32-bit physical address. The difference between the two modes lies in how the base address is calculated.

Relocatability is a property of programs or data such that they may be located in different places in memory at different times without requiring modification to system or application software. Segment relocation is done in the 80386 real mode as it is in the 8086. The 16-bit value in a segment selector is shifted left by four bits (multiplied by 16) to form the 20-bit base address of a segment. The effective address is extended with four high-order zeros (to give a 20-bit value) and added to the base to form a linear address. This linear address is equivalent to the physical address because paging is not used in real-address mode.

Interrupts and exceptions are breaks in the normal flow of a system or routine. Interrupts and exceptions in 80386 real-address mode work exactly as they do on the 8086. (See Chapter 3 for a list of the interrupts recognized by the 80386.) In real mode, the Interrupt Descriptor Table (IDT) is an 8086 real interrupt vector table, starting at real zero and extending through real 1024 (4 bytes per interrupt with 256 possible entries).

The only way to leave real-address mode is to explicitly switch to protected mode. The 80386 enters the protected mode when a MOV to CR0 (Move to Control Register Zero) instruction sets the protection enable (PE) bit in CR0. For compatibility with the 80286, the LMSW (Load Machine Status Word) instruction may also be used to set the PE bit.

The processor re-enters real-address mode if software clears the PE bit in CR0 with a MOV to CR0 instruction.

Protected Mode. The complete capabilities of the 80386 are available when it operates in protected mode. Software can perform a task switch to enter tasks designated as virtual 8086 mode tasks. Each such task behaves with 8086 semantics (the relationship between symbols and their intended meanings independent of their interpretation devices). This allows 8086 software—an application program or an entire operating system—to execute on the 80386. At the same time, the virtual 8086 tasks are isolated and protected from one another and from the host 80386 operating system.

Like real mode, Protected mode uses a 16-bit selector to specify an index into an operating system-defined table that contains the 32-bit base address of a given segment. The physical address is formed by adding the base address obtained from the table to the offset.

In general, programs designed for the 80286 will run without modification on the 80386. Also, the 80386 supports the descriptors used by the 80286, as long as the Intel-reserved word (low-order word) of the descriptor is zero.

DATA TYPES

The 80386 divides memory into 8-bit bytes, 16-bit words, and 32-bit double words (DWords). A byte is eight contiguous bits starting at any logical address and the bits are numbered 0 through 7, with bit zero as the least significant bit. Figure 1-5 shows a comparison of the basic data types.

Words are stored in high-byte, low-byte order. The value which in AX would be 0201_{16} would appear in memory as 0102. (It seems that byte-oriented transfers and reverses to/from registers are with us forever.) Thus, words contain 16 bits, with the low-order byte at the lower address and the high-order byte at the higher address.

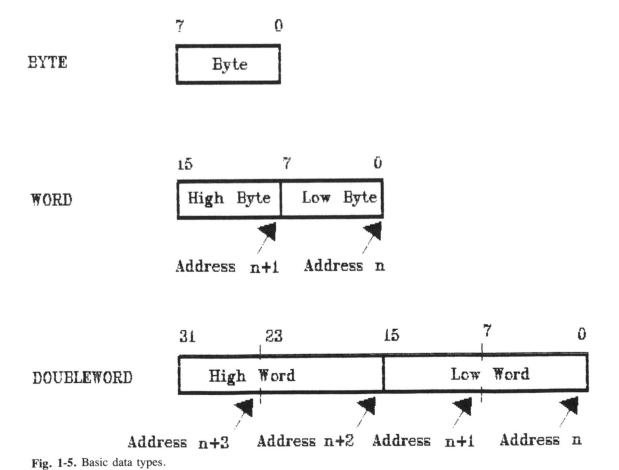

Fig. 1-5. Basic data types.

Each byte within a word has its own address. The address of the word or DWord is the byte address of the low-order byte.

To allow maximum flexibility in data structures and efficient memory utilization, words need *not* be aligned at even-numbered addresses. Nor do doublewords need to be aligned at addresses evenly divisible by four. However, when used in a system configuration with a 32-bit bus, data transfers between processor and memory take place in units of doublewords, beginning at addresses evenly divisible by four. The processor converts the requests for misaligned words or doublewords into the sequence of requests that is acceptable to the memory interface. Thus, a misalignment of data reduces performance by increasing the number of memory cycles. For the best performance, align data structures and stacks so that word operands start at even addresses and doubleword operands start at addresses evenly divisible by four.

Since prefetching and queuing occur within the CPU, instructions needn't be aligned on word or doubleword boundaries. There is a slight increase in speed if they *are,* however.

In addition to bytes, words, and doublewords, the 80386 also supports these additional data types:

UNPACKED BINARY CODED DECIMAL (BCD)—An unpacked byte representation of a decimal digit in the range 0 through 9. Unpacked decimal numbers are stored as unsigned byte values, with one digit in each byte. The magnitude of the number is determined from the low-order half-byte (or nibble). The high-order half-byte must be zero for division and multiplication, but it may contain any value for subtraction or addition.

PACKED BCD—A packed byte representation of two decimal digits, each in the range of 0 through 9. One digit is stored in each half-byte. The digit in the high-order half-byte is the most significant. The range of a packed decimal byte is 0 through 99.

BIT FIELD—A contiguous sequence of bits in which the position of each binary digit is considered as an independent unit. A bit field may begin at any bit location of any byte and may be up to 32 bits long.

BIT STRING—Like a bit field, a bit string is a contiguous sequence of bits. A bit string may begin at any bit position of any byte and may be up to $2^{32} - 1$ bits long.

NEAR POINTER—A 32-bit logical address that represents the offset within a segment. Near pointers are used in either a flat or a segmented model of memory organization.

FAR POINTER—A 48-bit logical address of two components: a 16-bit segment selector and a 32-bit offset. Far pointers are used by programmers only when system designers choose a segmented memory organization.

INTEGER—A signed binary value contained in a 32-bit doubleword, a 16-word, or an 8-bit byte. All operations assume a 2's complement representation. The sign bit is located in bit 7 in a byte, bit 15 in a word, and bit 31 in a doubleword. It is zero for positive integers and one for negative. Since this high-order bit is used as the sign, and 8-bit (byte) integer can range from -128 to $+127$, a 16-bit (word) integer may range from $-32,768$ through $+32,767$, and a 32-bit integer (doubleword or Dword) ranges from -2^{31} to $+2^{31} - 1$. The value zero has a positive sign.

ORDINAL—An unsigned binary value contained in an 8-bit byte, a 16-bit word or a 32-bit doubleword. All bits are considered in determining the magnitude of the number. The value range of a byte is 0 through 255. A word can range from 0 through 65536 and a doubleword form 0 through $2^{32} - 1$.

STRING—A contiguous sequence of bytes, words or double words. A string may contain from zero through $2^{32} - 1$ bytes, or 4 gigabytes.

REGISTERS

A register is a temporary storage device that is used to facilitate arithmetical, logical, and transfer operations. The 80386 registers are a superset of the previous 8086, 80186, and 80286 registers. All the previous generations' 16-bit registers are contained within the 32-bit architecture.

REGISTER	USE IN REAL MODE		USE IN PROTECTED MODE		USE IN VIRTUAL 8086 MODE	
	LOAD	STORE	LOAD	STORE	LOAD	STORE
General Registers	Yes	Yes	Yes	Yes	Yes	Yes
Segment Registers	Yes	Yes	Yes	Yes	Yes	Yes
Flag Register (EFLAGS)	Yes	Yes	Yes	Yes	IOPL	IOPL
Control Registers	Yes	Yes	PL=0	PL=0	No	Yes
GDT Register (GDTR)	Yes	Yes	PL=0	Yes	No	Yes
LDT Register (LDTR)	No	No	PL=0	Yes	No	Yes
IDT Register (IDTR)	Yes	Yes	PL=0	Yes	No	No
Transaction Register	No	No	PL=0	Yes	No	No
Debug Control	Yes	Yes	PL=0	PL=0	No	No
Test Registers	Yes	Yes	PL=0	PL=0	No	No

PL=0 — The register can be accessed only when the current privilege level (CPL) is zero.

IOPL — The PUSHF and POPF instructions are made I/O Privilege Level sensitive in Virtual 8086 Mode.

Fig. 1-6. Register availability.

The 80386 includes six directly accessible segment selector registers, which contain values that point to the segments. These selector values can be loaded as a program executes and also are task-specific, which means that the segment registers are automatically reloaded when the 80386 switches tasks. (Note: in ''back'' of the segment selector registers are actual segment cache registers which contain the description of the segment indicated by the selector. This is done in the hardware to avoid an additional memory fetch when segment description is needed.)

There are a few differences regarding the availability of the registers in real and protected mode. Figure 1-6 summarizes them.

General Registers

The eight general-purpose registers are 32 bits long and hold addresses or data. They support data operands of 1, 8, 16, 32 and (by using two registers) 64 bits; bit fields of 1 to 32 bits; 16- and 32-bit address operands. These registers are named EAX, EBX, ECX, EDX, ESI, EDI, EBP, and ESP.

The least significant 16 bits of the registers are separately accessible. This is done in most assemblers by using the 16-bit names of the registers: AX, BX, CX, DX,

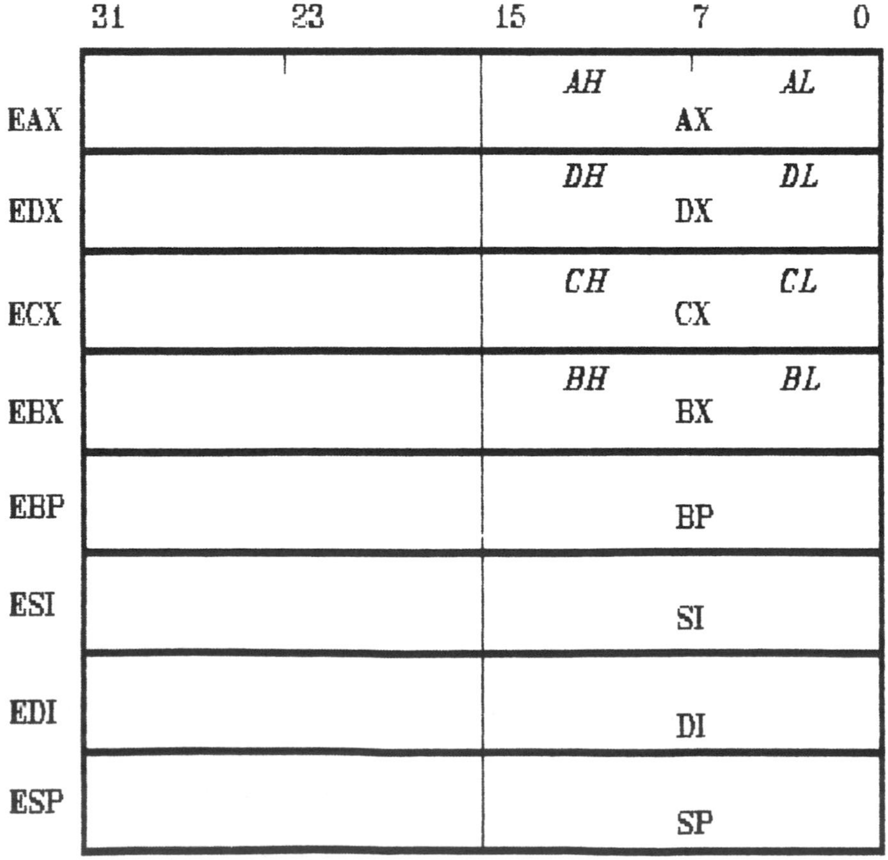

Fig. 1-7. General registers.

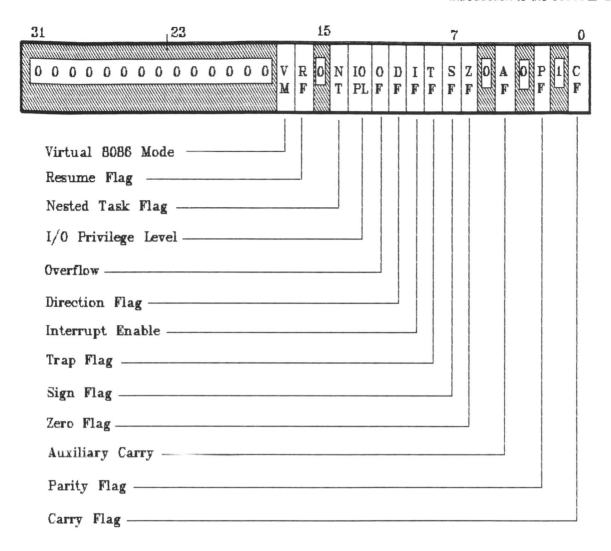

A 1 or 0 indicates Intel Reserved. Do not define.

Fig. 1-8. EFLAGS register.

SI, DI, BP, and SP. Figure 7 shows the format of the general registers.

8-bit operations can individually access the low byte (bits 0-7) and the high byte (bits 8-15) of the general registers AX, BX, CX, and DX. The low bytes are named AL, BL, CL, and DL, respectively, while the high bytes are named AH, BH, CH, and DH. Again, this selection is done by most assemblers by using the register names.

System Flags Register

The EFLAGS register controls I/O, maskable interrupts, debugging, task switching, and enabling of virtual 8086 execution in a protected, multitasking environment;

all this, in addition to providing status flags which represent the result of instruction execution. Figure 1-8 shows the EFLAGS register contents. The low 16 bits (0-15) of EFLAGS contain the 80286 16-bit status or flag register named FLAGS, which is most useful when executing 8086 and 80286 code.

In the following descriptions, the term "set" means "set to 1," and "reset" means "clear to zero."

VM (Virtual 8086 Mode Bit 17—The VM bit provides Virtual 8086 Mode within the protected mode. If set while the processor is in protected mode, the 80386 switches to Virtual 8086 operation. The VM bit can be set *only* two ways: in protected mode by the IRET instruction and only if Current Privilege Level is zero; and by task switches at any privilege level.

RF (Resume Flag) Bit 16—This flag temporarily disables debug exceptions (breaks to normal program flow) so that an instruction can be restarted after a debug exception without immediately causing another debug exception.

NT (Nested Task) Bit 14—The 80386 uses this flag to control chaining of interrupted and *CALL*ed tasks. A CALL transfers the program execution sequence on a temporary basis to a subroutine or subprogram. On termination of that subroutine, execution is resumed at the instruction following the CALL. NT influences the operation of the IRET instruction.

IOPL (Input/Output Privilege Level) Bits 12-13—This two-bit field applies to protected mode. IOPL shows the highest current privilege level (CPL) value permitted to execute I/O instructions without generating an exception 13 fault or consulting the I/O Permission Bitmap. It also shows the highest CPL value that allows change of the IF (INTR Enable Flag) bit when new values are popped (See POP and PUSH in Chapter 10) into the EFLAGS register.

OF (Overflow Flag) Bit 11—OF is set if the operation resulted in carry/borrow into the sign bit (high-order bit) of the result but did not result in a carry/borrow out of the high-order bit, or vice-versa.

DF (Direction Flag) Bit 10—DF defines whether the ESI and/or EDI registers are to decrement or increment during string operations. If DF = 0, the registers increment; if DF = 1, they decrement.

IF (Interrupt-Enable) Bit 9—Setting IF allows the CPU to recognize external (maskable) interrupt requests. Clearing this bit disables these interrupts. IF has no effect on either nonmaskable external interrupts or exceptions.

TF (Trap Flag) Bit 8—Setting TF puts the processor into single-step mode for debugging. The CPU automatically generates an Exception 1 after each instruction, which allows a program to be inspected as it executes each instruction. When TF is reset, exception 1 traps occur only as a function of the breakpoint addresses loaded into debug registers DR0-DR3. Further information is given in an upcoming discussion of the debug registers.

SF (Sign Flag) Bit 7—SF is set if the high-order bit of the result is set. It is reset otherwise. For 8-, 16-, and 32-bit operations, SF reflects the state of bit 7, 15, and 31, respectively.

ZF (Zero Flag) Bit 6—ZF is set if all bits of the result are 0. Otherwise, it is reset.

AF (AUXILIARY CARRY FLAG) BIT 4—This flag is used to simplify the addition and subtraction of packed BCD quantities. Regardless of the operand length (8, 16 or 32 bits), AF is set if the operation resulted in a borrow into bit 3 (which is a subtraction) or a carry out of bit 3 (which is an addition). Otherwise, AF is reset. Remember that BCD uses bits 0 through 3 to represent decimal digits.

PF (PARITY FLAG) BIT 2—PF is set if the low-order eight bits of the operation contains an even number of "1's" (even parity). PF is reset if the low-order eight bits have odd parity. PF is always a function of only the low-order eight bits, regardless of operand size.

CF (CARRY FLAG) BIT 0—CF is set if the operation resulted in a carry out of the high-order bit (an addition), or a borrow into the high-order bit (a subtraction). Otherwise, CF is reset. For 8-, 16-, or 32-bit operations, CF is set according to the carry/borrow at bit 7, 15, or 31, respectively.

Segment Registers

Six 16-bit segment registers hold the segment selector values that identify the currently addressable memory segments. The registers are:

CODE SEGMENT (CS)—CS points to the segment that contains the currently executing sequence of instructions. The 80386 fetches all instructions from this segment, using the contents of the instruction pointer as an offset. CS is changed as the result of inter-segment control-transfer instructions, interrupts and exceptions. The CS cannot be explicitly loaded.

STACK SEGMENT (SS)—Subroutine calls, parameters and procedure activation records usually require a region of memory that is allocated for a stack. All stack operations use SS to locate that stack. Unlike the CS register, the SS register can be loaded explicitly by program instructions.

The next four registers are data segment registers (DS, ES, FS, GS), each of which is addressable by the currently executing program. Having access to four separate data areas aids program efficiency by allowing them to access different types of data structures. These four registers can be changed under program control.

To use the data segment registers, the 80386 associates a base address with each segment selected. To address a data unit within a segment, a 32-bit offset is added to the segment's base address. Once a segment is selected, by loading the segment selector into a segment register, a data manipulation instruction needs only to specify the offset.

Registers that hold Segment descriptors are not programmer visible. Inside the 80386, a descriptor register is associated with each programmer-visible segment register. Each descriptor register holds a 32-bit segment base address, a 32-bit segment limit, and the other necessary segment attributes.

When a selector value is loaded into a segment register, the processor automatically updates the associated descriptor register. In protected mode, the base address, the limit (the field that defines the size of the segment), and the attributes are all updated according to the contents of the segment descriptor indexed by the selector. In real address mode, only the base address is updated directly, by shifting the selector value four bits to the left, since the segment maximum limit and attributes are fixed in real mode.

Segmented Memory Management Registers

These registers are also known as *System Address Registers.* Four registers locate the data structures that control segmented memory management. These registers are defined to reference the tables or segments supported by the 80286/80386 protection model.

The addresses of these tables and segments are stored in special System Address and System Segment Registers. Chapter 2 describes the Global Descriptor Table, the Local Descriptor Table, and the Interrupt Descriptor Table in detail.

GDTR (GLOBAL DESCRIPTOR TABLE REGISTER)—This register holds the 32-bit linear base address and the 16-bit limit of the Global Descriptor Table.

LDTR (LOCAL DESCRIPTOR TABLE REGISTER)—This register holds the 16-bit selector for the Local Descriptor Table. Since the LDT is a task-specific segment, it's defined by selector values stored in the system segment registers. There is a programmer-invisible segment descriptor register associated with the LDT.

IDTR (INTERRUPT DESCRIPTOR TABLE REGISTER)—This register points to a table of entry points for interrupt handlers (the IDT). The register holds the 32-bit linear base address and the 16-bit limit of the Interrupt Descriptor Table.

TR (TASK REGISTER)—This register points to the information needed by the processor to define the current task. The register holds the 16-bit selector for the Task State Segment descriptor (See Chapter 2 for further information). Since the TSS segment is task-specific, it is defined by selector values stored in the system segment registers. Note that a programmer-invisible segment descriptor register is associated with each system segment register.

Instruction Pointer

The Extended Instruction Pointer (EIP) is a 32-bit register. EIP contains the offset address of the next sequential instruction to be executed. This offset is relative to the start (or base address) of the current code segment. The EIP is not directly visible to programmers, but is controlled explicitly by control-transfer instructions, interrupts, and exceptions.

The low-order 16 bits of EIP are named IP and can be used by the processor as a unit. This feature is useful when executing instructions designed for the 8086 and 80286 processors, which only have an IP.

Control Registers

The 80386 has three 32-bit control registers (CR0, CR2, and CR3—CR1 is reserved by Intel) to hold machine states or statuses of a global nature. A global status is one that can be accessed by (or that controls) any of the logical units of the system. Along with the System Address Registers, these registers hold machine state information that affects all tasks in the system. Load and store instructions have been defined to access the control registers.

Control registers are accessible to systems programmers only via variants of the

MOV instruction which allows them to be loaded from or stored in general registers. Figure 1-9 shows the formats of the four control registers.

CR0—Contains flags which control or indicate conditions that apply to the system as a whole, not to an individual task. The low-order 15 bits of this register is the Machine Status Word (MSW), bits 0-15, for compatibility with 80286 protected mode.

PG (PAGING) BIT 31—PG indicates whether the 80386 uses page tables to translate linear addresses into physical addresses.

ET (EXTENSION TYPE) BIT 4—ET indicates the type of coprocessor present in the system, either a 80287 or 80387.

TS (TASK SWITCHED) BIT 3—The processor sets TS with every task switch. It also tests TS when it interprets coprocessor instructions because the only time coprocessor status needs to be saved is when a new task requires the coprocessor. Loading into the CR0 register can reset TS. Also the CLTS instruction specifically resets the TS.

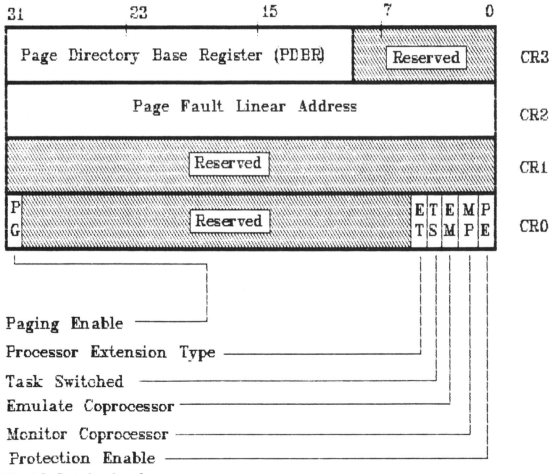

Fig. 1-9. Control register formats.

EM (EMULATION) BIT 2—EM indicates whether coprocessor functions are to be emulated. Emulation is designed to imitate one system or process with another so that the imitating system accepts the same data, executes the same programs, and achieves the same results as the imitated system or function. Setting EM often occurs when there is no coprocessor present.

MP (MATH PRESENT) BIT 1—MP controls the function of the WAIT instruction, which is used to coordinate a coprocessor.

PE (PROTECTION ENABLE) BIT 0—Setting PE causes the processor to begin executing in protected mode. Resetting PE returns to real-address mode.

CR1—Reserved for future Intel processors.

CR2—Used for handling page faults when the PG flag in CR0 is set. The 80386 stores in CR2 the linear address that triggers the fault. The error code pushed onto the page fault handler's stack when it is invoked provides additional status information on this page fault.

CR3—Used when PG (Paging) is set in CR0. CR3 enables the processor to locate the page table directory for the current task. This register contains the physical base address of the page directory table. The 80386 page directory table is always page-aligned (4 Kbyte-aligned). The lowest twelve bits of CR3 are ignored when written and they store as undefined.

A task switch through a TSS that changes the value in CR3 (or as an explicit load to CR3) invalidates all cached page table entries in the paging unit cache. Note that if the value in CR3 does not change during the task switch, the cached page table entries are not flushed.

Debug Registers

The six programmer-accessible debug registers (DR0-DR3, DR6, and DR7) bring advanced debugging capabilities to the 80386, including data breakpoints and the ability to set instruction breakpoints without modifying code segments. Registers DR0-DR3 specify the four linear breakpoints. DR4 and DR5 are reserved by Intel for future development. DR6 displays the current state of the breakpoints. DR7 is used to set the breakpoints.

Translation Lookaside Buffer (TLB)

The Translation Lookaside Buffer (TLB) is a cache used for translating linear addresses to physical addresses. *Warning:* the TLB testing mechanism is unique to the 80386 and may not be continued in the same way in future processors. Software that uses this mechanism as it currently is may be incompatible with future processors.

The TLB is a four-way, set-associative memory. A set is a collection of elements that have some feature in common or which bear a certain relation to one another. Figure 10 shows the TLB structure. In the TLB, there are:

CONTENT-ADDRESSABLE MEMORY - CAM. CAM holds 32 linear addresses and associated tag bits, which are used for data protection and cache implementation.

RANDOM ACCESS MEMORY - RAM. RAM holds the upper 20 bits of the 32 physical addresses that correspond to the linear addresses in the CAM.

Logic implements the four-way cache and includes a 2-bit replacement pointer that decides which of the four sets into which a new entry is directed during a write to the TLB.

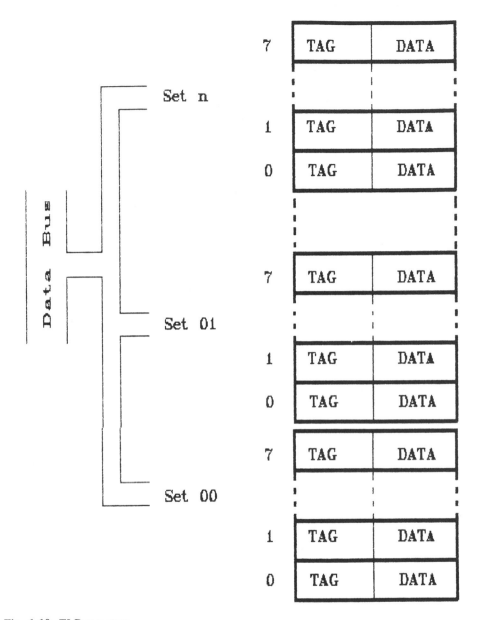

Fig. 1-10. TLB structure.

Addresses and commands are written to the TLB through the command register, while *data* is read from or written to the TLB through the data register. Test Register Six (TR6) is the command register for TLB accesses while Test Register Seven (TR7) is used as the data register.

Test Registers. Two test registers are used to control the testing of the RAM/CAM (Content Addressable Memories) in the translation lookaside buffer (TLB), the cache used for storing information from page tables. TR6 is the command test register and

TR7 is the data register which contains the data of the TLB test. (TR0 through TR5 do not exist.)

These registers are accessed by variants of the MOV instruction, which is defined in both real-address mode and protected mode. In the protected mode, the MOV instruction that accesses them can be executed only at privilege level 0. Any attempt to read or write either of the TRs when executing in any other privilege level causes a general protection exception. Figure 1-11 shows the formats of the test registers TR6 and TR7.

Fields for TR6 are:

LINEAR ADDRESS—BITS 12 - 31. On a TLB write, a TLB entry is allocated to this linear address. The rest of the TLB entry is set depending on the value of TR7 and the value just written into TR6. On a TLB lookup, the TLB is interrogated per this value. If one and only one TLB entry matches, the rest of the fields of TR6 and TR7 are set from the matching TLB entry.

V—BIT 11. This is the valid bit. The TLB uses it to identify entries that contain valid data. Valid means a successful translation has been made. Entries in the TLB that have not been assigned values have zero in the valid bit. All valid bits can be cleared by writing to Control Register 3 (CR3).

D, D#—BITS 10 AND 9. Bit 10 is the dirty bit (the entry has been changed) and bit 9 is its complement for/from the TLB entry.

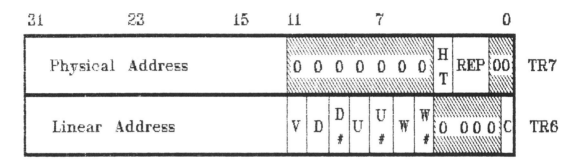

Fig. 1-11. Test register formats.

U, U#—BITS 8 AND 7. Bit 8 is the U/S (User accessible) bit and bit 7 is its complement for/from the TLB entry.

W, W#—BITS 6 AND 5. Bit 6 is the R/W (Writeable) bit and bit 5 is its complement for/from the TLB entry.

C—BIT 0. TR6 contains a command and an address tag. To cause an immediate TLB lookup, move a doubleword into TR6 that contains a 1 in this bit. To cause an immediate write to the TLB, move a doubleword that has a 0 in this bit.

The fields of TR7 are:

PHYSICAL ADDRESS—BITS 31 - 12. This is the data field of the TLB. On a write to TLB, the TLB entry allocated to the linear address in TR6 is set to this value. On a TLB lookup, if HT is set, the data field (physical address) from the TLB is read out to this field. If HT bit is not set, this field is undefined.

HT—BIT 4. For a TLB write, HT must be set to 1. For a TLB lookup, the HT bit indicates whether the lookup was a hit (HT=1) or a miss (HT=0).

REP—BITS 3 AND 2. For a TLB write, one of four associative blocks of the TLB is to be written. These bits indicate which. For a TLB read, if HT is set, REP shows in which of the four associative blocks the tag was found. If HT is not set on a TLB read, REP is undefined.

2

Selectors and Descriptors

In the 80386, selectors and descriptors are those items that provide the hardware with the software's expected image of what is located where.

SELECTORS

A selector is a 16-bit pointer that, when loaded into a register or used with certain instructions, selects certain descriptors. In a logical address, the selector portion identifies an individual descriptor by first specifying the descriptor table and then indexing to the descriptor within that table. Figure 2-1 shows a general selector format. The various terms (such as Global Descriptor Table and descriptor) are defined later in this chapter.

The fields are:

INDEX—Selects one of up to 8192 descriptors in a descriptor table. The 80386 multiplies this index value by eight (the length of a descriptor) and then adds the result to the base address of the descriptor table. This accesses the correct entry in the table.

TABLE INDICATOR (TI)—This bit specifies the descriptor table to which the selector refers: a zero points to the GDT (Global Descriptor Table) and a one indicates the current LDT (Local Descriptor Table).

REQUESTED PRIVILEGE LEVEL (RPL)—Used by the system protection mechanism. See Chapter 6 for more on protection and privilege.

The first entry of the GDT is not used by the processor. A selector that has an index of zero and a table indicator of zero (that is, a selector that points to the first entry in the GDT) is called a *null selector*. The 80386 does not cause an exception when a segment register, other than CS or SS, is loaded with a null selector. It *does* cause an exception when the segment register is used to access memory. This is useful to trap accidental references.

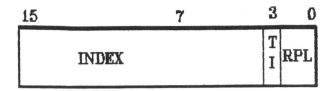

Fig. 2-1. Selector format.

TI — Table Indicator

RPL — Requestor's Privilege Level

SEGMENT DESCRIPTORS

Descriptors are those objects to which the segment selector point. They are 8-byte quantities that contain attributes about a given linear address space (that is, about a segment). These attributes include the segment 32-bit base linear address, the segment's 20-bit length and granularity, the protection level, read, write or execute privileges, the default size of the operands (16- or 32-bit), and the type of segment.

All descriptor attribute information is contained in 12 bits of the segment descriptor. Segments on the 80386 have three attribute fields in common: the *P* (Present) bit, the *DPL* (Descriptor Privilege Level) bits, and the *S* (Segment Descriptor) bit.

Segment descriptors are stored in either a Global Descriptor Table (GDT) or Local Descriptor Table (LDT). The 80386 locates the GDT and the current LDT in memory by means of the GDTR and LDTR registers.

A segment descriptor provides the 80386 with the data it needs to map a logical address into a linear address. These descriptors are not created by programs, but by compilers, linkers, loaders, or the operating system. Figure 2-2 shows the general segment-descriptor format.

The fields are:

BASE—This defines the location of the segment within the 4 gigabyte linear address space. The 80386 concatenates the three fragments of the base address to form a single 32-bit value.

LIMIT—This field defines the size of the segment. The 80386 links the two parts of the LIMIT field, to form a 20-bit result. The processor then interprets the LIMIT field in one of two ways, depending on the setting of the Granularity Bit.

1. In units of one byte, to define a LIMIT of up to 1 megabyte.

2. In units of 4 Kilobytes (one page), to define a LIMIT of up to 4 gigabytes. The LIMIT is shifted left by 12 bits when loaded, and low-order one-bits are inserted.

GRANULARITY BIT—This bit specifies the units with which the LIMIT field is interpreted. When G=0, LIMIT is interpreted as units of one byte. If G=1, LIMIT is interpreted in units of 4 Kilobytes.

S BIT—The Segment bit determines if a given segment is a system segment (S=0), or a code or data segment (S=1).

TYPE—This differentiates between the kinds of descriptors. Code and data descrip-

Descriptor Used for Special System Segments

31	23				15			7		0
Base 31..24	G	X	0	A V L	Limit 19..16	P	DPL	S	Type	Base 23..16
Segment Base 15..0					Segment Limit 15..0					

Descriptor Used for Applications Code and Data Segments

31	23				15			7			0
Base 31..24	G	X	0	A V L	Limit 19..16	P	DPL	S	Type	A	Base 23..16
Segment Base 15..0					Segment Limit 15..0						

A   = Accessed
AVL = Available for Programmer Use
DPL = Descriptor Privilege Level
G   = Granularity
P   = Segment Present
S   = System Descriptor
        S=0 for Special Segment
        S=1 for Code/Data Segment

Fig. 2-2. General segment descriptor format.

tors split TYPE into a 3-bit TYPE and 1-bit of Accessed Flag. System segments use the following set of values in TYPE:

0	=	Invalid	8	=	Invalid
1	=	Available 286 TSS	9	=	Available 386 TSS
2	=	LDT	A	=	Intel Reserved
3	=	Busy 286 TSS	B	=	Busy 386 TSS
4	=	286 Call Gate	C	=	386 Call Gate
5	=	Task Gate (286 or 386)	D	=	Intel Reserved
6	=	286 Interrupt Gate	E	=	386 Interrupt Gate
7	=	286 Trap Gate	F	=	386 Trap Gate

DPL (Descriptor Privilege Level)—This is used by the protection mechanism.

Segment-Present Bit—If this bit holds a zero value, the descriptor is not valid for use in address translation. The 80386 signals an exception when a selector for the descriptor is loaded into a segment register. Figure 2-3 shows the format of a Not-Present Descriptor.

Accessed Bit—The 80386 sets this bit when the segment is accessed in data and code descriptors. Operating systems that implement virtual memory at the segment level may monitor the frequency of segment usage by periodically testing and clearing this bit.

In addition to the selector value, every segment register has an "invisible" segment descriptor cache register associated with it. When the segment register's contents are changed, the 8-byte descriptor associated with that selector is automatically loaded (cached). Once loaded, all references to that segment use the cached descriptor information instead of reaccessing the descriptor.

To provide operating system compatibility between the 80286 and 80386, the 80386 processor supports all the 80286 segment descriptors. The only differences between the two formats are that the values of the type fields, and the limit and base address fields have been expanded for the 80386.

The 80286 system segment descriptors contain a 24-bit address and a 16-bit limit. The 80386 system descriptors, on the other hand, have a 32-bit base address, a 20-bit

Descriptors Used for Applications Code and Data Segments

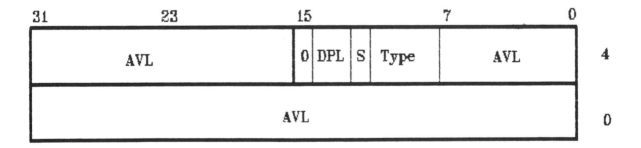

```
AVL  —  Available for use by Systems Programmers
DPL  —  Descriptor Privilege Level
S    —  Segment Present
0    —  Present Bit contains a zero value
```

Fig. 2-3. Format of not-present descriptor.

limit and a granularity bit (G Bit). To tell the difference, if the upper word of the descriptor is zero, then it is an 80286-type descriptor.

The only other difference between 80286 and 80386 style descriptors is the interpretation of the word count field of call gates and the B bit. The word count field specifies the number of 16-bit quantities to copy for 80286 call gates and the 32-bit quantities for 80386 call gates. The B bit controls the size of PUSHes when using a call gate. If B=0, the PUSHes are 16 bits; if B=1, the PUSHes are 32 bits.

DESCRIPTOR TABLES

Descriptor tables define all the segments which are used in the 80386 system. The three types of tables are the Global Descriptor Table (GDT), the Local Descriptor Table (LDT), and the Interrupt Descriptor Table (IDT). The registers that point to these tables (and contain the 32-bit linear base address and the 16-bit limit of each table) are, respectively, the GDTR, LDTR, and IDTR. These registers were initially discussed in Chapter 1.

Descriptor tables are variable length memory arrays, with 8-byte entries that contain descriptors. In the 80386, they range in size from 8 bytes to 64 Kbytes and each table holds up to 8192 8-byte descriptors. The upper 13 bits of a selector are used as an index into the descriptor table. Since the operating system maintains these tables, Load Descriptor Table instructions are privileged instructions. The first entry of the GDT (where INDEX=0) is not used by the 80386.

The 80386 stores descriptor information in segment registers. This way, the processor does not have to index into a table each time it refers to the information. There are two classes of instructions to do this: Implied load instructions, such as CALL and JMP, and Direct load instructions, such as POP, MOV, LDS, LFS.

Each register has a programmer-visible portion and a programmer-invisible portion. Using either the direct load or the implied load instructions, the visible portions of these segment address registers are manipulated by programs as if they were simply 16-bit registers. The invisible portions are manipulated by the processor; it fetches the base address, limit, type, and other information from a descriptor table and loads them into the invisible portion of the segment register.

Global Descriptor Table (GDT)

Every 80386 system contains a Global Descriptor Table (GDT). The GDT holds descriptors that are available to all the tasks in a system. Except for descriptors which control interrupts or exceptions, the GDT can contain any other kind of segment descriptor.

Generally, the GDT contains three types of descriptors: code and data segments used by the operating system, descriptors for the Local Descriptors in a system, and task state segments. The first slot of the GDT is not used; it corresponds to the null selector, which defines a null pointer value.

Local Descriptor Table (LDT)

Operating systems are generally designed so that each task has a separate Local Descriptor Table (LDT). LDTs provide a way for isolating a given task's code and data segments from the rest of the operating system. The GDT contains descriptors for segments that are common to all tasks. The LDT is associated with a given task and may contain only code, data, stack, task gate and call gate descriptors.

A segment cannot be accessed by a task if its segment descriptor does not exist in either the current LDT or the GDT. This both isolates and protects that task's segments, while still allowing global *data* to be shared among tasks.

The GDT and IDT registers consist of a 16-bit limit value and a 32-bit linear address. (The 16 plus the 32 add to 48 bits, or 6 bytes.) Unlike the 6-byte GDT or IDT registers which contain both the base address and limit, the programmer-visible portion of the LDT register contains only a 16-bit selector. This selector refers to an LDT descriptor in the GDT.

Interrupt Descriptor Table (IDT)

The Interrupt Descriptor Table (IDT) contains the descriptors that point to the location of up to 256 interrupt service routines. The IDT can only contain trap gates, task gates, and interrupt gates. (*Gates* are circuits having one output and several inputs, the output remaining unenergized until certain input conditions have been met.) The IDT should be at least 256 bytes in size so it can hold the descriptors for the 32 Intel-Reserved Interrupts. *Every interrupt used by the system must have an entry in the IDT.*

3

INTERRUPTS
AND EXCEPTIONS

Both hardware- and software-generated interrupts can alter the programmed execution of the 80386. A hardware-generated interrupt occurs in response to an active input on one of two 80386 interrupt inputs: NMI, which is non-maskable, or INTR, which is maskable. A software-generated interrupt (a fault, trap or abort) occurs in response to an INT instruction or an exception, a software condition that requires servicing. Figure 3-1 shows a schematic representation of maskable and non-maskable interrupts.

MASKABLE INTERRUPTS (INTR)

The 80386 INTR input allows external devices to interrupt the executing program. To ensure recognition, the INTR input must be held high until the 80386 acknowledges the interrupt by performing the interrupt acknowledge sequence. The INTR input is sampled at the beginning of every instruction. It must be high at least eight CLK2 periods prior to the instruction to guarantee recognition as valid—CLK2 is a double-frequency clock signal for synchronous operation. Figure 3-2 shows the relationship between CLK and CLK2. This reduces the possibility of false inputs from voltage glitches. Also, maskable interrupts must be enabled in software for interrupt recognition. See Chapter 7 for more information on the system clocks.

The INTR signal is usually supplied by the 8259A Programmable Interrupt Controller. The Controller is, in turn, connected to devices that require interrupt servicing. The 8259A appears to the 80386 as a set of I/O ports. It accepts interrupt requests from devices connected to it, determines the priority of those requests, activates the INTR input, and then supplies the appropriate service routine vector when requested. The service routine vector is the entry in the IDT that points to a service routine for handling the interrupt. The mechanism is the same as used in the INT instruction.

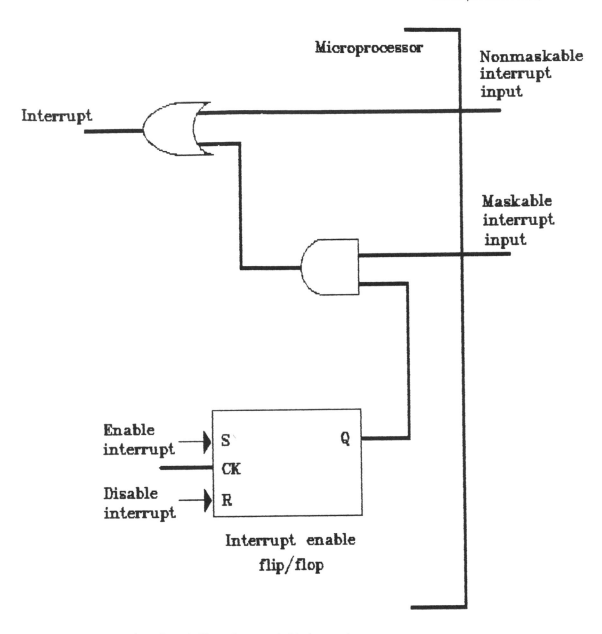

Fig. 3-1. Representation of maskable and nonmaskable interrupts.

NONMASKABLE INTERRUPTS (NMI)

The 80386 NMI input generally signals a catastrophic event such as an imminent power loss, a memory error, or a bus parity error. NMI is edge-triggered (on a low-to-high transition) and asynchronous. A valid signal is low for eight CLK2 periods before the transition and high eight CLK2 periods after the transition.

An NMI automatically causes the 80386 to execute the service routine that cor-

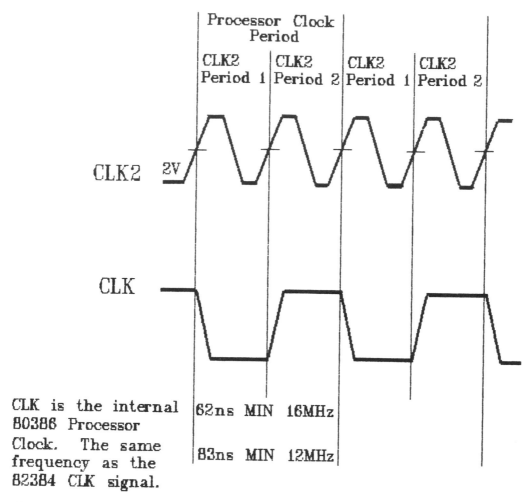

CLK is the internal 80386 Processor Clock. The same frequency as the 82384 CLK signal.

Fig. 3-2. CLK and CLK2 relationship.

responds to location 2 in the IDT. The 80386 will not service subsequent NMI requests until the current one has been serviced. The 80386 disables INTR requests in real mode, although these can be re-enabled in the service routine. In protected mode, the disabling of the INTR request depends on the gate in IDT location 2.

The NMI and the software exceptions recognized by the processor are assigned predetermined identifiers in the range zero (0) through 31. At the present time, some numbers are reserved by Intel for future use.

In the case of maskable interrupts, external interrupt controllers (such as Intel's 8259A Programmable Interrupt Controller) determine the identifier and communicate it to the processor during the processor's interrupt-acknowledge sequence. In response to an interrupt request, the 80386 accepts and then services the interrupt. That is, it transfers program execution to an interrupt service routine. Any number from 32 through 255 can be assigned to the service routines. Table 3-1 shows the assigned and unassigned identifiers.

Table 3-1. Interrupt and Exception ID Assignments.

Identifier	Description
0	Divide Error
1	Debug Exceptions
2	Nonmaskable interrupt
3	Breakpoint
4	Overflow
5	Bounds Check
6	Invalid Opcode
7	Coprocessor not available
8	Double Fault
9	(Reserved)
10	Invalid TSS
11	Segment Not Present
12	Stack Exception
13	General Protection
14	Page Fault
15	(Reserved)
16	Coprocessor Error
17-31	(Reserved)
32-255	Available for External Interrupts via the INTR Pin

INTERRUPT DESCRIPTOR TABLE

The entry point descriptors to the service routines or the interrupt tasks are stored in memory in a table, the Interrupt Descriptor Table or IDT. The IDT associates each interrupt or exception identifier with a descriptor for the instructions that service the associated event.

To access a particular service routine, the 80386 obtains a vector, or index, to the table location that contains the descriptor. The source of this vector depends on the type of interrupt. If the interrupt is maskable (INTR input active), the vector is supplied by the 8259A Interrupt Controller. If the interrupt is nonmaskable (NMI input is active), location 2 in the IDT is used.

The IDT is an array of 8-byte descriptors. The first entry of the IDT can contain a descriptor, unlike the first entry of the Global Descriptor Table (GDT) or the Local Descriptor Table (LDT). To locate the correct descriptor, the processor multiples the identifier by eight. The IDT can contain up to 256 identifiers and can reside in any location in memory. The processor finds it by using the IDT register (IDTR). The instructions LIDT (Load Interrupt Descriptor Table Register) and SIDT (Store Interrupt Descriptor Table Register) operate on the IDTR.

LIDT loads the IDT register with the linear base address and limit values contained in the memory operand. This instruction is executed only when the CPL is zero. It is used normally by the initialization of the operating system when it creates the IDT. The operating system can use the instruction to change from one IDT to another.

SIDT copies the base and limit value stored in the IDTR to a memory location. SIDT can be executed at any privilege level.

EXCEPTIONS

Exceptions are classified as *faults, aborts,* or *traps,* depending on the way they are reported and also whether restart of the instruction that caused the exception is supported. Faults are exceptions that are either detected before the instruction begins to execute or during execution. If detected during execution, the fault is reported with the machine restored to a state that permits the instruction to be restarted. The CS (Code Segment) Register and EIP (Instruction Pointer) values, saved when a fault is reported, point to the instruction causing the fault.

A trap is reported at the instruction boundary immediately after the instruction in which the exception was detected. The CS and EIP values, stored when the trap is reported, point to the instruction after the instruction causing the trap. The reported values of CS and EIP reflect alterations of program flow if a trap is detected during an instruction that alters that program flow. If a trap is detected in a JMP (JUMP) instruction, for example, the CS and EIP values pushed onto the stack point to the *target* of the JMP, *not* to the instruction immediately after the JMP.

An abort allows neither the restart of the program that caused the exception nor the identification of the precise location of the instruction causing the exception. Aborts are used to report severe errors such as illegal and/or inconsistent values in system tables or hardware errors.

The time that elapses before an interrupt request is serviced depends on several factors. The interrupt source must take this delay into account. The following all can affect elapsed time:

- If the interrupt is masked, an INTR request will not be recognized until interrupts are re-enabled.
- If a nonmaskable interrupt is currently being serviced, an incoming nonmaskable interrupt request will not be recognized until the 80386 encounters the IRET (interrupt return) instruction.

- Saving the Flags register and other registers requires time.
- If interrupt servicing requires a task switch, time must be allowed for saving and restoring the task state.
- If the 80386 is currently executing an instruction, the instruction must be completed. With certain exceptions (such as a string move, which allows an interrupt after each block move) an interrupt request is recognized *only* on an instruction boundary.

The longest delay occurs when the interrupt request arrives while the 80386 is executing a long instruction such as multiplication, division, or a task-switch in the protected mode. If the instruction sets the interrupt flag, thereby enabling interrupts, an interrupt is not processed until *after* the next instruction.

INTERRUPT CONTROLLER

The 8259A Programmable Interrupt Controller manages interrupts for an 80386 system. The programmable features allow it to be used in a variety of ways to fit the interrupt requirements of a particular system. A single 8259A can accept interrupts from up to eight external sources, and up to 64 requests can be accommodated by cascading several 8259A chips.

The 8259A resolves priority between active interrupts, then interrupts the processor and passes it a code to identify the interrupting source.

INTERRUPT AND EXCEPTION PRIORITIES

If more than one interrupt or exception is waiting at an instruction boundary, the processor services them one at a time in order of highest priority. Highest in the priority list are faults (except debug faults), trap instructions (INT0, INT n, INT3), debug traps for this instruction, debug faults for next instruction, and NMI interrupts. The lowest priority is the INTR interrupt.

When the processor selects an interrupt to service, any exceptions of lower priority are delayed until their priority is reached. These low-priority exceptions will be rediscovered when the interrupt handler returns control to the point of interruption. Lower-priority interrupts are retained and held pending.

INTERRUPT TASKS AND PROCEDURES

An interrupt or exception can call an interrupt handler that is either a procedure or a task. An interrupt gate or trap gate points indirectly to a procedure which executes in the context of the currently executing task. The gate selector points to an executable-segment descriptor in either the GDT or the current LDT. The offset field of the gate points to the beginning of the interrupt or exception handling procedure. The 80386 invokes an interrupt or exception handling procedure in much the same manner as it CALLs a procedure. Figure 3-3 shows the formats of the IDT Gate Descriptors.

An interrupt procedure differs from a normal procedure in the method used to leave the procedure. The IRET (Interrupt Return) instruction is used to exit from an interrupt procedure. IRET is similar to RET (Return) except that IRET increments

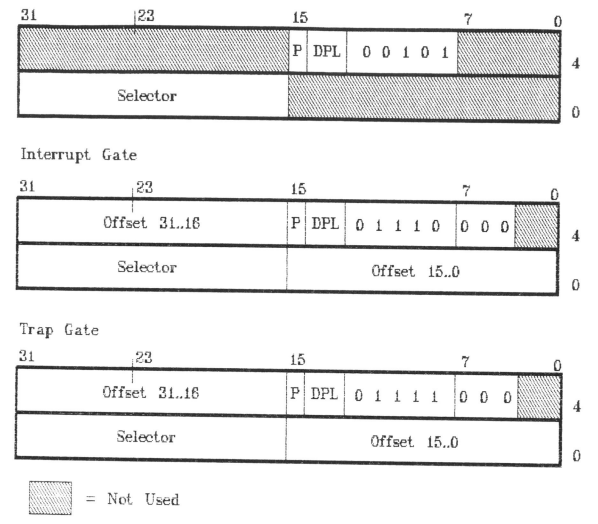

Fig. 3-3. IDT gate descriptors for the 80386.

the ESP by an extra four bytes, because the flags are on the stack. IRET then moves the saved flags into the EFLAGS register.

An interrupt that vectors through an interrupt gate resets IF (Interrupt-Enable Flag). This prevents other interrupts from impacting or tampering with the current interrupt handler. The IRET instruction at the end of the interrupt procedure restores IF to the value in the EFLAGS image on the stack. In contrast, an interrupt through a trap gate does *not* change the IF.

The processor does not permit an interrupt to transfer control to a procedure in a segment of lesser privilege; that is, one with a numerically higher privilege level than the current level. Violation of this rule results in a general protection exception.

Because it is difficult to predict the occurrence of an interrupt, there are restrictions placed on the privilege levels at which interrupt and exception handling procedures can execute. Use one of the following methods to ensure privilege levels are not violated.

- Place the handler procedure in a privilege level zero segment.
- Place the handler in a conforming segment. This method suits handlers for certain exceptions, such as divide error. Such an interrupt handler must use only the data available to it from the stack. If it needs data from a data segment, the data segment must have a privilege level of three, making it unprotected.

ERROR CODES

When the processor finds an exception that relates to a specific segment, the 80386 pushes the appropriate error code onto the exception handler stack. The error code format looks like that of a selector, except that it has two one-bit items instead of an RPL field. The format of the error code is shown in Figure 3-4.

The fields are:

SELECTOR INDEX—Indexes into the error handling tables.

TI—Bit 2. Table Indicator. If the I-bit is not set and TI=0, TI indicates the error code refers to the Global Descriptor Table (GDT). If I-bit is not set, and TI=1, TI refers to the Local Descriptor Table (LDT).

I—Bit 1. The 80386 sets this IDT (Interrupt Descriptor Table) bit if the index portion of the error code refers to a gate descriptor in the IDT.

EX—Bit 0. The 80386 sets the External (EX) bit if the exception was caused by an event external to the program.

The 80386 recognizes sixteen defined error codes.

Interrupt 0—Divide Error. The divide-error occurs during a DIV (Unsigned Divide) or IDIV (Signed Divide) instruction when the divisor is zero.

Interrupt 1—Debug Exceptions. The 80386 generates this interrupt for five general conditions.

1. Task-switch breakpoint trap.
2. General detect fault.
3. Data address breakpoint trap.
4. Instruction address breakpoint fault.
5. Single-step trap.

Whether the exception is a trap or a fault depends on the condition. The 80386 does not push an error code onto the stack for this exception. Create an exception handler that checks the debug registers (DR0-DR7) to determine which condition triggered the exception.

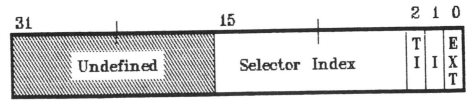

Fig. 3-4. Error code format.

Interrupt 3—Breakpoint. INT 3 (Call to Interrupt Procedure) causes this trap. INT 3 is one byte long, which makes it easy to replace an opcode in an executable segment with the breakpoint opcode. The saved CS:EIP (Code Segment, Instruction Pointer) points to the byte following the breakpoint.

Interrupt 4—Overflow. When the processor executes an INTO (Call to Interrupt Procedure for Overflow) *and* the OF (Overflow) flag is set, this interrupt is triggered. Both signed and unsigned arithmetic use the same arithmetic instructions. The 80386 cannot judge which is meant. Therefore, it does not cause overflow exceptions automatically.

It does set the OF flag when the results would be out of range if interpreted as signed numbers.

Interrupt 5—Bounds Check. While executing a BOUND (Check Array Index Against Bounds) instruction, if the 80386 finds that the operand is greater than the limit, the processor signals this fault. Software can also use BOUND to check a signed array index against signed limits that are defined in a block of memory.

Interrupt 6—Invalid Opcode. This fault occurs if an invalid opcode is found by the execution unit. That exception is not detected until the processor attempts to execute it. That is, prefetching an invalid opcode does not trigger this interrupt. Also, no error code is pushed on the stack. An exception can be handled within the same task.

Another problem can cause this exception. If the type of operand is invalid for a given opcode, this fault is triggered. For example, an interrupt will occur if an LES (Load Full Pointer into ES Register) uses a register source operand.

Interrupt 7—Coprocessor Not Available. This exception occurs in one of two conditions:

1. The processor encounters either the WAIT instruction or an ESC (Escape, the signal that this is a coprocessor instruction) and both the MP (Monitor Coprocessor) and the TS (Task Switched) bits of Control Register Zero (CR0) are set.

2. The 80386 finds an ESC instruction and the EM (Emulate) bit if CR0 is set.

Interrupt 8—Double Fault. Generally, the 80386 handles exceptions serially. If it cannot, it signals a double-fault exception. To be able to determine if the error is a double-fault condition, the 80386 divides exceptions into three classes: benign exceptions, contributory exceptions, and page faults. The 80386 always pushes an error code onto the stack of the double-fault handler. That error code is *always* zero. The faulting instruction may not be restarted. If another exception occurs while the processor is attempting to handle a double fault, the processor shuts down. Figure 3-5 shows the three classes.

Interrupt 9—Coprocessor Segment Overrun. In the protected mode, if the processor detects a page or segment violation while transferring the middle portion of a coprocessor operand to the NPX, this exception is raised.

Interrupt 10—Invalid Task State Segment (TSS). An attempt to switch to an invalid TSS causes this exception. Twelve conditions can cause a TSS to be considered invalid and Fig. 3-6 lists the conditions. An error code is pushed onto the stack to help identify which cause it is. The EXT (External) bit indicates if the exception

Class	Identification	Description
Benign Exceptions	1 2 3 4 5 6 7 16	Debug Exceptions NMI Breakpoint Overflow Bounds Check Invalid Opcode Coprocessor Not Available Coprocessor Error
Contributory Exceptions	0 9 10 11 12 13	Divide Error Coprocessor Segment Overrun Invalid TSS Segment Not Present Stack Exception General Protection
Page Fault	14	Page Fault

Fig. 3-5. Three classes of double-faults.

was caused by a condition outside the control of the program, such as an external interrupt via a task gate which triggered the switch to the invalid TSS. To ensure a correct TSS to process this condition, the exception handler must be a task called via a task gate.

Interrupt 11—Segment Not Present. This exception occurs when the 80386 finds that the P (Present) bit of a descriptor is zero. This fault is restartable. The exception handler makes the segment present and returns. The interrupted program then resumes execution. Generally, an operating system uses this exception to implement virtual memory at the segment level.

Interrupt 12—Stack Exception. Interrupt 12 occurs in either of two conditions:
    1. When the processor attempts to load the SS register with a descriptor that is marked as not-present but is otherwise valid. This can occur in an interlevel CALL, an interlevel return, in a task switch, an LSS instruction, or a MOV or POP instruction to SS.

ERROR CODE	CONDITIONS
TSS id + EXT	The limit in the TSS descriptor is less than 103
LTD id + EXT	Invalid LDT selector, or LDT not present
SS id + EXT	Stack segment selector is outside table limit
SS id + EXT	Stack segment is not a writeable segment
SS id + EXT	Stack segment DPL does not match new CPL
SS id + EXT	Stack segment selector RPL not equal to CPL
CS id + EXT	Code segment selector is outside table limit
CS id + EXT	Code segment selector does not refer to code segment
CS id + EXT	DPL of non-conforming code segment is not equal to the new CPL
CS id + EXT	DPL of conforming code segment is greater than new CPL
DS/ES/FS/GS id + EXT	DS, ES, FS, or GS segment selector is outside table limits
DS/ES/FS/GS id + EXT	DS, ES, FS, or GS is not a readable segment

Fig. 3-6. Conditions invalidating a TSS.

2. In any operation that refers to the SS register and has a limit violation. This includes stack-oriented instructions such as ENTER, LEAVE, POP, and PUSH. It also includes other memory references that imply use of SS.

An instruction that causes this interrupt is restartable in all cases. The return pointer pushed onto the exception handler's stack points to the instruction to be restarted.

Interrupt 13—General Protection Exception. This exception is the "catch-all." All protection violations that do not cause another exception cause a general exception. The following are sample causes:

1. Exceeding segment limit when referencing a descriptor table.
2. Writing into a read-only data segment or into a code segment.
3. Reading from an execute-only segment.
4. Loading DS, ES, FS, GS or SS with the descriptor of a system segment.
5. Switching to a busy task.
6. Violating privilege rules.
7. Loading CR0 with PG=1 (Paging is enabled) and PE=0 (Protection Enable is not).
8. Exceeding segment limit when using CS, DS, ES, FS, or GS.
9. Transferring control to a segment that is not executable.

Interrupt 14—Page Fault. Interrupt 14 occurs when paging is enabled (PG=1) and the processor finds one of the two following conditions while translating a linear address to a physical address:

1. The current procedure does not have enough privilege to access the indicated page.
2. The page-table entry or page-directory that is needed for the address translation has a zero in its present bit.

The 80386 makes available to the page fault handler two pieces of information to aid diagnosis of the error and how to recover from it:

1. Control Register 2 (CR2). The 80386 stores the linear address, used in the access that caused the exception, into CR2. The exception handler uses this to locate the corresponding page table and page directory entries.
2. An error code on the stack. This error code has a different format from other exceptions. The code tells the exception handler (1) whether the exception is due to a not-present page or to an access rights violation, (2) whether the memory access that caused the exception was a read or a write, and (3) whether the 80386 was executing at user or supervisor level at the time of the exception.

Interrupt 15—Reserved for Future Intel Use.

Interrupt 16—Coprocessor Error. The 80386 issues an Interrupt 16 if it detects a signal on its own ERROR# pin, from the numeric coprocessor (the 80287 or 80387). The 80386 only tests this ERROR# pin twice: at the beginning of certain ESC (Escape) instructions and when the 80386 finds a WAIT instruction while the EM (Emulate) bit of the MSW (Machine Status Word) is zero (that is, no emulation). Figure 3-7 gives a summary of the error information that is available with each exception.

Coprocessor Error Codes

The 80386 processor can operate with either an 80287 or 80387 math coproces-

Number	Description	Return to Faulting Instruction	Caused By
0	Divide Error	Yes	DIV, IDIV
1	Debug Exceptions	Yes	Any
3	Breakpoint	No	One-byte INT3
4	Overflow	No	INTO
5	Bounds Check	Yes	BOUND
6	Invalid Opcode	Yes	Any illegal
7	Coprocessor Not Available	Yes	ESC, WAIT
8	Double Fault	Yes	Any that can generate an exception
9	Coprocessor Segment Overrun	No	Any operand of ESC that wraps a segment
10	Invalid TSS	Yes	JMP, CALL, IRET, or any interrupt.
11	Segment Not Present	Yes	Any segment-register modifier
12	Stack Exception	Yes	Any memory reference through SS
13	General Protection	Yes	Any memory reference or code fetch
14	Page Fault	Yes	Any memory reference or code fetch
16	Coprocessor Error	Yes	ESC, WAIT
0-255	Two-Byte SW Interrupt	No	INTn

Fig. 3-7. Exception summary.

sor. The ET (Processor Extension Type) bit in Control Register Zero (CR0) shows which coprocessor is present. ET is set during RESET, according to the level detected on the ERROR# input. If necessary, ET can be set or reset by loading CR0 with a MOV instruction. If ET=1, the 80386 uses the 80387 32-bit protocol. If ET=0, it uses the 16-bit protocol of the 80287.

The 80386 recognizes the bit pattern ''11011'' in the first five bits of an instruction as an opcode intended for a coprocessor. Instructions with that pattern are called ESCAPE or ESC. When the 80386 finds an ESC code, it does three things: tests the emulation mode (EM) flag to see whether coprocessor functions are being emulated by software, tests the TS (Task Switched) flag to see if there has been a context change since the last ESC, and for some ESCs, tests the ERROR# pin to see if the coprocessor detected an error in the previous ESC instruction.

The EM and MP bits of CR0 control how the 80386 reacts to coprocessor instructions. The EM bit shows whether the coprocessor functions are to be emulated. If the 80386 finds EM set when it executes an ESC instruction, it signals an Exception 7 which gives the exception handler a chance to emulate the ESC instruction. The MP bit indicates if a coprocessor is attached and controls the function of the WAIT instruction. If the 80386 finds MP set while executing a WAIT instruction, it tests the TS (Task Switch) flag. If TS is set, the CPU signals Exception 7.

Both EM and MP can be changed with a MOV instruction, using CR0 as the destination. They can be read with a MOV, by using CR0 as the source operand. These forms of MOV can only be executed at privilege level zero.

The TS bit in CR0 helps to evaluate if the context of the coprocessor matches the task being currently executed by the 80386. The processor sets TS each time it performs a task switch, whether that switch is triggered by software or hardware. If the CPU finds TS already set when interpreting one of the ESC instructions, the 80386 causes Exception 7. WAIT also causes an Exception 7 if both TS and MP are set. Valid only at privilege level zero, CLTS (Clear Task Switched Flag) resets the TS flag.

Three exceptions interface with the coprocessor: Interrupt 7 (coprocessor not available), Interrupt 9 (coprocessor segment overrun) and Interrupt 16 (Coprocessor error). These three interrupts are included in the general interrupts, as described above. They are expanded slightly here.

Interrupt 7—Coprocessor Not Available. This exception occurs in one of two ways:

1. The CPU finds either the WAIT instruction or an ESC instruction when both MP (Monitor Coprocessor) and TS (Task Switched) are set. If this occurs, the exception handler should update the coprocessor state, if necessary.

2. The CPU finds an ESC instruction and EM (a flag that says the coprocessor functions are to be emulated) is set. In this instance, the exception handler should emulate the instruction that caused the exception. TS (Task Switched) may also be set.

Interrupt 9—Coprocessor Segment Overrun. This coprocessor exception occurs in the protected mode in several conditions:

1. Both the first byte and the last byte of the operand (when considering

wrap-around) are at addresses located in the segment and in present and accessible pages and the address wraps.

2. When the operand of a coprocessor instruction wraps around an *addressing limit:* 0FFFFH for small segments, 0FFFFFFFFH for big segments, and zero for expand-down segments. The operand can wrap around an addressing limit when the segment limit is near an addressing limit and the operand is near the largest valid address in the segment. The beginning and ending addresses of such an operand will be near the opposite ends of the segment because of the wrap-around.

3. When the operand spans inaccessible addresses.

The address of the failing numeric instruction and data operand may be lost. An FSTENV does not return reliable addresses. Coprocessor segment overruns should be handled by executing an FNINIT instruction—a FINIT without a preceding WAIT. The return address on the stack does not necessarily point to the failing instruction nor to the following instruction. The failing numeric instruction is *not* restartable.

Interrupt 16—Coprocessor Error. The 80287/80287 detects six different exception conditions during instruction execution. If this exception is not masked by a bit in the control word, the coprocessor signals the CPU that an error occurred. The signal is at the ERROR# pin. The 80386 causes interrupt 16 the next time it checks the ERROR# pin, which it does only at certain ESC instructions or at the beginning of a subsequent WAIT. If the exception is masked, the coprocessor handles the exception according to on-board logic. It does not signal the ERROR# pin in this latter case.

Memory

Memory is a basic component of a computer system; it stores information for future use. Not only must the memory unit store large amounts of information, it must be designed to allow rapid access to any particular portion of that information. Speed, size, and cost are the crucial criteria in any storage unit. This chapter digs further into the 80386 and describes memory organization, memory interfacing and cache memory.

MEMORY ORGANIZATION

Internal memory forms an integral physical part of any computer and is controlled by the processor (with some assists by direct memory access facilities). Organizational techniques for dividing memory aid programmers in making the best possible use of the total computer system. Two common organizational models, flat and segmented, are discussed below.

Segmentation

Segmentation is the division of memory into logical blocks for use by a computer. Memory segmentation allows efficient management of the logical address space. Segments are used to enclose regions of memory which have common attributes.

Memory is organized into one or more variable-length segments, from one byte up to four gigabytes in size. Every task in an 80386 can have up to 16,381 segments (each up to four gigabytes long), thus providing 64 terabytes of virtual memory. Any given region of the linear address space (a segment of the physical memory) has several attributes associated with it. These include its size, location, type (stack, code, or data), and protection characteristics.

The memory organization model seen by programmers is determined at system design. The 80386 architecture gives the designers the freedom to choose a model for each task. The most common models are:

FLAT—An address space consisting of a single array of up to 4 gigabytes. In this model, the processor maps the 4 gigabyte flat space onto the physical address space by address translation mechanisms. A pointer into this space is a 32-bit number that may range from 0 to $2^{32} - 1$. Relocation of separately-compiled modules in this space must be performed by systems software, such as loaders, linkers, binders, and so on.

SEGMENTED—An address space that consists of a collection of up to 16,383 linear address spaces of up to 4 gigabytes each. The total space, as viewed by a program, can be up to 2^{46} bytes (64 terabytes). The processor maps the logical address space onto the physical address space by address translation mechanisms.

Programmers view the segmented model (also called logical address space) as a collection of up to 16,383 one-dimensional subspaces, each with some specified length. Each of these linear subspaces is a *segment,* a unit of contiguous address space. A complete pointer into this address space consists of two parts: a segment selector, which is a 16-bit field that identifies a segment and an offset which is a 32-bit value that points to a byte within the segment.

Address Space

As noted above, physical memory is organized as a sequence of 8-bit bytes. Each byte is assigned a unique address that ranges from zero to $2^{32} - 1$, or 4 gigabytes. The 80386 has three distinct address spaces: physical, logical, and linear.

Physical addresses are the actual addresses used to select the physical memory chips which contain the data. A logical address consists of a segment selector and an offset into that segment. A linear address is the address formed by adding the offset to the base address of the segment. In a segmented memory model, logical address space is much larger space as viewed by a program and can be up to 2^{46} bytes, or 64 terabytes. The 80386 maps the logical space onto the physical space by address translation mechanisms.

The 80386 converts logical addresses into physical addresses in two steps: first, it performs a segment translation, by converting a logical address consisting of a segment selector and segment offset into a linear address; second, it does a page translation, by converting a linear address into a physical address. The second step is optional, depending on how the system was designed to run.

Paging and Page Translation

Paging is another type of memory management useful in a multitasking operating system. Paging operates only in protected mode and provides a means of managing the very large segments of the 80386. Paging divides programs into uniformly sized pages, unlike segmentation which modularizes programs and data into variable length segments. In a real sense, paging operates beneath segmentation. That is, the paging mechanism translates the protected linear address, which comes from the segmentation unit, into a physical address. Figure 4-1 illustrates the 80386 paging mechanism.

In the second phase of address translation, the 80386 changes a linear address into a physical address, by specifying a page table, a page within that table, and an

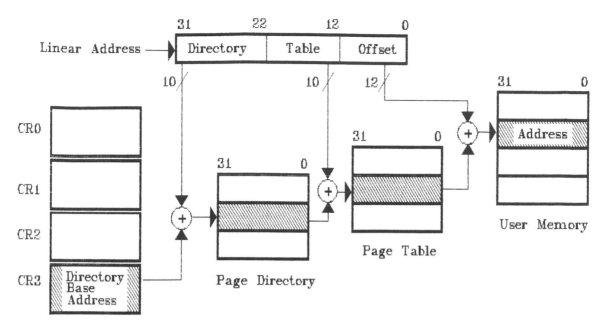

Control Registers

Fig. 4-1. Memory paging mechanism.

offset within that page. The page-translation step is optional. Page translation is in effect only when the PG bit of CR0 (Control Register Zero) is set. This bit is generally set by the operating system during software initialization. This PG bit must be set if the operating system is to use multiple virtual 8086 tasks, page-oriented virtual memory, or page-oriented protection.

A linear address is composed of three fields: DIR, PAGE, and OFFSET. Figure 4-2 shows how the 80386 converts the linear address into the physical address. The addressing mechanism uses the DIR field as an index into a page directory, and uses the OFFSET field to address a byte within the page determined by the page table.

A *page frame* is a block of 4K bytes in physical memory. Pages begin on 4K byte boundaries and are fixed in size. The pages bear no direct relation to the logical structure of a program. The page frame address specifies the physical starting address of a page and the low-order 12 bits are always zero. In a page directory, the page frame address is the address of a page table. In a second-level page table, the page frame address is the address of the page frame that contains the desired memory operand.

Page Tables. A page table is an array of 32-bit page specifiers. The table is, itself, a page and contains 4 Kilobytes of memory or up to 1K 32-bit entries. Figure 4-3 shows the format of a page table entry.

The fields are:

D (DIRTY) BIT 6, AND A (ACCESSED) BIT 5—These bits provide data about page usage and are set by hardware. The processor sets the accessed bits in both levels of page tables to the value of one before a read or write operation to a page. Then the processor sets the dirty bit in the second-level page table to the value of one be-

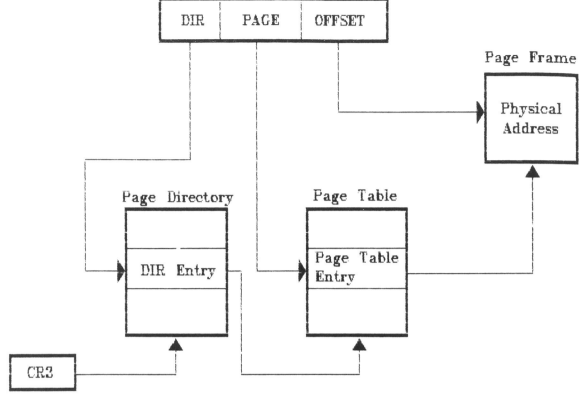

Fig. 4-2. Page translation.

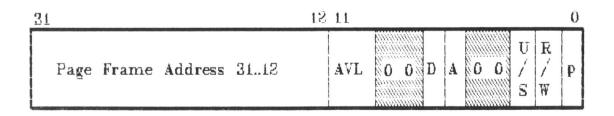

AVL	— Available for Programmer Use
D	— Dirty
A	— Accessed
U/S	— User/Supervisor
R/W	— Read/Write
0	— Intel Reserved

Fig. 4-3. Format of a page table entry.

fore a write to an address covered by that page table entry. The dirty bit in directory entries is undefined.

In an operating system that supports paged virtual memory, these bits are used to determine which pages can be eliminated from physical memory when the demand for memory exceeds the available physical memory. The operating system holds the responsibility for testing and clearing these two bits.

U/S (USER/SUPERVISOR) BIT 2 AND R/W (READ/WRITE) BIT 1—These bits are used for page-level protection which the 80386 performs at the same time as address translation.

P (PRESENT) BIT 0—The Present bit indicates whether a page table entry can be used in address translation. If so, P=1. If P=0, in either level of page tables, the entry is *not* valid for address translation and the remainder of the entry is available for software use.

If P=0 in either level of page tables and an attempt is made to use a page-table entry for address translation, the 80386 signals a page exception.

Page Translation and Segment Combinations. It may be expedient to turn off the 80386 segmentation when the 80386 is used to execute software designed for special architectures that do not have segments. The processor does not have a specific mode to disable segmentation. However, the same effect is achieved by initially loading the segment registers with selectors for descriptors that encompass the entire 32-bit linear address space. Once the descriptors are loaded, the segment registers are not changed. The 80386 instructions' 32-bit offsets address the entire linear-address space.

Segments can be larger or smaller than a page (4 kilobytes). If the required data structure is larger than a page and the operating system supports paged virtual memory, the operating system (OS) divides the structure into pages, any number of which may be present at any one time. This is transparent to the applications programmer. If the required information is smaller than a page, the OS may be designed to combine several data structures within a page.

The 80386 architecture does not force any one-to-one relationship between the boundaries of pages and segments. Thus, a segment can contain the end of one page and the beginning of another. Similarly, a page can contain the end of one segment and the beginning of another. Memory management software may be of simpler design, however, if it enforces some correlation between page and segment boundaries. For example, the logic for segment and page allocation can be combined if segments are allocated only in units of one page. In this case, there is no need for logic to account for partially used pages.

DMA Controller

A Direct Memory Access (DMA) controller performs DMA transfers between main memory and an I/O device, typically a hard disk, floppy disk, or communications channel. In a DMA transfer, a large block of data can be copied from one place to another without the intervention of the CPU.

The 82258 Advanced DMA (ADMA) Controller offers four channels and provides all the signals necessary to perform DMA transfers. The main features of the 82258 are:

• One of the four high-speed channels can be replaced with as many as 32 lower-

speed, multiplexed channels.
- Command chaining to perform multiple commands.
- Data chaining to scatter data to separate memory locations—for example, separate pages—and to gather data from separate locations.
- Compare, translate, and verify functions.
- Automatic assembly and disassembly to convert from 16-bit memory to 8-bit I/O, or vice versa.

MEMORY INTERFACING

To achieve the performance potential of the 80386, a system must use relatively fast memory. The design problem lies in: the faster the memory, the more it costs. The cost-performance tradeoff can be settled by dividing functions and using a combination of both fast and slow memories. By placing the most frequently used functions in fast memory and all other functions in slow memory, high performance for most operations can be achieved at a cost much less than that of a fast memory subsystem.

In high-performance systems, overall system delivery is linked closely to how well memory subsystems perform. To get all the potential promised by the 80386, fast memory must be used, although it is more costly. To get the best cost-performance tradeoff, a mix of fast and slower memory is used.

Main memory is a basic part of a microcomputer and is used to store program instructions and data. Generally, the main memory is random access and made up of a number of words, each consisting of a number of bits. An address is assigned to each word so that it may be uniquely accessed.

Basic Memory Interface

Configuring a memory system from memory units may be thought of as filling a memory space. The space can be viewed as a rectangular area that is divided into rows corresponding to possible address combinations. Each row consists of the number of bits making up a data word. Once the memory units have been placed into the space, it remains to specify the necessary interconnections.

The data lines of every memory unit are each connected to the corresponding line of the processor data bus. The address lines are used to first select a memory unit or a parallel group of units and then a word location within the selected unit or units.

The block diagram in Figure 4-4 shows how bus control logic provides the control signals for data buffers, the memory latches, and memory devices. It also returns READY# active to end the 80386 bus cycle and NA# to control address pipelining. Based on the address outputs of the 80386, the address decoder generates chip-select signals and the BS16# signals.

Static RAM (SRAM) Interface

Static RAMs (SRAMs) store information until power is cut off. A SRAM consists of two transistor states that are cross-coupled to operate in a bistable manner; that is, they stay in either of two stable states—on or off.

Two complementary data lines in each column convey information to or from

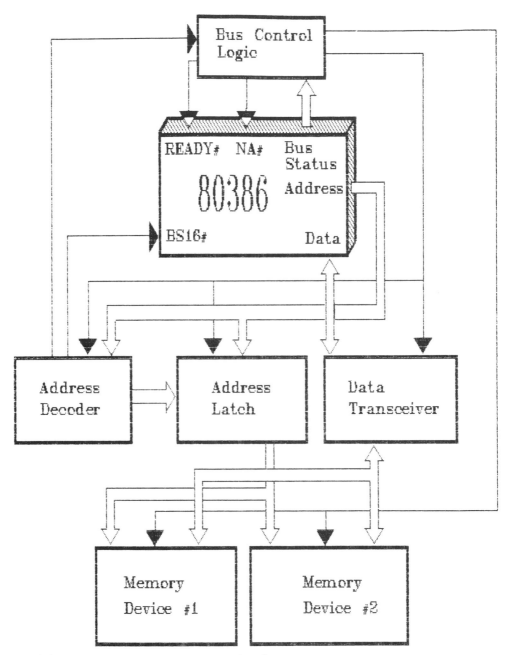

Fig. 4-4. Block diagram of a basic memory interface.

the element in the selected row. The memory elements in each column are coupled to the data lines with n-channel, normally off MOS transistors. The gates of the coupling transistors for each row connect to a corresponding row-select line. The row-select lines are the output lines of an address decoder. Therefore, only those coupling transistors in the selected row (as determined by the specified address to the decoder) are turned on. In this way, information is channeled between data lines and the selected element in each column.

Dynamic RAM (DRAM) Interface

Dynamic RAM (DRAM) memory subsystems provide relatively fast access times at a low cost per bit. On the other hand, DRAMs require a brief idle time between accesses to recharge or refresh the data. Refreshing is done by performing a read and/or write operation. Each refresh operation restores the contents of several word locations in a memory unit. If this time is not allowed, data stored in the DRAM can be lost. If back-to-back accesses are needed to the same bank of DRAMs, the second access is delayed by this recharge time. To avoid this delay, arrange memory so that each subsequent access is most likely to be directed to a different DRAM bank.

For most DRAMs, periodic activation of each of the row address signals internally refreshes the data in every column of the row. Most DRAMs allow a RAS-only (Row Address Select) refresh cycle, the timing of which is the same as a read cycle, except that only the RAS signals are activated (no Column Address Select—CAS— signals) and all the data pins are in the high impedance state.

The frequency of refreshing and the number of rows to be refreshed depend on the type of DRAM. For the DRAMs 64K x N and larger, only the lower eight multiplexed address bits (A7-A0, 256 rows) must be supplied for the refresh cycle. The upper address bits are ignored. Larger DRAMs generally require refresh every 4 milliseconds. Once the system is initialized, the integrity of the DRAM data and states is maintained (even during an 80386 HALT or shutdown state or hardware reset) because all DRAM system functions are performed in hardware external to the CPU.

Some DRAMs require a number of warm-up cycles before they can operate. Generally, there are two ways to provide these cycles: (1) using external logic, activate the RFRQ signal for a preset amount of time. This causes the DRAM control hardware to run several refresh cycles; or (2) as part of the 80386 initialization process, perform several dummy DRAM cycles. One way to do these dummy cycles is to set up the 80386 registers and perform a REP LODS instruction.

80386 CACHE MEMORY

A cache memory is a mechanism interposed in the memory hierarchy between main memory and the processor to improve effective memory transfer rates and to raise processor speeds. The name refers to the fact that the mechanism appears transparent to the user. Cache is usually implemented in semiconductor devices whose speeds are compatible with that of the processor, while the main memory uses a less costly, lower-speed technology.

The cache concept anticipates the likely use of the CPU of data in main storage by organizing a copy of it in cache memory. The concept is extended to include data that is adjacent to data that has been used. It is usual to transfer a block of several words from memory to the cache even though the immediate need is for only one word. If the required word is part of a stream of sequential instructions, it is likely that subsequent instructions will be retrieved with the required first work, which makes repeated access to main memory unnecessary.

All data is stored in main memory. With a cache system, some of that data is

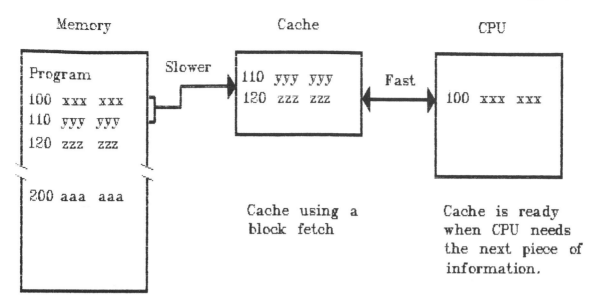

Fig. 4-5. Using cache to look ahead.

duplicated in the cache. When the processor needs to read or write memory, it checks first in the cache. If the necessary data is there (called a cache hit), the 80386 can use it quickly and easily, because cache uses the fastest memory available. If the data is not in cache (called a cache miss) when the processor needs it, the data is fetched from main memory and written to cache.

The cache hit rate is the percentage of all accesses that are hits; that is, they found either the code or data already in cache. This percentage is affected by cache size and physical organization, the program being run, and the cache algorithm. A successful cache is one that has the ability to maintain data in a way that increases the hit rate.

If cache is organized so that the code and data the processor needs most often is in cache, the cache significantly reduces average memory access time. Programs execute more rapidly when most operations are transfers to and from the faster cache memory.

Mainframe computers have used cache memories for a long time. The arrival of fast 32-bit processors created the need for such hardware in smaller machines. The 80386 works with an off-chip cache. The one described here consists of 10 discrete ICs. The physical address cache requires no overhead, in contrast to the logical address caching implemented by CPUs with on-board caches. The objective is to sustain a 3.5 to 4-MIPS (millions of instructions per second) operations with a 90 percent hit rate, given the following elements: a 32-Mbyte bus, two clock bus cycles, a 16-MHz 80386, the 80387 numeric coprocessor and a 32-Kbyte physical address code and data cache.

Predicting the location of the next memory access would be nearly impossible if programs accessed memory totally at random. Actually, programs tend to access memory near the most previous access. This principle is called *program locality* or *locality of reference*. Program locality is what makes a cache system effective. For

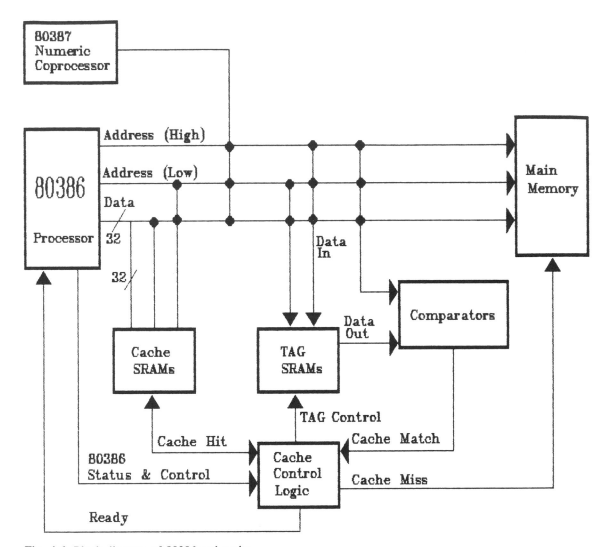

Fig. 4-6. Block diagram of 80386 and cache.

instance, stacks grow and shrink from one end so that the next few accesses are all near the top of stack (TOS).

To increase the hit rate, the processor uses a block fetch. The cache controller divides main memory into blocks (also known as line size) that are generally 2, 4, 8, or 16 bytes long. Block size is one of the most important parameters in the design of a cache memory system. If the block is too small, main memory fetch effectiveness and the hit rate are both reduced. Too large a block reduces the number of blocks that fit into the cache. It also tends to require a wider bus between the cache and main memory, as well as more static and dynamic memory, which results in increased cost.

A 32-bit processor usually uses two or four words per block. When a cache miss occurs, the cache controller moves the entire block that contains the word from main memory into cache.

The block fetch can bring in the data located *before* the requested byte (called lookbehind), the data that *follows* it (called lookahead), or both. When locations are accessed in ascending order (for example, code accesses), an access to the first byte in the block results in a lookahead fetch. When memory locations are accessed in descending order (such as stack PUSHing), the fetch is lookbehind.

Cache Organization

Most programs refer to code segments, subroutines, lists, buffers located in different parts of address space, and various stacks. An effective cache must hold several noncontiguous blocks of data.

Fully Associative Cache. A fully associative cache determines which blocks are stored in the cache at any time. In this cache, there is no single relationship between all the addresses of the blocks, so the cache has to store the entire address of each block as well as the block itself. When the processor needs data from memory, the cache controller compares the address of the data with each of the addresses in the cache. This is relatively slow and expensive; it violates the main principle of limiting the number of required address comparisons.

Direct Mapped Cache. Each direct mapped cache address has two parts. The first (the cache index field) contains enough bits to specify a block location within the cache. The second (the tag field) contains enough bits to distinguish a block from other blocks that may be stored at a particular cache location.

The many address comparisons of the fully associative cache are required because any block from main memory can be stored in any location of the cache. That is what forces the address comparison of all blocks. The direct mapped cache, on the other hand, reduces the number of comparisons needed by allowing each block from main memory only one possible location in the cache.

The direct mapped cache has its drawbacks. If the processor makes frequent requests from a pair of locations where two pieces of memory are mapped to the same cache, the controller must access main memory frequently, because only one of these locations can be in the cache at a time.

Set Associative Cache. The set associative cache is a compromise between the fully associative and the direct mapped caches. The set associative cache has several groups of direct mapped blocks that operate in parallel. For each cache index, there are several block locations allowed, one in each set or group. A block of arriving data can go into any block location of its set.

The excessive main memory traffic that is a drawback of a direct mapped cache is reduced and the hit rate increased, because the set associative cache has several places for blocks with the same cache index in their addresses. The set associative cache, however, is more complex than the direct mapped cache.

In a two-way set associative cache, there are two locations in cache where each block can be stored. The controller must make two comparisons to determine in which block the requested data is located or if it is there at all. A set associative cache also needs a wider tag field and more SRAM space to store the tags. Next, the cache controller must decide which block of the cache to overwrite when a block fetch is executed since there are several locations in which the data from main memory can be stored. Finally, when information is stored in a set associative cache, additional logic comes into play for the decision that must be made as to which block should store the information.

Cache Updating

The main thing to remember in a cache system is that at least two copies of the same data can exist at once: one in the cache and the other in main memory. If one copy is changed and the other is not, two sets of information are now identified by the same address. The cache must contain an updating system to prevent stale data

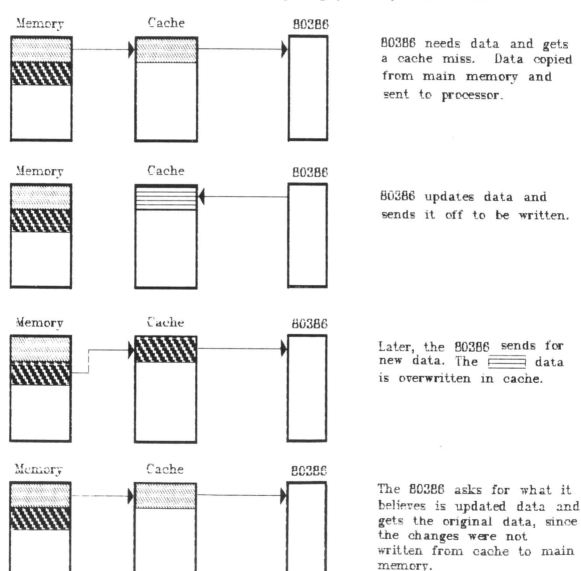

80386 needs data and gets a cache miss. Data copied from main memory and sent to processor.

80386 updates data and sends it off to be written.

Later, the 80386 sends for new data. The ▭ data is overwritten in cache.

The 80386 asks for what it believes is updated data and gets the original data, since the changes were not written from cache to main memory.

Fig. 4-7. Creation of stale or incorrect data.

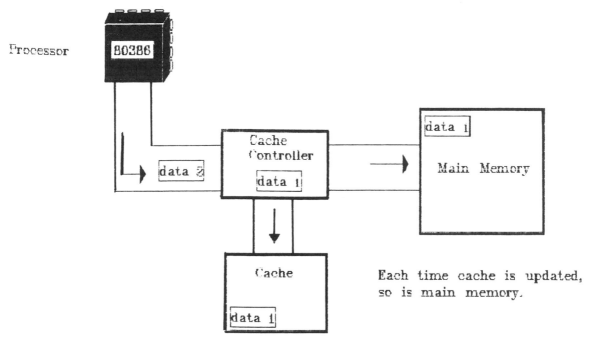

Fig. 4-8. Example of write-through.

from being used as good data. Figure 4-7 illustrates how data can become stale and incorrect. To ensure cache coherency, there are three general methods used: write-through, buffered write-through, and write-back.

Write-Through. With the write-through method of cache updating, the cache controller copies updated data back to main memory immediately. Main memory stays current with cache. That immediate updating allows any block in cache to be over-written at any time without loss of data. The write-through update system is simple, but the time required to write the data to main memory reduces performance and increases bus traffic (a major problem in a multiprocessing system).

Buffered Write-Through. In a buffered write-through update scheme, any write to main memory is buffered; that is, it is delayed in the cache prior to being copied into main memory (the cache circuits control the access to main memory asynchronously to CPU execution). The processor then begins a new cycle before the write cycle to main memory is completed. If a write is followed by a read that is a cache hit, the read can be done while the cache controller is busy updating main memory. This buffering avoids the decrease in performance of the write-through system.

There is one major drawback. Since there is generally only a single write buffered, two consecutive writes to main memory require that the processor wait. In addition, a write followed by a read miss also requires the processor to wait. A *wait state* is an internal state entered by a processor when a synchronizing signal is not present. The wait state is used to synchronize the processor to slower memory.

Write-Back. In a write-back updating scheme, an "altered" bit in the tag field is used. This bit is set if the block has been updated with new data and is more recent

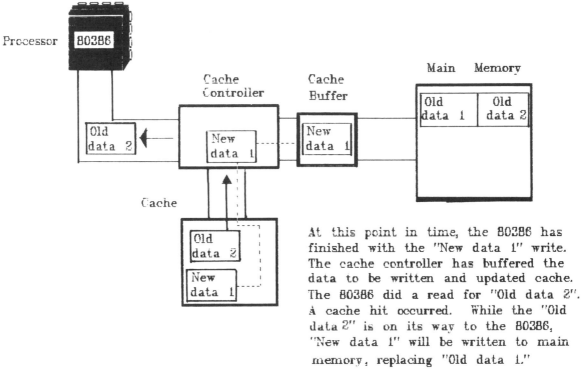

At this point in time, the 80386 has finished with the "New data 1" write. The cache controller has buffered the data to be written and updated cache. The 80386 did a read for "Old data 2". A cache hit occurred. While the "Old data 2" is on its way to the 80386, "New data 1" will be written to main memory, replacing "Old data 1."

Fig. 4-9. Example of buffered write-through.

than its original copy in main memory. Before the cache controller overwrites a block in cache, it checks this altered bit. If the bit is set, the controller writes the block to memory before loading new data into the cache.

Write-back is faster than write-through because, in general, the number of times a block is altered and must be written to main memory is less than the number of times that blocks are read and overwritten.

Write-back has several disadvantages, however. The first is that all altered blocks must be written to main memory *before* another device can access them. Second, in case of catastrophic failure such as a power failure, where cache is lost but main memory is preserved, there is no way to tell which locations in main memory contain stale data. Finally, a write-back cache controller must contain more (and more complex) logic than a write-through. For example, when a write-back system writes an altered block to memory, it constructs the write address from the tag and performs the write-back cycle as well as the newly requested access.

Cache coherency. Stale data in main memory, caused by write operations, is virtually eliminated with write-through and write-back. There is a sub-category of stale data that occurs when caches are used in a system that has more than one device assessing the main memory. For instance, suppose two devices copy a section of memory and device 1 updates it first. When device 2 writes back, it will destroy any changes made by device 1. The coherency of the cache is said to be destroyed. In general, there are three cache coherency approaches:

CACHE FLUSHING—A cache flush writes altered data to main memory and clears the contents of the cache. If all caches in the system flush before a device writes to shared memory, potential for stale data in any cache is eliminated. The advantage of flushing is that it takes very simple hardware. The major disadvantage is that a memory access that follows a flush must, by definition, be a cache miss until the cache is filled with new data.

HARDWARE TRANSPARENCY—A hardware solution to stale data ensures that all accesses to main memory (that memory that is mapped by a cache) are seen by the cache. This can be done by either (1) copying all cache writes both to main memory and to all other caches that share the memory or (2) routing all cache writes through a single cache. Figure 4-10 shows various hardware approaches.

NON-CACHEABLE MEMORY—Another way to solve cache concurrency problems is to designate shared memory as non-cacheable. In a system using this method, all accesses to shared memory are designated cache misses because this memory is *never* copied to cache. The non-cacheable memory can be identified by using high-address bits or chip-select logic.

System designers tend to use some combination of the three methods to ensure data validity. For example, one system may use non-cacheable memory for slow I/O tasks such as printing and hardware transparency for time-critical I/O operations such as paging.

80386 Cache

The prototype cache is a 64 Kbyte, direct mapped cache, organized as 16,384 entries. Each entry contains 32 bits of data along with 16 bits of tag information. The line size (the unit of transfer) between the cache and DRAM is 32 bits. The 10 cache memory chips consist of eight 8K × 8-bit data SRAMs and two 8K × 8-bit tag field SRAMs. Two comparators and two PALs (Programmable Array Logic) are used for the cache control. Eight more discrete logic chips provide interface and buffers.

No present bits are necessary since each entry is presumed to contain a valid 32-bit doubleword at all times. The cache subsystem uses a buffered write-through to update the DRAMs. To the 80386, the cache/DRAM combination achieves zero wait-states during read hits and typically 1 wait state during writes. The processor uses about 4 wait states during read misses.

In a direct-mapped cache, each DRAM location is mapped to only one location within the cache. The mapping is done by dividing the processor's 30-bit physical address into two parts: a 16-bit tag and a 14-bit index. The tag is assigned to the upper address lines (A16-A31). The index corresponds to the lower address lines (A2-A15). Since each DRAM location with the same A2-A15 maps to the same location in cache, only one of these DRAM locations can be present in the cache at any one time.

Together, the tag and index fields uniquely identify a doubleword location in main memory. Additionally, the index selects one of the 16,384 cache memory locations. The lowest two address bits are encoded in the form of four byte enables; A31 differentiates between non-cacheable EPROM addresses and cacheable DRAM addresses.

If the requested data is in cache, a read can be performed in 2 clock cycles. Otherwise, reads require six clocks. The key to success in cache design is to maximize

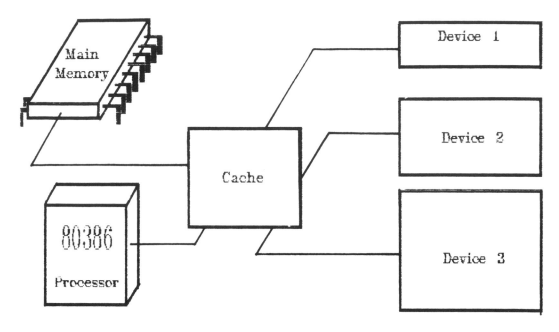

Routing all cache writes through a single cache

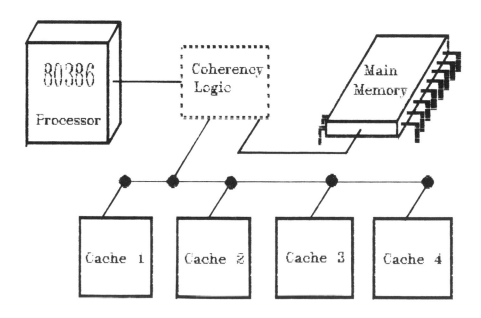

Each write updates main memory and all caches that share the memory.

Fig. 4-10. Hardware cache concurrency.

the number of 2-clock bus cycles relative to six-clock cycles. This is done by making cache memory large, 16 to 64 Kbytes.

The cache uses the buffered write-through to update the DRAMs. During the write cycles, new data is written into the cache and simultaneously into DRAM. By use of a buffer, the DRAM write cycle is overlapped with a subsequent bus cycle. This overlap allows writes to be performed in only three clocks.

Buffered write-through is implemented by separating the state machine that controls cache from the state machine that runs the DRAMs. Since both cache and DRAM has its own controller, overlapped operation is possible. A state machine within the cache PAL knows when a memory cycle is necessary, while the DRAM state machine checks this request only when ready to start a new cycle.

5

Interfacing:
Local Bus and Input/Output

The 80386 features 32-bit wide internal and external data paths and eight general-purpose 32-bit registers. The processor outputs 32-bit physical addresses directly, for a physical memory of four gigabytes. This chapter explores more of the sub-systems that surrounds the 80386, by discussing local bus interface, Input/Output and I/O interfacing.

LOCAL BUS INTERFACE

A bus is a path over which data are transferred, from any of several sources to any of several destinations. It acts as a common connection among a number of locations such as between the CPU, memory, and peripheral devices. Bus lines act as the means of communications. Figure 5-1 shows a block diagram of a general bus interface.

The 80386 performs a variety of bus operations in response to both internal and external conditions, such as to service interrupts. The 80386 communicates with external memory, I/O, and other devices through a parallel bus interface. This interface consists of a bi-directional data bus, a separate address bus, five bus status pins, and three bus control pins. Those functions operate as follows:

BI-DIRECTIONAL DATA BUS—There are 32 pins (D31-D0) and 8, 16, 24, or 32 bits of data can be transferred at once.

ADDRESS BUS—This bus generates 32-bit addresses and consists of 30 address pins (A31-A2) and four byte-enable pins (BE3#-BE0#). Each of these byte-enable pins corresponds to one of our bytes of the 32-bit data bus. The address pins identify a 4-byte location. The byte-enable pins select the active bytes within the 4-byte location.

BUS STATUS—These pins establish the type of bus cycle to be done. The outputs show the following conditions:

    1. LOCK#—Locked bus cycle

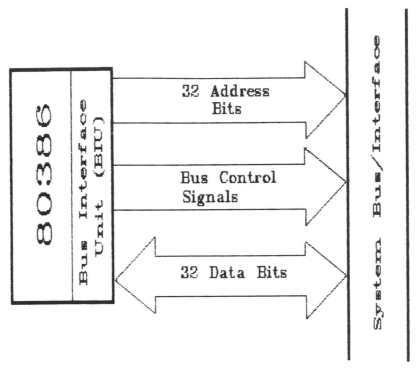

Fig. 5-1. General bus interface.

    2. Address Status (ADS#)—Address bus outputs valid
    3. Data/Control (D/C#)—Data or Control cycle
    4. Memory/I/O (M/I/O)—Memory or I/O cycle
    5. Write/Read (W/R#)—Write or Read cycle

BUS CONTROL—These pins allow external logic to control the bus cycle on a cycle-by-cycle basis. The inputs do the following:

    1. READY#—Ends the current bus cycle. It controls the bus cycle duration.
    2. Next Address (NA#)—This pin allows address pipelining. That is, it emits address and status signals for the next bus cycle during the current cycle.
    3. Bus Size 16 (BS16#)—The bus activates this pin, to indicate that it is a 16-bit bus and will pass 16-bit information. Data is transferred on the lower 16 bits of the data bus. An extra cycle provides for transfers of more than 16 bits.

The following seven pins control the execution of instructions in the 80386 and interface with external bus masters. The processor provides both a standard interface to communicate with other bus masters and a special interface support for a numeric coprocessor.

    1. RESET—This input forces the 80386 to a known reset state.

2. INTR (Maskable Interrupt) and NMI (Nonmaskable Interrupt)—These inputs cause the processor to interrupt its current instruction stream and begin execution of an interrupt service routine.

3. CLK2—This input provides a double-frequency clock signal for synchronous operation. A 16-MHz 80386 uses a 32-MHz CLK2 signal. That is, CLK is divided by two internally so the 80386 frequency is half the CLK2 signal frequency.

4. BUSY#, ERROR#, and PEREQ (Coprocessor Request)—These signals make up the interface to an external numeric coprocessor. ERROR# and BUSY# are status signals from the coprocessor. PEREQ allows the coprocessor to request data from the 80386.

5. HOLD—This signal can be generated by another bus master, to request that the 80386 release control of the bus. The 80386 activates the HLDA (Hold Acknowledge) signal as it gives up control of the local bus.

Figure 5-2 summarizes the 80386 Signal Pins. See Chapter 7 for a full list of the 80386 pins.

There are seven types of bus operations: memory read, memory write, I/O read, I/O write, instruction fetch, interrupt acknowledgment, and Halt/Shutdown.

Each bus cycle is started when the address is valid on the address bus, and the bus status pins are driven to states that correspond to the type of bus cycle. Memory read and memory write cycles can be locked to prevent another bus master (See Chapter 12 and Appendix 4 for more information on the MULTIBUS masters/slaves.) from using the local bus and also to allow for indivisible read-modify-write operations.

Address pipelining allows bus cycles to be overlapped, which increases the amount of time available for the memory or I/O to respond. The first bus cycle after an idle bus state is always non-pipelined. To initiate address pipelining, this cycle must be extended by at least one CLK cycle so that the address and status can be output before the end of the cycle. Subsequent cycles can be pipelined as long as no idle bus cycles occur.

Bus States

The 80386 processor uses a double-frequency clock (CLK2) that generates the 80386's internal processor clock signal (CLK). This internal clock matches the external 82384 (Clock Generator) CLK. The 82384 CLK is allowed to lag CLK2 slightly, but never to lead CLK2. The 82384 CLK can be used reliably as a phase status indicator.

Each bus cycle is made up of at least two bus states: T1 and T2. Each of the bus states in turn is comprised of two CLK2 cycles, which can be thought of as Phase 1 and Phase 2 of the bus state. During the first bus state (T1), both address and bus status pins go active. During the second state (T2) which is the end of the second CLK cycle, the bus cycle terminates. When no bus cycles are needed by the 80386, the 80386 remains in idle bus state (T1).

The maximum data transfer rate for a bus operation is determined by the 80386 internal clock, and is 32 bits for every two CLK cycles. That works out to 32 megabytes per second (CLK2 = 32 MHz, internal CLK = 16 MHz).

A handy feature of the 80386 is that the timing of address and status outputs can

Signal Name	Signal Function	Active State	Input/ Output	Input Synch or Asynch to CLK2	Output High Impedence during HLDA ?
CLK2	Clock	--	I	--	--
D0–D31	Data Bus	HIGH	I/O	S	Yes
BE0#–BE3#	Byte Enables	LOW	O	--	Yes
A2–A31	Address Bus	HIGH	O	--	Yes
W/R#	Write–Read Indicator	HIGH	O	--	Yes
D/C#	Data–Control Indicator	HIGH	O	--	Yes
M/IO#	Memory I/O Indicator	HIGH	O	--	Yes
LOCK#	Bus Lock Indicator	LOW	O	--	Yes
ADS#	Address Status	LOW	O	--	Yes
NA#	Next Address Request	LOW	I	S	--
BS16#	Bus Size 16	LOW	I	S	--
READY#	Transfer Acknowledge	LOW	I	S	--
HOLD	Bus Hold Request	HIGH	I	S	--
HLDA	Bus Hold Acknowledge	HIGH	O	--	No
PEREQ	Coprocessor Request	HIGH	I	A	--
BUSY#	Coprocessor Busy	LOW	I	A	--
ERROR#	Coprocessor Error	LOW	I	A	--
INTR	Maskable Interrupt Request	HIGH	I	A	--
NMI	Non–Maskable Interrupt Request	HIGH	I	A	--
RESET	Reset	HIGH	I	S	--

Fig. 5-2. Summary of 80386 signal pins.

be controlled so the outputs become valid before the end of the previous bus cycle. This overlapping allows bus cycles to be pipelined. The address pipelining increases bus throughput without decreasing allowable memory or I/O access time. A 16-MHz 80386 transfers data at the maximum rate of 32 megabytes per second while it allows an address access time of three CLK cycles (187.5 nanoseconds at CLK=16 MHz, neglecting signal delays). Without address pipelining, the access time is only two CLK cycles (125 nanoseconds at CLK=16 MHz).

The 80386 addresses up to four gigabytes (2^{32} bytes, addresses 00000000H to FFFFFFFFH) of physical memory and 64 kilobytes (2^{16} bytes, addresses 00000000H to 0000FFFFH) of I/O. The processor maintains separate physical memory space and I/O space.

The memory spaces and I/O space are sequences of 32-bit doublewords (2^{30} 32-bit memory locations and 2^{14} 32-bit I/O ports maximum). Each doubleword begins at a physical address that is a multiple of four. The doubleword also has four individually addressable bytes at consecutive addresses. 80386 pins A31-A2 correspond to the most significant bits of the physical address. Note that these pins address doublewords of memory.

For each bus cycle of a data transfer, data can be transferred in groups of 8, 16, 24, or 32 bits. These transfers need two bus cycles, which are automatically made available by the 80386. Certain combinations of BE3#-BE0# are never produced because the 80386 only operates on bytes, words, and doublewords. For instance, a bus cycle is never done with only BE0# and BE2# active because such a transfer would be an operation on two noncontiguous bytes at the same time.

Read and Write Cycles

In a local bus interface, read cycles are of two types: pipelined address cycles and non-pipelined address cycles. In a pipelined address cycle, the address bus and bus status signals are output *before* the beginning of the cycle to allow longer memory access times. In a non-pipelined address cycle, the address bus and the bus status signals become valid during the first CLK period of the cycle.

Like Read Cycles, Write Cycles are of two types: pipelined address and non-pipelined address.

Interrupts

The 80386's execution can be altered by both hardware- and software-generated interrupts. A hardware interrupt occurs when an active input is placed on one of two 80386 interrupt request inputs (NMI—Non-Maskable Interrupts, and INTR—Maskable Interrupt). The software interrupt occurs when the 80386 encounters either an INT (Interrupt) instruction or finds a software condition (an exception) that needs servicing.

Interrupt Latency is the elapsed time before an interrupt request is serviced. Any of the following causes can affect interrupt latency:

- If the interrupt service routine saves registers that are not automatically saved by the 80386. These instructions also delay the beginning of interrupt servicing.
- Saving the Flags Register (EFLAGS) and CS:EIP (Code Segment, Instruction Pointer) register which contains the return address.
- If interrupts are masked, an INTR will be recognized only after interrupts are re-enabled.
- If the processor is currently executing an instruction, the instruction must be completed. An interrupt request is recognized only on an instruction boundary, with the single exception that Repeat String instructions are interruptable after each iteration.
- If the interrupt servicing needs a task switch, registers must be saved and others restored.

Interrupt Acknowledge Cycle. As part of the acknowledge cycle, an unmasked interrupt causes the 80386 processor to suspend execution of the current program and perform some instructions from another program. This second program is called a *service routine* (or sometimes *handler*).

The 80386 performs two back-to-back interrupt acknowledgment cycles in response to an active INTR input. These interrupt acknowledgment cycles, special bus cycles, activate the 8259A programmable interrupt controller which, in turn, supplies the interrupt vector on D0-D7 of the data bus.

System logic must delay READY# to extend the cycle to the minimum pulse-width requirements of the 8259A. In addition, the 80386 inserts at least a 160 nanosecond bus idle time (four T1 states) between the two cycles to match the recovery time of the 8259A.

BS16# Cycle. The 80386 performs data transfers for both 16- and 32-bit data buses. A control input, BS16#, allows the bus size to be specified for each bus cycle. This dynamic sizing is what allows the 80386 to handle both widths of data.

If the highest possible internal communication speed is necessary, a direct bus interconnection can be used. The use of a 16-bit data bus can be advantageous for some systems. Memory that is implemented as 16-bit (rather than 32-bit) reduces support chip count, i.e., buffers, latches and so on. Moreover, I/O addresses that are located at word boundaries (rather than doubleword boundaries) can be software compatible with other systems that use 16-bit microprocessors.

When the 80386 receives the BS16# input, the processor transfers data for a 16-bit data bus, using data bus signals D15-D0. If there is no input, the 80386 transfers 32-bit data. The 80386 automatically performs two or three cycles for data transfers larger than 16 bits and for misaligned (odd-addressed) 16-bit transfers. BS16# is supplied by external hardware, either directly from the addressed device or through chip select decoding. BS16# is sampled at the start of Phase 2 only in CLK cycle as long as ADS# is not active. If BS16# and READY# are sampled low in the same CLK cycle, the 80386 assumes a 16-bit data bus.

The BS16# affects the data transfer speed only for transfers in which BE0# and BE1# are active and BE2# or BE3# active at the same time. In these transfers, the 80386 performs two bus cycles using only the lower half of the data bus. If a BS16# cycle needs one more cycle, the 80386 retains the current address for the second cycle. Because address pipelining requires that the next address be generated on the bus before the end of the current bus cycle, address pipelining can not be used with BS16# cycles. That is why both signals are sampled at the same sampling window. BS16# must be active before (or at the same time) as NA# (Next Address) to guarantee 16-bit operation. Once NA# is sampled active in a bus cycle and BS16# is *not* active at that time, BS16# is locked out internally.

Halt/Shutdown Cycle. The 80386 halts in response to a HLT instruction. The shutdown condition occurs when the 80386 is processing a double fault and encounters a protection fault. The 80386 can not recover from this and shuts down. Externally, a shutdown cycle differs from a halt cycle only in the resulting address bus outputs. The following outlines the steps:

• M/IO# and W/R# are driven high. D/C# is driven low to indicate a halt cycle.

- All address bus outputs are driven low.

    > For a Halt condition, BE2# is active.
    > For a Shutdown condition, BE0# is active.

- READY# must be asserted to complete the halt or shutdown cycle. The 80386 remains in halt or in shutdown until:

    > NMI goes high. Then the 80386 services the interrupt.
    > RESET goes high. The 80386 is reinitialized.

In the halt condition, if maskable interrupts are enabled, an active INTR input causes the 80386 to end the halt cycle and service the interrupt. This is not true in the shutdown condition. The 80386 can service processor extensions (PEREQ input) requests and HOLD (HOLD input) requests while in both the halt or shutdown conditions.

Bus Lock and HOLD

Locked cycles must be used when it is critical that two or more bus cycles follow one another immediately, especially in a system in which more than one device may control the local bus. If locked cycles are not used, the cycles can be separated by a cycle from another bus master.

As a rule of thumb, any bus cycles that must be performed back-to-back (without any intervening bus cycles from another bus master) should be locked. The 80386 LOCK# output signals the other bus masters that they *may not* gain control of the bus. Also, the 80386 with LOCK# asserted will not recognize a HOLD request from another bus master.

The LOCK prefix on certain instructions activates the LOCK# signal. The XCHG instruction, a descriptor update, interrupt acknowledgment cycles and a page table update will each automatically assert the LOCK# signal.

The maximum time of the LOCK# depends on the instruction being executed and the number of wait states per cycle. The longest period in real mode is two bus cycles plus about two clocks. This happens during the XCHG instruction and in LOCKed read-modify-write operations. The longest duration in protected mode is five bus cycles and about 15 clocks. This occurs when a hardware or software interrupt happens and the 80386 performs: a LOCKed read of the gate in the IDT, a read of the target descriptor, and a write of the accessed bit in the target descriptor.

To get control of the local bus, the requesting bus master drives the 80386 HOLD input active. The 80386 finishes its tasks and then sets all outputs (except for HLDA) to the three-state OFF condition to remove itself from the bus. Then the 80386 drives HLDA active to signal the requesting bus master that it can take control. The requesting master must maintain HOLD active until the master no longer needs the bus. The 80386 is waiting for HOLD to go low, when the processor will drive HLDA low and begin a bus cycle (if one is pending).

The 80386 is not idle during the HOLD; it continues executing instructions in its Prefetch Queue. Program execution is halted if a read cycle is needed while the 80386 cannot get the local bus. The 80386 queues one write cycle internally, awaiting the return of the bus access. If more than one write is needed, the 80386 must delay further execution until the writes have been done.

While HOLD has priority over most bus cycles, there are three instances where it is not recognized: (1) between two interrupt acknowledgment cycles; (2) during locked cycles; and (3) between two repeated cycles of a BS16 cycle.

The 80386 ignores all inputs while in the HOLD state, except for these three: (1) One NMI request is recognized and latched. It will be serviced after HOLD is released. (2) RESET takes precedence over HOLD. An active RESET input reinitializes the 80386. (3) HOLD is monitored to see when the 80386 can regain control of the bus.

INPUT/OUTPUT AND I/O INTERFACING

The 80386 processor supports 8-, 16-, and 32-bit Input/Output (I/O) devices where I/O can be mapped either (1) onto the 4 gigabyte physical memory address space using general-purpose operand manipulation instructions or (2) onto the 64-kilobyte I/O address space, using specific I/O instructions. I/O mapping and memory mapping differ in three major ways.

- Memory mapping offers more flexibility in protection than I/O mapping does because memory-mapped devices are protected by protection and memory management features. Depending on where the device is mapped in memory space, a device can be inaccessible to a task, can be visible but protected, or can be fully accessible. Paging gives the same protection levels to each 4-kilobyte page and shows whether that page has been written to or not.
- The address decoding necessary to generate chip selects for I/O mapped devices is generally simpler than for memory-mapped devices. In addition, I/O-mapped devices reside in the 64 kilobyte I/O space of the 80386, while memory-mapped devices reside in much larger memory space that makes use of more address lines, the 4 gigabytes.
- Memory-mapped devices can be accessed using any 80386 instruction. This allows efficient coding of I/O-to-memory, memory-to-I/O, and I/O-to-I/O transfers. I/O-mapped devices can be accessed through four instructions: IN, INS, OUT, OUTS. All I/O transfers are done via the AL (8-bit), AX (16 bit), or EAX (32 bit) registers. The first 256 bytes of I/O space are directly addressable and the entire 64-kilobyte I/O space is indirectly addressable through the DX register.

Interfaces to peripheral devices depend not only upon data width, but also on the signal requirements of the device and its location within the memory or I/O space. Address decoding to generate the correct chip selects must be done whether I/O devices are memory-mapped or I/O-mapped. Addresses can be assigned to I/O devices arbitrarily within the I/O or memory space. These addresses should be selected to minimize the number of address lines needed.

The 80386 has a separate I/O address space that is distinct from physical memory and that can be used to address the input/output ports that are used for external 16-bit devices. This I/O address space is made up of 2^{16} (65K) individually addressable 8-bit ports. Any even-numbered consecutive 8-bit ports can be treated as a 16-bit port and any doubleword-addressed consecutive 8-bit ports can be treated as a 32-bit port. That means that the total I/O address space accommodates up to 64K of 8-bit ports (numbered 0 through 65535), up to 32K 16-bit ports (numbered 0, 2, 4, up to 65534), or up to 16K 32-bit ports (numbered 0, 4, 8, up to 65532).

Memory-mapped I/O allows programming flexibility. Any instruction that references memory can be used to access an I/O port located in the memory space. Memory-mapped I/O is performed using the full instruction set and maintains the full complement of addressing modes for selecting the desired I/O device. However, memory-mapped I/O, like any of the other memory references, is still subject to access protection and control when executing in protected mode.

I/O Instructions

The 80386 I/O instructions give access to the processor's I/O ports for transfer of data to and from peripheral devices. These instructions have as one operand the address of a port in the I/O space. There are two classes of I/O instructions: those that transfer strings of items located in memory (known either as ''string I/O instructions'' or ''block I/O instructions'') and those that transfer a single byte, word, or doubleword located in a register.

The block I/O instructions INS and OUTS move blocks of data between I/O ports and memory space. These instructions use the DX register to specify the address of a port in the I/O address space. The 8-bit ports are numbered 0 through 65535. The 16-bit ports are numbered 0, 2, 4, and up to 65534. The 32-bit ports are numbered 0, 4, 8, and up to 65532.

The IN and OUT instructions move data between I/O ports and the AL (for 8-bit I/O), AX (for 16-bit I/O) and EAX (for 32-bit I/O). IN and OUT address I/O ports either directly (with the addresses of one of up to 256 port addresses coded in the instruction) or indirectly (using the DX register to one of up to 64K port addresses).

Protection, Privilege, and I/O

The I/O privilege level offers protection by allowing a task to access all I/O devices or by preventing a task from accessing any I/O device. In virtual-8086 mode, the I/O permission bitmap can be used to select the privilege level for any combination of I/O bytes.

I/O protection is provided in two ways: the I/O permission bit map of a 80386 TSS segment defines the right to use ports in the I/O address space; and the IOPL (I/O Privilege Level) in the EFLAGS register defines the right to use I/O related instructions. These mechanisms work only in protected mode, which includes the virtual 8086 (V86) mode. They do *not* work in real mode. In real mode, any procedure executes I/O instructions and any I/O port can be addressed by any of those instructions.

I/O Permission Bit Map. Instructions that directly use addresses in the 80386's I/O space are IN, INS, OUT, and OUTS. The 80386 can selectively trap references to specific I/O addresses. The mechanism that allows this trapping is the I/O Permis-

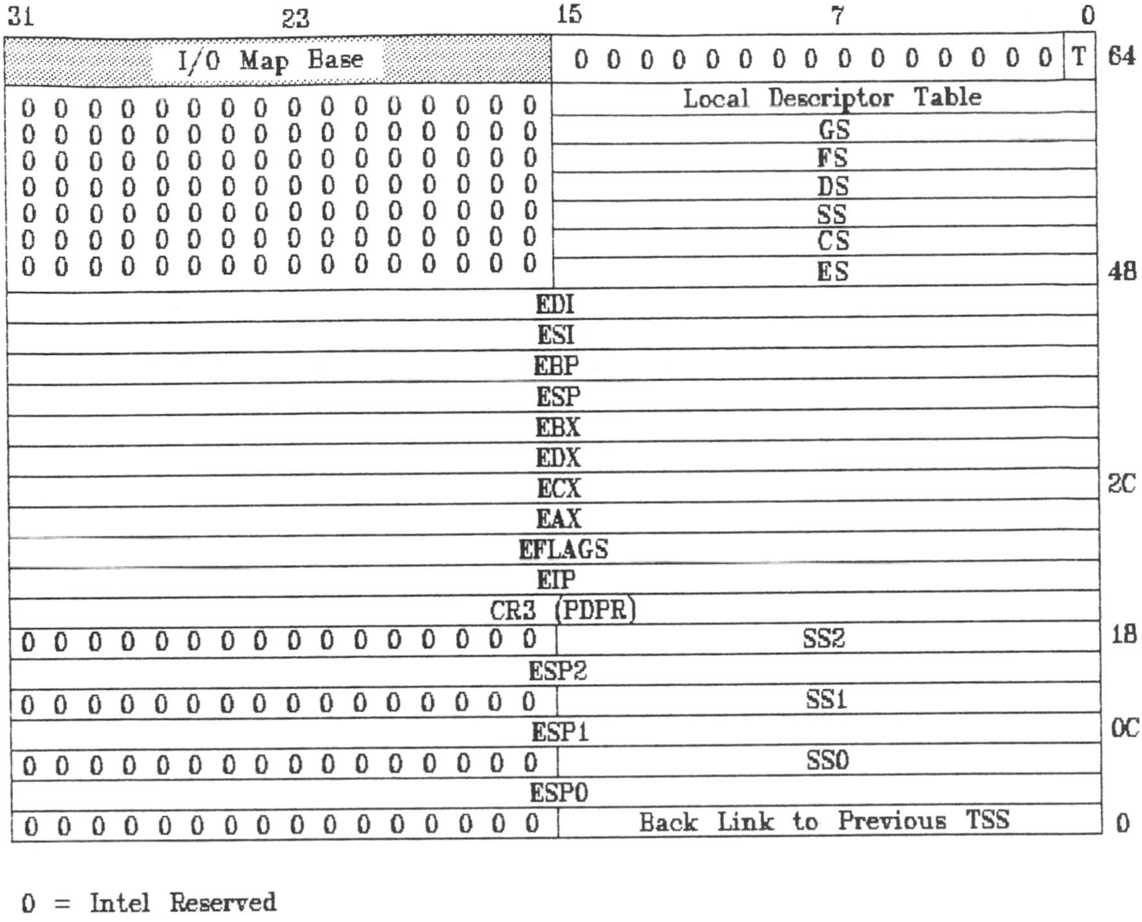

31	23	15	7	0	
I/O Map Base		0 0 0 0 0 0 0 0 0 0 0 0 0 0 0 T			64
0 0 0 0 0 0 0 0 0 0 0 0 0 0 0		Local Descriptor Table			
0 0 0 0 0 0 0 0 0 0 0 0 0 0 0		GS			
0 0 0 0 0 0 0 0 0 0 0 0 0 0 0		FS			
0 0 0 0 0 0 0 0 0 0 0 0 0 0 0		DS			
0 0 0 0 0 0 0 0 0 0 0 0 0 0 0		SS			
0 0 0 0 0 0 0 0 0 0 0 0 0 0 0		CS			
0 0 0 0 0 0 0 0 0 0 0 0 0 0 0		ES			48
EDI					
ESI					
EBP					
ESP					
EBX					
EDX					
ECX					2C
EAX					
EFLAGS					
EIP					
CR3 (PDPR)					
0 0 0 0 0 0 0 0 0 0 0 0 0 0 0		SS2			18
ESP2					
0 0 0 0 0 0 0 0 0 0 0 0 0 0 0		SS1			
ESP1					0C
0 0 0 0 0 0 0 0 0 0 0 0 0 0 0		SS0			
ESP0					
0 0 0 0 0 0 0 0 0 0 0 0 0 0 0		Back Link to Previous TSS			0

0 = Intel Reserved

Fig. 5-3. TSS with I/O map.

sion Bit Map in the TSS segment. Figure 5-3 shows where the I/O Map appears in the TSS.

The Map is a bit vector and its size and location in the TSS segment are variable. The 80386 locates the Map by means of the 16-bit *I/O Map Base* field in the fixed portion of the TSS which contains the offset of the beginning of the Map. The upper limit of the I/O Permission Map is the same as the limit of the TSS segment. Because the I/O Permission Map is in the TSS, different tasks can have different Maps. Thus, the operating system can allocate ports to a task by changing the I/O Permission Map in the task's TSS.

Each bit in the Map corresponds to an I/O port byte address. That is, the bit for port 41 is found at I/O Map Base + 5, bit offset 1. The 80386 tests all bits that correspond to the I/O addresses spanned by an I/O operation. That is, a doubleword operation will test four bits that correspond to four adjacent byte addresses. If any tested bit is set, the 80386 signals a general protection exception. If all tested bits are zero, the I/O operation proceeds.

When the 80386 encounters an I/O instruction in protected mode, it first checks whether CPL (Current Privilege Level) is less than or equal to IOPL. If true, the I/O operation proceeds. If not true, the 80386 checks the I/O Permission Map. (Note that in virtual 8086 mode, the 80386 checks the Map without regard for IOPL.) If the I/O Map Base is greater than or equal to TSS limit, the TSS segment has no I/O Permission Map and *all* I/O instructions cause exceptions when CPL is greater than IOPL.

Instructions that deal with I/O not only need to be restricted, they need to be executed by procedures which execute at privilege levels other than zero. To allow this, the 80386 uses two bits of the flags register to store the IOPL. The IOPL defines the privilege level needed to execute I/O related instructions. The following six instructions can be executed only if CPL is less than or equal to IOPL. The instructions are called "sensitive" because they are sensitive to the value stored in IOPL.

IN	Input
INS	Input String
OUT	Output
OUTS	Output String
CLI	Clear Interrupt-Enable Flag
STI	Set Interrupt-Enable Flag

To use sensitive instructions, a procedure executes at a privilege level at least as privileged as that stored in the IOPL. Any attempt by a less privileged procedure to use one of the six instructions produces a general protection exception.

Each task in the system has its own unique copy of the flags register. Therefore each task can have a different IOPL. A task can change the IOPL *only* with a POPF instruction. Such changes are privileged. No procedure may alter IOPL in the flag register unless the procedure is executing at privilege level zero. Any less privileged instruction or procedure attempting to alter IOPL does not result in an exception; IOPL remains unchanged.

Basic I/O Interface

In a typical 80386 system design, a number of slave I/O devices are controlled through the same local bus interface. Other I/O devices, especially those who can control the local bus, require more complex interfaces.

The performance and flexibility of the 80386 local bus interface plus the increased availability of programmable and semi-custom logic make it feasible to design custom bus control logic that meets the requirements of any particular system. The basic I/O interface is shown in the Fig. 5-4.

The following components are compatible with this interface:

8041, 8042	Universal Peripheral Interface
8237	DMA Controller (remote node)
8253, 8254	Programmable Interval Timer
8255	Programmable Peripheral Interface
8259A	Programmable Interrupt Controller

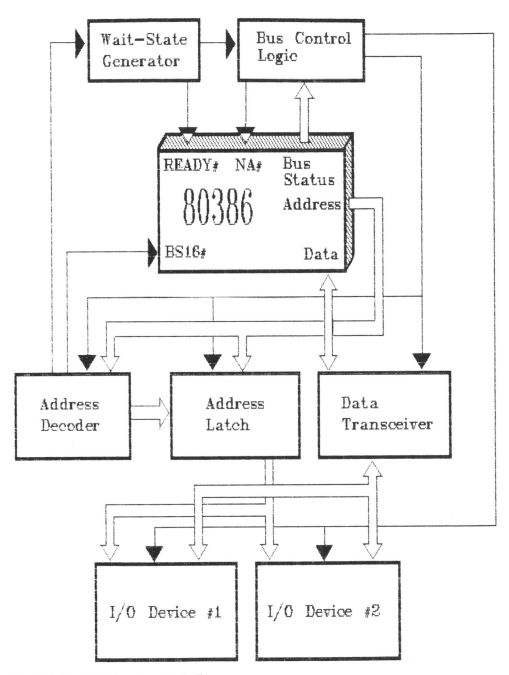

Fig. 5-4. Basic I/O interface block diagram.

8272	Floppy Disk Controller
8274	Multi-Protocol Serial Controller
82062, 82064	Fixed Disk Controller
82258	Advanced DMA Controller (remote node)

8-, 16-, and 32-bit I/O. Eight-bit I/O devices can be connected to any of the four 8-bit sections of the data bus. In a write cycle, if BE3# and/or BE2# (the top doubleword) is active but not BE1# or BE0#, the top half of the data bus is duplicated on the bottom half. If the addresses lie within the same doubleword boundaries (the address of the two devices differ only in the values of BE3#-BE0#), BE#3-BE0# must be decoded to provide a chip select signal. This signal prevents a write to one device from performing an erroneous write to the other. The chip select can be done by using either TTL logic or an address decoder PAL device.

Another interfacing technique with 8-bit peripherals is shown in Fig. 5-5. The 32-bit data bus is multiplexed onto an 8-bit data bus to allow for byte-oriented DMA (Direct Memory Access) or block transfers to memory-mapped 8-bit I/O devices. Because only one 8-bit section of the data bus is enabled at any one time, the addresses assigned to devices connected can be closely spaced.

16-bit I/O devices should be assigned to even addresses, to avoid extra bus cycles and to simplify device selection. If addresses are located on adjacent word boundaries, address decoding has to generate the Bus Size 16 (BS16#) signal so that the 80386 does a 16-bit bus cycle. If the addresses are located on every other word boundary (that is, on every doubleword address), BS16# is not needed.

32-bit devices should be assigned to addresses that are even multiples of four, to avoid extra bus cycles and to simplify device selection. Chip select for such a 32-bit device should be conditioned by all byte enables (BE3#-BE0#) being active.

Systems with 14 or fewer I/O ports that reside only in the I/O space or that require more than one active select can use linear chip selects to access the I/O devices. Latched address lines (A2-A15) connect directly to I/O device selects.

Address Latch. Latches are circuits that maintain their contents for a specified period of time. Latches are used to maintain the I/O address for the duration of the bus cycle. The 74×373 Latch Enable (LE) input is controlled by the Address Latch Enable (ALE) signal that comes from the bus control logic. LE goes active at the start of each bus cycle. The 74×373 Output Enable (OE#) is always active.

Address Decoder. The address decoder consists of two 1-of-4 decoders, one decoding memory addresses and the other for decoding I/O addresses. In Fig. 5-5, an output from the memory address decoder activates the I/O address decoder for I/O accesses. Only address bits A4 and A5 are needed to generate the correct chip-select signal because of the way the addresses for the I/O devices are located.

Also in Fig. 5-5, the address decoder converts the 80386 address into chip-select signals. The decoder is located before the address latches. The decoder can also be placed after the latches. If placed before, the chip-select signal becomes valid as early as possible but must be latched with the address. That means the number of address latches needed is determined by the location of the address decoder as well as the number of address bits and chip-select signals required by the interface. Chip-select signals are sent to the bus control logic, which sets the current number of wait states for the accessed device.

Data Transceiver. Standard 8-bit transceivers (as shown in Fig. 5-5) provide isolation and additional drive capability for the 80386 data bus. Transceivers prevent the contention on the data bus that occurs if some devices are slow to remove read data from the bus after a read cycle. If a write cycle follows a read cycle, the 80386

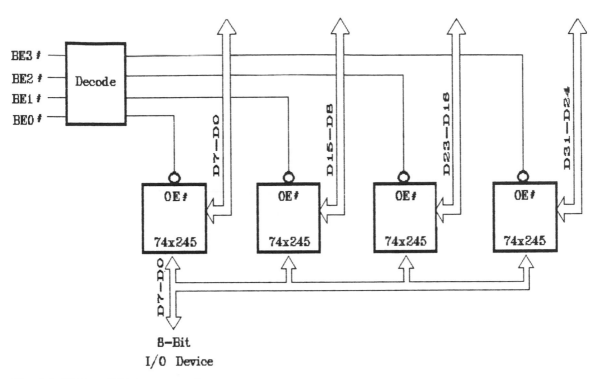

Fig. 5-5. 32-bit to 8-bit bus conversion.

may drive the data bus before a slow device has totally removed its outputs. This may cause bus contention problems.

A bus interface includes enough transceivers to accommodate the device with the most inputs and outputs on the data bus. Only two 8-bit transceivers are needed if the widest device has 16 data bits and if the I/O addresses are located so that all devices are connected only to the lower half of the data bus. Generally, 32-bit wide memories which require four 8-bit transceivers are used in an 80386 system.

Bus Control Logic. The bus control logic for the basic I/O interface is the same as for the memory interface. The bus controller decodes the 80386 status outputs (W/R#, M/IO#, and D/C#) and activates a command signal for the type of bus cycle requested. The bus controller also controls the READY# input to the 80386 that ends each bus cycle. The PAL-2 (bus control PAL) counts wait states and returns READY# after the number of wait states needed by the accessed device.

6

Privilege and Protection, Pipelining, Multitasking, and Multiprocessing

This chapter discusses how the 80386 works with pipelining, multitasking with its associated Task State Segments (TSSs) and descriptors, and Multiprocessing. First, here are some additional terms that appear in the discussion.

PRIVILEGE—A privilege is a property (generally established during system design) that determines which computer operations are allowed at any point in time and which accesses to memory are legal. Privilege is used to provide security in a computer system.

PL—Privilege Level. One of four 80386 hierarchical privilege levels. Level 0 is the *most* privileged level and level 3 is the *least*.

RPL—Requester Privilege Level. A requestor is a program or device which desires to use system resources. RPL is the privilege level requested by the original supplier of the selector. RPL is determined by the *least two* significant bits of a selector.

CPL—Current Privilege Level. The privilege level at which a task is currently executing. CPL normally equals the privilege level of the code segment being executed. (It can be different if the code segment is a conforming segment.) CPL also can be determined by examining the lowest 2 bits of the CS (Code Segment) register, except for conforming code segments.

DPL—Descriptor Privilege Level. The DPL is the least privileged level at which a task may access that descriptor, and access the segment associated with that descriptor. DPL is determined by bits 6:5 in the Access Right Byte of a descriptor.

EPL—Effective Privilege Level. The EPL is the least privileged of the RPL and DPL. Note that smaller privilege level values indicate greater privilege. The EPL is the numerical maximum of RPL and DPL.

PRIVILEGE AND PROTECTION

Privilege and protection are a means of controlling access to operating system code and to data. The security of the system is maintained, as is the integrity of the information. Privilege and protection became a necessity of programming life when the concept of multiple users or multiple uses became a reality.

Privilege

The concept of privilege is central to several facets of protection. Applied to procedures, privilege is the degree to which the procedure can be *trusted* not to make a mistake that might affect other procedures or data. Applied to data, privilege is the *degree of protection* that a data structure should have from less trusted procedures.

Privilege Levels and Rules

The 80386 uses four levels of protection to optimize support of multitasking. Privilege is implemented by assigning a value from zero to three to key objects which are recognized by the processor. This value is called the *privilege level*. The value zero is the greatest privilege, while the value three is the least privileged. The key items that the processor recognizes are:

DESCRIPTOR PRIVILEGE LEVEL—DPL. Descriptors contain a field called the DPL. This is the least privilege that a task must have to access the descriptor.

REQUESTER'S PRIVILEGE LEVEL—RPL. The RPL represents the privilege level requested by the procedure that originates a selector.

CURRENT PRIVILEGE LEVEL—CPL. Generally, the CPL is equal to the segment DPL of the code segment which the processor is currently executing. CPL changes when control transfers to segments with differing DPLs.

Figure 6-1 shows how the four privilege levels are interpreted as rings of protection. The center, level 0, is for segments containing the most critical software, usually

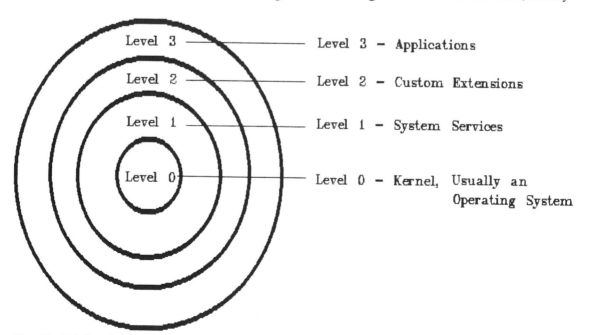

Fig. 6-1. Privilege levels.

the kernel of the operating system. The outer rings are for segments of less critical software and data. It is not necessary to use all four privilege levels. Existing software that was designed with fewer levels can simply ignore the other levels offered. It is advised that a one-level system use privilege level zero. A two-level system should use privilege levels zero and three. If you have second thoughts, you can move from kernel up and application down, expanding your design to use three or four levels.

The 80386 automatically verifies a procedure's right to access another segment by comparing the procedure's CPL to one or more other privilege levels. This verification occurs at the time a descriptor selector is loaded into a segment register.

Privileged Instructions

Privileged instructions that affect system data structures can only be executed when the CPL is zero. If the processor finds one of these instructions when CPL is greater than zero, it signals a general protection exception. These instructions, described more fully in Chapter 10, are:

CLTS	Clear Task-Switched Flag
HLT	Halt Processor
LGDT	Load Global Descriptor Table
LIDT	Load Interrupt Descriptor Table
LLDT	Load Local Descriptor Table
LMSW	Load Machine Status Word
LTR	Load Task Register
MOV to/from CRn	Move to Control Register n
MOV to/from DRn	Move to Debug Register
MOV to/from TRn	Move to Test Register

Sensitive Instructions

Instructions that deal with I/O need to be restricted to protect system operating code and various levels of data. However, they also may need to be executed by procedures that execute at privilege levels other than zero. This can reduce the need for state switches.

Protection

The 80386 is designed with built-in protection methods to help detect and identify bugs. The segment is the basic unit of protection and segment descriptors store the necessary protection parameters. Figure 6-2 shows the protection-related fields of segment descriptors.

The type fields of data and executable code segments include bits which further define the purpose of the segment. Bit 9 is interpreted differently in executable and data segments.

1. Readable bit—In an executable-segment, Bit 9 indicates if instructions are allowed to read data from the segment. Reading from an executable segment can be attempted either via the CS register by using a ''CS:'' override prefix,

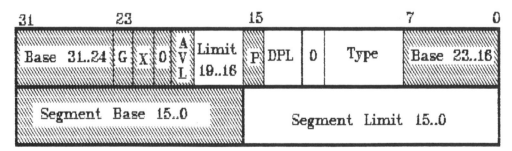

Fig. 6-2. Protection fields of segment descriptors.

or by loading a selector in the descriptor into a data segment register (DS, ES, FS, or GS).

2. Writeable bit—In a data segment, Bit 9 specifies whether instructions can write into the segment.

Before a memory cycle starts, the hardware checks each reference to memory to verify that the reference satisfies the protection criteria. Any violation prevents that cycle from starting and results in an exception. Because the checks are performed concurrently with address translation, there is little or no performance penalty.

Protection parameters are stored in the segment descriptors by systems software at the time a descriptor is created. When a program loads the selector into a segment register, the 80386 loads not only the base address of the segment but also protection information. Each segment register has bits in the programmer-invisible portion for storing base, limit, type and privilege level. Any subsequent protection checks on the same segment do not consume additional memory access cycles.

Protection has eight aspects: type checking, limit checking, restriction of access to data, restriction of procedure entry points, restriction of instruction set, pointer validation, descriptor validation, and page and segment protection.

TYPE Checking

The TYPE field of a descriptor distinguishes between differing descriptor formats and it specifies the intended usage of a segment. Type checking can be used to detect programmer errors that would attempt to use a segment in ways not intended by the programmer. The processor checks type information on two occasions.

1. When an instruction implicitly or explicitly refers to a segment register. Some segments can be used by instructions only in predefined ways. For example:
> If the writeable bit is not set, no instruction may write into a data segment.
> Unless the readable bit is set, no instruction can read an executable segment.
> No instruction may write into an executable segment.

2. When a descriptor selector is loaded into a segment register. Some segment registers can contain only certain descriptor types. For example:
> Only selectors of writeable data segments can be loaded into the SS register.
> The CS register can be loaded only with the selector of an executable segment.
> Selectors of executable read-protected segments cannot be loaded into data-segment registers.

Limit Checking. Limit checking catches programming errors such as invalid pointer calculations or runaway subscripts. These errors are detected when they occur, which makes it much easier to determine the cause. Without limit checking, such errors could corrupt other modules. This corruption would only be discovered later when the corrupted module runs incorrectly. At that point, error identification is much more difficult.

In a segment descriptor, the processor uses the LIMIT field to prevent programs from addressing outside the segment. The processor uses the G (granularity) bit to interpret the LIMIT. For data segments, the processor also uses the E (Expansion-direction) bit and the B (Big) bit. Table 1 shows some combinations of the bits.

When G=0, LIMIT is the value of the 20-bit LIMIT field as it appears in the descriptor. LIMIT can range from 0 to 0FFFFFH ($2^{20} - 1$, or 1 megabyte). When G=1, the 80386 appends 12 low-order one-bits to the value of the LIMIT field. In this case, the actual limit can range from 0FFFH ($2^{12} - 1$, or 4 kilobytes) to 0FFFFFFFFH ($2^{32} - 1$, or 4 gigabytes).

Table 6-1. Combinations of E, G, and B Bits.

CASE	1	2	3	4
Expansion Direction	U	U	D	D
G Bit	0	1	0	1
B Bit	X	X	0	1
Lower bound is:				
0	X	X		
LIMIT + 1			X	
shl(LIMIT,12,1)+1				X
Upper bound is:				
LIMIT	X			
shl(LIMIT,12,1)		X		
64K - 1			X	
4G - 1				X
Max Segment Size is:				
64K	X			
64K - 1			X	
4G - 4K		X		
4G				X
Min Segment Size is:				
0	X		X	
4K		X		X

Note: shl(x,12,1) = Shift X left by 12 bits,
                    inserting one-bits on the right

The processor uses the LIMIT field of descriptors for descriptor tables to prevent programs from selecting a table entry outside the descriptor table. The descriptor table LIMIT identifies the last valid byte of the last descriptor in that table. Since the descriptor is eight bytes long, the limit value is (N * 8 − 1) for a table that contains N descriptors.

The expand-down feature allows a stack to expand by copying it to a larger segment without needing also to update intra-stack pointers.

For all types of segments except expand-down data segments, the value of LIMIT is one less than the segment size, expressed in bytes. The 80386 causes a general protection exception in any of the following cases:

> Attempt to access a memory doubleword (DWord) at an address > = (LIMIT − 2).
> Attempt to access a memory word at an address > = LIMIT.
> Attempt to access a memory byte at an address > LIMIT.

For expand-down data segments, LIMIT has the same function but is interpreted differently. For these data segments, the range of valid addresses is (LIMIT + 1) to either 64K − 1, 2^{32} − 1, or 4 gigabytes, depending on the B-bit. An expand-down segment reaches maximum size when LIMIT is zero. The B-bit also controls the default size PUSHed or POPed (or otherwise transferred) to or from a stack. When B=1, 32-bit sizes are used; otherwise, 16-bit sizes are used.

Restriction of Access to Data. Before the processor can address operands in memory, an 80386 program loads the data segment selector into a data-segment register (DS, ES, FS, GS, or SS). Then the 80386 compares the privilege levels to evaluate access to that data. As Fig. 6-3 shows, three different privilege levels enter into this check: the current privilege level (CPL), the requester's privilege level (RPL) of the selector used to specify the target segment, and the descriptor privilege level (DPL) of the target segment.

Instructions are allowed to load a data-segment register and its target segment only if the DPL of the target segment is numerically greater than (lesser privilege level) or equal to the maximum of the CPL and the selector's RPL. This can be used to prevent applications from changing or reading operating system tables.

Less common is the use of code segments to store data. Code segments can hold constants, but it is not possible to write to a segment defined as a code segment. There are three methods of reading data in code segments:

1. Use a "CS:" override prefix to read a readable, executable segment whose selector is already loaded in the CS register.
2. Load a data-segment register with a selector for a non-conforming, readable, executable segment.
3. Load a data-segment register with a selector of a conforming, readable, executable segment.

Case 1 is always valid because the DPL of the code segment in CS is, by definition, equal to CPL. Case 2 uses the same rules as for access to data segments. Case

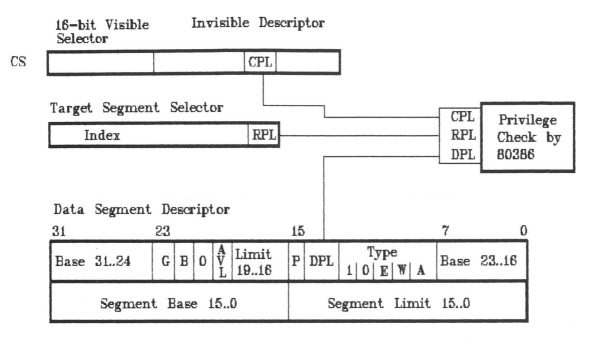

CPL = Current Privilege Level

RPL = Requestor's Privilege Level

DPL = Descriptor Privilege Level

Fig. 6-3. Data access privilege check.

3 is always valid because the privilege level of a segment whose conforming bit is set is effectively the same as CPL, regardless of its DPL.

Control Transfers. The 80386 transfers control by use of exceptions, interrupts, and by the instructions CALL, JMP, INT, IRET, and RET. Exceptions and interrupts are special cases and are covered in Chapter 3. This section discusses forms of the instructions. There are both "near" and "far" forms of the CALL, JMP, and RET instructions.

The "near" form transfers within the current code segment and therefore is subject only to limit checking. The 80386 simply ensures that the destination of the instruction is within the current executable segment. Since this limit is cached in the CS register, protection checks for near transfers require no extra clock cycles.

"Far" CALLs and JMPs transfer to other segments. Because of this, the 80386 checks the privilege levels. There are two ways a CALL or JMP can refer to another segment: the operand selects a call gate descriptor; or the operand selects the descriptor of another executable segment.

Two different privilege levels enter into the privilege check for a control transfer that does not use a call gate: the current privilege level (CPL); and the descriptor privilege level (DPL) of the descriptor of the target segment. Generally, the CPL is equal to the DPL of the segment currently being executed. The CPL, however, may be greater than the DPL if the conforming bit is set in the descriptor of the current executable segment.

An executable segment whose descriptor has the conforming bit (bit 10) set is called a *conforming segment*. The conforming-segment allows sharing of procedures that may be called from differing privilege levels but should execute at the privilege level of the calling procedure. When control is transferred to a conforming segment, the CPL does not change. This is the only case when CPL may be unequal to the DPL of the currently executable segment.

The 80386 allows a CALL or JMP directly to another segment only if: the conforming bit of the target code-segment descriptor is set *and* the DPL of the target is less than or equal to the CPL; or the DPL of the target is equal to the CPL.

Most code segments are *not* conforming. For these segments, control can be transferred without a gate only to executable segments at the same privilege level. To transfer control to numerically smaller privilege levels, the CALL instruction is used with call-gate descriptors. The JMP instruction may never transfer control to a nonconforming segment whose DPL does not equal CPL.

Through the use of gate descriptors, the 80386 provides protection for control transfers among executable segments at differing privilege levels. There are four: Task gates, Trap gates, Interrupt gates, and Call gates. Task gates are used for task switching and are discussed in another section which discusses Tasks. Trap gates and interrupt gates are used by exceptions and interrupts and are described in those sections. This section is concerned with CALL gates only.

A CALL gate is used to specify the privilege level and to define an entry point of a procedure. Call gate descriptors are used by CALL and JMP instructions in the same way as code segment descriptors. When the hardware recognizes that the destination selector refers to a gate descriptor, the instruction operation is executed depending on the contents of the call gate.

Where protection comes in is that the selector and offset fields are 'guaranteed' to be a pointer to the entry point of a procedure. All transitions from another segment go to a valid entry point, rather than possibly into the middle of a procedure or into the middle of an instruction. The point is that the operating system controls the building and can ensure that trusted code is going to be executed. This allows the proper granting of increased privilege.

The processor checks four different privilege levels to validate the control transfer via a call gate: the current privilege level (CPL), the descriptor privilege level (DPL) of the gate descriptor, the requester's privilege level (RPL) of the selector that specifies the call gate, and the DPL of the target executable segment's descriptor.

Only CALL instructions can use gates to transfer to smaller privilege levels. A gate may be used by a JMP instruction only to transfer to an executable segment with the same privilege level or to a conforming segment.

An interlevel transfer is being requested if the destination code segment of the call gate is at a different privilege level than the CPL. To keep system integrity, each privilege level has a separate stack. These stacks ensure that sufficient stack space is allocated to process calls from less privileged levels. Without the stack, a trusted procedure would work incorrectly if the calling procedure provided insufficient space on the caller's stack.

The 80386 locates these stacks via the Task State Segment (TSS). Since each task has a separate TSS, it follows that each task has a separate stack. Systems software creates the TSSs and places correct stack pointers in them; the initial pointers are read-only values. The 80386 *never* changes them during the course of execution. The systems software also ensures that each stack contains enough space to hold the old SS:ESP (Stack Segment, Extended Stack Pointer), the return address, and all parameters and local variables that may be needed to process a call.

When a call gate is used to change privilege levels, a new stack is selected by loading a pointer value from the TSS. The 80386 uses the DPL of the target code segment (which is the new CPL) to index the initial stack pointer for PL 0, 1, or 2. The TSS does not have a stack pointer for a PL 3 stack, because privilege level 3 cannot be called by any procedure at any other privilege level. If the DPL of the new stack data segment does not equal the CPL, a stack exception occurs.

To ease privilege transitions, the 80386 copies the parameters to the new stack. It uses the count field of the call gate as to how many doublewords (the maximum is 31) it is to copy from the caller's stack to the new stack. If the count is zero, it copies no parameters. Procedures that are called from another privilege level and that require more than the 31 doublewords must use the saved SS:ESP link to access all parameters beyond the last doubleword copied.

The "near" forms of the RET instruction transfer control within the current code segment. They are, therefore, subject only to limit checking. To do this, the offset of the instruction following the corresponding CALL is popped from the stack. The 80386 checks that this offset does not exceed the limit of the current executable segment.

On the other hand, the "far" form of RET pops the return pointer that was pushed onto the stack by a prior far CALL. Normally, the return pointer will be valid because of its relation to the prior CALL or INT. The processor still performs privilege checking because of the possibility that the current procedure failed to correctly maintain the stack or altered the pointer. The RPL of the CS selector popped off the stack by the return instruction identifies the privilege level of the calling procedure. An intersegment return instruction *can* change privilege levels, but only toward procedures of lesser privilege.

Restriction of Instruction Set. Certain instructions can affect the protection mechanism or influence general system performance. These instructions can only be executed by trusted procedures. The 80386 has two classes of restricted instructions: privileged instructions and sensitive instructions. They are described more fully under the preceding section on Privilege.

Pointer Validation. Validity checking refers to finding the limits that data can have. Validation of pointers is an important part of finding programming errors. It is also necessary for maintaining isolation between privilege levels and consists of the following three steps: First, check if the segment type is appropriate to its intended use. Second, check if the pointer violates the segment limit. Third, check if the supplier of the pointer is entitled to access the segment.

The 80386 automatically checks steps 1 and 2 during instruction execution but software must assist in performing step 3. The unprivileged instruction ARPL (Adjust RPL Field of Selector) does this. Software can also do steps 1 and 2, rather than waiting for an exception. The unprivileged instructions LAR (Load Access Rights Byte), LSL (Load Segment Limit), VERR (Verify a Segment for Reading), and VERW (Verify a Segment for Writing) help do this. LAR verifies that a pointer refers to a segment of the proper privilege level and type. LSL allows software to test the limit of a descriptor. VERR and VERW determines whether a selector points to a segment that can be read or written at the current privilege level. Neither VERR or VERW causes a protection fault if the result is negative.

The Requester's Privilege Level (RPL) can aid prevention of the faulty use of pointers that could corrupt the operation of more privileged code or data from a less privileged level. The RPL field allows a privilege attribute to be assigned to a selector, which normally shows the privilege level of the code which generated the selector. The 80386 automatically checks the RPL of any selector loaded into a segment register to verify that the RPL allows access.

Page and Directory Protection. Each page table entry has two bits associated with type protection. The U/S bit and the R/W bit. The Present bit can be used to restrict the addressable domain. At the level of page addressing, two types are defined: Read-only access, where R/W = 0; and Read/write access, where R/W = 1.

When the processor executes at a supervisor level (CPL < 3), the setting of U/S and R/W are ignored. All pages are both readable and writeable. At user level (CPL = 3), only pages that belong to the user level (U/S = 1) *and* are marked for write access (R/W = 1) are writeable. Pages that belong to the supervisor level are neither readable nor writeable from the user level. The ''ownership'' of pages is established through page restriction.

Page restriction is implemented by assigning each page to one of two levels:

    1. User level (Bit 2 of the Page Table Entry U/S = 1) This is for applications procedures and data.
    2. Supervisor level (Bit 2 of the Page Table Entry, U/S = 0). This is for operating system and other systems software and related data.

The current level (U or S) is related to CPL. If CPL is 0, 1, or 2, the processor is executing at supervisor level. If CPL is 3, the processor is executing at user level. When the processor executes at supervisor level, all pages are addressable. At the user level, only pages that belong to the user level can be addressed.

The 80386 computes the effective protection attributes for a page by examining the protection attributes in *both* the directory and the page table. For any one page, the protection attributes of its page directory entry may be different from those of its page table entry.

There are overrides to page protection. Certain accesses are checked as if they are privilege-level 0 references, even if CPL = 3. Those are any LDT, GDT, TSS, and IDT references or access to inner stack during ring crossing CALL/INT.

When paging is enabled, the processor first checks segment protection, then evaluates page protection. If the 80386 detects a protection violation at either the segment or the page level, the requested operation is not allowed to proceed. A protection exception is generated.

PIPELINING FOR PERFORMANCE

System performance measures how fast a microprocessor system performs a given task or set of instructions. Through increased processing speed and data throughput, an 80386 operating at the heart of a system can improve overall performance. One of the greatest benefits of instruction pipelining is that it is transparent to the user. When implemented properly, the performance of instructions can be increased significantly without affecting the code already written. See Chapter 14 for additional, background information on pipelining.

Because a system will include devices whose response is slow relative to the 80386 bus cycle, the overall system performance is often less than the potential the 80386 offers. Two techniques for accommodating slow devices are address pipelining and slowing the system clock.

Address Pipelining

The actual execution of an instruction is divided into four distinct parts. First the instruction is fetched from memory. Second, it is interpreted or decoded. Third, the operand or operands are fetched from memory. Finally, the instruction is executed. If all these operations are performed serially for successive instructions (as on an assembly line), the next instruction is fetched while the first one is decoded, and so on. The pipe can be kept full so the incremental time to complete an instruction can be reduced to just the execution time.

Address pipelining increases the time that a memory has to respond by one CLK cycle without lengthening the bus cycle. This extra CLK cycle eliminates the output delay of the 80386 address and status outputs. Address pipelining overlaps the address and status outputs of the next bus cycle from the point of view of the accessed memory device. An access that requires two wait states without address pipelining would require one wait state with pipelining.

Address pipelining is advantageous for most bus cycles, but if the next address is not available before the current cycle ends, the 80386 cannot pipeline the next address. In this case, the bus timing is identical to a non-pipelined bus cycle. Also, the first bus cycle after an idle bus must always be nonpipelined because there is no previous cycle in which to generate the address early. If the next cycle is to be pipelined, the first cycle must be lengthened by at least one wait state so that the new address can be output before the end of the cycle.

Address pipelining is less effective for I/O devices requiring several wait states. The larger the number of wait states required, the less significant the elimination of one wait state through pipelining becomes. This fact coupled with the relative infrequency of I/O accesses means that address pipelining for I/O devices usually makes little difference to system performance.

The 80386 offers both pipelined and nonpipelined bus cycles. When pipelining is selected, the 80386 overlaps bus cycles which allows longer access times. Since cache memory can be accessed without wait states, non-pipelined cycles are often preferred. Using non-pipelined cycles minimizes latency between the processor requesting information from the outside world and data becoming available at the 80386 pins. Since performance benefits of a cache result from its ability to provide a 32-bit doubleword in 2 clock cycles, address pipelining is recommended only for systems with slower memory devices that would otherwise require one or more wait states.

Slowing the 80386

While pipelining instructions is one way of allowing slower devices to "feed" the fast 80386, a less-common way to accommodate memory speed is to reduce the 80386 operating frequency. That is, slow it down. Clock frequency is the periodic pulses that are used to schedule computer operations. Clock generators produce clock and processor time-phasing signals. The rate at which these signals pulse determine the rate at which logical gating and movement is performed within the computer system.

Because a slower clock frequency increases the bus cycle time, fewer wait states may be required for particular memory devices. On the other hand, system performance depends directly on the clock frequency. Execution time increases in direct proportion to the increase in clock period. A 12.5 MHz 80386 requires almost 33 percent more time to execute a program than a 16 MHz 80386 operating with the same number of wait states. Table 6-2 gives some comparisons.

MULTITASKING

Multitasking is a technique that manages a computer system's work when that work consists of multiple activities such as editing a file, compiling a program or performing inter-system transfers. Individual tasks execute as if they run on dedicated processors and share a common memory. It appears that, except for pauses to communicate or synchronize with other tasks, each task runs in parallel with all other tasks. The 80386 contains hardware to support efficient multitasking.

To switch tasks efficiently, the 80386 uses special high-speed hardware. Only a single instruction or interrupt is needed for the processor to do a switch. Running at 16 MHz, the processor can save the state of one task (all registers), load the state of another task, and resume execution in less that 16 microseconds.

The 80386 uses no special instructions to control multitasking. Instead, it interprets ordinary control-transfer instructions differently when they refer to the special data structures. The registers and data structures that support multitasking are: Task State Segment, task state segment descriptor, task register, and task gate descriptor.

Table 6-2. Wait States Versus Operating Frequency.

Number of Wait States	Without Pipelining 16 MHz	12.5 MHz	With Pipelining 16 MHz	12.5 MHz
0	1.00	0.78	0.91	0.71
1	0.81	0.64	0.76	0.59
2	0.66	0.52	0.63	0.49
3	0.57	0.45	----	----

In addition to the simple task switch, the 80386 offers two other task-management features:

- With each task switch, the processor can also switch to another LDT and to another page directory. Thus each task can have a different logical-to-linear mapping and a different linear-to-physical mapping. Using this feature, tasks can be isolated and prevented from interfering with one another.
- Interrupts and exceptions can cause task switches if needed in the system design. The 80386 not only switches to the task that handles the interrupt or exception, but it automatically switches back to the interrupted task when the interrupt or exception has been serviced.

In reality, the multitasking simulates multiple processors by providing each task with a virtual processor. That is, at any one instant, the operating system assigns the real processor to any one of the virtual processors, which then runs that virtual processor's task. To do this, the 80386 uses Task State Segments (TSS) and instructions that switch tasks.

Task State Segment (TSS)

A TSS is a data structure that holds the state of a task's virtual processor. The TSS is divided into two parts. The first class of information is the dynamic set that the processor updates with each switch from the task. This set includes fields that store the following:

SEGMENT REGISTERS—GS, FS, DS, SS, CS, and ES
GENERAL REGISTERS—EDI, ESI, EBP, ESP, EBX, EDX, ECX, and EAX
FLAGS REGISTER—EFLAGS
INSTRUCTION POINTER—EIP

- The selector of the TSS of the previously executing task. This is updated only when a return is expected.

The second class of information in the TSS is a static set that the processor reads but does not change. This set includes fields that store the following:

- The I/O map base
- The debug trap bit, T-bit, which causes the 80386 to raise a debug exception when a task switch occurs.
- The selector of the task's LDT
- The stack definitions for level 0, 1, or 2 interrupt handlers which are to execute in the task's environment
- The CR3 register (PDBR) that contains the base address of the task's page directory. It is read only when paging is enabled.

A TSS may reside anywhere in the linear space. The single caution is when the TSS spans a page boundary and the higher-addressed page is not present. In this case, the 80386 raises an exception if it encounters the not-present page while reading the

TSS during a task switch. To avoid this, either allocate the TSS so that it does not cross a page boundary or ensure that both pages are either both present or both not-present at the time of a task switch. In this latter case, if both pages are not-present, the page-fault handler makes both pages present before restarting the instruction that caused the page fault. Figure 6-4 shows the 80386 32-bit Task State Segment.

When creating a new task, the operating system creates the TSS and initializes it to the values the task should have when it begins execution. The information is updated when any of the values change.

31	23	15	7	0	
I/O Map Base		0 0 0 0 0 0 0 0 0 0 0 0 0 0 0		T	64
0 0 0 0 0 0 0 0 0 0 0 0 0 0 0 0			LDT		60
0 0 0 0 0 0 0 0 0 0 0 0 0 0 0 0			GS		5C
0 0 0 0 0 0 0 0 0 0 0 0 0 0 0 0			FS		58
0 0 0 0 0 0 0 0 0 0 0 0 0 0 0 0			DS		54
0 0 0 0 0 0 0 0 0 0 0 0 0 0 0 0			SS		50
0 0 0 0 0 0 0 0 0 0 0 0 0 0 0 0			CS		4C
0 0 0 0 0 0 0 0 0 0 0 0 0 0 0 0			ES		48
EDI					44
ESI					40
EBP					3C
ESP					38
EBX					34
EDX					30
ECX					2C
EAX					28
EFLAGS					24
Instruction Pointer (EIP)					20
CR3 (PDBR)					1C
0 0 0 0 0 0 0 0 0 0 0 0 0 0 0 0			SS2		18
ESP2					14
0 0 0 0 0 0 0 0 0 0 0 0 0 0 0 0			SS1		10
ESP1					0C
0 0 0 0 0 0 0 0 0 0 0 0 0 0 0 0			SS0		8
ESP0					4
0 0 0 0 0 0 0 0 0 0 0 0 0 0 0 0		Back Link to Previous TSS			0

Fig. 6-4. Task state segment for 80386.

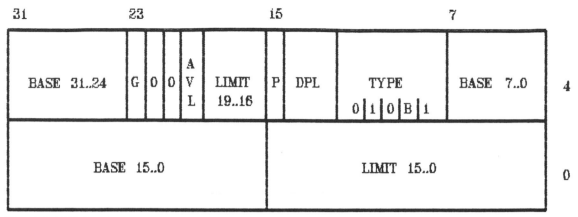

Fig. 6-5. TSS descriptor.

Task State Segment Descriptor

Like all segments, the TSS is defined by a descriptor. This descriptor resides only in the Global Descriptor Table (GDT). An attempt to identify a TSS with a selector that has TI = 1 (Table Indicator flag to indicate the current LDT) generates an exception. Also, even if it has access to a TSS descriptor, a procedure does not have the right to read or modify the TSS. Reading and changing can be done only with another descriptor that redefines the TSS as a data segment. An attempt to load a TSS descriptor into any of the segment registers (CS, DS, ES, FS, GS, or SS) causes an exception. Figure 6-5 shows the format of a TSS descriptor.

Tasks are *not* re-entrant because both the LDT selector and CR3 (Control Register 3) for the task are stored in the TSS. The B-bit (busy) of the TYPE field allows the processor to detect an attempt to switch to a task that is already busy. A TYPE code of 9 shows the task is not-busy. A TYPE code of 11 indicates it is busy.

The BASE, LIMIT and DPL (Descriptor Privilege Level) fields and the G-bit (Granularity) and P-bit (Present) have functions similar to their counterparts in data-segment descriptors. The BASE defines the location of the segment within the linear address space. The LIMIT defines the size of the segment. With the TSS descriptor, the LIMIT must contain a value of 103 or higher because the TSS itself requires 104 bytes. An attempt to switch to a task whose LIMIT has less than 103 causes an exception.

Task Switching

The 80386 schedules and executes tasks based on a priority set by the operating system. To do this, the 80386 uses a *Task Register* (TR) in which it keeps a selector and a descriptor for the running task's TSS. The TR has both a visible and an invisible portion. The visible and changeable portion can be read and modified by instructions. The invisible portion is maintained by the processor to correspond to the changeable portion and cannot be read by any instruction.

Two instructions (Load Task Register, LTR, and Store Task Register, STR) read and modify the changeable portion of the TR. Both instructions take one operand, which is a 16-bit selector located in memory or in a general register.

The LTR instruction loads the changeable portion of the task register with the selector operand which must select a TSS descriptor in the GDT. The execution of LTR also loads the invisible portion with information from the TSS descriptor selected by the operand. LTR is a privileged instruction. That is, it may be executed only if CPL (Current Privilege Level) is zero. Generally, LTR is used during system initialization to give an initial value to the task register. After that, the contents of TR are changed by task switch operations.

The STR instruction stores the changeable portion of the TR in a general register or memory word. STR is not a privileged instruction.

A task gate descriptor gives an indirect, protected reference to a TSS. The 80386 uses task gates, in addition to TSS descriptors, to satisfy three needs.

1. Because the busy-bit is stored in the TSS descriptor, each task should have only one such descriptor. However, there may be several task gates that select the single TSS descriptor.

2. With task gates, systems software can limit the right to cause task switches to specific tasks.

3. Task gates may also reside in the IDT, so it is possible for interrupts and exceptions to cause task switching.

To switch tasks, the operating system issues a Jump (JMP) or Call (CALL) instruction whose operand is a selector for the TSS or the task gate of the new task.

The 80386 first checks that the current task is allowed to switch to the designated task. Data access privilege rules apply in the cases of JMP or CALL instructions. The DPL (Descriptor Privilege Level) of the TSS descriptor or task gate must be less than or equal to the maximum of CPL (Current Privilege Level) or the RPL (Requesters Privilege Level) of the gate selector.

Next, the TSS descriptor is checked to see if it is marked present and has a valid limit. A detected error up to this point occurs in the context of the *outgoing* task. Errors are restartable and can be handled in a way that makes it applications transparent.

The processor next executes the JMP TSS instruction by first storing its current registers in the current TSS. The EIP (instruction pointer) is loaded with the address of the instruction after the one that caused the task switch.

It then loads the TR with the selector specified in the JMP instruction. It marks the incoming task's TSS descriptor as busy and sets the TS (task switched) bit of the MSW (Machine Status Word). Since it now has the new TSS, the 80386 loads its registers with the values in this new TSS. Execution continues at the instruction pointed to by the new task's Instruction Pointer. Any errors detected in this step occur in the context of the incoming task.

To an exception handler, it appears as if the first instruction of the new task has not yet executed. Exception handlers that field task-switch exceptions in the incoming task should be cautious about taking action that might load the selector that caused the exception. Unless the handler first examines the selector and fixes any potential problems, such an action may well cause another exception.

Every task switch sets the TS (Task Switch) bit in the MSW. The TS flag is useful when a coprocessor, such as the numeric coprocessor, is used. The TS bit signals that the context of the coprocessor *may not* correspond to the current 80386 task.

To resume execution of the old task, the operating system issues a JMP instruction to the old task's TSS. The process repeats with the storing of current registers, loading of new registers, and continuing execution. The task switch takes about 17 microseconds.

The privilege level at which execution restarts in the incoming task is not restricted by the privilege level of the outgoing task. The tasks are isolated by their separate address spaces and TSSs and privilege access rules are used to prevent improper access to a TSS. Thus, no special privilege rules are needed to constrain the relations between the CPLs of the individual tasks. The new task simply begins executing at the privilege level indicated by the RPL of the CS selector value which is loaded from the TSS.

JMP, CALL, IRET, interrupts and exceptions are all ordinary mechanisms that can be used when a task switch is not required. Either the type of descriptor reference or the NT (Nested Task) bit in the flag word distinguishes between the standard mechanism and the variant that causes a task switch.

MULTIPROCESSING

Multiprocessing is the execution of several programs or program segments concurrently with a processor per program. Execution and I/O may occur in parallel using shared resources such as memory and I/O devices.

The components of a general 80386 multiprocessing system include the LOCK# signal, the LOCK instruction prefix which gives programmed control of the LOCK# signal, and automatic assertion of the LOCK# signal with implicit memory updates by the processor.

LOCK and LOCK# Signal

Both the LOCK instruction prefix and its output signal, LOCK#, are used to prevent other system elements from interrupting a data movement operation. LOCK has limits in that it can be used only with the following sixteen 80386 instructions. An undefined opcode exception results from using LOCK before any other instruction than listed here.

- Exchange: XCHG
- Bit Change and Test: BT, BTC, BTR, BTS
- One-operand arithmetic and logical: DEC, INC, NEG, NOT
- Two-operand arithmetic and logical: ADD, ADC, AND, OR, SBB, SUB, XOR

The area of memory defined by the destination operand is guaranteed to be locked against processor access *only* on the same memory area; that is, an operand with *identical* starting address and *identical* length. Only the area of memory defined by the destination operand is *guaranteed* to lock with a lock instruction. LOCK can lock a larger memory area. For example, both the 8086 and 80286 configurations lock the entire physical memory space.

Sometimes, the 80386 itself initiates activity on the data bus and wants the activity to complete correctly. It issues the LOCK# signal. Generally, there are five instances when this happens:

1. Executing XCHG instructions. The 80386 *always* issues a LOCK during an XCHG that references memory, even if the LOCK prefix is not used.

2. Loading of Descriptors. When the 80386 copies the contents of a descriptor table into a segment register, the 80386 issues a LOCK# so that the descriptor is not modified while it's being loaded.

3. Acknowledging interrupts. The interrupt controller uses the data bus, after an interrupt request, to send the interrupt ID of the interrupt source to the 80386. The processor issues a LOCK# to keep all other data off the bus during this time.

4. Setting the busy bit of the TSS descriptor. The 80386 tests and then sets the busy-bit in the TSS Descriptor TYPE field. To keep two different processors from switching to the same task, the 80386 issues the LOCK# while testing and setting this bit.

5. Updating Page Table A-bit (Accessed) and D-bit (Dirty). The 80386 issues LOCK# while it updates the A and D bits of the page-table entries. Note that the 80386 bypasses the page-table cache and directly updates these bits in memory.

7

Hardware and
Hardware Subsystems

Hardware interfacing is important in designing the best possible system. Often, programmers' knowledge of hardware, and of its internal functioning, allows them to choose the best software design or set of instructions to promote system efficiency. Once aware of what hardware is *supposed* to do, a programmer can quickly determine whether a bug lies in hardware or in the software use of that hardware. This chapter overviews the remaining hardware requirements and concepts not handled earlier.

The 80386 processor is packaged in a high density package, the *pin grid array* (PGA). The PGA looks like a square bed of nails extending from a ceramic base. It uses a ceramic substrate, has 0.100 inch pin spacings, excellent thermal characteristics, and provides for very high density. The 80386 is built on a 32-bit internal and external bus architecture. All instruction prefetch operations are made on a 32-bit basis that takes advantage of the bandwidth of the memory bus.

CONTROLLERS

A controller is that element or group of elements in a computer system that directs a series of operations and sends the proper signals to other computer circuits to carry out the instructions. Included in this discussion is the 8259A Interrupt Controller, the 8274 Serial Controller, and the 82258 Advanced Direct Memory Access Controller.

8274 Serial Controller

The 8274 is a Multi-Protocol Serial Controller (MPSC). It is designed to interface high-speed serial communications lines using a variety of communications protocols. These protocols include asynchronous, IBM bisynchronous, and HDLC/SDLC (High Level Data Link Control or Synchronous Data Link Control). The 8274 has two independent full-duplex channels and can serve as a high-performance replacement for two 8251A Universal Synchronous/Asynchronous Receiver Transmitters

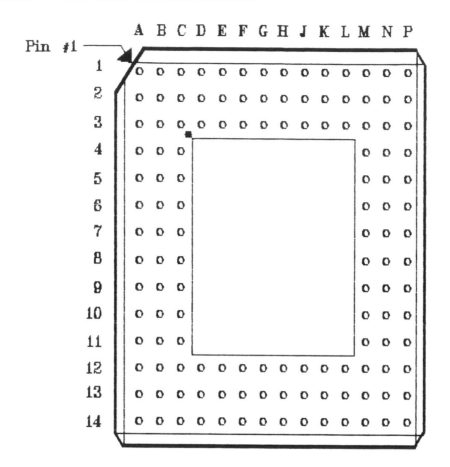

Listing by Pin Number

Pin	Signal		Pin	Signal		Pin	Signal
A1	Vcc		B1	Vss		C1	A8
A2	Vss		B2	A5		C2	A7
A3	A3		B3	A4		C3	A6
A4	N.C.		B4	N.C.		C4	A2
A5	Vcc		B5	Vss		C5	Vcc
A6	Vss		B6	N.C.		C6	N.C.
A7	Vcc		B7	INTR		C7	N.C.
A8	ERROR#		B8	NMI		C8	PEREQ
A9	Vss		B9	BUSY#		C9	RESET
A10	Vcc		B10	W/R#		C10	LOCK#
A11	D/C#		B11	Vss		C11	Vss
A12	M/IO#		B12	N.C.		C12	Vcc
A13	BE3#		B13	BE2#		C13	BE1#
A14	Vcc		B14	Vss		C14	BS16#

Fig. 7-1. Pin assignment of 80386.

Pin	Signal
D1	A11
D2	A10
D3	A9
D12	Vcc
D13	NA#
D14	HOLD

Pin	Signal
E1	A14
E2	A13
E3	A12
E12	BE0#
E13	N.C.
E14	ADS#

Pin	Signal
F1	A15
F2	Vss
F3	Vss
F12	CLK2
F13	N.C.
F14	Vss

Pin	Signal
G1	A16
G2	Vcc
G3	Vcc
G12	Vcc
G13	READY#
G14	Vcc

Pin	Signal
H1	A17
H2	A18
H3	A19
H12	D0
H13	D1
H14	D2

Pin	Signal
J1	A20
J2	Vss
J3	Vss
J12	Vss
J13	Vss
J14	D3

Pin	Signal
K1	A21
K2	A22
K3	A25
K12	D7
K13	D5
K14	D4

Pin	Signal
L1	A23
L2	A24
L3	A28
L12	Vcc
L13	D8
L14	D6

Pin	Signal
M1	A26
M2	A29
M3	Vcc
M4	Vss
M5	D31
M6	D28
M7	Vcc
M8	Vss
M9	D20
M10	Vss
M11	D15
M12	D10
M13	Vcc
M14	HLDA

Pin	Signal
N1	A27
N2	A31
N3	Vss
N4	Vcc
N5	D27
N6	D25

Pin	Signal
P1	A30
P2	Vcc
P3	D30
P4	D29
P5	D26
P6	Vss

Pin	Signal		Pin	Signal
N7	Vcc		P7	D24
N8	D23		P8	Vcc
N9	D21		P9	D22
N10	D17		P10	D19
N11	D16		P11	D18
N12	D12		P12	D14
N13	D11		P13	D13
N14	D9		P14	Vss

Listing by Function

Signal	Pin		Signal	Pin		Signal	Pin
A31	N2		D31	M5		ADS#	E13
A30	P1		D30	P3		BE3#	A13
A29	M2		D29	P4		BE2#	B13
A28	L3		D28	M6		BE1#	C13
A27	N1		D27	N5		BE0#	E12
A26	M1		D26	P5		BS16#	C14
A25	K3		D25	N6		BUSY#	B9
A24	L2		D24	P7		D/C#	A11
A23	L1		D23	N8		ERROR#	A8
A22	K2		D22	P9		LOCK#	C10
A21	K1		D21	N9		M/IO#	A12
A20	J1		D20	M9		NA#	D13
A19	H3		D19	P10		READY#	G13
A18	H2		D18	P11		W/R#	B10
A17	H1		D17	N10			
A16	G1		D16	N11		CLK2	F12
A15	F1		D15	M11		HOLD	D14
A14	E1		D14	P12		HLDA	M14
A13	E2		D13	P13		INTR	B7
A12	E3		D12	N12		NMI	B8
A11	D1		D11	N13		PEREQ	C8
A10	D2		D10	M12		RESET	C9
A9	D3		D9	N14			
A8	C1		D8	L13			
A7	C2		D7	K12			
A6	C3		D6	L14			
A5	B2		D5	K13			
A4	B3		D4	K14			
A3	A3		D3	J14			
A2	C4		D2	H14			
			D1	H13			
			D0	H12			

Signal	Pin	Signal	Pin	Signal	Pin
Vcc	A1	Vss	A2	N.C.	A4
Vcc	A5	Vss	A6	N.C.	B4
Vcc	A7	Vss	A9	N.C.	B6
Vcc	A10	Vss	B1	N.C.	B12
Vcc	A14	Vss	B5	N.C.	C6
Vcc	C5	Vss	B11	N.C.	C7
Vcc	C12	Vss	B14	N.C.	E13
Vcc	D12	Vss	C11	N.C.	F13
Vcc	G2	Vss	F2		
Vcc	G3	Vss	F3		
Vcc	G12	Vss	F14		
Vcc	G14	Vss	J2		
Vcc	L12	Vss	J3		
Vcc	M3	Vss	J12		
Vcc	M7	Vss	J13		
Vcc	M13	Vss	M4		
Vcc	N4	Vss	M8		
Vcc	N7	Vss	M10		
Vcc	P2	Vss	N3		
Vcc	P8	Vss	P6		
		Vss	P14		

(USARTs). See Chapter 12 for more information on USARTs. The 8274 requires a minimum recovery time between back-to-back access that is provided for in the basic I/O interface hardware.

8259A Interrupt Controller

The 8259A Programmable Interrupt Controller manages the interrupts for an 80386 system. One 8259A can accept interrupts from as many as eight external sources, although as many as 64 requests can be handled by cascading several 8259A chips. The 8259A arbitrates the priority of simultaneous interrupts, then interrupts the processor and passes a code to the 80386 to identify the interrupting source.

Single and Cascaded Interrupt Controller. When an interrupt occurs, the 8259A Programmable Interrupt Controller activates its own Interrupt (INT) output. This output is connected to the 80386 Interrupt Request (INTR). The 80386 automatically executes two back-to-back interrupt acknowledge cycles. The 8259A timing requirements are:

- Four idle bus cycles must be inserted between the two interrupt-acknowledge cycles. The 80386 automatically inserts these idle cycles.
- Each interrupt-acknowledge cycle must be extended by at least one wait state. Wait-state generator logic must provide for this extension.

Several 8259As can be cascaded to handle up to 64 interrupt requests. In this type of cascaded system, one 8259A is designated the master controller. It receives input from the other 8259As, known as slave controllers. Each slave controller resolves priority between up to eight interrupt requests and transmits a single interrupt request to the master controller. The master, in turn, resolves interrupt priority between the slaves and transmits a single interrupt request to the 80386.

The timing of the interface is essentially the same as that of a single 8259A. During the first interrupt-acknowledge cycle, all the 8259As freeze the states of their interrupt request inputs. When the master outputs the cascade address to select the slave controller with the highest priority request, the selected slave outputs an interrupt vector to the 80386. This occurs during the second 80386 interrupt-acknowledge cycle.

If the 80386 system needs more than 64 interrupt request lines, a third level of 8259As can be added. When one of the third level slave controllers receives an interrupt request, it drives active one of the interrupt request inputs of a second level. After the priorities have been determined, the second level slave sends the service-routine vector to the 80386. The service routine must contain commands to poll the third level of interrupt controllers to determine the source of the interrupt request. The extra 8259A and their chip-select logic are the only additional hardware required to handle more than 64 interrupts. It's recommended, for maximum performance, that third-level interrupt controllers should be used only for noncritical, infrequently used interrupts.

82258 ADMA Controller

A Direct Memory Access (DMA) controller handles DMA transfers between main memory and one of the following: an I/O device (typically a hard disk), a floppy disk, or a communications channel. The DMA transfer occurs without the assistance of the CPU. This shift of responsibility from the CPU and to another system element improves overall system performance because the CPU does not have to switch context for every memory transfer.

The 82258 Advanced DMA (ADMA) Controller has four channels. It provides all the signals required to perform DMA transfers. It also has the following features:

- The option to replace one of the four high-speed channels with as many as 32 lower-speed multiplexed channels.
- Automatic assembly and disassembly, to convert from 16-bit memory to 8-bit I/O, or vice versa.
- Compare, translate, and verify functions.
- Command chaining, to perform multiple commands.
- Data chaining, to scatter data to separate memory locations (for example, to separate pages) and gather data from separate locations.

Paired with the 82288 Bus Controller, the 82258 is able to be a bus master on a common local bus. Further, it can also be a system bus with the 80386 and its bus controller. To do either of these tasks, the 82258 requires both a local bus interface to act as a bus master, and an 80386 interface to communicate directly with the CPU processor.

The ADMA does most of its communication with the 80386 via memory. Occasionally, the 80386 performs bus cycles directly to the 82258, such as when the 80386 does a direct access to set the general mode register during initialization. The access happens asynchronously over the 82258 slave mode interface that consists of four kinds of pins: (1) Chip Select (CS#) that enables the slave mode interface; (2) Data (D15-D0) that transfers data to and from the 82258; (3) Control (RD# and WR#) that indicates bus cycle type; and (4) Register Address (A7-A0) that selects an 82258 internal register.

COPROCESSORS

Many applications run faster and more efficiently if the computer uses specialized coprocessors. Coprocessors furnish the hardware with the ability to perform functions that must otherwise be emulated by software. In addition, they extend the instruction set of the main processor.

Numeric Coprocessor

The numeric coprocessor interface in the 80386 supports the 80287 and 80387 numeric processors, both of which are software compatible with the earlier 8087.

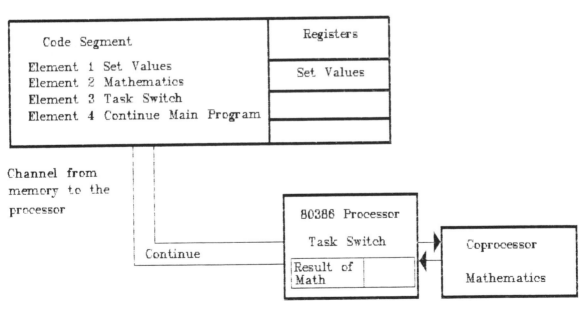

The processor passed the math to the coprocessor. While waiting for the results, the processor goes to the next step in the program.

Fig.7-2. Processor passes math to coprocessor.

For those applications which benefit from high-precision integer and floating-point calculations, both coprocessors provide full support for the IEEE floating-point standard.

The 80386 offers system designers the choice of low-cost or high-performance numeric solutions. At 16 MHz, the 80387 operates over six times faster than a 5 MHz 80287, even though the 80287 is fast enough for most applications and is a cost-effective solution for many designs.

When the 80386 encounters a coprocessor instruction, and it's interacting with the 80287, the 80386 performs all necessary bus cycles to memory and transfers data to and from the 80287 on the lower half of the data bus. The 80386 automatically converts 32-bit memory transfers to 16-bit transfers and vice versa.

When the 80386 runs with the 80387, the 80386 performs all necessary bus cycles to memory and transfer data to and from the 80387. All 80387 transfers are 32 bits wide. Read cycles (transfers from the 80387 to the 80386) require at least one wait state, whereas the write cycles to the 80387 require no wait states.

The 80387 coprocessor achieves significant enhancements in performance and instruction capabilities over the 80287. It runs at internal clock rates of up to 16 MHz. To achieve its best speed, the interface with the 80386 is synchronous and includes a full 32-bit data bus. The 80387 is designed to run either fully synchronously or pseudo-synchronously with the 80386. In the pseudo-synchronous mode, the 80387 interface logic runs with the clock signal of the 80386, whereas internal logic runs with a different clock signal. Figure 7-3 shows how the 80386 connects to an 80287 coprocessor.

The connections between the 80386 processor and the 80287 are as follows:

- The 80287 BUSY#, ERROR#, and PEREQ outputs connect to corresponding 80386 pins.
- The 80287 RESET input connects to the 82384 (Clock Generator) RESET output.
- The 80287 Numeric Processor Select chip-select inputs (NPS1# and NPS2) connect to the latched M/IO# and A31 outputs, respectively.
- The 80287 Command inputs (CMD1 and CMD0) tell the difference between data and commands. These inputs connect to ground and the latched A2 output, respectively. (Note: the 80386 outputs address 800000F8H when it writes a command, and address 800000FCH when it writes or reads data.
- The lower half of the data bus connects to the 16 data bits of the 80287. The 80386 transfers data to and from the coprocessor only over the D15-D0 lines.
- The 80287 Numeric Processor Read (NPRD#) and Numeric Processor Write (NPWR#) inputs connect to the I/O read and write signals from local bus control logic.
- The 80287 Processor Extension Acknowledge (PEACK#) input is pulled high. In an 80286 system, the 80286 generates PEACK# to disable the PEREQ output of the 80287 so that extra data is not transferred. PEACK# is not needed or used in the 80386 system.

The connections between the 80386 processor and the 80387 are as follows:

- The 80387 BUSY#, ERROR#, and PEREQ outputs connect to the correspond-

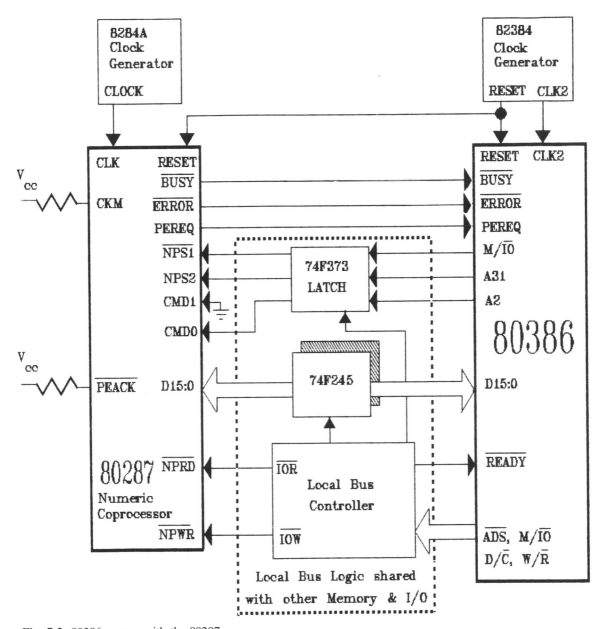

Fig. 7-3. 80386 system with the 80287 coprocessor.

ing 80386 inputs.

- The 80387 RESETIN input connects to the 82384 RESET output.
- The 80387 Numeric Processor Select chip-select inputs (NPS1# and NPS2) connect directly to the 80386 M/IO# and A31 outputs, respectively. For coprocessor cycles, A31 is always high and M/IO# is always low.
- The 80387 Command (CMD0#) input tells the difference between data and commands. This input connects to the 80386 A2 output. The 80386 outputs ad-

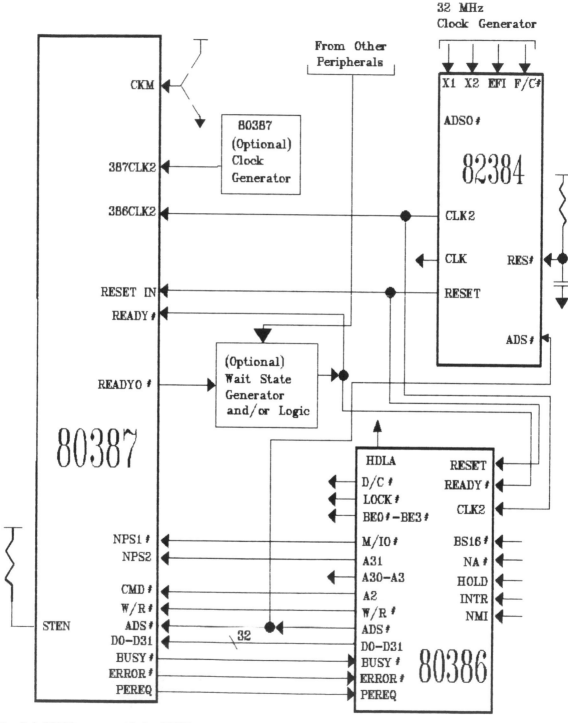

Fig. 7-4. 80386 system with the 80387 coprocessor.

dress 800000F8H when writing a command or reading status, and address 800000FCH when reading or writing data.

- All 32 bits (D31-D0) of the 80386 data bus connect directly to the data bus of the 80387. Any local bus transceivers must be disabled when the 80386 reads data from the 80387 because of the directly connected data lines.
- The 80387 READY#, ADS#, and W/R# inputs connect to the corresponding 80386 pins. The 80387 uses READY# and ADS# to track bus activity and determine when W/R#, NPS1#, NPS2, and the Status Enable (STEN) can be sampled.
- STEN is an 80387 chip select. It can be pulled high. If multiple 80387s are used by the same 80386, STEN can be used to activate one 80387 at a time.
- Ready Out (READYO#) is an optional output. It can be used to generate the wait state required by a coprocessor. External logic can also generate these wait states since the number of wait states is constant.

When the 80386 finds a coprocessor instruction, it automatically generates one or more I/O cycles to addresses 800000F8H and 800000FCH. The processor performs all necessary bus cycles to memory and transfers data to and from the 80387. All 80387 transfers are 32 bits wide. If for some reason the memory subsystem is only 16 bits wide, the 80386 automatically performs the conversion before transferring data to or from the numeric coprocessor.

Transfers of data from the 80387 and the 80386 need at least one wait state. Write cycles to the 80387 require no wait states.

Because the interface to the 80386 is always synchronous, the 80387 CLK2 signal must be connected to the 80386 CLK2 input. The state of the 80387 CKM input determines which of two modes it operates in:

1. In pseudo-synchronous mode, CKM is low. A frequency source for the 80387 CLK2 input must be provided. Only the interface logic of the 80387 is synchronous with the 80386. The internal logic of the 80387 operates from the 80387 CLK2 clock source. Its frequency may be 10/16 to 16/10 times the speed of CLK2.

2. In synchronous mode, CKM is high and the 80387 CLK2 is not connected. The 80387 operates from the CLK2 signal. The operation of the numeric coprocessor is fully synchronous with the 80386.

Both the 80387 and the 80287 coprocessors use two methods to interact with the 80386 processor. The first is when the 80386 initiates coprocessor operations. This occurs during the execution of a coprocessor instruction (an ESC instruction) and occur under program control. The second method is when the coprocessor uses the PEREQ signal to request that the 80386 initiate operand transfers to or from system memory. These transfers occur when the coprocessor requests them. Therefore, they are asynchronous to the instruction execution of the 80386. Data transfers for the coprocessor have the same bus priority as programmed data transfers.

Two, three, four, or five bus cycles may be necessary for each operand transfer. These cycles include one coprocessor cycle plus one of the following:

- One memory cycle for an aligned operand.

- Two memory cycles for a misaligned operand.
- Two or three memory cycles for misaligned 32-bit operands to 16-bit memory.
- Four memory cycles for misaligned 64-bit operands to 16-bit memory.

Local Area Network Coprocessor

The 82586 Local Area Network (LAN) Coprocessor is an intelligent, high-performance communications controller designed to perform most tasks required for controlling access to a local area network (LAN). Generally, the 82586 is the communications manager for a station connected to a LAN. This coprocessor performs all functions associated with data transfer between the shared memory and the LAN link, including: address filtering, Link management, framing, error detection, data encoding, network management, direct memory access, and buffer chaining. Figure 7-5 shows a block diagram of this LAN coprocessor.

This type of station usually includes a host CPU, a Serial Interface Unit, shared memory, a transceiver, and a LAN link. The 82586 has two interfaces: a network interface to the Serial Interface Unit, and a bus interface to the 80386 local bus.

The 82586 is a master on the 80386 local bus. It communicates directly with the 80386 through its Channel Attention (CA) and interrupt (INT) signals.

Dedicating a CPU (such as an 80186 or 80188) to control the 82586 LAN coprocessor results in a high-performance, high-cost interface. The CPU executes the data link layer of software and sometimes the network, transport, and session layers. (These are four of the standard layers in data communications architecture.) The dedicated CPU saves the 80386 from having to do the network tasks.

82384 CLOCK GENERATOR

Microprocessor systems require some type of clock pulse in order to perform and time the various functions. The clock is the very heart of the system because it generates accurately timed pulses and because the logic subsystems are gated or enabled by these pulses.

The Clock Generator is a multifunction component that provides clocking for synchronous operation for the 80386 processor and its components. The Clock does so as follows:

- Both CLK2 and CLK are generated. CLK2 is a double-frequency clock for the 80386 processor and some of the support devices. CLK is the system clock for other support devices. The phase of the 82384 CLK matches that of the CLK signal internally generated by the 80386.
- The 82384 uses 80386 ADS# output, which guarantees setup and hold time to CLK2, to generate an ADSO# signal, which is functionally equal to ADS# but also guarantees setup and hold times with respect to CLK.
- The RES# (RESET Signal) input of the 82384 accepts an asynchronous input from a simple RC circuit or similar source, synchronizes the signal with CLK, and then outputs the active-high RESET signal to the 80386 and other system components.

The 82384 can be driven by either an external frequency source or a third over-

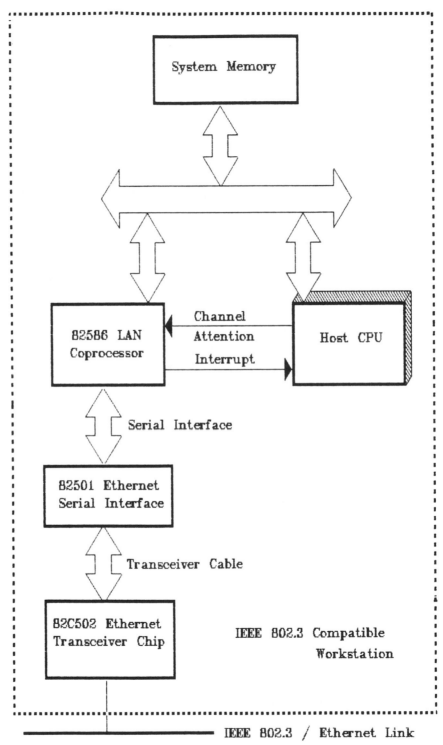

Fig. 7-5. Block diagram of a LAN station.

tone crystal. The F/C# input indicates the signal source. If F/C# is tied low, the crystal connected to the X1 and X2 pins of the 82384 is its frequency source. If F/C# is pulled high, the 82384 recognizes the signal on its External Frequency Input (EFI) pin as the frequency source. Figure 7-6 shows the connections of the 82384 to an 80386.

Clock Speeds and Timing

Clock speed is limited by response time of the ICs used in the system. Clocks vary from simple local devices to very diverse and complex systems. All other things being equal, the faster the clock frequency, the more functions that can be performed.

Both the CLK and CLK2 outputs of the 82384 are MOS-level outputs with output high voltage levels of VCC -0.6V and adequate drive for TTL (Transistor-to-transistor Logic) inputs. CLK2 is twice the frequency of CLK. The internal 80386 CLK signal is matched to the CLK output of the 82384 by the falling edge of the RESET signal.

The skew between 82384 CLK2 and CLK signals is maintained at 0-16 nanoseconds, regardless of clock frequency. For closely timed interfaces, peripheral devices must be timed by CLK2. Devices that can not be operated at this double-clock speed must use the CLK output.

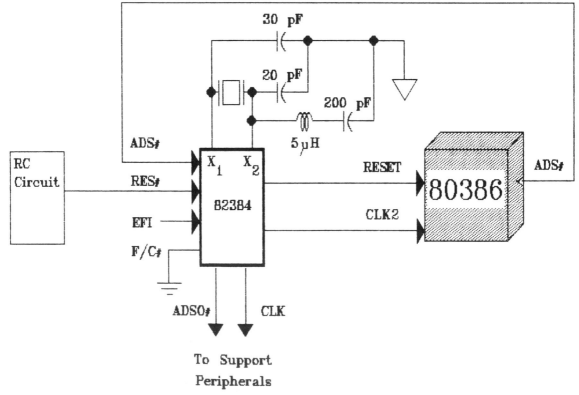

Fig. 7-6. Connecting 82384 to 80386.

Waveforms

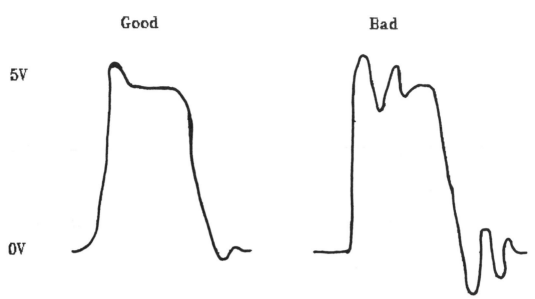

Fig. 7-7. CLK2 waveforms.

Clock Distribution and Termination

The 82384 Clock Generator provides the timing for the 80386 and its support components. The 82384 provides both the standard clock (CLK2) and a half-frequency (CLK) to indicate the internal phase of the processor. The 82384 clock pulses also drive the 80286-compatible devices that may be included in the system.

For high frequency performance, the CLK2 clock signal must be free of noise and within specification and provided with the Intel 80386 data sheet (Contact vendor for the latest information). Generally, the requirements can be met by following the following guidelines:

1. Put no more than two loads on a single trace to avoid signal reflection.
2. Use an oscilloscope to compare CLK2 waveforms to the ones shown in Fig. 7-7.
3. Use the 82384 Clock Generator to provide both CLK and CLK2 signals.
4. Obtain a clean signal by terminating the CLK2 output with a series resistor. Calculate the resistor value by measuring the total capacitive load on the CLK2 signal to Fig. 7-8. If the total capacitive load is less than 80 picofarads, add capacitors to make up the difference. Carbon resistors are recommended because of the high frequency of CLK2.

$$C_L = C_{IN} (80386) \; C_{IN}(80387) + C_{IN} (PALs) + \ldots + C_{BOARD}$$

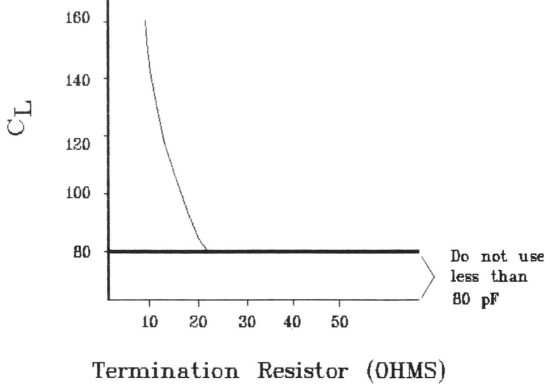

Fig.7-8. Series termination for CLK2.

C_{BOARD} = Calculated from layout and board parameters: thickness, dielectric constant, distance to ground D/VCC planes

Termination resistor must be low inductance type.

POWER AND GROUND REQUIREMENTS

Since power dissipation depends mostly on frequency, there is almost no dc power dissipation for the CHMOS III 80386. The 80386's power is primarily capacitive. Internal power varies with operating frequency and, to some extent, with wait states and software.

Accounting for about one-fifth of the total power dissipation, I/O power varies with frequency and voltage. It also depends on capacitive bus load and performance will be reduced if loading exceeds recommended maximums. Although the 80386 demands less power than the 80286, the possibility of power surges is increased, due to higher frequency and pin count.

Power and ground planes (as opposed to lines) must be used in 80386 systems to minimize noise. Since power and ground lines have inherent inductance and capacitance, an impedance $Z = (L/C)^{1/2}$ must be considered in the design if they're used. The 80386 has 20 VCC pins and VSS pins. All power and ground pins must be connected to a plane. Ideally, the 80386 is located at the center of the board to take full advantage of these planes.

At high signal frequencies, the transmission line properties of signal paths in a circuit must be considered. Reflections, interference and noise can cause false signal transitions, input voltage level violations, and data errors. These errors can be transient and difficult to debug.

Input voltage level violations are usually due to voltage spikes that raise input levels over the maximum (called *overshoot*) or under the minimum (called *under-shoot*). These voltage levels cause excess current on input gates that could damage the device permanently.

Interference is the result of electrical activity in one conductor causing transient voltages to appear in another conductor. There are two types of interference: electromagnetic interference (EMI) and electrostatic interference (ESI). EMI (also called crosstalk) is caused by the magnetic field that exists around any current-carrying conductor. ESI is caused by the capacitive coupling of two adjacent conductors. The conductors act as the plates of a capacitor. A charge built on one induces the opposite charge on the other.

THERMAL CHARACTERISTICS

Acceptable thermal (heat) levels are critical for correct performance of any electronic component, especially a processor. The heat at the surface of a chip is called the junction temperature. This temperature can be determined from external measurements, using the known heat characteristics of the electronic package. To calculate the junction temperature, use the following equations (which are courtesy of Intel Corporation):

$$T_j = T_a + (O_{ja} * PD)$$
$$T_j = T_c + (O_{jc} * PD)$$

Where:

$$
\begin{aligned}
T_j &= \text{Junction Temperature} \\
T_a &= \text{Ambient Temperature} \\
T_c &= \text{Case Temperature} \\
O_{ja} &= \text{Junction-to-ambient Temperature Coefficient} \\
O_{jc} &= \text{Junction-to-case Temperature Coefficient} \\
PD &= \text{Power Dissipation}
\end{aligned}
$$

There are advantages to using case equations to compute ambient temperatures. Because the measurement is localized to a single point, the top center of the package, case temperature is easier to calculate and measure than ambient temperature. In addition, the worst-case junction temperature (shown as T_j in the equations) is lower when figured with case temperature because the junction-to-case thermal coefficient (O_{jc}) is lower than the junction-to-ambient thermal coefficient (O_{ja}). This means that computed junction temperature varies less with power dissipation (PD).

Ambient temperature is the still air surrounding a power supply or component. The temperature of circulating air, such as a chamber with a fan, is not a correct ambient-temperature measurement since the components are being cooled by the circulating air. When using case-temperature specifications, the system designer can either set the ambient temperature or use fans to control case temperature. Conductive cooling or finned heat sinks also may be used where fans are precluded.

Consult the current data sheet to determine the values of O_{ja} for the system's air flow and ambient temperature; this should give the desired case temperature.

HARDWARE BUILDING AND DEBUGGING

A designer first considers the entire system, while knowing that the core portions must be tested prior to actually building that system. Designing and building an 80386 system incrementally is a short-cut to coming live in the shortest amount of time. Once the basic system is designed, built, and finally debugged, more software and enhancements can be added.

Incremental System Design Guidelines

Intel design engineers suggest the following guidelines to use in conjunction with the latest hardware data sheets.

1. First, install the 82384 Clock Generator and its crystal. Check that the CLK2 signal is clean and then connect the CLK2 to the 80386.

2. Connect the 82384 RESET output to the 80386 RESET input. With CLK2 running, check that the 80386 RESET state is correct.

3. Tie the 80386 INTR, NMI and HOLD input pins low. So that the first bus cycle will not end, tie the READY# pin high. Reset the 80386. Check that the processor emits the correct signals to perform its first code fetch from physical address FFFFFFF0H. Then connect the address latch and verify that the address is driven at its outputs.

4. Connect the address decoding hardware to the 80386. After reset, check that the processor attempts to select the EPROM device which stores the initial code to be executed.

5. Connect the data transceiver to the system. After reset, check that the transceiver control pins are being driven for a read cycle. Connect all the EPROM sockets' address pins. Also after reset, check that the address pins are receiving the correct address for the first code fetch cycle.

After installing the EPROMs, tie the READY# high so that the 80386 begins its first bus cycle after reset and continues to add wait states. Use a voltmeter or oscilloscope and probe the circuits while the system is in this state to verify signal states.

When the 80386, address decoder, address latch, 82384, crystal, data transceiver and READY# generation logic (which includes the wait-state generation) are functioning correctly, the 80386 can run the software stored in the EPROMs. A simple debug program (as suggested by Intel) shown in Fig. 7-9 can be run to verify that the parts of the system work together. If the program does not run, use a logic analyzer to determine where the problem is.

```
                         ASSUME CS:SIMPLEST_CODE

     0000               SIMPLEST_CODE    SEGMENT
     FFF0                                ORG 0FFF0H

     FFF0 90            START:           NOP
     FFF1 90                             NOP
     FFF2 EB FC                          JMP START

     FFF4               SIMPLEST_CODE    ENDS
                                         END
```

Fig. 7-9. A sample 4-byte diagnostic program.

When the EPROM programmed with the diagnostic program is installed, and the 80386 is executing the code, the LED indicator for ADS# glows, if the indicator has been included in the system, because ADS# is generated for each bus cycle. Check that the EPROMs are selected for each code fetch cycle.

The sample program loops back on itself and runs continuously. When the READY# input is connected to the READY# generation logic, run the program and test the results.

Check that the address latches have latched the first latch and if the address decoder is applying a chip-select signal to the EPROMs. The EPROMs should emit the first four opcode bytes of the first code to be executed: 90H, 90H, EBH, and FCH for the 4-Byte program in Fig. 7-9. The opcode should propagate through the data transceivers to the 80386 data pins.

Debugging Guides

The 80386 can stop running for any of three reasons: (1) it encounters a predefined shutdown condition. In real mode, a shutdown generally indicates that the 80386 has detected garbage on the data bus. (2) The 80386 enters a HALT state due to a HALT instruction. (3) The READY# signal is never asserted to end the bus cycle.

The 80386 emits codes on its W/R#, D/C#, and M/IO# pins and address outputs to indicate the halt or shutdown. If the shutdown occurs and the 80386 stops running, check the EPROM contents, the wiring of the address and data paths and the data transceivers. Use the 4-byte diagnostic program to investigate the system. Make this program work before attempting more complex software.

If the 80386 stops, check the READY# generation circuit. It probably hasn't activated the READY# to complete the bus cycle. The processor is adding wait states to the cycle, waiting for that READY# signal to go active. Check the circuit with a logic analyzer.

PERFORMANCE CONSIDERATIONS

At its most basic level, system performance measures how fast a microprocessor system performs a task or set of instructions. Often because the system includes devices whose response time is slow relative to the processor, overall system performance

is less than its potential. When evaluating which device to give the most consideration for performance improvements, realize that the impact of memory speed on performance is much greater than that of I/O device speeds, because most programs access
memory more than I/O.

The first method generally used to interface slower devices to fast processors
is by use of a wait state. Wait states are extra clock cycles added to the bus cycle.
On the 80386, some external logic generates the wait by delaying the READY# input. That means, for an 80386 running at 16 MHz, one wait state adds 62.5 nanoseconds to the time available for memory to respond.

A second method is to pipeline addresses. Unlike the wait state, address pipelining increases the time memory has to respond by one clock cycle *without* lengthening
the bus cycle. This extra clock cycles virtually eliminate the output delay of the 80386
status and address outputs. Address pipelining is advantageous for most bus cycles.
However, if the next address is not available before the current cycle ends, the 80386
obviously cannot pipeline the next address because it has not yet arrived. In this case,
the bus timing is identical to a non-pipelined bus cycle. Note also that the first bus
cycle after an idle bus always is non-pipelined because there was no previous cycle
in which to output the address. And, if the next cycle is to be pipelined, the first cycle
must be lengthened by at least one wait state so that the address can be output before
the end of the cycle.

Address pipelining is less effective for I/O devices which require several wait
states. In fact, the larger the number of waits required, the lesser the significance
of eliminating a single wait through pipelining. Couple this fact with the *relative* infrequency of I/O accesses and it becomes clear why address pipelining for I/O devices
usually makes little difference to system performance.

A third, and interesting, approach to accommodating slower memory speed is
to reduce the 80386's clock frequency. This approach requires a very fine tuning because a somewhat slower clock increases the bus cycle time, which means fewer wait
states may be required for particular memory devices. Note that, at the same time,
overall system performance depends directly on the clock frequency. Execution time
increases in direct proportion to the reduction in clock frequency. A 12.5 MHz 80386
takes almost 33 percent more time to execute a program than a 16 MHz 80386 operating with the same number of WAITs.

PAL DESCRIPTIONS

PALs borrow from proven fusible-link technology so the users can "write in silicon" the desired digital functions. PALs are the equivalent of four or five IC packages and fit in complexity between small- and medium-scale logic parts and the very
complex gate arrays.

Programmable Array Logic (PAL) Interface

Programmable Logic Devices (PLDs) are ICs that can be programmed to perform specific logic functions. Most PLDs consist of two arrays of logic gates: an AND
array followed by an OR array. The PLD input signals must first pass through the
array of AND gates where special combinations of input signals are formed. Each

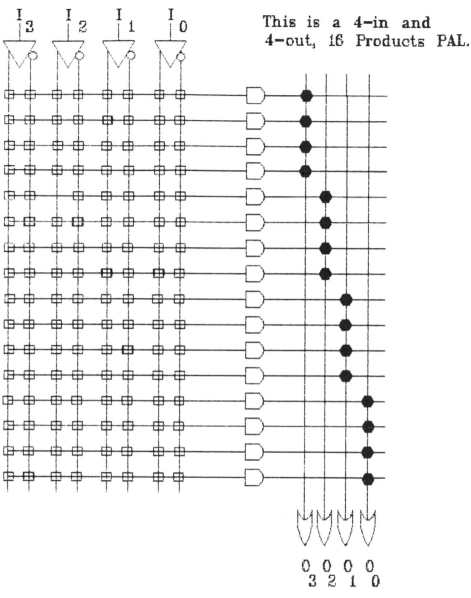

This is a 4-in and 4-out, 16 Products PAL.

Programmable AND Array   Fixed OR Array

● = Fixed Connection
□ = Fuse-Link Crosspoint Connection

Fig. 7-10. Simplified diagram of a PAL device.

group of AND combinations is called a product line, in PLD terms. The product lines are then summed in OR gate arrays.

There are three basic types of PLDs: Programmable Read-Only Memories (PROMs), Programmable Logic Arrays (PLAs), and Programmable Array Logic (PAL) devices. In a PROM, the AND array is fixed and the OR is programmable. In a PLA, both are programmable. PAL devices, on the other hand, have a programmable AND array and a fixed OR array. Within the limits of the number of PAL inputs, outputs and equation terms, any sum-of-products can be realized by specifying the correct AND array connections.

Having a programmable AND array allows a user to program only the desired input combinations. Fixing the OR array requires that certain product lines be tied to specific outputs, generally eight product lines per output. Figure 7-10 is a simplified diagram showing the programmable-AND/fixed-OR array structure of a PAL device.

Early PALs, such as the 10LB and 14LB (which have 10 and 14 inputs and 8 and 4 outputs, respectively), were combinatorial and had sparse arrays. PALs come in different speeds. Generally, the suffix on the part number tells the part's speed and power consumption. Parts with standard speed (50 nanoseconds) and power (generally 0.2 watt) have no suffix.

A PAL device can be used as a state machine or a signal decoder. The advantages of PALs include: programability which allows the PAL functions to be changed easily which simplifies prototype development; PALs are inexpensive compared to dedicated bus controllers; and the designer determines the PAL pinout and can simplify the board layout by moving signals as required.

On the other hand, PALs have three disadvantages: first, the PAL drive capability may be insufficient for some applications where buffering is required; second, PAL pin counts or speeds can restrict some designs; and, third, most PALs do not have buried state registers, that is, those not connected to outputs. Therefore, in state-machine implementations, registered output pins must be used to store the current state.

The trend seems to be toward making generic PALs that can replace most others. The generic PAL can have its output macrocell (a logic block between the fuse array and the output pin that can be configured by programming certain fuses to act in any of several ways) programmed to emulate the output structure of any existing 20-pin PAL.

Some PALs are erasable. They are useful in debugging logic equations before moving the final product to a one-time programmable PAL. Another advantage is that they allow the manufacturer to test the logic device and erase it, to ensure that the device is not defective.

The PAL's logic functions are first described as a set of Boolean equations. These equations are translated to a fuse map by a compiler that knows the target PAL's structure. The resulting fuse map is expressed in a Joint Electron Device Engineering Council (JEDEC) file which can be read by most PAL programming hardware. The JEDEC file is loaded into the PAL programmer and the fuses are blown.

Many manufacturers provide PALs with security fuses that, when blown, inhibit the ability to read or verify the contents of the PAL's fuse array, while still letting the PAL function in a circuit.

The setup, hold, and propagation delay times for each PAL input and output can be determined from PAL data sheets, available from the manufacturer and from most sales offices. As with other hardware details, the manufacturer retains the right to make adjustments as required and update the appropriate data sheets. Figure 7-11 illustrates PAL equations. These equations are for a DRAM Refresh Controller and are courtesy of Intel Corporation.

DRAM Refresh Controller Equations

```
module refresh;
flag '-r3';
title 'DRAM refresh controller  Intel Corporation'

pall device 'p16r8';
h,1,c,x = 1,0,.C.,.x.;

gnd pin 10;
vcc pin 20;

clk2 pin1;        "80386 CLK2
clk pin 2;        "82384 CLK
refreq pin 3;     "High to request refresh cycle
refout pin 5;     "Low to force all DRAM RAS lines active
refgate pin 6;    "High to disable refresh--if necessary
oe pin 11;

tc0 pin 14;       "Bit 0 of refresh timer
tc1 pin 15;       "Bit 1 of refresh timer
tcout pin 16;     "Carry from Bits 0 and 1 of refresh timer
q0 pin 17;        "State variable q0
q1 pin 18;        "State variable q1
refin pin 19;     "Low to request DRAM refresh cycle

"refresh state machine

state_diagram [refin,q0,q1];
state [1,1,1]:    "Idle
   if (refreq & clk) then [1,0,1]
   else [1,1,1];

state [1,0,1]:    "Check refresh enable
   if (refout & !refgate & clk) then [0,1,1]
   else [1,0,1];

state [0,1,1]:    "Request refresh
```

Fig. 7-11. DRAM refresh controller equations (courtesy of Intel Corp.).

```
         if (!refreq & clk) then [1,1,0]
         else [0,1,1];

state [1,1,0]:     "Recovery
   if (!refreq & clk) then [1,1,1]
   else [1,1,0];

state [0,0,0]: goto [1,1,1];    "Illegal
state [0,0,1]: goto [1,1,1];    "Illegal
state [0,1,0]: goto [1,1,1];    "Illegal
state [1,0,0]: goto [1,1,1];    "Illegal

"Lowest 2 bits of refresh timer

state-diagram [tc1,tc0];
state [0,0]:
   if (clk) then [0,1]
   else [0,0];

state [0,1]:
   if (clk) then [1,0]
   else [0,1];

state [1,0]:
   if (clk) then [1,1]
   else [1,0];

state [1,1]:
   if (clk) then [0,0]
   else [1,1];

"Refresh timer carry

state-diagram [tcout];
state 0: if (tc1 & !tc0 & clk) then 1
         else 0;

state 1: if (clk) then 0
         else 1;

test_vectors ([clk2,clk,refreq,refout,refgate] -> [refin])

      [c,h,1,h,1] -> [h];        "Idle
      [c,h,1,h,1] -> [h];        "Idle
      [c,h,1,h,1] -> [h];        "Idle
```

```
[c,h,h,1,1] -> [h];          "Wait
[c,h,h,1,1] -> [h];          "Wait
[c,h,h,1,1] -> [h];          "Wait
[c,h,h,1,1] -> [h];          "Refresh
[c,h,h,h,1] -> [1];          "Refresh
[c,h,h,h,1] -> [1];          "Refresh
[c,h,h,1,1] -> [h];          "Refresh
[c,h,1,1,1] -> [h];          "Refresh
[c,h,1,1,1] -> [h];          "Refresh

[c,h,1,h,1] -> [h];          "Idle
[c,h,1,h,1] -> [h];          "Idle

test_vectors ([clk2,clk] -> [tc1,tc0,tcout])

[c,h] -> [h,1,1];            "Count 2
[c,h] -> [h,h,h];            "Count 3, Carry
[c,h] -> [1,1,1];            "Count 0
[c,h] -> [1,h,1];            "Count 1
[c,h] -> [h,1,1];            "Count 2
[c,h] -> [h,h,h];            "Count 3, Carry
[c,h] -> [1,1,1];            "Count 0
[c,h] -> [1,h,1];            "Count 1

end refresh;
```

Note: This set of PAL equations has been "paper tested" only. It is included here for reference. PAL equation courtesy of Intel Corporation.

Local Bus Control PALs

Intel implemented the Bus Controller in two PALs. The first, PAL-1, follows the processor bus cycles and generates the overall bus cycle timings. The second, PAL-2, generates most of the bus control signals. Both PALs are clocked by CLK2, so the choice of PALs is limited to only 20-pin B-Series PALs. CLK2 gives the following advantages over CLK:

- The PAL can provide delays in 31-nanosecond increments, rather than being limited to 62-nanosecond ones.
- The skew from clock to command signal is reduced, which allows higher performance with slower devices.
- The processor's ADS# and READY# signals can be sampled directly.

PAL-1 Functions. As implemented, PAL-1 is two main state machines. The first, BUSSTATE, is used to follow the 80386 bus cycles. It is specified by the state of two signals IDLE and PIPE and follows the 80386 bus by sampling ADS# and READY#. The second, LOCALSTATE, keeps track of the local bus state. Signals L0, L1, and L2 specify LOCALSTATE. LOCALSTATE uses the processor's W/R# signal and various chip-select inputs to determine what type of cycle to run.

PAL-2 Functions. PAL-2 generates the majority of the bus control signals. This includes all five command signals, READY#, and the latch and transceiver enable signals. PAL-2 inputs the three LOCALSTATE (See PAL-1) signals and the three 80386 bus cycle definition pins: WR#, M/IO#, and D/C#. It does this to follow the local bus state. Also, PAL-2 inputs the 0-wait state chip-select signal to set output signals quickly enough for zero wait states.

DRAM State PAL

The DRAM State PAL judges when to run a new DRAM cycle. It also tracks the state of the DRAM through the cycle. This PAL's inputs sample DRAM requests from the 80386 as well as refresh requests. The PAL outputs store information and generate two Row Address Select (RAS) signals.

This DRAM PAL is implemented in a 16R8 PAL if the RAS signals are registered internally. It is implemented in a 16R6 PAL if external registers are used. For a 16-MHz 80386 system, B-series PAL speeds are required.

DRAM Control PAL

The majority of the control signals for the DRAM circuit are generated by the DRAM Control PAL. The PAL's inputs sample the 80386 byte-enable outputs and W/R# as well as the DRAM State PAL status signals. The PAL outputs generate the four Column Address Select (CAS) signals, the signals for the processor's READY# and Next Address (NA#) logic, and two transceiver control signals.

A 16R8 PAL is needed to register the CAS signals internally. A 16R4 PAL is needed when the external registers drive the CAS signals. For a 16-MHz 80386 system, B-series PAL speeds are required.

Refresh Interval Counter PAL

The Refresh Interval Counter PAL periodically generates fresh requests to the DRAM State PAL. The Refresh Interval Counter PAL operates as a counter decremented every CLK cycle. When the counter reaches a preset value, it resets its value to 255 and activates its refresh request (RFRQ). The RFRQ remains active until both refresh acknowledge (REFACK) inputs are sampled simultaneously active.

Refresh Address Counter PAL

The Refresh Address Counter PAL keeps track of the address of the next DRAM row to be refreshed. After each refresh cycle, the PAL increments this address. A 16R8 PAL can be used since most DRAMs need only 8-bits or fewer for the refresh row address. If required, a 20X10 PAL can be used to provide 10 bits of row address. For an 80386 system operating at any speed, standard PAL speeds are fast enough.

8

Programming The 80386

This chapter discusses software development strategy in general, virtual-8086 (V86) environment, the 80286 protected-mode and 80386 real-address mode. Chapter 9 reviews general programming guidelines and lists programming notes of special cases for the 80386 programmers. Chapter 10 discusses the complete 80386 instruction set, which is a superset of all the instructions for the previous generations: 8086/88 through 80286.

SOFTWARE SYSTEM DESIGN

Software design is the application of principles, skills and a subtle art to the design and construction of programs and systems. The environment for these programs consists of the computer system on which the program runs.

A software system has these properties:

- The program(s) are implemented under one authority, generally the operating system that runs on the main, central processor.
- The hierarchy of other software is subservient to this major authority, generally running at different priority and/or privilege levels.
- Inner levels of the operating system are hidden from computer system end-users. These inner levels are held to be "sacred" and unchangeable by end-users.

The design of a software system is the creation of a complete and precise description of the system. That description is a collection of sub-descriptions of the software and hardware components and their interactions. The complete description of a software component is a program, written in a well-defined programming language. The semantics of the programming language must be known prior to actual start of programming, to ensure that all the software components can be implemented correctly in that language.

A software designer strives to achieve four goals: required function, correctness, performance, and reliability.

Required function is achieving the desired and correct output, given known inputs. Input is comprised of all the information taken in by the software system. Output is the information delivered. *Correctness* is the definition of how closely the software system meets the objectives as specified by the design.

Performance is the speed and effectiveness of a software system as it uses resources toward meeting the objectives of the original design. Finally, *reliability* is the ability of a software system to perform its function correctly in spite of failures of computer system components. Failure, here, means a temporary or permanent change in the component's characteristics that alters its function. Most programmers do not feel, for instance, that software *fails*; it is merely *incorrect*.

"Modular" means "constructed with standardized units or dimensions for flexibility and variety in use." Applied to software engineering, modularity refers to the building of software systems by putting together parts called *program modules*. A large system is a precise representation of a system that is composed of many interacting parts or modules.

LANGUAGE ELEMENTS

Very simply, a language or an instruction set is made up of those elements (mnemonics) which a set of designers found necessary to do a set of predefined tasks. For instance, if there is no need to do floating-point arithmetic, then there will be no instructions to do it.

The limits and rules within the language or instruction set were defined during design. One major requirement for the 80386 was the support of previous generations' instruction set. Another important fact that influenced the design of the 80386 instruction set was the requirement for implementing privilege levels; as software systems become more powerful, security becomes an increasingly important issue. Third, a powerful operating system needs to be protected from applications programs; a protected system is a controlled environment in which some well-defined boundaries and ground rules exist to restrict communication and movement.

ADDRESSING MODES

Some instructions access memory to obtain or store data involved in the operation of the instruction. Other instructions refer to memory to indicate the location to which a program jump is to be made. In either case, the instruction must specify the address of the memory location being referenced. The part of the instruction that provides the memory location is called the *address field*. The contents of the address field is the *stated address* and the address of the referenced memory location is the *effective address*.

In *direct addressing*, the effective address is given in the instruction. If all the locations in the computer memory are to be addressed directly, then the instruction must consist of several words. The operand for the instruction is part of the instruction itself in *immediate addressing*. The location of the operand immediately follows the memory location that contains the operation portion of the instruction.

A useful and important addressing mode is *indirect addressing*, where the stated address in the address field of the instruction is a pointer to the location that contains the effective address. Some microprocessors allow the stated address in an instruction to be added to the contents of a specified register. This is called *indexed* addressing and the specified register is an *index register*. Closely related to indexed addressing is *relative addressing* where the stated address in the instruction is added to the content of the instruction pointer to form the effective address. The stated address is regarded as a signed quantity so that relative addressing in a jump instruction allows a jump forward or backward (from the location indicated by the instruction pointer) by the amount shown in the address field of the instruction.

The 80386 has nine instruction types: arithmetic, bit manipulation, data transfer, high level language support, logical and shift/rotate, processor control, program control, protection, and string manipulation. The instructions in each type are listed below. In addition, to provide software compatibility with the 8086, the 80386 can execute 16-bit instructions in real and protected modes.

The processor itself determines the default operand size of the instructions it is executing by examining the "D bit" in the CS Segment Descriptor. If D=0, all operand lengths and effective addresses are assumed to be 16 bits long. If D=1, the operands and addresses are 32 bits long. However, in real mode, the default operand and address size is 16 bits (no 80386 descriptors in real mode).

Regardless of default size, two prefixes (The Operand Size Prefix and the Address Length Prefix) override the D bit value on an individual instruction basis. These prefixes are automatically added by Intel assemblers.

INSTRUCTION SET OVERVIEW

Instructions in a set can be considered as tools of a trade. Each tool was designed to perform a specific task which satisfied some requirement. Useful, high-quality tools are closely associated with quality end-products.

The 80386 instruction set is a superset of that developed for the 8086/8088 and 80286 processors. Four major highlights of the 80386's extensions to the previous instruction sets are:

- A scaled index address mode has been added for instructions that use memory references. This mode allows the contents of an index register to be scaled (multiplied by 1, 2, 4, or 8) before being added to the base. This scaling allows efficient indexing into data arrays with multiple-byte entries.
- Instructions such as multiply (MUL) are optimized by using an early-out algorithm which detects when the most significant bits of the multiplier are zero and completes the instruction. This allows the instruction to execute faster.
- Support for 32-bit operands and addresses is added for both real and protected mode. In real mode, the operand and address default size is 16 bits, to maintain compatibility with 8086/8088 and 80286. This default can be overridden by a prefix byte. In protected mode, operand and address size is governed by a bit in the segment descriptor which may be overridden with an instruction prefix.

- A 64-bit barrel shifter in the execution unit (EU) optimizes shift, divide, and multiply operations. With this shifter, multiple-bit shift operations can execute in one clock cycle. For instance, the SHRD and SHLD instructions use two 32-bit registers to allow a 64-bit string to be shifted multiple positions in a single clock cycle.

Designed to sustain an execution rate of between 3 and 4 million instructions per second (MIPS), the 80386 has a high system throughput. To do this, it uses instruction pipelining (see Chapter 6 for an overview of pipelining), on-chip address translation and high bus bandwidth.

The 80386 instruction set offers 8-, 16-, and 32-bit data types. As stated above, the 80386 instructions are divided into nine functional categories. The instructions are listed in summary form below. In Chapter 10, each instruction will be defined and described in detail.

Arithmetic

Addition
ADD   Add operands
ADC   Add with carry
INC   Increment operand by 1
AAA   ASCII adjust for addition
DAA   Decimal adjust for addition

Subtraction
SUB   Subtract operands
SBB   Subtract with borrow
DEC   Decrement operand by 1
NEG   Negate operand
CMP   Compare operands
DAS   Decimal adjust for subtraction
AAS   ASCII adjustment for subtraction

Multiplication
MUL   Multiply Double/Single precision
IMUL   Integer multiply
AAM   ASCII adjust after multiply

Division
DIV   Divide unsigned
IDIV   Integer divide
AAD   ASCII adjust before division

Bit Manipulation

Single Bit Instructions
BT   Bit Test
BTS   Bit Test and Set

BTR	Bit Test and Reset
BTC	Bit Test and Complement
BSF	Bit Scan Forward
BSR	Bit Scan Reverse

Data Transfer

General Purpose

MOV	Move Operand
PUSH	Push operand onto stack
POP	Pop operand off stack
PUSHA	Push all registers on stack
POPA	Pop all registers off stack
XCHG	Exchange Operand, Register

Conversion

MOVZX	Move byte or Word, Dword, with zero extension
MOVSX	Move byte, Word, Dword, sign extended
CBW	Convert byte to Word in AX
CWDE	Convert Word to DWord in EAX
CWD	Convert Word to DWord in DX, AX
CDQ	Convert DWord to QWord in EDX, EAX

Input/Output

IN	Input operand from I/O space
OUT	Output operand to I/O space

Address Object

LEA	Load Effective Address
LDS	Load pointer into D segment register
LES	Load pointer into E segment register
LFS	Load pointer into F segment register
LGS	Load pointer into G segment register
LSS	Load pointer into S (Stack) segment register

Flag Manipulation

LAHF	Load A register from Flags
SAHF	Store A register in Flags
PUSHF	Push flags onto stack
POPF	Pop flags off stack
PUSHFD	Push EFLAGS onto stack
POPFD	Pop EFLAGS off stack
CLC	Clear Carry Flag
CLD	Clear Direction Flag
CMC	Complement Carry Flag

| STC | Set Carry Flag |
| STD | Set Direction Flag |

High Level Language Support

BOUND	Check Array Bounds
ENTER	Set up Parameter Block for entering procedure
LEAVE	Leave procedure
SETcc	Byte set on condition

Logical Instructions and Shift/Rotate

Logical

NOT	"NOT" operands
AND	"AND" operands
OR	"Inclusive OR" operands
XOR	"Exclusive OR" operands
TEST	"Test" operands

Shifts

SHL/SHR	Shift logical left or right
SAL/SAR	Shift arithmetic left or right
SHLD/SHRD	Double shift left or right

Rotates

| ROL/ROR | Rotate left/right |
| RCL/RCR | Rotate through carry left/right |

Processor Control

ESC	Processor Extension Escape
HLT	Halt
LOCK	Lock bus—Instruction Prefix
MOV	Move To/From Control Registers
NOP	No operation
WAIT	Wait until BUSY # negated

Program Control

Conditional Transfers

JA/JNBE	Jump if above/not below nor equal
JAE/JNB	Jump if above or equal/not below
JB/JNAE	Jump if below/not above nor equal
JBE/JNA	Jump if below or equal/not above
JC/JNC	Jump if carry/Not carry
JE/JZ	Jump if equal/zero

JG/JNLE	Jump if greater/not less nor equal
JGE/JNL	Jump if greater or equal/not less
JL/JNGE	Jump if less/not greater nor equal
JLE/JNG	Jump if less or equal/not greater
JNE/JNZ	Jump if not equal/not zero
JNO	Jump if not overflow
JNP/JPO	Jump if not parity/parity odd
JNS	Jump if not sign
JO	Jump if overflow
JP/JPE	Jump if parity/parity even
JS	Jump if sign

Unconditional Transfers

CALL	Call a procedure or task
RET	Return from a procedure
JMP	Jump

Iteration Controls

LOOP	Loop
LOOPE/LOOPZ	Loop if equal/zero
LOOPNE/LOOPNZ	Loop if not equal/not zero
JCXZ	Jump if register CX=0
JECXZ	Jump short if ECX=0

Interrupts

INT	Interrupt
INTO	Interrupt if overflow
IRET	Return from Interrupt/Task
CLI	Clear interrupt enable
STI	Set interrupt enable

Protection

CLTS	Clear Task Switched Flag
SGDT	Store Global Descriptor Table
SIDT	Store Interrupt Descriptor Table
STR	Store Task Register
SLDT	Store Local Descriptor Table
LGDT	Load Global Descriptor Table
LIDT	Load Interrupt Descriptor Table
LTR	Load Task Register
LLDT	Load Local Descriptor Table
ARPL	Adjust Requested Privilege Level
LAR	Load Access Rights
LSL	Load Segment Limit

VERR/VERW	Verify segment for reading or writing
LMSW	Load Machine Status Word
SMSW	Store Machine Status Word

String Manipulation

MOVS	Move byte or Word, DWord string
INS	Input string from I/O space
OUTS	Output string to I/O space
CMPS	Compare byte or Word, DWord string
SCAS	Scan byte or word, DWord string
LODS	Load byte or Word, DWord string
STOS	Store byte or Word, DWord string
REP	Repeat Prefix
REPE/REPZ	Repeat while equal/zero
RENE/REPNZ	Repeat while not equal/not zero
XLAT	Translate String

The average instruction is 3.2 bytes long. Since the 80386 has a 16-byte instruction queue, an average of 5 instructions will be prefetched. All instructions operate on either 0, 1, 2, or 3 operands. The operands reside in a register, in the instruction itself, or in memory. Most zero-operand instructions take only one byte, while two-operand instructions are generally two bytes long. However, prefixes can be added to all instructions to override the default length of the operand.

Operands can be 8-, 16-, or 32-bits long. Normally, when executing 32-bit code written for the 80386, they are 8 or 32 bits. When executing existing 80286 or 8086 code, operands are 8 or 16 bits. Prefixes can be added to operands to override the operand default lengths; that is, use 32-bit operands for 16-bit code and vice versa.

Memory is addressed with either 16- or 32-bit addresses. Each instruction that accesses memory has an address-size attribute of 16 or 32 bits. A 16-bit address both indicates the use of a 16-bit displacement in the instruction and an effective address calculation; that is, it means the generation of a 16-bit address offset, a segment relative address. The 32-bit addresses use a 32-bit displacement and the creation of a 32-bit address offset. Any instruction that reads or writes a 16-bit word or a 32-bit doubleword has an operand-size attribute of either 16 or 32 bits.

Instructions that implicitly use a stack—such as POP EAX—also have a stack address-size attribute of either 16 or 32 bits. To form the address of the top of the stack, the 16-bit addresses use the 16-bit SP (stack pointer register). Instructions with a stack address-size attribute of 32 bits use the 32-bit ESP (Extended Stack Pointer register). The stack address-size attribute is shown by the B-bit of the data-segment descriptor in the SS (Stack Segment) register. A zero B-bit selects a stack address-size attribute of 16. A one selects an attribute of 32.

Programs executed in real mode or virtual-8086 mode have 16-bit addresses and operands by default. On the other hand, in the protected mode, the D-bit (in executable-segment descriptors) determines the default size attribute for both operands and addresses. These default attributes apply to the execution of all instructions in the segment. If the D-bit is zero, the default address and operand sizes are 16 bits. If it's a one, the default is 32 bits.

There is an override for the default segment attribute. The internal encoding of an instruction can include two byte-long prefixes: the address-size prefix (67H) and the operand-size prefix (66H). Table 8-1 shows how each prefix affects the combinations of defaults and overrides.

To help programming, the 80386 has testability and debug features. They include a self-test and direct address to the page translation cache. In addition, the 80386 has four breakpoint registers that provide breakpoint traps on code execution or data access.

VIRTUAL 8086 ENVIRONMENT

The 80386 allows 8086/88 and 80186/188 application programs to execute unchanged in real mode. A protected mode operating system also can run their programs unchanged. 8086 applications and operating systems run in protected mode as part of a virtual (V86) task that takes advantage of the hardware support of multitasking offered by protected mode.

The V86 task forms a "virtual machine" that consists of the 80386 hardware and systems software. The software controls the V86 external interfacing, the interrupts and I/O. The hardware provides the TSS which contains the virtual registers, a virtual memory space which is the task's first megabyte of the linear address space, and executes the instructions that deal with the registers and address space.

Entering and Leaving Virtual 8086 Mode

The 80386 systems software does not manipulate the VM (Virtual Mode) flag

Table 8-1. Size Attributes.

Segment Default D =	0	0	0	0	1	1	1	1
Operand-size Prefix (66H)	N	N	Y	Y	N	N	Y	Y
Address-size Prefix (67H)	N	Y	N	Y	N	Y	N	Y
Operand Size	16	16	32	32	32	32	16	16
Address Size	16	32	16	32	32	16	32	16

N = No, this instruction prefix is not present

Y = Yes, this instruction is present

in EFLAGS directly. It changes the EFLAGS image that is stored in the TSS or on the stack. A V86 monitor would set the VM bit in the EFLAGS image when first creating a V86 task. The exception and interrupt handlers examine the VM bit as stored on the stack. If VM is set, the interrupted procedure was executing in V86 mode and the handler may need to invoke the V86 monitor.

The 80386 can enter virtual 8086 mode in two ways:

- An IRET from a procedure of an 80386 task that loads EFLAGS from the stack. If the VM flag is 1, the 80386 returns control to an 8086 procedure. The Current Privilege Level (CPL) must be zero when IRET is executed or the 80386 does not change VM.
- A switch to an 80386 task that loads the EFLAGS from the new Task State Segment. The new TSS must be an 80386 TSS, not an 80286 TSS, because the 80286 TSS does not store the high-order word of EFLAGS, which contains VM. If VM is 1, the new task is executing 8086 instructions and the 80386 forms base addresses as if it were an 8086 processor.

The 80386 leaves virtual mode when it handles an interrupt or an exception. There are two possibilities:

- If the interrupt or exception vectors to a privilege level zero procedure, the 80386 stores the current EFLAGS on the stack and clears the VM flag. That causes the interrupt or exception handler to execute as native 80386 protected mode code. If the interrupt or exception vectors to a conforming segment or to a privilege level other than 3, the 80386 signals a general protection exception. The exception error code is the selector of the executable segment to which transfer was attempted.
- The interrupt or exception causes a task switch. A task switch from a V86 task to any other loads EFLAGS from the new task's TSS. If the new TSS is an 80386 TSS and the VM flag is zero, or the new TSS is an 80286 TSS, the processor resets the VM flag, loads the segment registers from the new TSS using 80386 address formation, and then begins to execute the new task instructions according to 80386 protected mode.

Figure 8-1 shows how the 80386 enters and leaves an 8086 program.

A switch to or from the V86 task may be due to several things. It can be an interrupt that vectors to a task gate, an IRET when the NT (Nested Task) flag is set, or an action of the scheduler of the 80386 operating system. Regardless of which occurred, the 80386 changes the VM flag in EFLAGS in the new TSS. If the new TSS is an 80286 TSS, the processor clears VM, because the high-order word is not in the TSS. The 80286 updates VM before loading the segment registers from the images in the new TSS. The new setting of VM determines whether the 80386 interprets the new segment register images as 80386/80286 or 8086 selectors.

Interrupt and Trap Gates. If the 80386 leaves V86 mode as the result of an exception or interrupt that vectors via a trap or interrupt gate to a privilege level zero procedure, the exception or interrupt handler returns to the 8086 code by executing

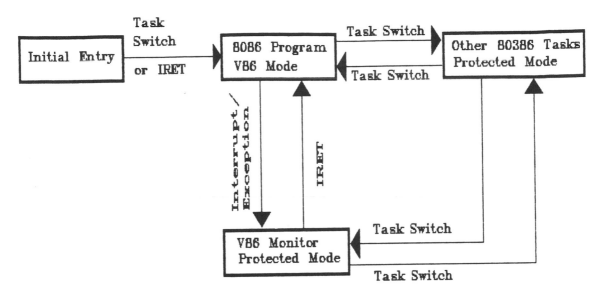

Fig. 8-1. 80386 enters and leaves virtual 8086.

an IRET. Since it was designed for execution by an 8086, the 8086 program has an 8086-style interrupt table that starts at linear address zero. The 80386 does not use this table; it vectors through the IDT for all exceptions and interrupts that occur in V86 mode. The IDT entry for interrupts or exceptions that occur in V86 mode must contain a trap gate, an 80386 trap gate (type 14), or an 80386 interrupt gate (type 15). The type 14 and 15 gates must point to a nonconforming, privilege level zero code segment.

If the interrupt is to be reflected to the virtual 8086 task's interrupt handler, the 80386 interrupt handler emulates an 8086-style interrupt for the task.

Interrupts and exceptions, with 80386 trap or interrupt gates in the IDT, vector to the appropriate handler procedure at privilege level zero. The 80386 stores the contents of the 8086 segment registers on the PL0 stack. Then it loads all the segment registers with zeros before beginning to execute the handler procedure. Interrupt procedures that expect values in the segment registers or that return values via segment registers must use the register images stored on the PL0 stack. Interrupt handlers that need to know if the interrupt occurred in V86 mode examine the VM flag in the stored EFLAGS.

After processing the interrupt or exception, the 80386 returns to the 8086 code in the following steps:

1. Locate the appropriate handler procedure by referring to the 8086 interrupt vector.
2. Store the 8086 program state on PL3 (Privilege Level three) stack.
3. Modify the return link on the PL0 stack to point to the PL3 handler procedure.
4. Execute IRET to pass control to the handler.
5. When the PL3 handler's IRET traps to the V86 monitor, restore the return line on PL0 to point to the originally interrupt, privilege level three procedure.

6. Execute an IRET to pass control back to the original, interrupted procedure.

Virtual 8086 Mode Addressing

The 80386 executes V86 mode when the VM (Virtual Mode) flag is set in the EFLAGS register. The processor tests the VM flag when decoding instructions to determine which instructions are sensitive to IOPL (I/O Privilege Level), and when loading segment registers to determine if it is to use 8086-style address formation.

All 80386 registers are accessible to V86, including the segment registers FS and GS, Control and Test Registers, and the Debug registers. V86 code also may use the new 80386 instructions that explicitly operate on FS and GS, along with the segment-override prefixes that cause instructions to use FS and GS for address calculations. The new instructions are: LSS, LFS, and LGS, bit scan, double-shift, byte set on condition, long-displacement conditional jumps, move with sign/zero extension and a generalized multiply.

Address Formation

When in the V86 mode, the 80386 does not interpret 8086 selectors by referring to descriptors. It forms linear addresses as if it were an 8086. The selector is shifted left by four bits to form the 20-bit base address. The effective address is extended with four high-order zeros and added to the base address. There is a possibility of a carry, so the resulting linear address can contain up to 21 significant bits. The 8086 program running in V86 can generate linear addresses in the range of 0 to 10FFEFH, one megabyte plus approximately 64K bytes.

V86 tasks actually generate 32-bit linear addresses. While the 8086 program only uses the low-order 21 bits (of that 32-bit address), the linear address can be mapped via page tables to a 32-bit physical address. Using the address-size prefix, 32-bit effective addresses can be generated, unlike the 8086 and 80286 processors. However, if the value of the 32-bit addresses exceeds 65535, it creates an exception (interrupt 12 or 13 with no error code).

Virtual 86 Task

A virtual 8086 task must be represented by an 80386 TSS, which the 80386 uses to execute the 8086 program before it returns to protected mode to execute the 80386 tasks. The V86 task consists of two parts: the 8086 program to be executed, and 80386 code that serves as the virtual machine monitor.

The V86 monitor is actually 80386 protected mode code that executes at privilege level zero, and consists mainly of initialization and exception handling procedures. The monitor, as with any other 80386 program, uses executable segment descriptors that must exist in the GDT or in the task's LDT. The monitor may also need data segment descriptors to allow it to examine the interrupt vector table or other parts of the 8086 program that are in the first megabyte of address space.

Operating system services can be left as part of the 8086 code or emulated in the V86 monitor. The major reasons for choosing to leave them are that the application code modifies the operating system and the development group may not have sufficient development time to reimplement the 8086 operating system in 80386 code.

Some reasons to implement or emulate in the V86 monitor are that the functions of the 8086 operating system often can be easily emulated by CALLs to the 80386 operating system and that operating system functions (and system resources such as hard disks and printers) can be more easily coordinated among several V86 tasks. Regardless how V86 is implemented, note that different V86 tasks can use different 8086 operating systems, which opens choices available to systems programmers.

Paging is not required for a single V86 task but it is useful in order to:

- redirect or trap references to memory-mapped I/O devices.
- share 8086 operating system code or ROM code that is common to several 8086 programs that may be executing simultaneously.
- create a virtual address space larger than the physical address space.
- create multiple V86 tasks, in which each task must map the lower megabyte of linear addresses to different physical locations.
- emulate the megabyte wrap of the 8086.

The 80386 does not refer to descriptors while executing 8086 programs, so it does not use the protection mechanisms offered by descriptors. There are a couple of approaches that can be used to protect the systems software in a V86 task from the 8086 program. The software designer may choose to use the U/S bit of the page table entries to protect the virtual machine monitor and other systems software that is in each V86's task space. When the 80386 is in V86 mode, the Current Privilege Level (CPL) is 3, which means that the 8086 program has only user privileges. If the virtual machine monitor's pages have supervisor privileges, they cannot be accessed by the 8086 program.

Another way to protect the V86 system from a V86 application is to reserve the first megabyte and 64 kilobytes of each task's linear address space for the 8086 program. The 8086 tasks cannot generate addresses outside that range.

Sensitive Instructions in Virtual 8086 Mode

When the 80386 executes in V86 mode, the instructions IN, INS, OUT and OUTS are *not* sensitive to the IOPL bits in EFLAGS, although they are normally sensitive in protected mode. There are several instructions that are sensitive to the IOPL bits that are not normally sensitive. Those are: CLI (Clear Interrupt Enable Flag), INT*n* (Software Interrupt), IRET (Interrupt Return), LOCK (Assert Bus Lock Signal), POPF (Pop Flags), PUSHF (Push Flags), and STI (Set Interrupt Enable Flag). These instructions are made sensitive to IOPL so that their function can be simulated by the V86 monitor.

In virtual 8086 mode, the Current Privilege Level is always three. If IOPL is less than three, these seven instructions trigger a general protection exception.

Many 8086 operating systems are called by pushing parameters onto the stack and then executing an INT*n* instruction. INT*n* is sensitive so that the V86 monitor can intercept calls to the 8086 operating system if IOPL is less than three. The V86 monitor can then emulate the required function of the 8086 operating system or direct the interrupt back to the 8086 operating system.

The instructions POPF, PUSHF and IRET are sensitive to IOPL so that the V86 monitor can control any changes to the Interrupt Enable flag (IF). CLI and STI are sensitive to IOPL in both 8086 code and 80386 code.

Virtual Mode Input/Output

There are 8086 programs that were designed to operate on a single-task system and that use I/O devices directly. These programs are disruptive when running in a multitasking environment. Instead of direct control, system designers may take other approaches. The method chosen to control the I/O depends on whether the I/O ports are memory mapped or I/O mapped. Some options for control are:

- Selectively trap and then emulate references that a task makes to specific I/O ports.
- Trap or redirect references to memory-mapped I/O addresses.
- Emulate the 8086 operating system as an 80386 program and require it to do I/O via software interrupts to the operating system. Trap all attempts to do I/O directly.

I/O-mapped input/output in the V86 differs from protected mode in one way. The protection mechanism does not consult IOPL when it executes the IN, INS, OUT and OUTS instructions; only the I/O permission Bit Map controls whether the V86 tasks execute these I/O instructions. The I/O Permission Bit Map traps I/O instruction selectively, depending on the I/O address to which they refer. Because each task has its own I/O Permission Bit Map, the addresses trapped for one task may be different for those trapped for others.

Each task that executes memory-mapped I/O must have a page (or several pages) for the memory-mapped address space. The V86 monitor can control the memory-mapped I/O by either (1) causing a monitor trap which forces a page fault on the memory-mapped page (read-only pages will trap writes and not-present pages will trap both reads and writes), or (2) assigning the memory-mapped page to appropriate physical addresses. Intervening for each I/O may be excessive for some kinds of I/O devices. In this case, a page fault can intervene on the first I/O operation. Then the monitor can make sure that the task has exclusive access to the device and can change the page status to present and read/write. This allows subsequent I/O to proceed at full speed.

Differences Between Virtual-8086 and 8086

In general, most software operates the same on an 8086 processor and on the 80386 in virtual mode. There are some differences to keep in mind.

- Opcodes that were not defined for the 8086 and 8088 processors cause an Exception 6. However, if the undefined 8086/88 opcode translates to a defined 80386 opcode, it will execute in the 80386 manner.
- Since the 80386 takes fewer clocks for most instructions than does the 8086 or 8088, two affected areas can be: assumed delays with the 8086/88 operating in parallel with an 8087 numerics coprocessor, and delays required by I/O devices between I/O operations.

- The 80386 generates the largest negative number as a quotient for the IDIV instruction. The 8086/88 causes an exception zero.
- On both the 8086 and 8088, divide exceptions leave the instruction pointer (CS:IP) pointing to the instruction *after* the failing one. The 80386 CS:IP points directly at the failing instruction.
- The 8086/88 has no instruction length limit. The 80386 sets a 15 byte limit on instruction length and exception 13 occurs if this limit is violated. The only way to exceed the 80386 limit is to put redundant prefixes before the instruction.
- Flags bit positions 12 through 15 differ, depending on whether they were stored in real or virtual-8086. The 8086 stores them as ones. V86 stores bit 15 *always* as zero and bits 14 through 12 as whatever the last value loaded into them.
- The 8087 INT signal uses an interrupt controller but the 80387 error signal to the 80386 does not go through an interrupt controller. Coprocessor instructions that deal with the interrupt controller may need to be deleted.
- On the 8086/8088 systems, the saved CS:IP points to the ESC instruction itself. On the 80836, the value of CS:IP (saved for coprocessor exceptions) points at any prefixes *before* the ESC.
- If an 8086/88 system uses a vector other than 16 for the 8087 interrupt, both vectors should point to the coprocessor-error exception handler. Any 80386 system with a coprocessor must use interrupt vector 16 for coprocessor error exceptions.
- An 8086/88 processor PUSHes the value of SP *after* it is incremented. The 80386 PUSHes the value of SP *before* it is incremented as part of the PUSH operation.
- The 80386 masks all shift and rotate counts to the low-order five bits. This MOD 32 operation limits the count to a maximum of 31 bits. This limits the time that interrupt response is delayed while the instruction executes.
- On the 8086, an offset 0 (for example, to PUSH a word when SP=1) or an attempt to access a memory operand that crosses offset 65535 (e.g., a MOV of a word to offset 65535) causes the offset to wrap around, modulo 65536. The 80386 raises an exception in these cases: 12 if the segment is a stack segment or 13 if the segment is a data segment.
- On the 8086, if sequential access goes past offset 65535, the 8086 fetches the next instruction byte from offset 0 of the same segment. The 80386 raises Exception 13 in this case.

The 80286 processor implements the bus lock function differently than the 80386. Depending on how the V86 monitor handles LOCK, this difference may or may not be apparent to 8086 programs. If 8086 programs execute LOCK directly, programs that use forms of memory locking specific to the 8086 may not execute properly on the 80386 system.

EXECUTING 80286 PROTECTED-MODE CODE

Programs designed for execution in protected mode on an 80286 execute without change on the 80386 because of the design requirement that the 80386 be a superset of the 8086 and 80286.

Descriptors used in the 80286, executable segments, task gates, and local descriptor tables are used in both the 80286 and 80386. The 80386 has new versions of TSS descriptors, but both the 80286 and 80386 descriptors can be used simultaneously in the same system. For the common descriptors, the 80386 looks for zeros in the final word to determine if it should interpret the descriptor as a 80286 descriptor.

When moving 80286 software to the 80386, consider the following two cases:

CASE 1: Porting selected 80286 applications to the 80386 environment with an 80386 system builder, loader, and operating system.

The TSSs used to represent the 80286 should be changed to 80386 TSSs. It is not necessary to change the 80286 object modules. TSSs are usually constructed by the operating system, loader or the system builder.

CASE 2: Porting an entire 80286 system, complete with 80286 operating system, loader and system builder.

All tasks have 80286 TSSs. The 80386 acts as a fast 80286.

Restricted LOCK

LOCK and its corresponding output signal should be used to prevent other bus masters from interrupting a data movement operation. In typical 8086 and 80286 configurations, LOCK locked the entire physical memory space. With the 80386, memory is guaranteed to be locked against access by a processor executing a locked instruction on *exactly* the same memory; that is, an operand with identical starting address and identical length.

LOCK can be used only with the following instructions when they modify memory: BT, BTS, BTR, BTC, XCHG, INC, DEC, NOT, NEG, ADD, ADC, SUB, SBB, AND, OR and XOR. Using LOCK before any other instruction generates an undefined opcode.

The bus lock function is implemented differently in the 80286 and the 80386. Software that uses forms of memory locking that are specific to the 80286 *may* not run correctly when transported to a specific application of the 80386.

80286 Address Wraparound

With the 80286, base and offset combinations that address beyond 16M bytes wrap around to the first megabyte of the 80286 address space. The 80386's greater physical address space has these addresses fall into the 17th megabyte. If software depends on the 80286 wraparound, the same effect can be simulated by using paging to map the first 64K bytes of the 17th megabyte of the logical addresses to physical addresses in the first megabyte.

80386 REAL-ADDRESS MODE

The 80386 real-address mode executes object code designed for the 8086, 8088, 80186, 80188, and 80286 real-address mode. The 80386 architecture is nearly identical to that of the 8086/88 and 80186/188. From a programmer's view, the 80386 in real-address mode is a high-speed 8086 with some extensions to the registers and the instruction set.

Entering and Leaving Real-Address Mode

Real-address mode is automatically in effect after the RESET signal. Even when the system is intended to be used in protected mode, the start-up program (system initialization or boot) executes in real-address mode temporarily initializing for protected mode.

Switching to protected mode is the only way to leave real-address mode. The 80386 enters protected mode when a MOV to CR0 instruction sets the PE (Protection Enable) bit in CR0. If maintaining 80286 compatibility, the LMSW instruction can be used to set the PE bit.

If software clears the PE bit in CR0 with a MOV to CR0 instruction, the 80386 re-enters real-address mode. Be sure to take the necessary steps. For instance:

1. If paging is enabled:

- Transfer control to linear addresses that have their linear addresses equal to physical addresses.
- Clear the PG (Paging) bit in CR0.
- Move zeros to CR3 to clear the paging cache.

2. Transfer control to a segment with a 64K limit. This loads the CS register with the limit it needs for real mode.

3. Load segment registers (SS, DS, ES, FS, and GS) with a selector that points to a descriptor that contains the appropriate values for real mode:

- Base = any value
- Limit = 64K
- Byte granular, G = 0
- Expand up, E = 0
- Writeable, W = 1
- Present, P = 1

4. Disable interrupts, perhaps with a CLI instruction that disables INTR interrupts. NMIs can be disabled with external circuitry.

5. Clear the PE bit.

6. Jump to real mode code to be executed. Use a far JMP which flushes the instruction queue and puts the correct values in the access rights of CS.

7. Ensure that the 8086 interrupt vectors are set in locations 0 through 4*(Highest interrupt possible) − 4.

8. Enable interrupts.

9. Load the segment registers, as needed, by the real-mode code.

Real-Address Physical Address Formation

For an 8086 program, the 80386 provides byte memory space of one megabyte plus 64K. Segment relocation is done as in the 8086: the 16-bit value stored in a segment selector is shifted left by four bits (with zeros added) to form the segment base address. The effective address is extended with four high-order zeros and added to the base to form a linear address. The linear address is equivalent to the physical address since paging is not used in real-address mode. There can be a carry when the linear address is formed. On the 8086, this carry is truncated. On the 80386, the carried bit is stored in the linear address bit position 20.

The 80386 can generate a 32-bit effective address via the address-size prefix, unlike the 8086 and 80286. The value of that address must be in the range of 0 to 65,536 or it causes an exception: Interrupt 12 or 13 with no error code. This is for compatibility with the 80286.

New 80386 Exceptions

For a detailed description of all the exceptions and interrupts recognized by the 80386, see Chapter 3. There are eight *new* exceptions:

EXCEPTION 5—A BOUND instruction was executed with a register value outside the limit values.

EXCEPTION 6—An undefined opcode was found or LOCK was used improperly before an instruction which it does not apply.

EXCEPTION 7—The EM (Coprocessor Emulation) in the MSW (Machine Status Word) is set when an ESC instruction is found. This exception also occurs when a WAIT instruction is encountered if TS (Task Switch) is set.

EXCEPTION 8—An interrupt or exception vectored to an interrupt table entry beyond the interrupt table limit in IDTR. This occurs only if the LIDT instruction changed the limit from the default value of 3FFH, which can hold all 256 interrupt IDs.

EXCEPTION 12—The operand crosses extremes of stack segment, for example MOV operation at 0FFFFH or PUSH, CALL, or INT with SP = 1.

EXCEPTION 13—An operand crosses extremes of a segment other than a stack segment. Or sequential instruction execution attempts to proceed beyond offset 0FFFFH. Or an instruction is longer than 15 bytes, including the prefixes.

EXCEPTION 14—Paging is enabled and an attempt to translate encounters a page directory or page table entry which is marked non-present or would violate access privilege.

EXCEPTION 16—A coprocessor error signaled by the 80287/80387 on the 80386 ERROR# pin, which is detected at the beginning certain ESC instructions.

Differences between Real-Mode and 8086

In real-address mode, the 80386 generally correctly executes ROM-based software designed for 8086/8088 and 80186/80188. The following is an overview of the differences programmers find.

- Opcodes that were not defined for the 8086 and 8088 processors cause an Exception 6. If the undefined 8086/88 opcode translates to a defined 80386 opcode, it will execute in the 80386 manner.
- The 80386 generally takes fewer clock counts for most instructions than did the 8086 or 8088. Two affected areas can be: assumed delays with 8086/88 operating in parallel with an 8087 numeric coprocessor, and delays required

by I/O devices between I/O operations.

- The 80386 generates the largest negative number as a quotient for the IDIV instruction. The 8086/88 causes exception zero.
- On both the 8086 and 8088, Divide (DIV) exceptions left the instruction pointer (CS:IP) pointing to the *next* instruction *after* the failing one. The 80386 CS:IP points directly at the failing instruction.
- The 8086/88 have no instruction limit. The 80386 sets a 15 byte limit on instructions and Exception 13 occurs if this limit is violated. The only way to exceed the 80386 limit is to put redundant prefixes before the instruction.
- Flags bit positions 12 through 15 differ, depending on whether they were stored in 8086 or virtual-8086. The 8086 stores them as ones. V86 stores bit 15 *always* as zero and bits 14 through 12 as whatever the last value loaded into them.
- The 8087 INT signal uses an interrupt controller but the 80387 error signal to the 80386 does not go through an interrupt controller. Some coprocessor instructions may need to be deleted if they deal with the interrupt controller.
- On the 8086/88 systems, the saved CS:IP points to the ESC instruction itself. On the 80836, the value of CS:IP (saved for coprocessor exceptions) points at any prefixes *before* the ESC.
- If an 8086/88 system uses a vector other than 16 for the 8087 interrupt, both vectors should point to the coprocessor-error exception handler. Any 80386 system with a coprocessor must use interrupt vector 16 for coprocessor error exceptions.
- The additional six exceptions arise only if the 8086 program has a hidden bug. Exception handlers should be added that treat these exceptions as invalid operations. Since these interrupts do not normally occur, this additional software does not significantly affect existing 8086 code. Note: these interrupt handlers should not already have been used by the 8086 software because they are in a range that was reserved by Intel.
- An 8086/88 processor PUSHes the value of SP *after* it is incremented. The 80386 PUSHes the value of SP *before* it is incremented as part of the PUSH operation.
- The 80386 masks all shift and rotate counts to the low-order five bits. This MOD 32 operation limits the count to a maximum of 31 bits. This limits the time that interrupt response is delayed while the instruction executes.
- On the 8086, an offset 0 (for example, to PUSH a word when SP=1) or an attempt to access a memory operand that crosses offset 65535 (e.g., a MOV of a word to offset 65535) causes the offset to wrap around modulo 65535. The 80386 raises an exception in these cases: 12 if the segment is a stack segment or 13 if the segment is a data segment.
- On the 8086, if sequential access goes past offset 65535, the 8086 fetches the next instruction byte from offset 0 of the same segment. The 80386 raises exception 13 in this case.
- After the 80386 recognizes a NMI interruption, the NMI is masked until an IRET is executed.
- The 80386 always asserts LOCK during an XCHG with memory, even if the LOCK prefix is not used. An undefined-opcode exception (Interrupt 6) results

if LOCK is used before any instruction other than: ADD, ADC, AND, BTS, BTR, BTC, DEC, INC, NEG, NOT, OR, SBB, SUB, XCHG, or XOR.
- On the 8086 family of processors, it is possible to specify addresses greater than one megabyte. The 8086 can form addresses only up to 20 bits long. It truncates the high-order bit, which "wraps" the overflowing address to the range 00000H to 0FFEFH.

Differences between Real-Mode and 80286

The differences between real-address mode on the 80386 and 80286 are not likely to affect existing 80286 programs, with the possible exception of system initialization. The four differences are:

1. Certain general registers may contain different values after RESET on the 80386 than on the 80286. The compatibility problems should be minimized because these registers are undefined in the 8086.

2. The 80286 initializes the MSW register (in CR0 in the 80386) to FFF0H. The 80386 initializes this register to 0000H. Programs that read the MSW value may have problems, but these bits are undefined on the 80286 and should not have been used.

3. The 80286 implements bus lock differently than the 80386. 80286 programs which use forms of memory locking that are specific to the 80286 may not execute properly on the 80386. Typical 8086 and 80286 configurations lock the entire physical memory space. With the 80386, the defined area of memory is guaranteed to be locked against access by a processor executing a locked instruction on exactly the same memory, that is, with identical starting address and length.

4. The 80286 uses a starting location of 0FFFFF0H, sixteen bytes from the end of 24-bit address space. The 80386 uses the starting location of 0FFFFFFF0H, sixteen bytes from the end of 32-bit address space. Many 80286 ROM initialization programs work correctly. Others will by redefining external hardware signals on A_{31-20}.

RESET AND INITIALIZATION

RESET starts or restarts the 80386. When the processor detects a low-to-high transition on RESET, it terminates all activities. When RESET goes low again, the 80386 initializes to a known internal state and fetches instructions from the reset address.

The 82384 (Clock Generator) generates the RESET signal. The RESET input to the 80386 must remain high for at least 15 CLK2 periods to be sure of proper initializations or at least 80 CLK2 periods if self-test is to be performed. RESET should be kept high for at least one millisecond after Vcc and CLK2 have reached their dc and ac specifications. Prior to its first instruction fetch, the 80386 makes no internal bus requests and, therefore, relinquishes bus control if it receives a HOLD request. Sometime between 350 and 450 CLK2 cycles after the high-to-low RESET transition, the 80386 fetches its first instruction from linear address 0FFFFFFF0H. Generally, this location contains a JMP instruction that points to the beginning of the bootstrap program.

RESET causes data bus pins to enter the three-state condition and the following pins to enter either high, low, or three-state.

D31-D0	Three-State
W/R#, M/IO#, HLDA, BE3#-BE0#	Low
LOCK#, D/C#, ADS#, A31-A2	High

Registers after Reset

EAX contents depend on the result of the power-up self test. EAX holds zero if the 80386 passed the test. A nonzero in EAX after self-test indicates that this particular 80386 may be faulty.

Figure 8-2 shows how DX holds a component identifier and revision number after RESET. DH contains a "3" which indicates an 80386 processor. DL contains a unique revision level identifier.

Figure 8-2 also shows the contents of Control Register Zero (CR0). The ET bit is set, which tells which coprocessors resides in the system. If ET is reset, the system either contains an 80287 or does not have a numeric coprocessor; software must distinguish between the two possibilities. The remaining registers and flags are set as follows and the settings imply that the 80386 begins in real-address mode with interrupts disabled. Any register not shown here is considered to be undefined.

Register	Contents
CS Selector	0000H
DS Selector	0000H
ES Selector	0000H
FS Selector	0000H
GS Selector	0000H
SS Selector	0000H
EFLAGS	00000002H
IP	0000FFF0H
IDTR	Base = 0, Limit = 03FFH

Software Initialization for Real-Address Mode

Before programs can take advantage of real-address mode, a few structures must be initialized in real-address mode. The stack-segment register (SS) must be loaded before any instructions that reference the stack can be used. SS must point to an area in RAM.

Address lines A_{31-20} are automatically asserted for instruction fetches after RESET. This allows system designers to use a ROM at the high end of address space to initialize the system. Together with the initial values of CS:IP, this address line assertion causes instruction execution to begin at physical address FFFFFFF0H. Intrasegment (near) forms of control transfer instruction can be used to pass control

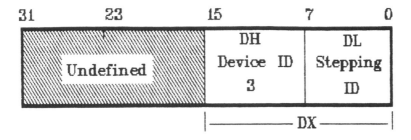

Contents of EDX after RESET

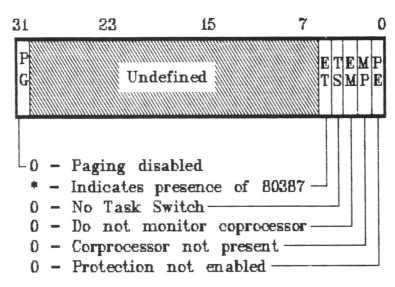

Fig. 8-2. Contents of EDX and CRO after RESET.

to other addresses in the upper 64K bytes of the address space. The first inter-segment (far) JMP or CALL causes A_{31-20} to drop low. The 80386 continues executing instructions in the lower one megabyte of physical memory.

Interrupts are disabled during the initial state of the 80386. The processor still tries to access the interrupt table if an exception or nonmaskable interrupt occurs. Initialization software should choose one of the following actions:

- Put pointers to valid interrupt handlers in all positions of the IDT that might be used by exceptions or interrupts.
- Change the IDTR to point to a valid interrupt table.
- Change the IDTR limit value to zero which causes a shutdown if an exception or nonmaskable interrupt occurs.

Software Initialization for Protected Mode

Generally, most initialization needed for protected mode is done either before or immediately after switching to protected mode. If the initialization is done after switching, the procedures used afterward must not use protected-mode features that are not yet initialized.

The initialization procedure can run in protected mode before initializing the Task Register. Before the first task switch, however, the following must be done:

      1. The task register must point to an area in which to save the current task state. After the first switch, the information dumped in this area is not needed and the area can be used for other things.

      2. There must be a valid TSS for the new task. The stack pointer in TSS (for privilege levels numerically less than or equal to the initial CPL) must point to valid stack segments.

The Stack Segment register (SS) may be loaded in either protected or real-address mode. If loaded in real-address mode, SS continues to point to the same linear base-address after the switch to protected mode.

The format of the interrupt table for protected mode is different than that for real-address mode. Since it is not possible to do both the change to protected mode and to change the interrupt table formats at the same time, it is inevitable if the IDTR selects an interrupt table that it will have the wrong format at some time. An interrupt or exception during this changeover will have unpredictable results. To avoid this, interrupts should be disabled until interrupt handlers are in place and a valid IDT has been created in protected mode.

Page tables and the PDBR in CR3 can be initialized in either protected or real-address mode. The PG bit (Paging Enabled) of CR0 can not be set until the 80386 is in protected mode. Before PG is set, initialize PDBR in CR3 with a physical address that points to a valid page directory. Adopt one of the following to ensure consistent addressing before and after paging is enabled:

- A JMP instruction should immediately follow the setting of PG.
- The page currently being executed should map to the same physical addresses both before and after PG is set.

The Global Descriptor Table Register (GDTR) must point to a valid GDT before any segment register is changed in protected mode. The GDT and LDTs should reside in RAM because the 80386 modifies the accessed bit of descriptors. Initialization of both the GDT and the GDTR can be done in real-address mode.

TESTABILITY AND DEBUGGING

The processor can do two types of internal tests: automatic self-test and Translation Lookaside Buffer (TLB) tests. The processor controls the self-test. The designer needs only to initiate the test and check the results. The TLB tests must be developed and applied externally. There, the 80386 provides an interface that simplifies this second test.

Self-Test

The 80386 processor can verify the functionality of its three major Programmable Array Logics (PALs)—the Entry Point, Control, and Test—in addition to the contents of its Control ROM (CROM). This self-test initiates when the BUSY# input is activated during initialization. The test result is stored in the EAX register. The part successfully passes self-test if the contents of the EAX register are zero(0). If they are not zero, then the self-test has detected a flaw.

The self-test takes about $2**19$ clocks or approximately 33 milliseconds with a 16 MHz processor. This test provides 100-percent coverage of single-bit faults. Single-bit faults statistically comprises a high percentage of total faults.

Translation Lookaside Buffer (TLB)

The TLB is discussed in some detail in Chapter 1. Here, its importance during testing is emphasized. The on-chip 80386 Page Descriptor Cache stores its data in the Translation Lookaside Buffer (TLB). The linear-to-physical mapping values for the most recent memory accesses are stored in the TLB, which allows fast translation for any subsequent accesses to those locations. The TLB consists of:

CONTENT-ADDRESSABLE MEMORY (CAM)—CAM holds 32 linear addresses—Page Directory and Page Table fields only—and associated tag bits used for data protection and cache implementation.

RANDOM ACCESS MEMORY (RAM)—RAM holds the 32 physical addresses—the upper 20 bits only—that correspond to the linear addresses in the CAM.

- Logic which implements the four-way cache and includes a 2-bit replacement pointer determines to which of the four sets a new entry is directed during a write to the TLB.

To translate a linear address to a physical address, the 80386 matches the Page Directory and Page Table fields of the linear address with an entry in the CAM. If a hit occurs, the corresponding 20 bits of physical address are retrieved from the RAM and added to the 132 bits of the Offset field of the linear address. This creates a 32-bit physical address. If a miss occurs, the 80386 brings the Page Directory and Page Table values into the TLB from memory.

There are two testing mechanisms for TLB tests. The first is to write entries into the TLB and, second, perform TLB lookups. The write takes the physical address contained in the data register and the linear address and tag bits contained in the command register and stores them into a TLB location designated by the data register. The lookup uses the linear address and tag bits contained in the command register. If a hit occurs, copy the corresponding physical address into the data register and set the value of the hit/miss bit in the data register. If a miss occurs, clear the hit/miss bit. In this case, the physical address in the data register is undefined.

Two 32-bit Test Registers (TR6 and TR7) are used. TR6 is the "test command register" and TR7 is the "test data register." An 80386 program can be written to generate test patterns that are applied to the TLB. However, during a test of the TLB, the 80386 Paging Mechanism must be disabled to avoid interference with the test data being written to the TLB.

80386 Programming Notes

In general, software developed for one generation of the Intel microprocessor family works without modification on the next higher level system. This chapter lists various facts you need to remember when you program or design around the 80386 chip.

The chapter first addresses the current software/hardware environment with a list of guidelines for software developers. Then the chapter reviews certain aspects of programming for the 80386.

SOFTWARE GUIDELINES

Applications that are designed for the 8086/8088 execute transparently in virtual-8086 mode. Virtual environments are used as bridges to provide upward compatibility with existing applications while offering a new environment with enhanced functions and performance. It must be remembered that performance of applications executed in virtual-8086 mode tends to be lower than in real mode in the same processor. This occurs because an operating system is intervening to handle interrupts and emulate certain instructions. To this intervention time is added the execution time of the code that saves and restores machine state and emulates the instruction. The primary impact is in interrupt-intensive programs because straight code tends to execute unimpeded in virtual-8086 mode.

Until a working operating system is designed for the 80386, certain guidelines should be kept in mind when developing a software product that is intended to run on the new 80386 systems.

Suggested guidelines are:

- If the software is intended to run on various levels of processors (8086/8088, 80286 or 80386), write to the least common denominator: the 8086/8088.
- Avoid any implicit or explicit use of register bits, flags, or data structures that are declared undefined or reserved for future Intel development.

- Routines written to run specifically on an 80386 system should be insensitive to the state of the PE (Protection Enable) bit in the Machine Status Word of CR0. Setting PE causes the processor to begin executing in protected mode. The visibility of the PE bit via the Store Machine Status Word (SMSW) may cause problems for code that attempts to act differently based on whether the 80386 is executing in real or protected mode.
- The value of various registers and flags after reset is different on the various processors. Do not depend on the power-on state of a particular processor. A program should explicitly load the required values.
- Do not use instruction opcodes that are not explicitly documented in Intel literature. An opcode that is not part of the supported instruction set may be defined differently in a later generation, even if it seemed to have a function in the earlier processor.
- The 80386 tends to execute specific code sequences significantly faster than earlier processors. Any code that interacts with real-time events or that depends on its execution time to perform its function should use a timing source independent of the 80386 clock speed.

PROGRAMMING FOR THE 80386

The 80386 provides compatibility with applications developed for earlier Intel processors, while providing a full 32-bit, large linear address programming environment. There are several issues to keep in mind when programming specifically for the 80386 environment that may not be clear from the documentation. Those issues are noted below.

Memory

1. Physical address formation in real-address mode: When calculating the effective address, unlike the 8086, the 80386's resulting linear address may have up to 21 significant bits. There is a possibility of a carry when the base address is added to the effective address. On the 8086, the carry bit is truncated. On the 80386, the carry bit is stored in bit position 20 of the linear address.

2. Unlike the 8086 and the 80286, 32-bit effective addresses can be generated via the address-size prefix. However, the value of a 32-bit address in real mode may not exceed 65536 or it will cause an exception.

3. With the 80286, any base and offset combination that addresses beyond 16 Mbytes wraps around to the first megabyte of the 80286 address space. With the 80386, since it has greater physical address space, any such address falls into the 17th megabyte. In the event that any software depends on this anomaly, the same effect can be simulated on the 80386 by using paging to map the first 64K bytes of the 17th megabyte of logical address to physical addresses in the first megabyte.

4. To allow maximum flexibility in data structures efficient memory utilization, words do *not* need to be aligned at even-numbered addresses. Also, doublewords do *not* need to be aligned at addresses evenly divisible by four. However, when using a system with a 32-bit bus, actual transfers of data between processor and memory take place in units of doublewords that begin at addresses evenly divisible by four.

The misaligned words causes an increase in the number of memory cycles to fetch data, thus decreasing performance.

5. It may be expedient to turn off the 80386 segmentation when the 80386 is used to execute software designed for special architectures that do not have segments. The processor does not have a specific mode to disable segmentation. However, the same effect is achieved by initially loading the segment registers with selectors for descriptors that encompass the entire 32-bit linear address space. Once the descriptors are loaded, the segment registers are not changed. The 80386 instructions' 32-bit offsets address the entire linear-address space.

6. In a write cycle (with 8-bit I/O devices), if BE3# and/or BE2# but not BE1# or BE0#, the write data on the top half of the data bus is duplicated on the bottom half. If the addresses of two devices differ only in the values of BE3#-BE0# (that is, the addresses lie within the same doubleword boundaries), BE3#-BE0# must be decoded to provide a chip select signal that prevents a write to one device from erroneously performing a write to the other. This chip select can be generated using an address decoder PAL device or TTL logic.

Descriptors

1. Because the 80386 uses the contents of the reserved word (the low order word) of every descriptor, 80286 programs that place values in this word may not execute correctly on the 80386.

2. Code that manages space in descriptor tables often uses an invalid value in the access-rights field of descriptor-table entries to identify unused entries. Access rights values of 80H and 00H remain invalid on the 80386. Other values that may have been invalid for the 80286 may now be valid for the 80386 because of new descriptor types.

3. To distinguish an 80286-type descriptor from an 80386-type descriptor, the processor checks the upper word. If the word is zero, then the descriptor is an 80286-type.

4. An executable segment whose descriptor has the conforming bit (bit 10) set is called a *conforming segment*. The conforming-segment allows sharing of procedures that may be called from differing privilege levels but should execute at the privilege level of the calling procedure. When control is transferred to a conforming segment, the CPL does not change. This is the only case when CPL may be unequal to the DPL of the currently executable segment.

Program Instructions

1. The 80286 implements the bus lock function differently than the 80386. Programs that use forms of memory locking specific to the 80286 may not execute correctly when transported to a specific program on the 80386.

2. LOCK may only be used with the following 80386 instructions when they modify memory. An undefined opcode exception results from using LOCK before any other instruction.

  • One-operand arithmetic and logical: INC, DEC, NOT, and NEG.

• Two-operand arithmetic and logical: ADD, ADC, SBB, SUB, AND, OR, and XOR.
  • Exchange: XCHG.
  • Bit test and change: BT, BTS, BTR, BTC.

3. The LOCK prefix and its corresponding output signal should only be used to prevent other bus masters from interrupting a data movement operation.

4. A locked instruction is guaranteed to lock only the areas of memory specifically defined by the destination operand. Typical 8086 and 80286 configurations lock the entire physical memory space. With the 80386, the defined area of memory is guaranteed to be locked against access by a processor executing a locked instruction on *exactly* the same memory area; that is, only with an operand with *identical* starting address and identical length.

5. The 80386 allows a CALL or JMP directly to another segment only if one of the following rules is satisfied: (1) the conforming bit of the target code-segment descriptor is set *and* the DPL of the target is less than or equal to the CPL; or (2) the DPL of the target is equal to the CPL. Most code segments are *not* conforming. For these segments, control can be transferred without a gate only to executable segments at the same privilege level. To transfer control to numerically smaller privilege levels, the CALL instruction is used with call-gate descriptors. The JMP instruction may never transfer control to a nonconforming segment whose DPL does not equal CPL.

6. Only CALL instructions can use gates to transfer to smaller privilege levels A gate may be used by a JMP instruction only to transfer to an executable segment with the same privilege level or to a conforming segment.

7. BSF—Bit Scan Forward. This instruction scans a word or doubleword for a one bit and stores the index of the first set bit into a register. The bit string being scanned may be either in a register or in memory. ZF is set if the entire word is zero; that is, no set bits are found. ZF is cleared if a one-bit is found.
NOTE: If no set bit is found, the value of the destination register is undefined.

8. DIV—Unsigned Integer Divide. Non-integer quotients are truncated to integers toward zero. The remainder is always less than the divisor. For unsigned byte division, the largest quotient is 255; for unsigned word division, it is 65535. For unsigned doubleword division, it is $2^{32} - 1$.

9. SAL—Shift Instructions. CF (Carry Flag) always contains the value of the last bit shifted out of the destination operand. In a single-bit shift, OF (Overflow Flag) is set if the value of the high-order (the sign) bit was changed by the operation. If the sign bit was not changed, OF is cleared. After a multi-bit shift, the contents of OF is *always* undefined.

10. The difference between TEST (Logical Compare) and AND is that TEST does *not* alter the destination operand. TEST differs from BT (Bit Test) in that TEST tests the value of multiple bits in one operation, while BT tests a single bit.

Registers

1. Certain bits in various registers are shown as either ''reserved'' or ''undefined.'' When using registers with these bits, treat the bits as truly undefined. Do

not depend on the states of any undefined bits when testing the values of defined register bits. Mask the undefined ones out.

Do not depend on the states of any undefined bits when storing them to memory or to another register or on the ability of these bits to retain information. When loading registers, always load the undefined or reserved bits as zeros or unchanged from their values as stored.

2. The VM bit of the EFLAGS register can be set only two ways: in protected mode, by the IRET instruction, and only if the current privilege level is zero; and by task switches at any privilege level.

3. The low-order 16 bits of the CR0 register is the 80286 Machine Status Word and can be addressed separately as the MSW.

Tasks

1. The only way to leave real-address mode is to deliberately switch to protected mode. The 80386 enters protected mode when a MOV to CR0 instruction sets the protection enable (PE) bit in CR0.

2. A Task State Segment (TSS) may reside anywhere in the linear address space. The single caution is when the TSS spans a page boundary. In this case, the 80386 raises an exception if it encounters the not-present page while reading the TSS during a task switch.

To avoid this, either allocate the TSS so that it does not cross a page boundary, or ensure that both pages are either both present or both not-present at the time of a task switch. In this latter case, if both pages are not-present, the page-fault handler makes both pages present before restarting the instruction that caused the page default.

3. Tasks are *not* re-entrant. The B-bit on the TSS descriptor allows the processor to detect an attempt to switch to a task that is already busy.

4. In the TSS descriptor, the LIMIT defines the size of the segment. This LIMIT must contain a value of 103 or higher. An attempt to switch to a task whose LIMIT has less than 103 causes an exception.

5. Every task switch sets the TS bit in the MSW (in CR0). The TS bit signals that the context of a numeric coprocessor *may not* correspond to the current 80386 task.

Privilege and Protection

1. The privilege level at which execution restarts in the incoming task is not restricted in any way by the privilege level of the outgoing task.

2. When paging is enabled, the processor first checks segment protection, then evaluates page protection. If the 80386 detects a protection violation at either level, it cancels the requested operation and generates a protection exception.

3. The processor examines type information (in segment descriptors) on two sets of occasions:

• When a selector of a descriptor is loaded into a segment register. Certain segment registers can contain only fixed descriptor types, such as:
> Only selectors of writeable data segments can be loaded into SS.

> The CS register can be loaded only with a selector of an executable segment.

> Selectors of executable segments (that are not readable) cannot be loaded into data-segment registers.

• When an instruction implicitly or explicitly refers to a segment register. Some segments can be used by instructions only in certain predefined ways, such as:
> Unless the readable bit is set, no instruction may read an executable segment.

> Unless the writeable bit is set, no instruction may write into a data segment.

> No instruction may write into an executable segment.

4. To combine page and segment protection: it is possible to define a large enough data segment that has some subunits that are read-only and other subunits that are read-write. If you do, the page directory or page table entries for the read-only subunits would have the U/S (User or Supervisor) and the R/W (Read/Write) bits set to x0. This indicates that there are no write rights for all the pages described by that directory entry or for the individual pages.

This technique could be useful in a UNIX-like system, to define a large data segment, part of which is read only (for shared data or ROMmed constants). This would enable the system to define a "flat" data space as one large segment, use "flat" pointers to address within this space, and yet be able to protect shared data, supervisor areas, and shared files mapped into virtual space.

5. Code segments can hold constants, but cannot be written to. There are three methods of reading data in code segments:

• Use a CS override prefix to read a readable, executable segment whose selector is already loaded in the CS register.
• Load a data-segment register with a selector or a non-conforming, readable, executable segment.
• Load a data-segment register with a selector of a conforming, readable, executable segment.

Case 1 is always valid because the DPL of the code segment in CS is, by definition, equal to CPL. Case 2 uses the same rules as for access to data segments. Case 3 is always valid because the privilege level of a segment whose conforming bit is set is effectively the same as CPL, regardless of its DPL.

Test and Debug

1. Since the first entry of the Global Descriptor Table (GDT) is not used by the processor, a selector that has an index of zero and a table indicator of zero can be used as a null selector. This process does *not* cause an exception when a segment register (other than CS or SS) is loaded with a null selector. It *will* cause an exception when the segment register is used to access memory. This feature is useful for initializing unused segment registers so as to trap accidental references.

2. The Translation Lookaside Buffer (TLB) is a cache used for translating linear addresses to physical addresses. Note that the TLB testing mechanism is unique to the 80386 and may not be continued in the same way in future processors. Software that uses this mechanism as it currently is may be incompatible with future processors.

3. The complement of the Dirty, User, and Writeable bits in Test Register 6 (TR6) are provided to force a hit or miss for TLB lookups. A lookup operation with a bit and its complement both low is forced to be a miss. If both bits are high, a hit is forced. A write operation is *always* performed when a bit and its complement have opposite values.

It is important to avoid writing the same linear address to more than one Translation Lookaside Buffer (TLB) entry. Otherwise, hit information returned during a TLB lookup operation is undefined.

4. TLB Test Operations—To lookup or read a TLB entry:

• Move a doubleword to TR6 that contains the appropriate linear address and attributes. Be sure C=1 for lookup.

• Store TR7. If the HT bit in TR7 is 1, then other values reveal the TLB contents. If HT=0, then the other values are undefined.

• For the purposes of testing, the V bit acts as another bit of address. The V bit for a lookup request should be set, so that uninitialized tags do not match. Lookups with V=0 are unpredictable if any tags are uninitialized.

To write a TLB entry:

• Move a doubleword to TR7 that contains the desired physical address, HT, and REP values. HT must contain a 1. REP must point to the associative block in which to place the entry.

• Move a doubleword to TR6 that contains the appropriate linear address, and values for V, D, U, and W. Be sure C=0 for write command.

• Be careful not to write duplicate tags. The results are undefined.

10

80386 Instruction Set

The 80386 instruction set is a superset of previous generations' instructions, with additional instructions for specific 80386 uses. The instruction set is listed in this chapter in alphabetic order by mnemonic. Along with each instruction, the forms are given for each operand combination, including the object code which is produced, the operands required, and a description of the instruction.

INSTRUCTION FORMAT

80386 instructions are made up of various elements and have various formats. Of the elements described below, only one (the opcode) is always present in each instruction. The others may not be present, depending on the operation involved and on the location and type of the operands.

Instructions are made up of optional instruction prefixes, one or two primary opcode bytes, possibly an address specifier which consists of the Mod R/M byte and the Scale Index Base byte, a displacement—if required, and an immediate data field—if required. All the instruction encodings are subsets of the general instruction format shown in Fig. 10-1.

The elements of an instruction are in their order of occurrence:

PREFIXES—One or more bytes preceding an instruction that modify the operation of that instruction. There are four types of prefixes:

1. Repeat—Used with a string instruction to cause the instruction to act on each element of the string.
2. Operand Size—Switches between 32-bit and 16-bit operands.
3. Address Size—Switches between 32-bit and 16-bit address generation.
4. Segment Override—Explicitly specifies which segment register an instruction should use. This overrides the default segment-register selection generally used by the 80386 for that instruction.

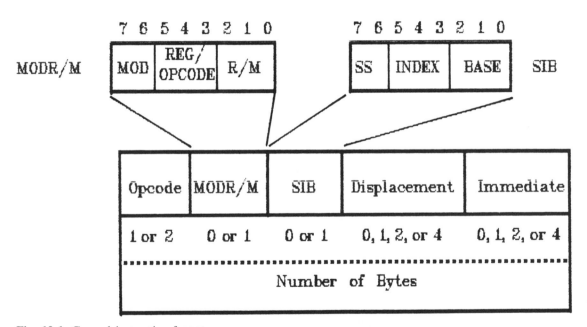

Fig. 10-1. General instruction format.

OPCODE—This specifies the operation performed by the instruction. Some operations have several different opcodes. Each specifies a different variant of the operation.

REGISTER SPECIFIER—The instruction may specify one or two register operands. Register specifiers may occur in either the opcode byte or the addressing-mode specifier byte.

ADDRESSING-MODE SPECIFIER—When present, this element specifies whether an operand is a register or a memory location. If it's in memory, this specifies whether a displacement, an index register, a base register, and scaling is to be used.

MOD R/M AND SIB (SCALE INDEX BASE) BYTES—Most instructions that can refer to an operand in memory have an addressing form byte following the primary opcode byte(s). This byte specifies the address form to be used. Some encodings of the MOD R/M byte indicate a second addressing byte, the Scale Index Base (SIB) byte. The MOD R/M and SIB bytes contain the following information:

- The indexing type or register number to be used in the instructions.
- The register to be used, or more information to select the instruction.
- The base, index, and scale information.

The MOD R/M byte contains these three fields:

MOD—bits 7 and 6, occupies the two most significant bits of the byte. They combine with the R/M field to form 32 possible values: eight registers and 24 indexing modes.

REG—bits 5, 4, and 3, specify either a register number or three more bits of opcode information. The meaning of REG is specified by the first (opcode) byte of the instruction.

R/M—bits 2, 1, and 0, can specify a register as the location of an operand, or it can form part of the addressing-mode encoding in combination with the MOD field as described above.

The SIB byte includes the these fields:

SS—bits 7 and 6, specifies the scale factor.

INDEX—bits 5, 4, and 3, specifies the register number of the index register.

BASE—bits 2, 1, and 0, specifies the register number of the base register.

Encoding of 32 bit address mode:

Register modifiers for address computation are all 32 bit registers (EAX for example). Address computation without Scale Index Base (SIB) byte include:

- A MOD of 00 which specifies address computation of DS:[r/m] which specifies a register as follows:

000	DS:[EAX]
001	DS:[ECX]
010	DS:[EDX]
011	DS:[EBX]
100	SIB Present
101	DS:32 bit displacement
110	DS:[ESI]
111	DS:[EDI]

Thus, the effective address is DS:32 bit modifier from register or memory.

- A MOD of 01 adds an 8 bit displacement to the above so that r/m of 000 is DS:[EAX + a displacement]

000	DS:[EAX + 8 bit displacement]
100	SIB Present
101	SS:[EBP + 8 bit displacement]

- A MOD of 10 adds a 32-bit displacement. An r/m of 000 is DS:[EAX + a displacement]

  000   DS:[EAX + 32 bit displacement]
  100   SIB Present
  101   SS:[EBP + 32 bit displacement]

- A MOD of 11 specifies a register in the r/m so that an r/m of:

  000   AL or EAX
  001   CL or ECX
  010   DL or EDX
  011   BL or EBX
  100   AH or ESP
  101   CH or EBP
  110   DH or ESI
  111   BH or EDI

The register selected depends on whether an 8 bit operation or a 32 bit operation is specified in the W bit.

The MOD value indicates the length of the displacement field to address:

  00 - no displacement, except for base 101
  01 - 8 bit displacement
  10 - 32 bit displacement

Therefore the SIB modifies the computed address (DS:[base + scaled index + displacement]), except for the case where the base is ESP or EBP and then the logical substitution of SS: is made for the segment, instead of DS:.

Where an SIB is present, r/m = 100 for MOD=00, 01, or 10. The address computation is done using a combination of the following:

A 32 bit scaled index value is computed as index $* 2^{scale}$ where scale is the first two bits of the SIB byte and specified by its binary value. The index register is specified as an index of:

  000   EAX
  001   ECX
  010   EDX
  011   EBX
  100   no index value, scale must be 0
  101   EBP
  110   ESI
  111   EDI

If the byte is laid out, the bits appear as SSIIIBBB, where SS is the scale, III is the index and BBB is the base. The base is selected as follows:

      000 EAX
      001 ECX
      010 EDX
      011 EBX
      100 ESP
      101 Special (a 32 bit displacement if MOD is
           00 and the EBP register otherwise)
      110 ESI
      111 EDI

DISPLACEMENT—When the addressing-mode specifier indicates that a displacement will be used to compute the address of an operand, the displacement is encoded in the instruction. A displacement is a signed integer of 8, 16 or 32 bits. The 8-bit form is used in the common case when the displacement is sufficiently small.

IMMEDIATE OPERAND—When present, this element provides the value of an operand of the instruction. Immediate operands may be 8, 16, or 32 bits wide. In cases where an 8-bit immediate operand is combined in some way with a 16- or 32-bit operand, the processor automatically extends the size of the 8-bit operand, by replicating its sign.

Description Notations

The following explains the notational conventions used and abbreviations used when illustrating the instruction set.

+rb, +rw, +rd   A register code, 0 through 7, which is added to the hexadecimal byte given at the left of the plus sign, in order to form a single opcode byte. The codes are:

rb			rw			rd		
AL	=	0	AX	=	0	EAX	=	0
CL	=	1	CX	=	1	ECX	=	1
DL	=	2	DX	=	2	EDX	=	2
BL	=	3	BX	=	3	EBX	=	3
AH	=	4	SP	=	4	ESP	=	4
CH	=	5	BP	=	5	EBP	=	5
DH	=	6	SI	=	6	ESI	=	6
BH	=	7	DI	=	7	EDI	=	7

/digit   The digit is generally between 0 and 7. It indicates that the MOD R/M byte of the instruction uses only the register or memory (r/m) operand. The reg field contains the digit that provides an extension to the instruction's opcode.

/r   This shows that the instruction's MOD R/M byte contains both a register operand *and* an r/m operand.

cb, cw, cd, cp   A 1-byte (cb), 2-byte (cw), 4-byte (cd), or a 6-byte (cp) value that follows the opcode is used to specify a code offset and possibly a new value for the code segment register.

ib, iw, id   A 1-byte (ib), 2-byte (iw), or 4-byte immediate operand to the instruction that follows the opcode, MOD R/M bytes or scale-indexing bytes. The opcode determines if the operand is a signed value. Note that all words and doublewords are given with the low-order byte first.

imm8   An immediate byte value. imm8 is a signed number between -128 and $+127$, inclusive. For those instructions where imm8 combines with a word or doubleword operand, the immediate value is sign-extended to form a word or doubleword. The upper byte of the word/doubleword is filled with the topmost bit of the immediate value.

imm16   An immediate word value. It's used for instructions whose operand-size attribute is 16 bits. Inclusive, this number runs from -32768 to $+32767$.

imm32   An immediate doubleword. imm32 is used for instructions whose operand-size attribute is 32 bits. The range of numbers is, inclusive, from -2147483648 to $+2147483647$.

m8   A memory byte. It is addressed by DS:SI or ES:DI.

m16   A memory word. It is addressed by DS:SI or ES:DI.

m32   A memory doubleword. It is addressed by DS:SI or ES:DI.

moffs8, moffs16, moffs32   A memory offset. A simple memory variable of type BYTE, WORD, or DWORD, used by some variants of the MOV instruction. The actual address is given by a simple offset relative to the segment base. The number shows with the ''moffs'' indicates its size, which is determined by the address-size attribute of the instruction. No MOD R/M byte is used in the instruction.

ptr16:16, ptr16:32   FAR pointer. Typically it is in a code segment different from that of the instruction. The notation 16:16 shows that the pointer value has two parts. The value to the left of the colon is the offset within the destination segment. The value to the right of the colon is a 16-bit selector or value destined for the code segment register. When the instruction's operand has a size attribute of 16, use 16:16. For the 32-bit attribute, use 16:32.

r8   One of the byte registers: AL, CL, DL, BL, AH, CH, DH, or BH.

r16   One of the word registers: AX, CX, DX, BX, SP, BP, SI or DI.

r32   One of the doubleword registers: EAX, ECX, EDX, EBX, ESP, EBP, ESI, or EDI.

rel8   A relative address in the range from 128 bytes before the end of the instruction to 127 bytes after the instruction's end.

rel16, rel32   A relative address within the same code segment as the instruction assembled. rel16 is applied to instructions whose operand-size attribute is 16 bits. rel32 is applied to the instructions with a 32-bit operand-size attribute.

r/m8   A one-byte operand. It is either the contents of a byte from memory or from a byte register—AL, BL, CL, DL, AH, BH, CH, or DH.

r/m16   A word register or memory operand. It is used for instructions whose operand-size attribute is 16 bits. The contents of memory are found at the address provided by the effective address computation. The word registers are: AX, BX, CX, DX, SP, BP, SI and DI.

r/m32   A doubleword register or memory operand. It is used for instructions whose operand-size attribute is 32 bits. The contents of memory are found at the address provided by the effective address computation. The doubleword registers are: EAX, EBX, ECX, EDX, ESP, EBP, ESI and EDI.

rrr   When rrr appears in the binary equivalent column, it appears as the last three digits of the binary figure and indicates a particular register is referenced. The rrr translates to the following:

000	= AX/EAX	100	= SP/ESP
001	= CX/ECX	101	= BP/EBP
010	= DX/EDX	110	= SI/ESI
011	= BX/EBX	111	= DI/EDI

Sreg   A segment register. The segment register bit assignments are ES=0, CS=1, SS=2, DS=3, FS=4, and GS=5.

Description of Modifiers and Specifications

In the figures that illustrate each instruction, there are some extension that show modifiers, register specifications and register/memory specifications. The notation ''mm 00 r/m'' specifies memory and ''mm 11 r/m'' specifies rrr. A further explanation of how those interact with the opcode follows:

where disp8 is an 8-byte displacement
disp16 is a 16-byte displacement
disp32 is a 32-byte displacement

8 Bit

rrr	8 bit registers	16 or 32 bit
000	AL	AX, EAX
001	CL	CX, ECX
010	DL	DX, EDX
011	BL	BX, EBX
100	AH	SP, ESP
101	CH	BC, EBP
110	DH	SI, ESI
111	BH	DI, EDI

16 Bit

r/m or mm	00	01	10	11
000	[BX+SI]	+ disp8	+disp16	rrr
001	[BX+DI]			

010	[BP+SI]			
011	[BP+DI]			
100	[SI]			
101	[DI]			
110	disp16	[BP]+disp8	[BP]+disp16	[BP]+disp 16
111	[BX]	+disp8	+disp16	

32 BIT

r/m & mm	00	01	10	11
000	[EAX]	+disp8	+disp32	rrr
001	[ECX]	+disp8		
010	[EDX]	+disp8		
011	[EBX]	+disp8		
100	SIB Follows			
101	disp32	[EBC]+disp8	[EBP]+disp32	
110	[ESI]	[EBC]+disp8		
111	[EDI]			

SCALED INDEX BYTE (SIB)

Where ss = the scale factor

SS	00	Times 1
	01	Times 2
	10	Times 4
	11	Times 8

Index	Base
000 EAX	000 EAX
001 ECX	001 ECX
010 EDX	010 EDX
011 EBX	011 EBX
100 None	100 ESP
101 EBP	101 Special
110 ESI	110 ESI
111 EDI	111 EDI

Instruction Demonstration

Most of the instruction shown in this section contain an actual use of that instruction as a demonstration. Instructions available only in protected mode are demonstrated in Appendix 5. Four other instructions (ESC, HLT, LOCK, and WAIT) are not demonstrated because of their action on the 80386, such as HLT which stops the processor.

Occasionally, instructions will be combined to show a "normal" use of the combined instructions. The major registers and flags are shown after each step, with text explaining what is occurring. The Instruction Pointer (IP) increments after each instruction, to point to the next instruction. An asterisk under the flags shows which flags changed as a result of this instruction being executed.

The instruction illustrations are intended to show the interactions of flags and so on. They are not intended to be a tutorial in the most efficient coding possible.

Flags and Registers Used

The following flags and registers are mentioned extensively in the detailed descriptions. Refer to this list if you have questions. Both the flags and registers are described in detail in Chapter 1.

AF	Auxiliary Carry	Bit 4 of EFLAGS Register
CF	Carry Flag	Bit 0 of EFLAGS Register
DF	Direction Flag	Bit 10 of EFLAGS Register
EIP	Instruction Pointer	32-Bit Register
EM	Emulation	Bit 2 of Control Register Zero CR0
ET	Extension Type	Bit 4 of Control Register Zero CR0
IF	Interrupt Enable	Bit 9 of EFLAGS Register
IOPL	I/O Privilege Level	Bit 12-13 of EFLAGS Register
MP	Math Present	Bit 1 of Control Register Zero CR0
NT	Nested Flag	Bit 14 of EFLAGS Register
OF	Overflow Flag	Bit 11 of EFLAGS Register
PE	Protection Enable	Bit 0 of Control Register Zero CR0
PF	Parity Flag	Bit 2 of EFLAGS Register
PG	Paging Bit	Bit 31 of Control Register Zero CR0
RF	Resume Flag	Bit 16 of EFLAGS Register
SF	Sign Flag	Bit 07 of EFLAGS Register
TF	Trap Flag	Bit 8 of EFLAGS Register
TS	Task Switched	Bit 03 of Control Register Zero CR0
VM	Virtual 8086 Mode	Bit 17 of EFLAGS Register
ZF	Zero Flag	Bit 06 of EFLAGS Register
AH	General Register	High Order 8 bits of AX
AL	General Register	Low Order 8 bits of AX
AX	General Register	Least significant 16 bits of EAX
BH	General Register	High order 8 bits of BX
BL	General Register	Low order 8 bits of BX
BX	General Register	Least significant 16 bits of EBX
CH	General Register	High Order 8 bits of CX
CL	General Register	Low order 8 bits of CX
CX	General Register	Least Significant 16 bits of ECX
DH	General Register	High order 8 bits of DX

DL	General Register	Low order 8 bits of DX
DX	General Register	Least significant 16 bits of EDX
EAX	General Register	32-bits
EBP	General Register	32-bits
EBX	General Register	32-bits
ECX	General Register	32-bits
EDI	General Register	32-bits
EDX	General Register	32-bits
EFLAGS	Flags Register	32-bit Flags Register
ESI	General Register	32-bits
ESP	General Register	32-bits - Stack Pointer
FLAGS	Flags Register	Least significant 16 bits of EFLAGS

ALPHABETICAL LISTING OF INSTRUCTIONS

AAA   ASCII Adjust after Addition

INSTRUCTION	OPCODE	BINARY
AAA	37	00110111

Purpose: AAA changes the contents of register AL to a valid unpacked decimal number and zeros the top 4 bits. AAA must always follow the addition of two unpacked decimal operands in AL. CF is set and AH is incremented if a carry is necessary.

Instruction Demonstration: This demonstration of the AAA instruction shows the adjustments made after addition to keep unpacked BCD as BCD even though the addition is binary.

The instruction sequence:

```
14EB:0100 B80800        MOV AX,0008
14EB:0103 0404          ADD AL,04

14EB:0105 37            AAA
14EB:0106 0404          ADD AL,04
14EB:0108 37            AAA
```

The registers and the flags at the start:

```
AX=0000   BX=0000   CX=0000   DX=0000   SP=EA04   BP=0000
SI=0000   DI=0000   DS=14EB   ES=14EB   SS=14EB   CS=14EB
IP=0100
                                        NV UP EI PL NZ NA PE NC
```

Note an asterisk appears under each flag that has changed in that step.

```
14EB:0100 B80800               MOV AX,0008
```

```
AX=0008   BX=0000   CX=0000   DX=0000   SP=EA04   BP=0000
SI=0000   DI=0000   DS=14EB   ES=14EB   SS=14EB   CS=14EB
IP=0103
                                   NV UP EI PL NZ NA PE NC
```

In order to set the values for AAA an add is done.

```
14EB:0103 0404              ADD AL,04
```

```
AX=000C   BX=0000   CX=0000   DX=0000   SP=EA04   BP=0000
SI=0000   DI=0000   DS=14EB   ES=14EB   SS=14EB   CS=14EB
IP=0105
                                   NV UP EI PL NZ NA PE NC
```

Note that the result 0C is not a decimal digit.

```
14EB:0105 37               AAA
```

```
AX=0102   BX=0000   CX=0000   DX=0000   SP=EA04   BP=0000
SI=0000   DI=0000   DS=14EB   ES=14EB   SS=14EB   CS=14EB
IP=0106
                                   NV UP EI PL NZ AC PE CY
                                                *       *
```

The AAA instruction has effectively subtracted 10(0A) from the 12(0C) in AL. The decimal carry is added to AH thus creating a two-digit BCD result. The adjust flag is set as is the carry flag indicating that a BCD carry has occurred.

```
14EB:0106 0404              ADD AL,04
```

```
AX=0106   BX=0000   CX=0000   DX=0000   SP=EA04   BP=0000
SI=0000   DI=0000   DS=14EB   ES=14EB   SS=14EB   CS=14EB
IP=0108
                                   NV UP EI PL NZ NA PE NC
                                                *       *
```

This add results in neither a carry nor an adjustment. Both flags are reset. The result of the addition is 06 a valid BCD digit.

```
14EB:0108 37               AAA
```

```
AX=0106   BX=0000   CX=0000   DX=0000   SP=EA04   BP=0000
SI=0000   DI=0000   DS=14EB   ES=14EB   SS=14EB   CS=14EB
IP=0109
                                   NV UP EI PL NZ NA PE NC
```

The result of the AAA is no change which is what would be expected since the value doesn't need any.

AAD   ASCII Adjust Register AX Before Division

INSTRUCTION	OPCODE	BINARY
AAD	D5 0A	11010101 00001010

Purpose: AAD modifies the numerator in AH and AL, to prepare for the division of two valid unpacked decimal operands so that the quotient produced by the division will be a valid unpacked decimal number. AH should contain the high-order digit and AL the low-order digit. AAD adjusts the value and places the result in AL. AH will contain zero.

Instruction Demonstration: The AAD and AAM are demonstrated together because they reverse each other's actions. The effect of each is shown below.

The instruction sequence:

```
14EB:0100 90          NOP
14EB:0101 B80508      MOV AX,0805
14EB:0104 D50A        AAD
14EB:0106 90          NOP
14EB:0107 D40A        AAM
14EB:0109 90          NOP
```

The registers and the flags at the start:

```
AX=0010   BX=0000   CX=0000   DX=0000   SP=EA04   BP=0000
SI=0000   DI=0000   DS=14EB   ES=14EB   SS=14EB   CS=14EB
IP=0101
                                        NV UP EI PL ZR NA PO NC
```

14EB:0101 B80508   MOV AX,0805

```
AX=0805   BX=0000   CX=0000   DX=0000   SP=EA04   BP=0000
SI=0000   DI=0000   DS=14EB   ES=14EB   SS=14EB   CS=14EB
IP=0104
                                        NV UP EI PL ZR NA PO NC
```

The MOV has loaded two BCD digits into AX. The setting of the flags is unaffected by MOV.

14EB:0104 D50A   AAD

```
AX=0055   BX=0000   CX=0000   DX=0000   SP=EA04   BP=0000
SI=0000   DI=0000   DS=14EB   ES=14EB   SS=14EB   CS=14EB
IP=0106
                                        NV UP EI PL NZ NA PE NC
                                                    *        *
```

The result of the AAD is to combine the BCD digits and convert them to their binary equivalent. (55 Hex = 85 decimal) The zero flag is set according to the result in AL (non zero in this case) as is the parity flag (to even in this case). If the sign flag were set to negative it would be set to positive for all valid conversions.

14EB:0106 90   NOP

```
AX=0055   BX=0000   CX=0000   DX=0000   SP=EA04   BP=0000
SI=0000   DI=0000   DS=14EB   ES=14EB   SS=14EB   CS=14EB
IP=0107
                                    NV UP EI PL NZ NA PE NC
```

14EB:0107 D40A   AAM

```
AX=0805   BX=0000   CX=0000   DX=0000   SP=EA04   BP=0000
SI=0000   DI=0000   DS=14EB   ES=14EB   SS=14EB   CS=14EB
IP=0109
                                    NV UP EI PL NZ NA PE NC
```

The result of the AAM is to convert the value in the AF register into two BCD digits in AH and AL.

AAM   ASCII Adjust AX Register After Multiplication

Instruction	Opcode	Binary
AAM	D4 0A	11010100 00001010

Purpose: AAM corrects the result of a multiplication of two valid unpacked decimal numbers. AAM must always follow the multiplication of two decimal numbers to produce a valid decimal result. The high-order digit is left in AH, the low-order in AL.

Instruction Demonstration: AAM is demonstrated with AAD since each reverses the other's results.

AAS   ASCII Adjust AL Register After Subtraction

Instruction	Opcode	Binary
AAS	3F	00111111

Purpose: AAS changes the contents of register AL to a valid unpacked decimal number and zeros the top 4 bits. AAS must always follow the subtraction of one unpacked decimal operand from another in AL. CF is set and AH decremented if a borrow is necessary.

Instruction Demonstration: This demonstration of the AAS instruction shows its effect in BCD subtraction.

The instruction sequence:

```
14EB:0100 90          NOP
14EB:0101 B80500      MOV   AX,0005
14EB:0104 2C04        SUB   AL,04
14EB:0106 3F          AAS
14EB:0107 2C04        SUB   AL,04
14EB:0109 3F          AAS
```

The registers and flags at the start:

```
AX=0000   BX=0000   CX=0000   DX=0000   SP=EA04   BP=0000
SI=0000   DI=0000   DS=14EB   ES=14EB   SS=14EB   CS=14EB
IP=0101
                                   NV UP EI PL NZ NA PO NC
```

```
14EB:0101 B80500      MOV AX,0005
```

```
AX=0005   BX=0000   CX=0000   DX=0000   SP=EA04   BP=0000
SI=0000   DI=0000   DS=14EB   ES=14EB   SS=14EB   CS=14EB
IP=0104
                                   NV UP EI PL NZ NA PO NC
```

```
14EB:0104 2C04        SUB AL,04
```

```
AX=0001   BX=0000   CX=0000   DX=0000   SP=EA04   BP=0000
SI=0000   DI=0000   DS=14EB   ES=14EB   SS=14EB   CS=14EB
IP=0106
                                   NV UP EI PL NZ NA PO NC
```

The result of the subtraction is still a positive value.

```
14EB:0106 3F          AAS
```

```
AX=0001   BX=0000   CX=0000   DX=0000   SP=EA04   BP=0000
SI=0000   DI=0000   DS=14EB   ES=14EB   SS=14EB   CS=14EB
IP=0107
                                   NV UP EI PL NZ NA PO NC
```

The AAS doesn't change the result or the flags.

```
14EB:0107 2C04        SUB AL,04
```

```
AX=00FD   BX=0000   CX=0000   DX=0000   SP=EA04   BP=0000
```

SI=0000   DI=0000   DS=14EB   ES=14EB   SS=14EB   CS=14EB
IP=0109

                                    NV UP EI NG NZ AC PO CY
                                              *   *   *

This subtract results in a negative value. The sign flag is set, the carry flag is set because of the 'borrow' required to set the sign flag. The adjust flag is set because of the borrow from the high nibble of AL.

14EB:0109 3F   AAS

AX=FF07   BX=0000   CX=0000   DX=0000   SP=EA04   BP=0000
SI=0000   DI=0000   DS=14EB   ES=14EB   SS=14EB   CS=14EB
IP=010A

                                    NV UP EI NG NZ AC PO CY

The result of the AAS is to set the proper decimal value in AL and to subtract one from AH.

ADC   Add Integers with Carry

Instruction	Opcode	Binary
ADC AL,imm8	14 ib	00010100
ADC AX,imm16	15 iw	00010101
ADC EAX,imm32	15 id	00010101
ADC r/m8,imm8	90 /2 ib	10010000 mm 010 r/m
ADC r/m16,imm16	90 /2 /w	10010000 mm 010 r/m
ADC r/m32,imm32	91 /2 id	10010001 mm 010 r/m
ADC r/m16,imm8	93 /2 ib	10010011 mm rrr r/m
ADC r/m32,imm8	93 /2 ib	10010011 mm rrr r/m
ADC r/m8,r8	10 /r	00010000 mm rrr r/m
ADC r/m16,r16	11 /r	00010001 mm rrr r/m
ADC r/m32,r32	11 /r	00010001 mm rrr r/m
ADC r8,r/m8	12 /r	00010010 mm rrr r/m
ADC r16,r/m16	13 /r	00010011 mm rrr r/m
ADC r32,r/m32	13 /r	00010011 mm rrr r/m

Purpose: ADC sums the operands, adds one if CF is set and replaces the destination operand with the result. If CF is cleared, ADC does the same operation as the ADD instruction. An ADD followed by multiple ADC instructions can be used to add numbers longer than 32 bits.

Instruction Demonstration: This demonstration of the ADC instruction shows the effect of the carry flag being set on when the instruction is executed. Note that the carry flag being set adds one to the sum.

The instruction sequence:

```
14EB:0100 90          NOP
14EB:0101 B80000      MOV AX,0000
14EB:0104 0440        ADD AL,40
14EB:0106 1440        ADC AL,40
14EB:0108 1440        ADC AL,40
14EB:010A 1440        ADC AL,40
14EB:010C 1440        ADC AL,40
14EB:010E 90          NOP
```

The registers and flags at the start:

```
AX=0000   BX=0000   CX=0000   DX=0000   SP=EA04   BP=0000
SI=0000   DI=0000   DS=14EB   ES=14EB   SS=14EB   CS=14EB
IP=0101
                                  NV UP EI PL NZ NA PO NC
```

14EB:0101 B80000   MOV AX,0000

```
AX=0000   BX=0000   CX=0000   DX=0000   SP=EA04   BP=0000
SI=0000   DI=0000   DS=14EB   ES=14EB   SS=14EB   CS=14EB
IP=0104
                                  NV UP EI PL NZ NA PO NC
```

The sequence of ADCs begins with an ADD which ignores the state of the carry flag. This would normally be the add of the lowest order numbers in the extended summation. The carry flag could have been forced off with the CLC (clear carry) instruction also.

14EB:0104 0440   ADD AL,40

```
AX=0040   BX=0000   CX=0000   DX=0000   SP=EA04   BP=0000
SI=0000   DI=0000   DS=14EB   ES=14EB   SS=14EB   CS=14EB
IP=0106
                                  NV UP EI PL NZ NA PO NC
```

14EB:0106 1440   ADC AL,40

```
AX=0080   BX=0000   CX=0000   DX=0000   SP=EA04   BP=0000
SI=0000   DI=0000   DS=14EB   ES=14EB   SS=14EB   CS=14EB
IP=0108
                                  OV UP EI NG NZ NA PO NC
                                  *              *
```

Note that because the sign bit (the high order bit of the register) has become set, that the minus flag has been set. Also note that the over-flow flag has been set because the result cannot be contained in the target register as a signed quantity.

14EB:0108 1440   ADC AL,40

AX=00C0   BX=0000   CX=0000   DX=0000   SP=EA04   BP=0000
SI=0000   DI=0000   DS=14EB   ES=14EB   SS=14EB   CS=14EB
IP=010A

NV UP EI NG NZ NA PE NC
*   *

Note that because the number of bits in AL (the low 8 bits of the result) is now even, the parity even flag is set. The overflow indication is turned off because the signed result can be contained in the register.

14EB:010A 1440   ADC AL,40

AX=0000   BX=0000   CX=0000   DX=0000   SP=EA04   BP=0000
SI=0000   DI=0000   DS=14EB   ES=14EB   SS=14EB   CS=14EB
IP=010C

NV UP EI PL ZR NA PE CY
* *   *

This addition caused a carry out of the register (AL). The carry flag is now set. Note the effect on the next ADC instruction. It also left a sum of zero as its result. This caused the zero flag to be set on. Since zero has a sign bit of zero, the sign flag is set to positive.

14EB:010C 1440   ADC AL,40

AX=0041   BX=0000   CX=0000   DX=0000   SP=EA04   BP=0000
SI=0000   DI=0000   DS=14EB   ES=14EB   SS=14EB   CS=14EB
IP=010E

NV UP EI PL NZ NA PE NC
*   *

Since the carry flag was on, an additional 1 was added in the operation. The result did not cause a carry so the carry flag is set off and since the result is non zero, the zero flag is also set off.

ADD   Add Integers

Instruction	Opcode	Binary
ADD AL,imm8	04 ib	00000100
ADD AX,imm16	05 /w	00000101
ADD EAX,imm32	05 id	00000101

ADD r/m8,imm8	80 /0 ib	10000000 mm 000 r/m
ADD r/m16,imm16	81 /0 iw	10000001 mm 000 r/m
ADD r/m32,imm32	81 /0 id	10000001 mm 000 r/m
ADD r/m16,imm8	83 /0 ib	10000011 mm 000 r/m
ADD r/m32,imm8	83 /0 ib	10000011 mm 000 r/m
ADD r/m8,r8	00 /r	00000000 mm rrr r/m
ADD r/m16,r16	01 /r	00000001 mm rrr r/m
ADD r/m32,r32	01 /r	00000001 mm rrr r/m
ADD r8,r/m8	02 /r	00000010 mm rrr r/m
ADD r16,r/m16	03 /r	00000011 mm rrr r/m
ADD r32,r/m32	03 /r	00000011 mm rrr r/m

Purpose: ADD replaces the destination operation with the sum of the source and destination operands. It sets CF if there is an overflow.

Instruction Demonstration: This demonstration of the ADD instruction shows that it executes its addition without interrogating the carry flag.

The instruction sequence:

```
14EB:0100 90            NOP
14EB:0101 B80000        MOV AX,0000
14EB:0104 0440          ADD AL,40
14EB:0106 0440          ADD AL,40
14EB:0108 0440          ADD AL,40
14EB:010A 0440          ADD AL,40
14EB:010C 0440          ADD AL,40
14EB:010E 90            NOP
```

The registers and flags at the start:

```
AX=0041   BX=0000   CX=0000   DX=0000   SP=EA04   BP=0000
SI=0000   DI=0000   DS=14EB   ES=14EB   SS=14EB   CS=14EB
IP=0101
                                    NV UP EI PL NZ NA PE NC
```

14EB:0101 B80000   MOV AX,0000

```
AX=0000   BX=0000   CX=0000   DX=0000   SP=EA04   BP=0000
SI=0000   DI=0000   DS=14EB   ES=14EB   SS=14EB   CS=14EB
IP=0104
                                    NV UP EI PL NZ NA PE NC
```

14EB:0104 0440   ADD AL,40

```
AX=0040   BX=0000   CX=0000   DX=0000   SP=EA04   BP=0000
SI=0000   DI=0000   DS=14EB   ES=14EB   SS=14EB   CS=14EB
IP=0106
                                    NV UP EI PL NZ NA PO NC
```
                                                        *

The ADD sets the parity flag to odd because the number of bits in the low 8 bits is odd.

l14EB:0106 0440   ADD AL,40

AX=0080   BX=0000   CX=0000   DX=0000   SP=EA04   BP=0000
SI=0000   DI=0000   DS=14EB   ES=14EB   SS=14EB   CS=14EB
IP=0108

                                   OV UP EI NG NZ NA PO NC
                                    *   *

The result of the addition cannot be contained as a signed 8 bit number so the overflow flag is set. The sign bit is also set which causes the sign flag to be set to negative.

14EB:0108 0440   ADD AL,40

AX=00C0   BX=0000   CX=0000   DX=0000   SP=EA04   BP=0000
SI=0000   DI=0000   DS=14EB   ES=14EB   SS=14EB   CS=14EB
IP=010A

                                   NV UP EI NG NZ NA PE NC
                                    *

The main change in the flags is to reset the overflow flag because the result can be contained in the target register as a signed value. The number of bits in the low 8 is 2 and thus the parity flag is set to even parity.

14EB:010A 0440   ADD AL,40

AX=0000   BX=0000   CX=0000   DX=0000   SP=EA04   BP=0000
SI=0000   DI=0000   DS=14EB   ES=14EB   SS=14EB   CS=14EB
IP=010C

                                   NV UP EI PL ZR NA PE CY
                                                *   *

This ADD causes a carry out of the target register. The carry flag is set. Since the result has a zero sign bit, the sign flag changes to positive. The result is a zero register so the zero flag is set.

14EB:010C 0440   ADD AL,40

AX=0040   BX=0000   CX=0000   DX=0000   SP=EA04   BP=0000
SI=0000   DI=0000   DS=14EB   ES=14EB   SS=14EB   CS=14EB
IP=010E

                                   NV UP EI PL NZ NA PO NC
                                                *   *   *

This ADD changes the zero flag to non zero, resets the carry flag and changes the parity flag to odd.

AND   Logical AND

INSTRUCTION	OPCODE	BINARY
AND AL,imm8	24 ib	00100100
AND AX,imm16	25 iw	00100101
AND EAX,imm32	25 id	00100101
AND r/m8,imm8	A0 /4 ib	10100000 mm 100 r/m
AND r/m16,imm16	A1 /4 iw	10100001 mm 100 r/m
AND r/m32,imm32	A1 /4 ib	10100001 mm 100 r/m
AND r/m16,imm8	A3 /4 ib	10100011 mm 100 r/m
AND r/m32,imm8	A3 /4 ib	10100011 mm 100 r/m
AND r/m8,r8	20 /r	00100000 mm rrr r/m
AND r/m16,r16	21 /r	00100001 mm rrr r/m
AND r/m32,r32	21 /r	00100001 mm rrr r/m
AND r8,r/m8	22 /r	00100010 mm rrr r/m
AND r16,r/m16	23 /r	00100011 mm rrr r/m
AND r32,r/m32	23 /r	00100011 mm rrr r/m

Purpose: AND is used to ensure that user-specified bits are off, e.g., the parity bit in an ASCII input stream from a terminal. When AND is used in conjunction with a compare, AND makes certain that the specified bits are on. In use, AND is executed prior to the compare. Both AND and the compare use known masks.

Instruction Demonstration: This demonstration of the AND instruction shows its effect as it is used to mask bits of its destination off.

The instruction sequence:

```
14EB:0101 B8EE11        MOV AX,11EE
14EB:0104 25FFFF        AND AX,FFFF
14EB:0107 25F1FF        AND AX,FFF1
14EB:010A 2511FE        AND AX,FE11
14EB:010D 25FFE0        AND AX,E0FF
```

The registers and flags at the start:

```
AX=0040   BX=0000   CX=0000   DX=0000   SP=EA04   BP=0000
SI=0000   DI=0000   DS=14EB   ES=14EB   SS=14EB   CS=14EB
IP=0101
                                 NV UP EI PL NZ NA PO CY

14EB:0101 B8EE11              MOV AX,11EE

AX=11EE   BX=0000   CX=0000   DX=0000   SP=EA04   BP=0000
SI=0000   DI=0000   DS=14EB   ES=14EB   SS=14EB   CS=14EB
IP=0104
                                 NV UP EI PL NZ NA PO CY
```

14EB:0104 25FFFF   AND AX,FFFF

AX=11EE   BX=0000   CX=0000   DX=0000   SP=EA04   BP=0000
SI=0000   DI=0000   DS=14EB   ES=14EB   SS=14EB   CS=14EB
IP=0107

                    NV UP EI PL NZ NA PE NC
                                 * *

Note that ANDing with a mask which has all bits set does not affect the target. It does set the carry flag off, sets the parity flag, and the zero flag according to the result. It also sets overflow off and the sign flag according to the result.

14EB:0107 25F1FF   AND AX,FFF1

AX=11E0   BX=0000   CX=0000   DX=0000   SP=EA04   BP=0000
SI=0000   DI=0000   DS=14EB   ES=14EB   SS=14EB   CS=14EB
IP=010A

                    NV UP EI PL NZ NA PO NC
                                 *

This AND has masked out the bits of the low nibble. The resulting parity in the low eight bits has changed as reflected in the parity flag.

14EB:010A 2511FE   AND AX,FE11

AX=1000   BX=0000   CX=0000   DX=0000   SP=EA04   BP=0000
SI=0000   DI=0000   DS=14EB   ES=14EB   SS=14EB   CS=14EB
IP=010D

                    NV UP EI PL NZ NA PE NC
                                 *

This AND has masked the value in AL to zero, leaving AX with only one bit in AH. Note the parity which is calculated on the low eight bits of the result is even. The zero flag is non zero because it is set based on the total result.

14EB:010D 25FFE0   AND AX,E0FF

AX=0000   BX=0000   CX=0000   DX=0000   SP=EA04   BP=0000
SI=0000   DI=0000   DS=14EB   ES=14EB   SS=14EB   CS=14EB
IP=0110

                    NV UP EI PL ZR NA PE NC
                                 *

This AND results in a zero result and sets the zero flag.

ARPL   Adjust Requestor Privilege Level of Selector

INSTRUCTION	OPCODE	BINARY
ARPL r/m16,r16	63 /r	01100011 mm rrr r/m

Purpose: ARPL is used by systems software to guarantee that selector parameters to a subroutine do not request more privilege than allowed to the caller.

ARPL has two operands. The first, a 16-bit word register or memory variable that contains the value of the selector. The second operand is generally a register that contains the caller's CS selector value.

Instruction Demonstration: The ARPL instruction is used by system software to validate selectors passed as parameter pointers. It checks a selector against a model which contains the maximum privilege allowed (usually the caller's CS selector is used) and adjusts the tested value to the lesser of the privilege levels (highest number). If no change is necessary, the zero flag is reset. If a change was needed, the zero flag is set (a possible attempt to breach security).

The instruction sequence:

```
0070:0100 8CCB        MOV    BX,CS
0070:0102 B87300      MOV    AX,0073
0070:0105 63C3        ARPL   BX,AX
```

The registers and flags at the start:

```
EAX=00000000    EBX=00000000    CS=0070
IP=0100
```

                                    NV UP EI PL NZ NA PO NC

For the purpose of the demo, we reverse the normal and set CS as the tested value (The demo was done at level 0).

```
0070:0100 8CCB            MOV    BX,CS

EAX=00000000    EBX=00000070    CS=0070
IP=0102
```
                                    NV UP EI PL NZ NA PO NC

We set a comparand with a lower privilege (3).

```
0070:0102 B87300          MOV    AX,0073

EAX=00000073    EBX=00000070    CS=0070
IP=0105
```
                                    NV UP EI PL NZ NA PO NC

We issue the ARPL that adjusts the tested descriptor to the least privilege, and sets the zero flag because the adjustment was needed.

0070:0105 63C3   ARPL   BX,AX

EAX=00000073   EBX=00000073   CS=0070
IP=0107

                             NV UP EI PL ZR NA PO NC

BOUND   Check Array Index Against Bounds

INSTRUCTION	OPCODE	BINARY
BOUND r16,m16&16	62 /r	01100010 mm rrr r/m
BOUND r32,m32&32	62 /r	01100010 mm rrr r/m

Purpose: BOUND verifies that the signed value contained in the specified register lies within specified limits. Interrupt 5 occurs if the value in the register is less than the lower bound or greater than the upper bound. The upper and lower limit values may each be a word or a doubleword.

The block of memory that specifies the lower and upper limits of an array may typically reside just before the array itself. This makes the array bounds accessible at a constant offset from the beginning of the array. Because the address of the array is already present in a register, this avoids extra calculations to obtain the effective address of the array bounds.

BOUND includes two operands. The first specifies the register being tested. The second contains the effective address of the two signed BOUND limit values. BOUND assumes that the upper limit and the lower limit are in adjacent memory locations. These limit values *cannot* be register operands. If they are, an invalid opcode exception occurs.

Instruction Demonstration: This demonstration of the BOUND instruction shows the execution of a valid BOUND check. An out of bound check is handled by the routine for INT 5.

The instruction sequence:

```
14EB:0100 B84000        MOV     AX,0040
14EB:0103 62060002      BOUND   AX,[0200]
14EB:0107 B80101        MOV     AX,0101
14EB:010A 62060002      BOUND   AX,[0200]
```

The registers and flags at the start:

AX=0040	BX=0000	CX=0000	DX=0000	SP=EA04	BP=0000
SI=0000	DI=0000	DS=14EB	ES=14EB	SS=14EB	CS=14EB

IP=0103   NV UP EI PL NZ NA PO NC

14EB:0103 62060002   BOUND AX,[0200]   DS:0200=0001
                                                           0202=0100

This execution of the bound instruction results in the execution of the next sequential instruction. AX is > = left bound and < = right bound. Note that no flags are affected.

AX=0040   BX=0000   CX=0000   DX=0000   SP=EA04   BP=0000
SI=0000   DI=0000   DS=14EB   ES=14EB   SS=14EB   CS=14EB
IP=0107
                                           NV UP EI PL NZ NA PO NC

14EB:0107 B80101   MOV   AX,0101

AX=0101   BX=0000   CX=0000   DX=0000   SP=EA04   BP=0000
SI=0000   DI=0000   DS=14EB   ES=14EB   SS=14EB   CS=14EB
IP=010A
                                           NV UP EI PL NZ NA PO NC

14EB:010A 62060002   BOUND AX,[0200]   DS:0200=0001
                                                           0202=0100

This execution of the BOUND instruction causes an INT 5 to be taken because AX is beyond the right bound.

BSF   Bit Scan Forward

INSTRUCTION	OPCODE	BINARY
BSF r16,r/m16	0F BC	00001111 10111100 mm rrr r/m
BSF r32,r/m32	0F BC	00001111 10111100 mm rrr r/m

Purpose: This instruction scans a word or doubleword for a one-bit and stores the number of the first set bit into a register. The bit string being scanned may be either in a register or in memory. ZF is set if the entire word is zero; that is, no set bits are found. ZF is cleared if a one-bit is found.

NOTE: If no set bit is found, the value of the destination register is undefined.

This instruction is new with the 80386. It is useful for scanning allocation bit maps for an allocatable or free bit. Returning the number of the bit provides the relative number of the item within the word being examined.

Instruction Demonstration: This demonstration of the Bit Scan Forward instruction shows its operation when finding a bit set. It should be noted that the operation is on a word of either 16 or 32 bits. The bits are numbered from right to left in the word. Note that the method of storage (low byte to high byte) is ignored. The word is fetched and then scanned.

The instruction sequence:

```
14EB:0100 B84000          MOV     AX,0040
14EB:0103 0FBC060002      BSF     AX,[200]
14EB:0108 90              NOP
```

The registers and flags at the start:

```
AX=0040   BX=0000   CX=0000   DX=0000   SP=EA04   BP=0000
SI=0000   DI=0000   DS=14EB   ES=14EB   SS=14EB   CS=14EB
IP=0103
                                    NV UP EI PL ZR NA PO NC
```

```
14EB:0103 0FBC060002      BSF  AX,[200]              DS:0200=0010
```

```
Binary      0000 0000 0001 0000
Bit No.     1        0 0        0
            5        8 7        0
```

```
AX=0004   BX=0000   CX=0000   DX=0000   SP=EA04   BP=0000
SI=0000   DI=0000   DS=14EB   ES=14EB   SS=14EB   CS=14EB
IP=0108
                                    NV UP EI PL NZ NA PO NC
                                                      *
```

The number of the first bit found is placed into the specified register. The zero flag is set non-zero to indicate that a bit was found.

The data as it resides in memory:

```
14EB:0200   10 00 00 01 00 00 00 00
```

BSR   Bit Scan Reverse

Instruction	Opcode	Binary
BSR r16,r/m16	0F BD	00001111 10111101 mm rrr r/m
BSR r32,r/m32	0F BD	00001111 10111101 mm rrr r/m

Purpose: This instruction scans a word or doubleword for a one-bit and stores the index of the first set bit into a register. The bit string being scanned may be either in a register or in memory. ZF is set if the entire word is zero; that is, no set bits are found. ZF is cleared if a one-bit is found. This is a new instruction with the 80386.

NOTE: If no set bit is found, the value of the destination register is undefined.

Instruction Demonstration: The BSR instruction operates like the BSF instruction except for the direction of scan. The bits in the designated word (or doubleword) are scanned from left to right (bit 31/15 to bit 0) and the number of the first bit found is placed in the register specified. If the word/doubleword is zero, the zero flag is set to zero.

The instruction sequence:

```
14EB:0100 B84000        MOV   AX,0040
14EB:0103 0FBD060002    BSR   AX,[0200]
14EB:0108 90            NOP
```

The registers and flags at the start:

```
AX=0040  BX=0000  CX=0000  DX=0000  SP=EA04  BP=0000
SI=0000  DI=0000  DS=14EB  ES=14EB  SS=14EB  CS=14EB
IP=0103
                                 NV UP EI PL ZR NA PE NC
```

```
14EB:0103 0FBD060002    BSR   AX,[0200]          DS:0200=0201
                          Binary      0000 0010 0000 0001
                          Bit No.      1      0 0        0
                                       5      8 7        0
```

```
AX=0009  BX=0000  CX=0000  DX=0000  SP=EA04  BP=0000
SI=0000  DI=0000  DS=14EB  ES=14EB  SS=14EB  CS=14EB
IP=0108
                                 NV UP EI PL NZ NA PE NC
                                              *
```

The word is scanned from bit 15 to the first bit which is set. The number of the bit is placed in the specified register and the zero flag is set non-zero.

The data in memory:

```
14EB:0200  01 02 00 01 00 00 00 00        ........
```

BT   Bit Test

INSTRUCTION	OPCODE	BINARY
BT r/m16,r16	0F A3	00001111 10100011 mm rrr r/m
BT r/m32,r32	0F A3	00001111 10100011 mm rrr r/m

BT r/m16,imm8	0F BA /r ib	00001111 10111010 mm 100 r/m
BT r/m32,imm8	0F BA /r ib	00001111 10111010 mm 100 r/m

Purpose: BT is a means of determining if a bit in a bit map is set or not. BT sets CF to the same value as the bit being tested. This instruction is new with the 80386.

Instruction Demonstration: This demonstration of the BT instruction shows its action in testing the value of the indicated bit.

The instruction sequence:

14EB:0100 B80900	MOV	AX,0009
14EB:0103 0FA3060002	BT	AX,[0200]
14EB:0108 90	NOP	

The registers and flags at the start:

```
AX=0009  BX=0000  CX=0000  DX=0000  SP=EA04  BP=0000
SI=0000  DI=0000  DS=14EB  ES=14EB  SS=14EB  CS=14EB
IP=0103
                              NV UP EI PL NZ NA PE NC
```

```
14EB:0103 0FA3060002      BT  AX,[0200]           DS:0200=0200
                          Binary       0000 0010 0000 0000
                          Bit No.        1      0 0        0
                                         5      8 7        0
```

```
AX=0009  BX=0000  CX=0000  DX=0000  SP=EA04  BP=0000
SI=0000  DI=0000  DS=14EB  ES=14EB  SS=14EB  CS=14EB
IP=0108
                              NV UP EI PL NZ NA PE CY
                                                       *
```

The bit specified in the register (9) is tested and is found on. That result is set in the carry flag. If the bit had been set off the carry flag would also be off.

The data in memory:

```
14EB:0200  00 02 00 01 00 00 00 00        ........
```

BTC   Bit Test and Complement

INSTRUCTION	OPCODE	BINARY
BTC r/m16,r16	0F BB	00001111 10111011 mm rrr r/m
BTC r/m32,r32	0F BB	00001111 10111011 mm rrr r/m
BTC r/m16,imm8	0F BA /7 ib	00001111 10111010 mm 111 r/m
BTC r/m32,imm8	0F BA /7 ib	00001111 10111010 mm 111 r/m

Purpose: BTC tests a specific bit, copies that bit to CF, and inverts the original bit, e.g., if the bit was a 1 it's changed to a 0. This instruction is new with the 80386.

Instruction Demonstration: This demonstrates the action of the BTC instruction. Note that the first execution finds the bit on, sets the carry on and sets the bit off. The second execution finds the bit off, sets the carry flag off and the bit on.

The instruction sequence:

```
14EB:0100 B80900          MOV AX,0009
14EB:0103 0FBB060002      BTC AX,[0200]
14EB:0108 0FBB060002      BTC AX,[0200]
14EB:010D 90              NOP
```

The data at the start:

```
14EB:0200  00 02 00 01 00 00 00 00        ........
```

The registers and flags at the start:

```
AX=0009   BX=0000   CX=0000   DX=0000   SP=EA04   BP=0000
SI=0000   DI=0000   DS=14EB   ES=14EB   SS=14EB   CS=14EB
IP=0103
                                   NV UP EI PL NZ NA PE NC
```

```
14EB:0103 0FBB060002          BTCAX,[0200]
```

```
AX=0009   BX=0000   CX=0000   DX=0000   SP=EA04   BP=0000
SI=0000   DI=0000   DS=14EB   ES=14EB   SS=14EB   CS=14EB
IP=0108
                                   NV UP EI PL NZ NA PE CY
                                                        *
```

```
14EB:0200  00 00 00 01 00 00 00 00        ........
```

The bit was on prior to execution. The bit is copied into the carry flag. The bit is then inverted in memory.

```
14EB:0103 0FBB060002          BTCAX,[0200]
```

```
AX=0009   BX=0000   CX=0000   DX=0000   SP=EA04   BP=0000
SI=0000   DI=0000   DS=14EB   ES=14EB   SS=14EB   CS=14EB
IP=010D
                                   NV UP EI PL NZ NA PE NC
                                                        *
```

```
14EB:0200  00 02 00 01 00 00 00 00        ........
```

The bit was off prior to execution. The bit is copied into the carry flag. The bit is then inverted in memory.

BTR   Bit Test and Reset

Instruction	Opcode	Binary
BTR r/m16,r16	0F B3	00001111 10110011 mm rrr r/m
BTR r/m32,r32	0F B3	00001111 10110011 mm rrr r/m
BTR r/m16,imm8	0F BA /6 ib	00001111 10111010 mm 110 r/m
BTR r/m32,imm8	0F BA /6 ib	00001111 10111010 mm 110 r/m

Purpose: BTR tests a specific bit, copies that bit to CF, and forces the original bit to zero. This instruction is new with the 80386.

Instruction Demonstration: This demonstrates the action of the BTR instruction. Note that the execution copies the bit into the carry flag and sets the bit off.

The instruction sequence:

```
14EB:0100 B80900          MOV    AX,0009
14EB:0103 0FB3060002      BTR    AX,[0200]
14EB:0108 90              NOP
```

The data at the start:

```
14EB:0200  FF FF 00 01 00 00 00 00        ........
```

The registers and flags at the start:

```
AX=0009  BX=0000  CX=0000  DX=0000  SP=EA04  BP=0000
SI=0000  DI=0000  DS=14EB  ES=14EB  SS=14EB  CS=14EB
IP=0103
                              NV UP EI PL NZ NA PE NC
```

```
14EB:01030 FB3060002          BTRAX,[0200]
```

```
AX=0009  BX=0000  CX=0000  DX=0000  SP=EA04  BP=0000
SI=0000  DI=0000  DS=14EB  ES=14EB  SS=14EB  CS=14EB
IP=0108
                              NV UP EI PL NZ NA PE CY
                                                    *
```

```
14EB:0200  FF FD 00 01 00 00 00 00       .}......
```

The bit was on prior to execution as is indicated by the carry flag. The bit is then forced off in memory.

BTS   Bit Test and Set

Instruction	Opcode	Binary
BTS r/m16,r16	0F AB	00001111 10101011 mm rrr r/m

BTS r/m32,r32	0F AB	00001111 10101011	mm rrr r/m
BTS r/m16,imm8	0F BA /5 ib	00001111 10111010	mm 101 r/m
BTS r/m32,imm8	0F BA /5 ib	00001111 10111010	mm 101 r/m

Purpose: BTS tests a specific bit, copies that bit to CF, and sets the original bit to 1. This instruction is new with the 80386.

Instruction Demonstration: This demonstrates the action of the BTS instruction. Note that the execution copies the bit into the carry flag and sets the bit on.

The instruction sequence:

```
14EB:0100 B80900          MOV    AX,0009
14EB:0103 0FAB060002      BTS    AX,[0200]
14EB:0108 90              NOP
```

The data at the start:

```
14EB:0200   FF FD 00 01 00 00 00 00        .}......
```

The registers and flags at the start:

```
AX=0009   BX=0000   CX=0000   DX=0000   SP=EA04   BP=0000
SI=0000   DI=0000   DS=14EB   ES=14EB   SS=14EB   CS=14EB
IP=0103
                                    NV UP EI PL NZ NA PE CY
```

```
14EB:0103 0FAB060002          BTSAX,[0200]
```

```
AX=0009   BX=0000   CX=0000   DX=0000   SP=EA04   BP=0000
SI=0000   DI=0000   DS=14EB   ES=14EB   SS=14EB   CS=14EB
IP=0108
                                    NV UP EI PL NZ NA PE NC
                                                          *
```

```
14EB:0200   FF FF 00 01 00 00 00 00        ........
```

The bit was off prior to execution as is indicated by the carry flag. The bit is then forced on in memory.

CALL   Call a Procedure

INSTRUCTION	OPCODE	BINARY	
CALL rel16	E8 cw	11101000	
CALL r/m16	FF /2	11111111	mm 010 r/m
CALL ptr16:16	9A cd	10011010	
CALL m16:16	FF /3	11111111	mm 011 r/m

CALL rel32	E8 cd	11101000
CALL r/m32	FF /2	11111111 mm 010 r/m
CALL ptr16:32	9A cp	10011010
CALL ptr32:32	9A cp	10011010
CALL m16:32	FF /3	11111111 mm 011 r/m

Purpose: CALL transfers control from one code segment location to another. These locations can be within the same code segment (*near*) or in different ones (*far*). Prior to actual transfer, CALL saves on the stack the address of the instruction following the CALL and the current value of EIP.

CALL instructions have relative, direct, and indirect versions. Indirect instructions specify an absolute address in one of two ways: (1) the 80386 can obtain the destination address from a memory operand specified in the instruction; or (2) the program CALLs a location specified by a general register (EAX, EDX, ECX, EBX, EBP, ESI, or EDI).

Instruction Demonstration: The CALL instruction, ENTER instruction, LEAVE instruction, and RET instruction are demonstrated together since they logically "fit" with each other and complement each other.

The CALLed routine's instructions:

14EB:0110 C80A0001	ENTER 000A,01
14EB:0114 90	NOP
14EB:0115 C9	LEAVE
14EB:0116 C3	RET

The CALL instruction:

14EB:0101 E80C00   CALL 0110

The area pointed to by SP:

14EB:E9D0   00 00 00 00 00 00 00 00-00 00 00 00 00 00 00 00   . . . .

The registers and flags at the start:

AX=0000	BX=0000	CX=0000	DX=0000	SP=EA04	BP=0000
SI=0000	DI=0000	DS=14EB	ES=14EB	SS=14EB	CS=14EB
IP=0101					

NV UP EI PL NZ NA PO NC

14EB:0101 E80C00   CALL 0110

AX=0000	BX=0000	CX−0000	DX=0000	SP=EA02	BP=0000
SI=0000	DI=0000	DS=14EB	ES=14EB	SS=14EB	CS=14EB
IP=0110					

NV UP EI PL NZ NA PO NC

We issue a CALL NEAR. Note that adding the adjusted IP to the near displacement results in an IP value of 0110. (0104 + 000C = 0110). Note also that SP has been decreased by 2. The IP value (0104) was placed on the stack prior to computing its new value.

14EB:0110 C80A0001   ENTER 000A,01

AX=0000   BX=0000   CX=0000   DX=0000   SP=E9F4   BP=EA00
SI=0000   DI=0000   DS=14EB   ES=14EB   SS=14EB   CS=14EB
IP=0114

                                        NV UP EI PL NZ NA PO NC

Note the effect of the ENTER instruction. BP is saved on the stack, set to the resulting value of SP then SP is decreased by the first operand's value.

14EB:0114 90   NOP

AX=0000   BX=0000   CX=0000   DX=0000   SP=E9F4   BP=EA00
SI=0000   DI=0000   DS=14EB   ES=14EB   SS=14EB   CS=14EB
IP=0115

                                        NV UP EI PL NZ NA PO NC

14EB:0115 C9   LEAVE

AX=0000   BX=0000   CX=0000   DX=0000   SP=EA02   BP=0000
SI=0000   DI=0000   DS=14EB   ES=14EB   SS=14EB   CS=14EB
IP=0116

                                        NV UP EI PL NZ NA PO NC

LEAVE reverses the effect of the ENTER. BP is copied to SP, then BP is POPed off the stack. This leaves the SP positioned for the RET.

14EB:0116 C3   RET

AX=0000   BX=0000   CX=0000   DX=0000   SP=EA04   BP=0000
SI=0000   DI=0000   DS=14EB   ES=14EB   SS=14EB   CS=14EB
IP=0104

                                        NV UP EI PL NZ NA PO NC

RET removes the IP value from the stack which causes the instruction following the CALL to be the next to be executed.

14EB:0104 90   NOP

AX=0000   BX=0000   CX=0000   DX=0000   SP=EA04   BP=0000
SI=0000   DI=0000   DS=14EB   ES=14EB   SS=14EB   CS=14EB
IP=0105

                                        NV UP EI PL NZ NA PO NC

CBW   **Convert Byte to Word**

CWDE   **Convert Word to Doubleword**

INSTRUCTION	OPCODE	BINARY
CBW	98	10011000
CWDE	99	10011001

Purpose: These instructions extend the sign bit into the top portion of the larger register so that arithmetic operations can occur with correct results.

Instruction Demonstration: This demonstrates the action of the CBW instruction. Both a positive and a negative value is extended.

The instruction sequence:

```
14EB:0100 B80504        MOV   AX,0405
14EB:0103 98            CBW
14EB:0104 B8F104        MOV   AX,04F1
14EB:0107 98            CBW
```

The registers and flags prior to the first CBW:

```
AX=0405   BX=0000   CX=0000   DX=0000   SP=EA04   BP=0000
SI=0000   DI=0000   DS=14EB   ES=14EB   SS=14EB   CS=14EB
IP=0103
                                    NV UP EI PL NZ NA PO NC
```

```
14EB:0103 98                CBW
```

```
AX=0005   BX=0000   CX=0000   DX=0000   SP=EA04   BP=0000
SI=0000   DI=0000   DS=14EB   ES=14EB   SS=14EB   CS=14EB
IP=0104
                                    NV UP EI PL NZ NA PO NC
```

Note that none of the flags were affected. AX now contains the word value previously in AL.

```
14EB:0104 B8F104              MOV    AX,04F1
```

```
AX=04F1   BX=0000   CX=0000   DX=0000   SP=EA04   BP=0000
SI=0000   DI=0000   DS=14EB   ES=14EB   SS=14EB   CS=14EB
IP=0107
                                    NV UP EI PL NZ NA PO NC
```

A negative value is placed in AL.

14EB:0107 98   CBW

```
AX=FFF1   BX=0000   CX=0000   DX=0000   SP=EA04   BP=0000
SI=0000   DI=0000   DS=14EB   ES=14EB   SS=14EB   CS=14EB
IP=0108
                                  NV UP EI PL NZ NA PO NC
```

AX now contains the sign extended negative value. No flags are changed.

CLC   Clear Carry Flag (CF)

INSTRUCTION	OPCODE	BINARY
CLC	F8	11111000

Purpose: This instruction sets the CF to zero. No other flags are affected.
Instruction Demonstration: This demonstrates the action of the CLC instruction.
The instruction sequence:

```
          14EB:0100 F9              STC
          14EB:0101 F8              CLC
          14EB:0102 90              NOP
```

The registers and flags at the start:

```
AX=FFF1   BX=0000   CX=0000   DX=0000   SP=EA04   BP=0000
SI=0000   DI=0000   DS=14EB   ES=14EB   SS=14EB   CS=14EB
IP=0101
                                  NV UP EI PL NZ NA PO CY
                                                       *
```

Note that the carry is set.

14EB:0101 F8   CLC

```
AX=FFF1   BX=0000   CX=0000   DX=0000   SP=EA04   BP=0000
SI=0000   DI=0000   DS=14EB   ES=14EB   SS=14EB   CS=14EB
IP=0102
                                  NV UP EI PL NZ NA PO NC
                                                       *
```

After the CLC, the carry is set to zero.

CLD   Clear Direction Flag (DF)

Instruction	Opcode	Binary
CLD	FC	11111100

Purpose: CLD sets DF to zero. No other flags are affected. By setting DF to zero, DF now signals the automatic indexing feature to increment. Automatic indexing is used by string instructions.

Instruction Demonstration: This demonstrates the CLD instruction's action. The instruction sequence:

14EB:0100 FD		STD
14EB:0101 FC		CLD

The registers and flags prior to the CLD:

```
AX=FFF1   BX=0000   CX=0000   DX=0000   SP=EA04   BP=0000
SI=0000   DI=0000   DS=14EB   ES=14EB   SS=14EB   CS=14EB
IP=0101
```

                                   NV DN EI PL NZ NA PO NC
                                                *

Note that the direction flag is set to 'down'.

14EB:0101 FC   CLD

```
AX=FFF1   BX=0000   CX=0000   DX=0000   SP=EA04   BP=0000
SI=0000   DI=0000   DS=14EB   ES=14EB   SS=14EB   CS=14EB
IP=0102
```

                                   NV UP EI PL NZ NA PO NC
                                                *

Note that the direction flag is reset to 'up', the IP register is advanced and that no other registers or flags are affected.

CLI   Clear Interrupt Flag (IF)

Instruction	Opcode	Binary
CLI	FA	11111010

Purpose: If the current privilege level is at least as privileged as the IOPL, CLI sets the interrupt flag to a zero. No other flags are affected.

NOTE: External interrupts are ignored at the end of CLI until the interrupt flag is set.

Instruction Demonstration: This demonstrates the action of the CLI instruction. The instruction sequence:

```
14EB:0100 FB              STI
14EB:0101 FA              CLI
14EB:0102 FB              STI
```

The registers prior to the CLI instruction:

```
AX=FFF1  BX=0000  CX=0000  DX=0000  SP=EA04  BP=0000
SI=0000  DI=0000  DS=14EB  ES=14EB  SS=14EB  CS=14EB
IP=0101
                              NV UP EI PL NZ NA PO NC
                                       *
```

Note that the interrupt flag is set (enabled).

```
14EB:0101 FA              CLI

AX=FFF1  BX=0000  CX=0000  DX=0000  SP=EA04  BP=0000
SI=0000  DI=0000  DS=14EB  ES=14EB  SS=14EB  CS=14EB
IP=0102
                              NV UP DI PL NZ NA PO NC
                                       *
```

The interrupt flag is reset (disabled), the IP register is advanced, and no other registers or flags are affected.

CLTS   Clear Task-Switched Flag in Control Register Zero (CR0)

INSTRUCTION	OPCODE	BINARY
CLTS	0F 06	00001111 00000110

Purpose: CLTS sets TS (in CR0) to zero. TS is set by the 80386 at each occurrence of a task switch.

NOTE: CLTS is used in systems programming. It is a privileged instruction, running at privilege level zero only.

Instruction Demonstration: The CLTS instruction clears the task switched flag in CR0. The CLTS instruction is used by a 80386 dispatcher to indicate to a coprocessor that all the data or results it contains pertain to the current task.

The task switched flag allows delay in saving the coprocessor state (often unnecessary if the switch was to a system task such as a spooler or interrupt handler). No flags are changed in the EFLAGS register.

The instructions:

```
0070:0100 0F20C0              MOV    EAX,CR0
```

```
0070:0103 0F06              CLTS
0070:0105 0F20C0            MOV    EAX,CR0
```

The registers and flags at the start:

EAX=00000000
IP=0100

NV UP EI PL NZ NA PO NC

```
0070:0100 0F20C0           MOV    EAX,CR0
```

Note that the task switched flag is on in the copy of CR0 copied to EAX.

EAX=7FFFFFE9
IP=0103

NV UP EI PL NZ NA PO NC

```
0070:0103 0F06             CLTS
```

The CLTS instruction makes no visible change.

EAX=7FFFFFE9
IP=0105

NV UP EI PL NZ NA PO NC

```
0070:0105 0F20C0           MOV    EAX,CR0
```

The task switched flag is now reset.

EAX=7FFFFFE1
IP=0108

NV UP EI PL NZ NA PO NC

CMC   Complement Carry Flag (CF)

Instruction	Opcode	Binary
CMC	F5	11110101

Purpose: CMC reverses the value of the carry flag, e.g., CF becomes a zero if it was a one. No other flags are affected.

Instruction Demonstration: This demonstrates the action of the CMC instruction. The instruction sequence:

```
14EB:0100 F5                        CMC
14EB:0101 F5                        CMC
```

The registers and flags prior to execution:

AX=FFF1   BX=0000   CX=0000   DX=0000   SP=EA04   BP=0000

SI=0000   DI=0000   DS=14EB   ES=14EB   SS=14EB   CS=14EB

IP=0100

                                    NV UP EI PL NZ NA PO CY
                                                 *

Note that the carry flag is set on.

14EB:0100 F5   CMC

AX=FFF1   BX=0000   CX=0000   DX=0000   SP=EA04   BP=0000

SI=0000   DI=0000   DS=14EB   ES=14EB   SS=14EB   CS=14EB

IP=010i

                                      NV UP EI PL NZ NA PO NC
                                               *

CMC inverts the flag from on to off or off to on, see below.

14EB:0101 F5   CMC

AX=FFF1   BX=0000   CX=0000   DX=0000   SP=EA04   BP=0000

SI=0000   DI=0000   DS=14EB   ES=14EB   SS=14EB   CS=14EB

IP=0102

                                      NV UP EI PL NZ NA PO CY
                                               *

CMP   Compare

INSTRUCTION	OPCODE	BINARY		
CMP AL,imm8	3C ib	00111100		
CMP AX,imm16	3D iw	00111101		
CMP EAX,imm32	3D id	00111101		
CMP r/m8,imm8	80 /7 ib	10000000	mm 111 r/m	
CMP r/m16,imm16	81 /7 iw	10000001	mm 111 r/m	
CMP r/m32,imm32	81 /7 id	10000001	mm 111 r/m	
CMP r/m16,imm8	83 /7 ib	10000011	mm 111 r/m	
CMP r/m32,imm8	83 /7 ib	10000011	mm 111 r/m	
CMP r/m8,r8	38 /r	00111000	mm rrr r/m	
CMP r/m16,r16	39 /r	00111001	mm rrr r/m	
CMP r/m32,r32	39 /r	00111001	mm rrr r/m	
CMP r8,m8	3A /r	00111010	mm rrr r/m	
CMP r16,r/m16	3B /r	00111011	mm rrr r/m	
CMP r32,r/m32	3B /r	00111011	mm rrr r/m	

Purpose: CMP subtracts the source operand from the destination operand. It updates OF, SF, ZF, AF, PF, and CF, but does not alter the source and destination operands.

Instruction Demonstration: This demonstrates the action of the CMP instruction. The instruction sequence:

```
14EB:0100 B8FEFE        MOV     AX,FEFE
14EB:0103 BBFD0F        MOV     BX,0FFD
14EB:0106 38E0          CMP     AL,AH
14EB:0108 38F8          CMP     AL,BH
14EB:010A 38D8          CMP     AL,BL
14EB:010C 38C7          CMP     BH,AL
14EB:010E 38C3          CMP     BL,AL
14EB:0110 90            NOP
```

The registers and flags prior to the CMP instruction:

```
AX=FEFE  BX=0FFD  CX=0000  DX=0000  SP=EA04  BP=0000
SI=0000  DI=0000  DS=14EB  ES=14EB  SS=14EB  CS=14EB
IP=0106
                                    NV UP EI NG NZ AC PO CY
```

```
14EB:0106 38E0              CMP              AL,AH
```

```
AX=FEFE  BX=0FFD  CX=0000  DX=0000  SP=EA04  BP=0000
SI=0000  DI=0000  DS=14EB  ES=14EB  SS=14EB  CS=14EB
IP=0108
                                    NV UP EI PL ZR NA PE NC
                                           *    *    *    *    *
```

The compare of −2 to −2 (FE to FE) results in a zero after the internal subtract. No carry, even parity, no adjust, a zero result, and a positive sign bit are the result. Note that other than the advance in IP that no other registers are affected.

```
14EB:0108 38F8              CMP              AL,BH
```

```
AX=FEFE  BX=0FFD  CX=0000  DX=0000  SP=EA04  BP=0000
SI=0000  DI=0000  DS=14EB  ES=14EB  SS=14EB  CS=14EB
IP=010A
                                    NV UP EI NG NZ AC PO NC
                                           *    *    *    *
```

The compare of 15 to −2 (0F to FE) results in a non zero after the internal subtract of 15 from −2 (−17). The negative flag is set, the zero flag is reset, an adjustment, and odd parity (the result EF has 7 bits on), and no carry.

14EB:010A 38D8   CMP   AL,BL

AX=FEFE BX=0FFD CX=0000 DX=0000 SP=EA04 BP=0000
SI=0000 DI=0000 DS=14EB ES=14EB SS=14EB CS=14EB
IP=010C

           NV UP EI PL NZ NA PO NC
                  *   *

The compare of −3 to −2 (FD to FE) results in a non zero after the internal subtract of −3 from −2 (1). The positive flag, non zero flag, adjust, odd parity and no carry flags are set.

14EB:010C 38C7   CMP   BH,AL

AX=FEFE BX=0FFD CX=0000 DX=0000 SP=EA04 BP=0000
SI=0000 DI=0000 DS=14EB ES=14EB SS=14EB CS=14EB
IP=010E

           NV UP EI PL NZ NA PE CY
                  *   *

The compare of −2 to 15 (FE to 0F) results in a non zero, positive result after the internal subtract of −2 from 15 (17 or hex 11). The changes in the flags reflect the even parity of the result and the carry because of the borrow.

14EB:010E 38C3   CMP   BL,AL

AX=FEFE BX=0FFD CX=0000 DX=0000 SP=EA04 BP=0000
SI=0000 DI=0000 DS=14EB ES=14EB SS=14EB CS=14EB
IP=0110

           NV UP EI NG NZ AC PE CY
                  *   *

The compare of −2 to −3 results in a non zero negative result after the internal subtraction (−1 or hex FF). A borrow is required and the result has a negative sign and an even (8) number of bits on. An adjust is also required.

CMPS	Compare String Operands
CMPSB	Compare String - Byte
CMPSW	Compare String - Word
CMPSD	Compare String - Doubleword

INSTRUCTION	OPCODE	BINARY
CMPS m8,m8	A6	10100110

CMPS m16,m16	A7	10100111
CMPS m32,m32	A7	10100111

NOTE: CMPSB is a common assembler mnemonic for CMPS m8,m8
CMPSW is a common assembler mnemonic for CMPS m16,m16
CMPSD is a common assembler mnemonic for CMPS m32,m32

Purpose: These instructions operate on strings rather than on logical or numeric values. They operate on one element of a string, which may be a byte, a word, or a doubleword. The string elements are addressed by the registers ESI and EDI. After each string operation, ESI and/or EDI are automatically updated to point to the next element of the string. If DF=0, the index registers are incremented. If DF=1, they are decremented. The amount incremented or decremented is 1, 2, or 4, depending on the size of the string element.

CMPS subtracts the destination string element (at ES:EDI) from the source string element (at DS:ESI). It then updates the flags AF, SF, PF, CF, and OF. If the string elements are equal, ZF=1. Otherwise, ZF=0. If DF=0, the 80386 increments the memory pointers ESI and EDI for two strings. The segment register used for the source address can be changed with a segment register override prefix. The destination segment register can *not* be overridden.

The assembler always translates CMPS into one of the other types. CMPSB compares bytes. CMPSW compares words. CMPSD compares doublewords.

If the REPE or REPNE prefix modifies this instruction, the 80386 compares the value of the current string element with the value in AL for byte elements, in AX for word elements, and in EAX for doubleword elements. Termination of the repeated operation depends on the resulting state of ZF as well as on the value in ECX.

Instruction Demonstration: This demonstration of the CMPS instruction includes an illustration of the use of the REP instruction prefix (in this case the REPZ prefix).

The data being compared:

        14EB:0200   41 42 43 41 42 43 41 42-44 41 42 42 41 42 43 00
        ABCABCABDABBABC.

to:

        14EB:0280   41 42 44 41 42 42 41 42-43 41 42 43 41 42 43 00
        ABDABBABCABCABC.

The instruction sequence:

14EB:0100 BE0002	MOV	SI,0200
14EB:0103 BF8002	MOV	DI,0280
14EB:0106 B90F00	MOV	CX,000F
14EB:0109 F3	REPZ	

```
14EB:010A A6          CMPSB
14EB:010B F3          REPZ
14EB:010C A6          CMPSB
14EB:010D F3          REPZ
14EB:010E A6          CMPSB
14EB:010F F3          REPZ
14EB:0110 A6          CMPSB
14EB:0111 F3          REPZ
14EB:0112 A6          CMPSB
```

The registers and flags at the start:

```
AX=0000   BX=0000   CX=0000   DX=0000   SP=EA04   BP=0000
SI=0200   DI=028F   DS=14EB   ES=14EB   SS=14EB   CS=14EB
IP=0103
                                        NV UP EI PL ZR NA PE NC
```

```
14EB:0103 BF8002          MOV     DI,0280
```

```
AX=0000   BX=0000   CX=0000   DX=0000   SP=EA04   BP=0000
SI=0200   DI=0280   DS=14EB   ES=14EB   SS=14EB   CS=14EB
IP=0106
                                        NV UP EI PL ZR NA PE NC
```

```
14EB:0106 B90F00          MOV     CX,000F
```

```
AX=0000   BX=0000   CX=000F   DX=0000   SP=EA04   BP=0000
SI=0200   DI=0280   DS=14EB   ES=14EB   SS=14EB   CS=14EB
IP=0109
                                        NV UP EI PL ZR NA PE NC
```

The DI, SI, and CX registers are now set for the comparison.

```
14EB:0109 F3          REPZ
14EB:010A A6          CMPSB
```

```
AX=0000   BX=0000   CX=000C   DX=0000   SP=EA04   BP=0000
SI=0203   D=0283    DS=14EB   ES=14EB   SS=14EB   CS=14EB
IP=010B
                                        NV UP EI NG NZ AC PE CY
                                             *    *    *      *
```

The first REP group compared the first 3 bytes of the strings at DS:SI and ES:DI until an unequal occurred. Note that at the end, SI and DI point at the bytes beyond the unequal one and that CX contains the count of bytes remaining. That is exactly what we need to be set up for the next REP. The results of the unequal compare are presented in the flags. (C (43 hex) − D (44 hex) = −1 (FF hex)) Setting carry, negative, adjust and non zero.

Since the registers are set we can continue:

```
14EB:010B  F3              REPZ
14EB:010C  A6              CMPSB
```

```
AX=0000   BX=0000   CX=0009   DX=0000   SP=EA04   BP=0000
SI=0206   DI=0286   DS=14EB   ES=14EB   SS=14EB   CS=14EB
IP=010D
                                NV UP EI PL NZ NA PO NC
                                      *        *  *  *
```

We have proceeded to the next unequal comparison. Again the registers are set to continue. The flags are set by the unequal compare (C (43 hex) − B (42 hex) = 1 (01 hex)) Setting positive, non-zero, no adjust, parity odd, and no carry.

Again we continue:

```
14EB:010D  F3              REPZ
14EB:010E  A6              CMPSB
```

```
AX=0000   BX=0000   CX=0006   DX=0000   SP=EA04   BP=0000
SI=0209   DI=0289   DS=14EB   ES=14EB   SS=14EB   CS=14EB
IP=010F
                                NV UP EI PL NZ NA PO NC
```

We have proceeded to the next unequal. The flags reflect the results of the D-C subtraction. (the same as the C-B above).

Again we continue:

```
14EB:010F  F3              REPZ
14EB:0110  A6              CMPSB
```

```
AX=0000   BX=0000   CX=0003   DX=0000   SP=EA04   BP=0000
SI=020C   DI=028C   DS=14EB   ES=14EB   SS=14EB   CS=14EB
IP=0111
                                NV UP EI NG NZ AC PE CY
                                      *        *  *  *
```

We have proceeded to the final unequal. The flags reflect the results of the B-C subtraction (the same as the C-D above).

We continue a final time:

```
14EB:0111 F3              REPZ
14EB:0112 A6              CMPSB
```

```
AX=0000   BX=0000   CX=0000   DX=0000   SP=EA04   BP=0000
SI=020F   DI=028F   DS=14EB   ES=14EB   SS=14EB   CS=14EB
IP=0113
                                        NV UP EI PL ZR NA PE NC
                                              *  *  *        *
```

The flags are set to the results of an equal comparison. The REP stopped because the count ran out in CX. This is signaled by the zero flag being set.

CWD	Convert Word to Doubleword
CDQ	Convert Doubleword to Quad-Word
CWDE	Convert Word to Doubleword Extended

INSTRUCTION	OPCODE	BINARY
CWD	99	10011001
CDQ	99	10011001

NOTE: CDQ is for 32 bit mode.

Purpose: CWD doubles the size of the source operand. CWD extends the sign of the word in register AX throughout register DX. CWD can be used to produce a doubleword dividend from a word before a word division.

CWDE extends the sign of the word in register AX throughout EAX.

CDQ extends the sign of the doubleword in EAX throughout EDX. CDQ can be used to produce a quad-word dividend from a doubleword before doubleword division.

Instruction Demonstration: This demonstrates the CWD instruction.

The instruction sequence:

```
14EB:0100 B80001         MOV   AX,0100
14EB:0103 99             CWD
14EB:0104 B800FF         MOV   AX,FF00
14EB:0107 99             CWD
```

The registers and flags after the MOV:

```
AX=0100   BX=0000   CX=0000   DX=FFFF   SP=EA04   BP=0000
SI=020F   DI=028F   DS=14EB   ES=14EB   SS=14EB   CS=14EB
```

IP=0103

NV UP EI PL ZR NA PE NC

14EB:0103 99   CWD

AX=0100   BX=0000   CX=0000   DX=0000   SP=EA04   BP=0000
SI=020F   DI=028F   DS=14EB   ES=14EB   SS=14EB   CS=14EB
IP=0104

NV UP EI PL ZR NA PE NC

Note that the only change is to DX which has had the AX sign bit propagated throughout the register. No flags change.

14EB:0104 B800FF   MOV   AX,FF00

AX=FF00   BX=0000   CX=0000   DX=0000   SP=EA04   BP=0000
SI=020F   DI=028F   DS=14EB   ES=14EB   SS=14EB   CS=14EB
IP=0107

NV UP EI PL ZR NA PE NC

14EB:0107 99   CWD

AX=FF00   BX=0000   CX=0000   DX=FFFF   SP=EA04   BP=0000
SI=020F   DI=028F   DS=14EB   ES=14EB   SS=14EB   CS=14EB
IP=0108

NV UP EI PL ZR NA PE NC

Again the sign bit is extended through the register.

DAA   Decimal Adjust AL Register After Addition

Instruction	Opcode	Binary
DAA	27	00100111

Purpose: DAA adjusts the result of adding two valid packed decimal operands in AL. DAA must always follow the addition of two pairs of packed decimal numbers (one digit in each half-cycle) to obtain a pair of valid packed decimal digits as results. CF is set if a carry was needed.

Instruction Demonstration: This demonstrates the DAA instruction. The DAA is used to adjust packed decimal values after an ADD.

The instruction sequence:

```
14EB:0100 B011            MOV     AL,11
14EB:0102 0409            ADD     AL,09
14EB:0104 27              DAA
14EB:0105 B099            MOV     AL,99
14EB:0107 0409            ADD     AL,09
14EB:0109 27              DAA
```

We start with the 11 in AL.

```
AX=FF11   BX=0000   CX=0000   DX=FFFF   SP=EA04   BP=0000
SI=020F   DI=028F   DS=14EB   ES=14EB   SS=14EB   CS=14EB
IP=0102
                                NV UP EI PL NZ AC PO CY
```

```
14EB:0102 0409            ADD              AL,09
```

```
AX=FF1A   BX=0000   CX=0000   DX=FFFF   SP=EA04   BP=0000
SI=020F   DI=028F   DS=14EB   ES=14EB   SS=14EB   CS=14EB
IP=0104
                                NV UP EI PL NZ NA PO NC
                                                 *        *
```

Note the ADD leaves a non BCD digit in the low nibble of AL.

```
14EB:0104 27              DAA
```

```
AX=FF20   BX=0000   CX=0000   DX=FFFF   SP=EA04   BP=0000
SI=020F   DI=028F   DS=14EB   ES=14EB   SS=14EB   CS=14EB
IP=0105
                                NV UP EI PL NZ AC PO NC
                                                        *
```

The DAA corrects the value by adding 6 to AL if the low nibble of AL is greater than 9 or if the adjust flag is set. If 6 is added, AC is set, otherwise it is cleared. If the high nibble of AL is greater than 9 or if the carry flag is set, 6 is added to the high nibble and the carry flag is set. Otherwise the carry flag is reset. Note that the high digit doesn't need adjustment in this example so the carry flag is reset.

```
14EB:0105 B099            MOV     AL,99
```

```
AX=FF99   BX=0000   CX=0000   DX=FFFF   SP=EA04   BP=0000
```

SI=020F   DI=028F   DS=14EB   ES=14EB   SS=14EB   CS=14EB
IP=0107

                                                  NV UP EI PL NZ AC PO NC

In order to demonstrate the action taken when both digits need adjustment we load 99 into AL.

14EB:0107 0409   ADD   AL,09

AX=FFA2   BX=0000   CX=0000   DX=FFFF   SP=EA04   BP=0000
SI=020F   DI=028F   DS=14EB   ES=14EB   SS=14EB   CS=14EB
IP=0109

                                                  NV UP EI NG NZ AC PO NC
                                                    *

We add 9 to the value in AL. The negative and adjust flags are set.

14EB:0109 27   DAA

AX=FF08   BX=0000   CX=0000   DX=FFFF   SP=EA04   BP=0000
SI=020F   DI=028F   DS=14EB   ES=14EB   SS=14EB   CS=14EB
IP=010A

                                                  NV UP EI PL NZ AC PO CY
                                                *   *

The values are adjusted causing a BCD carry which is reflected in the carry flag.

DAS   Decimal Adjust AL Register After Subtraction

INSTRUCTION	OPCODE	BINARY
DAS	2F	00101111

Purpose: DAS adjusts the result of subtracting two valid packed decimal operands in AL. DAS must always follow one subtraction of one pair of packed decimal numbers (one digit in each half-byte) from another to obtain a pair of valid packed decimal digits as results. CF is set if a borrow was needed.

Instruction Demonstration: The DAS instruction is used to adjust a packed BCD result after a subtract. Its action is similar to the DAA instruction except that it adjusts by subtracting 6 from the nibbles of AL instead of adding 6.

The instruction sequence:

```
14EB 0100 B011          MOV    AL,11
14EB:0102 2C19          SUB    AL,19
14EB:0104 2F            DAS
14EB:0105 B099          MOV    AL,99
14EB:0107 2C09          SUB    AL,09
14EB:0109 2F            DAS
```

After loading 11 into AL:

```
AX=FF11   BX=0000   CX=0000   DX=FFFF  SP=EA04   BP=0000
SI=020F   DI=028F   DS=14EB   ES=14EB  SS=14EB   CS=14EB
IP=0102
                                NV UP EI NG NZ NA PE NC
```

```
14EB:0102 2C19              SUB AL,19
```

```
AX=FFF8   BX=0000   CX=0000   DX=FFFF  SP=EA04   BP=0000
SI=020F   DI=028F   DS=14EB   ES=14EB  SS=14EB   CS=14EB
IP=0104
                                NV UP EI NG NZ AC PO CY
                                               *   *   *
```

The subtract sets NG, NZ, PO and CY as well as AC. AC is the important flag in this case because it triggers the adjust of the 8 in the low nibble.

```
14EB:0104 2F                DAS
```

```
AX=FF92   BX=0000   CX=0000   DX=FFFF  SP=EA04   BP=0000
SI=020F   DI=028F   DS=14EB   ES=14EB  SS=14EB   CS=14EB
IP=0105
                                NV UP EI NG NZ AC PO CY
```

DAS subtracts 6 from the low nibble because the AC flag is set. The high nibble is examined and has 6 subtracted from it because it is greater than 9. Because the high nibble was adjusted, the carry flag is set. If the high nibble had been a valid BCD digit, the carry flag would have triggered the adjustment.

```
14EB:0105 B099              MOV    AL,99
```

```
AX=FF99   BX=0000   CX=0000   DX=FFFF  SP=EA04   BP=0000
SI=020F   DI=028F   DS=14EB   ES=14EB  SS=14EB   CS=14EB
IP=0107
```

NV UP EI NG NZ AC PO CY

14EB:0107 2C09   SUB   AL,09

AX=FF90   BX=0000   CX=0000   DX=FFFF   SP=EA04   BP=0000
SI=020F   DI=028F   DS=14EB   ES=14EB   SS=14EB   CS=14EB
IP=0109

NV UP EI NG NZ NA PE NC
                      *   *   *

14EB:0109 2F   DAS

AX=FF90   BX=0000   CX=0000   DX=FFFF   SP=EA04   BP=0000
SI=020F   DI=028F   DS=14EB   ES=14EB   SS=14EB   CS=14EB
IP=010A

NV UP EI NG NZ NA PE NC

No adjustments are needed in this case so none are done.

==========

DEC   Decrement by 1

Instruction	Opcode	Binary
DEC r/m8	FE /1	11111110 mm 001 r/m
DEC r/m16	FF /1	11111111 mm 001 r/m
DEC r/m32	FF /1	11111111 mm 001 r/m
DEC r16	48 + rw	01001rrr
DEC r32	48 + rw	01001rrr

Purpose: DEC subtracts 1 from the destination operand. DEC does *not* update CF.

Instruction Demonstration: This demonstrates the DEC instruction and its effect on both the item being decremented and the flags.

The instruction sequence:

```
14EB:0100 B80200        MOV     AX,0002
14EB:0103 48            DEC     AX
14EB:0104 48            DEC     AX
14EB:0105 48            DEC     AX
```

Registers and flags after the value 2 is set into AX.

AX=0002	BX=0000	CX=0000	DX=FFFF	SP=EA04	BP=0000
SI=020F	DI=028F	DS=14EB	ES=14EB	SS=14EB	CS=14EB
IP=0103					

NV UP EI NG NZ AC PE NC

14EB:0103 48   DEC   AX

AX=0001	BX=0000	CX=0000	DX=FFFF	SP=EA04	BP=0000
SI=020F	DI=028F	DS=14EB	ES=14EB	SS=14EB	CS=14EB
IP=0104					

NV UP EI PL NZ NA PO NC
                               *   *   *

Note that one is subtracted from the target. The sign, zero, adjust and parity flags are set according to the result.

14EB:0104 48   DEC   AX

AX=0000	BX=0000	CX=0000	DX=FFFF	SP=EA04	BP=0000
SI=020F	DI=028F	DS=14EB	ES=14EB	SS=14EB	CS=14EB
IP=0105					

NV UP EI PL ZR NA PE NC
                              *   *

Note that one is subtracted from the target. The sign, zero, adjust and parity flags are set according to the result.

14EB:0105 48   DEC   AX

AX=FFFF	BX=0000	CX=0000	DX=FFFF	SP=EA04	BP=0000
SI=020F	DI=028F	DS=14EB	ES=14EB	SS=14EB	CS=14EB
IP=0106					

NV UP EI NG NZ AC PE NC
                              *   *   *

Note that one is subtracted from the target. The sign, zero, adjust and parity flags are set according to the result. Note that the carry flag is not affected.

DIV   Unsigned Integer Divide

INSTRUCTION	OPCODE	BINARY		
DIV AL,r/m8	F6 /6	11110110	mm 110	r/m
DIV AX,r/m16	F7 /6	11110111	mm 110	r/m
DIV EAX,r/m32	F7 /6	11110111	mm 110	r/m

Purpose: DIV divides an unsigned number in the accumulator by the source operand. The dividend (which is the accumulator) is twice the size of the divisor (which is the source operand). The quotient and the remainder have the same size as the divisor.

A divisor of zero or a quotient too large for the designated register cause an interrupt zero (0).

Note: Noninteger quotients are truncated to integers. The remainder is always less than the divisor. For unsigned byte division, the largest quotient is 255. For unsigned word division, the largest quotient is 65,535. For unsigned doubleword division, the largest quotient is $2^{32} - 1$.

Instruction Demonstration: This demonstrates the unsigned divide instruction. The instruction sequence:

```
14EB:0100 B80502        MOV     AX,0205
14EB:0103 B333          MOV     BL,33
14EB:0105 F6F3          DIV     BL
14EB:0107 F7F3          DIV     BX
```

The dividend is placed into AX.

```
AX=0205   BX=0033   CX=0000   DX=0000   SP=EA04   BP=0000
SI=0000   DI=0000   DS=14EB   ES=14EB   SS=14EB   CS=14EB
IP=0103
                                  NV UP EI PL NZ NA PE NC
```

Then we set the divisor in BL.

```
14EB:0103 B333                  MOV     BL,33
```

```
AX=0205   BX=0033   CX=0000   DX=0000   SP=EA04   BP=0000
SI=0000   DI=0000   DS=14EB   ES=14EB   SS=14EB   CS=14EB
IP=0105
                                  NV UP EI PL NZ NA PE NC
```

```
14EB:0105 F6F3                  DIV BL
```

```
AX=070A   BX=0033   CX=0000   DX=0000   SP=EA04   BP=0000
SI=0000   DI=0000   DS=14EB   ES=14EB   SS=14EB   CS=14EB
IP=0107
                                  NV UP EI NG NZ NA PE CY
```

Note that the short divide leaves the quotient in AL (517/51 = 10 with a remainder of 7) and the remainder in AH. The flags may be affected (NG and CY in this example) but their values are undefined.

```
14EB:0107 F7F3                  DIV BX
```

AX=0023   BX=0033   CX=0000   DX=0011   SP=EA04   BP=0000
SI=0000   DI=0000   DS=14EB   ES=14EB   SS=14EB   CS=14EB
IP=0109

NV UP EI PL NZ NA PE NC

Note that the long divide leaves the quotient in AX and the remainder in DX. Again, the flags are undefined.

ENTER   Make Stack Frame for Procedure Parameter

INSTRUCTION	OPCODE	BINARY
ENTER imm16,0	C8 iw 00	11001000
ENTER imm16,1	C8 /2 01	11001000
ENTER imm16,imm8	C8 iw ib	11001000

Purpose: ENTER creates a stack frame that can be used to implement the rules of block-structured high-level languages. A LEAVE instruction at the end of the procedure complements the ENTER.

ENTER has two parameters. The first specifies the number of bytes of dynamic storage to be allocated on the stack for the routine being entered. The second parameter corresponds to the lexical nesting level of the routine: 0 to 31. This level determines how many sets of stack frame pointers the CPU copies into the new stack frame from the proceeding frame. This list of stack frames is often called the *display*. Lexical level has *no* relationship to either the protection levels or to the I/O privilege level.

ENTER creates the new display for a procedure. Then it allocates the dynamic storage space for that procedure by decrementing ESP by the number of bytes specified in the first parameter. This new value of ESP serves as the starting point for all PUSH and POP operations within that procedure.

ENTER can be used either nested or non-nested. If the lexical level is zero, the non-nested form is used. The main procedure operates at the highest logical level, level 1. The first procedure it calls operates at the next deeper level, level 2. And so on. A level 2 procedure can access the variables in the main program because a program operating at a higher logical level (calling a program at a lower level) requires that the called procedure have access to the variables of the calling program.

A procedure calling another procedure at the *same* level implies that they are parallel procedures and should *not* have access to the variables of the calling program. The new stack frame does not include the pointer for addressing the calling procedure's stack frame. ENTER treats a reentrant procedure as a procedure calling another procedure at the same level.

Instruction Demonstration: The CALL instruction, ENTER instruction, LEAVE instruction, and RET instruction are demonstrated together since they logically "fit" with each other and complement each other. See the CALL instruction.

ESC Escape

INSTRUCTION	OPCODE	BINARY
ESC	D8 + TTT	11011TTT mod LLL r/m where TTT and LLL are opcode information for the coprocessor

Purpose: A numeric coprocessor provides an extension to the instruction set of the 80386. The coprocessor supports high-precision integer and floating-point calculations, in addition to containing a set of useful constants to enhance the speed of numeric calculations. The coprocessor operates in parallel with the CPU to provide maximum instruction throughput.

A program contains coprocessor instructions in the same instruction stream with the 80386 instructions. The system executes the coprocessor set in the same order as they appear in the stream.

ESC is a 5-bit sequence that begins with the opcodes that identify floating point numeric instructions. This sequence is "11011B." This pattern tells the 80386 to send the opcode and addresses of operands to the numerics coprocessor.

Instruction Demonstration: Not demonstrated because ESC is the signal that a coprocessor instruction needs decoding. Its action is nondemonstratable as are the prefixes, if no instruction followed them.

HLT Halt

INSTRUCTION	OPCODE	BINARY
HLT	F4	11110100

Purpose: HALT stops the execution of all instructions and places the 80386 in a HALT state. An NMI, reset, or an enabled interrupt will resume execution. A HLT would normally be the last instruction in a sequence which shuts down the system, i.e., for a checkpoint after a power failure is detected.

Instruction Demonstration: Not demonstrated since this instruction stops the processing.

IDIV Signed Divide

INSTRUCTION	OPCODE	BINARY	
IDIV r/m8	F6 /7	11110110	mm 111 r/m
IDIV AX,r/m16	F7 /7	11110111	mm 111 r/m
IDIV EAX,r/m32	F7 /7	11110111	mm 111 r/m

Purpose: IDIV does signed division. The dividend, quotient, and remainder are implicitly allocated to fixed registers (see box below), while only the divisor is given as an explicit r/m (register or memory) operand. The divisor determines which registers are to be used. Figure 10-2 shows which registers to use for IDIV.

An interrupt zero (0) is taken if a zero divisor or a quotient too large for the destination register is generated.

Size	Divisor	Quotient	Remainder	Dividend
Byte	r/m8	AL	AH	AX
Word	r/m16	AX	DX	DX:AX
Dword	r/m32	EAX	EDX	EDX:EAX

Fig. 10-2. Registers to use for IDIV.

Instruction Demonstration: This demonstrates the integer divide instruction. In some cases, various flags change as a result of the IDIV instruction; in these cases, the flags become undefined. That is, their new status is meaningless to the programmer. Their change is *not* indicated with an asterisk (*) in the following demonstration.

The instruction sequence:

```
14EB:0100 B803F8        MOV     AX,F803
14EB:0103 B370          MOV     BL,70
14EB:0105 F6FB          IDIV    BL
14EB:0107 B803F8        MOV     AX,F803
14EB:010A B390          MOV     BL,90
14EB:010C F6FB          IDIV    BL
14EB:010E B803F8        MOV     AX,F803
14EB:0111 F7FB          IDIV    BX
```

After loading the dividend (−2045) into AX:

```
AX=F803   BX=0000   CX=0000   DX=0000   SP=EA04   BP=0000
SI=0000   DI=0000   DS=14EB   ES=14EB   SS=14EB   CS=14EB
IP=0103
                                    NV UP EI PL NZ NA PE CY
```

We next load the divisor (112) into BX (and BL).

```
14EB:0103 B370               MOV     BX,70
```

AX=F803   BX=0070   CX=0000   DX=0000   SP=EA04   BP=0000
SI=0000   DI=0000   DS=14EB   ES=14EB   SS=14EB   CS=14EB
IP=0105

                                    NV UP EI PL NZ NA PE CY

14EB:0105 F6FB   IDIV   BL

AX=E3EE   BX=0070   CX=0000   DX=0000   SP=EA04   BP=0000
SI=0000   DI=0000   DS=14EB   ES=14EB   SS=14EB   CS=14EB
IP=0107

                                    NV UP EI PL NZ NA PE CY

The divide results in a signed (negative) quotient and remainder in AL and AH respectively. (−18 and −29)

We reload the dividend into AX.

14EB:0107 B803F8   MOV   AX,F803

AX=F803   BX=0070   CX=0000   DX=0000   SP=EA04   BP=0000
SI=0000   DI=0000   DS=14EB   ES=14EB   SS=14EB   CS=14EB
IP=010A

                                    NV UP EI PL NZ NA PE CY

We then change the divisor to −112 in BL.

14EB:010A B390   MOV   BL,90

AX=F803   BX=0090   CX=0000   DX=0000   SP=EA04   BP=0000
SI=0000   DI=0000   DS=14EB   ES=14EB   SS=14EB   CS=14EB
IP=010C

                                    NV UP EI PL NZ NA PE CY

14EB:010C F6FB   IDIV   BL

AX=E312   BX=0090   CX=0000   DX=0000   SP=EA04   BP=0000
SI=0000   DI=0000   DS=14EB   ES=14EB   SS=14EB   CS=14EB
IP=010E

                                    NV UP EI PL NZ NA PE NC

Note that the quotient is positive 18 while the remainder remains signed as was the dividend (negative).

Again, reloading the dividend:

14EB:010E B803F8   MOV   AX,F803

AX=F803   BX=0090   CX=0000   DX=0000   SP=EA04   BP=0000
SI=0000   DI=0000   DS=14EB   ES=14EB   SS=14EB   CS=14EB
IP=0111

                                  NV UP EI PL NZ NA PE NC

We divide the DX AX pair with the word in BX to get the following:

14EB:0111 F7FB   IDIV   BX

AX=01B8   BX=0090   CX=0000   DX=0083   SP=EA04   BP=0000
SI=0000   DI=0000   DS=14EB   ES=14EB   SS=14EB   CS=14EB
IP=0113

                                  NV UP EI NG NZ NA PE CY

We divide 63491 by 144 to get a quotient of 440 in AX and a remainder of 131 in DX. Note that the value in AX was negative if DX was not considered.

IMUL   Signed Integer Multiply

INSTRUCTION	OPCODE	BINARY
IMUL r/m8	F6 /5	11110110 mm 101 r/m
IMUL r/m16	F7 /5	11110111 mm 101 r/m
IMUL r/m32	F7 /5	11110111 mm 101 r/m
IMUL r16,r/m16	0F AF /r	00001111 10101111 mm rrr r/m
IMUL r32,r/m32	0F AF /r	00001111 10101111 mm rrr r/m
IMUL r16,r/m16,imm8	6B /r ib	01101011 mm rrr r/m
IMUL r32,r/m32,imm8	6B /r ib	01101011 mm rrr r/m
IMUL r16,imm8	6B /r ib	01101011 mm rrr r/m
IMUL r32,imm8	6B /r ib	01101011 mm rrr r/m
IMUL r16,r/m16,imm16	69 /r iw	01101001 mm rrr r/m
IMUL r32,r/m32,imm32	69 /r id	01101001 mm rrr r/m
IMUL r16,imm16	69 /r iw	01101001 mm rrr r/m
IMUL r32,imm32	69 /r id	01101001 mm rrr r/m

Purpose: IMUL performs a signed multiplication operation. This instruction has three variations:

    1. A one-operand form. The operand may be a byte, word or doubleword lo-

cated in memory or in a general register. IMUL uses EAX and EDX as implicit operands in the same way that MUL does.

2. A two-operand form. One of the source operands may be in any general register while the other may be either in memory or in a general-register. The product replaces the general-register operand.

3. A three-operand form. Two operands are source and one is destination. One of the source operands is an immediate value stored in the instruction. The second may be in memory or in any general register. The product may be stored in any general register. The immediate operand is treated as signed. If the immediate operand is a byte, the processor automatically sign-extends it to the size of the second operand before doing the multiplication.

Instruction Demonstration: This demonstrates signed multiplication. In some cases, various flags change as a result of the IMUL instruction; in these cases, the flags become undefined. That is, their new status is meaningless to the programmer. Their change is *not* indicated with an asterisk (*) in the following demonstration.

The instruction sequence:

```
14EB:0100 B8EEFF        MOV     AX,FFEE
14EB:0103 B370          MOV     BL,70
14EB:0105 F6EB          IMUL    BL
14EB:0107 B8EEFF        MOV     AX,FFEE
14EB:010A F7EB          IMUL    BX
```

Set up the registers for the multiply:

```
14EB:0100 B8EEFF                MOV     AX,FFEE
```

```
AX=FFEE   BX=0070   CX=0000   DX=0000   SP=EA04   BP=0000
SI=0000   DI=0000   DS=14EB   ES=14EB   SS=14EB   CS=14EB
IP=0103
                                NV UP EI NG NZ AC PO NC
```

We load a −18 into AX (and AL).

```
14EB:0103 B370                  MOV     BL,70
```

```
AX=FFEE   BX=0070   CX=0000   DX=0000   SP=EA04   BP−0000
SI=0000   DI=0000   DS=14EB   ES=14EB   SS=14EB   CS=14EB
IP=0105
                                NV UP EI NG NZ AC PO NC
```

A positive multiplier of 112 into BL.

```
14EB:0105 F6EB                  IMUL  BL
```

```
AX=F820   BX=0070   CX=0000   DX=0000   SP=EA04   BP=0000
SI=0000   DI=0000   DS=14EB   ES=14EB   SS=14EB   CS=14EB
IP=0107
```

OV UP EI NG NZ AC PO CY

The negative product is formed in AX −2016.
Restoring the value in AX,

```
14EB:0107 B8EEFF          MOV     AX,FFEE
```

```
AX=FFEE   BX=0070   CX=0000   DX=0000   SP=EA04   BP=0000
SI=0000   DI=0000   DS=14EB   ES=14EB   SS=14EB   CS=14EB
IP=010A
```

OV UP EI NG NZ AC PO CY

and multiplying by the word value in BX −

```
14EB:010A F7EB          IMUL    BX
```

```
AX=F820   BX=0070   CX=0000   DX=FFFF   SP=EA04   BP=0000
SI=0000   DI=0000   DS=14EB   ES=14EB   SS=14EB   CS=14EB
IP=010C
```

NV UP EI NG NZ AC PO NC

forms the product in the DX−AX register pair (in this case by extending the negative sign through DX).

IN   Input from Port

INSTRUCTION	OPCODE	BINARY
IN AL,imm8	E4 ib	11100100
IN AX,imm8	E5 ib	11100101
IN EAX,imm8	E5 ib	11100101
IN AL,DX	EC	11101100
IN AX,DX	ED	11101101
IN EAX,DX	ED	11101101

Purpose: IN brings a byte or word from a port and stores it in a register (AL, AX, or EAX). The port is specified by the second operand. The port is accessed by placing its number into the DX register and using an IN instruction with DX as the second parameter.

Instruction Demonstration: The IN, INS, OUT, and OUTS instructions are demonstrated together because of their relationship with each other. This demonstrates the use of the input and output group of instructions.

The instruction sequence:

```
14EB:0100 90              NOP
14EB:0101 E440            IN      AL,40
14EB:0103 90              NOP
14EB:0104 E640            OUT     40,AL
14EB:0106 90              NOP
14EB:0107 BA7803          MOV     DX,0378
14EB:010A EC              IN      AL,DX
14EB:010B 90              NOP
14EB:010C EE              OUT     DX,AL
14EB:010D 90              NOP
14EB:010E BF0002          MOV     DI,0200
14EB:0111 6C              INSB
14EB:0112 6D              INSW
14EB:0113 BE0002          MOV     SI,0200
14EB:0116 6E              OUTSB
14EB:0117 6F              OUTSW
```

The registers and flags at the start:

```
AX=0000  BX=0000  CX=0008  DX=0000  SP=EA04  BP=0000
SI=0000  DI=0000  DS=14EB  ES=14EB  SS=14EB  CS=14EB
IP=0101
                                 NV UP EI PL NZ NA PO NC

14EB:0101 E440                IN    AL,40


AX=001A  BX=0000  CX=0008  DX=0000  SP=EA04  BP=0000
SI=0000  DI=0000  DS=14EB  ES=14EB  SS=14EB  CS=14EB
IP=0103
                                 NV UP EI PL NZ NA PO NC
```

We read a byte value from port X'40' or 64 into AL.

```
14EB:0103 90                  NOP


AX=001A  BX=0000  CX=0008  DX=0000  SP=EA04  BP=0000
SI=0000  DI=0000  DS=14EB  ES=14EB  SS=14EB  CS=14EB
IP=0104
                                 NV UP EI PL NZ NA PO NC
```

14EB:0104 E640   OUT   40,AL

AX=001A   BX=0000   CX=0008   DX=0000   SP=EA04   BP=0000
SI=0000   DI=0000   DS=14EB   ES=14EB   SS=14EB   CS=14EB
IP=0106
                                   NV UP EI PL NZ NA PO NC

We output the byte in AL to port 40.

14EB:0106 90   NOP

AX=001A   BX=0000   CX=0008   DX=0000   SP=EA04   BP=0000
SI=0000   DI=0000   DS=14EB   ES=14EB   SS=14EB   CS=14EB
IP=0107
                                   NV UP EI PL NZ NA PO NC

14EB:0107 BA7803   MOV   DX,0378

AX=001A   BX=0000   CX=0008   DX=0378   SP=EA04   BP=0000
SI=0000   DI=0000   DS=14EB   ES=14EB   SS=14EB   CS=14EB
IP=010A
                                   NV UP EI PL NZ NA PO NC

14EB:010A EC   IN   AL,DX

AX=00AA   BX=0000   CX=0008   DX=0378   SP=EA04   BP=0000
SI=0000   DI=0000   DS=14EB   ES=14EB   SS=14EB   CS=14EB
IP=010B
                                   NV UP EI PL NZ NA PO NC

We read a byte from the port addressed by DX into AL. Note that the port address is above hex FF (the largest port addressable in an 8 bit immediate value.)

14EB:010B 90   NOP

AX=00AA   BX=0000   CX=0008   DX=0378   SP=EA04   BP=0000
SI=0000   DI=0000   DS=14EB   ES=14EB   SS=14EB   CS=14EB
IP=010C
                                   NV UP EI PL NZ NA PO NC

14EB:010C EE   OUT   DX,AL

AX=00AA   BX=0000   CX=0008   DX=0378   SP=EA04   BP=0000

SI=0000   DI=0000   DS=14EB   ES=14EB   SS=14EB   CS=14EB
IP=010D

                                      NV UP EI PL NZ NA PO NC

We output the byte to the port which has its address in DX.

14EB:010D 90   NOP

AX=00AA   BX=0000   CX=0008   DX=0378   SP=EA04   BP=0000
SI=0000   DI=0000   DS=14EB   ES=14EB   SS=14EB   CS=14EB
IP=010E

                                        NV UP EI PL NZ NA PO NC

14EB:010E BF0002   MOV   DI,0200

AX=00AA   BX=0000   CX=0008   DX=0378   SP=EA04   BP=0000
SI=0000   DI=0200   DS=14EB   ES=14EB   SS=14EB   CS=14EB
IP=0111

                                        NV UP EI PL NZ NA PO NC

14EB:0111 6C   INSB

AX=00AA   BX=0000   CX=0008   DX=0378   SP=EA04   BP=0000
SI=0000   DI=0201   DS=14EB   ES=14EB   SS=14EB   CS=14EB
IP=0112

                                        NV UP EI PL NZ NA PO NC

Note that the index (DI) has been stepped by one.

14EB:0112 6D   INSW

AX=00AA   BX=0000   CX=0008   DX=0378   SP=EA04   BP=0000
SI=0000   DI=0203   DS=14EB   ES=14EB   SS=14EB   CS=14EB
IP=0113

                                        NV UP EI PL NZ NA PO NC

Again DI is stepped but this time by the size of the word that was read.

14EB:0113 BE0002   MOV   SI,0200

AX=00AA   BX=0000   CX=0008   DX=0378   SP=EA04   BP=0000
SI=0200   DI=0203   DS=14EB   ES=14EB   SS=14EB   CS=14EB
IP=0116

                                        NV UP EI PL NZ NA PO NC

14EB:0116 6E   OUTSB

AX=00AA   BX=0000   CX=0008   DX=0378   SP=EA04   BP=0000
SI=0201   DI=0203   DS=14EB   ES−14EB   SS=14EB   CS=14EB
IP=0117

NV UP EI PL NZ NA PO NC

Note that the SI value has been incremented by the size of the value output.

14EB:0117 6F   OUTSW

AX=00AA   BX=0000   CX=0008   DX=0378   SP=EA04   BP=0000
SI=0203   DI=0203   DS=14EB   ES=14EB   SS=14EB   CS=14EB
IP=0118

NV UP EI PL NZ NA PO NC

Again the output pointer is incremented, this time by 2 for the size of a word. The data read with the INS instructions:

14EB:0200   AA AA 7F

INC   Increment by 1

INSTRUCTION	OPCODE	BINARY	
INC r/m8	FE /0	11111110	mm 000 r/m
INC r/m16	FF /0	11111111	mm 000 r/m
INC r/m32	FF /0	11111111	mm 000 r/m
INC r16	40 + rw	01000rrr	
INC r32	40 + rd	01000rrr	

Purpose: INC adds one to the destination operand, but (unlike ADD) INC does not affect CF.

Instruction Demonstration: This demonstrates the effects of the INC instruction. The instruction sequence:

```
14EB:0100 B8FE00          MOV     AX,00FE
14EB:0103 FEC0            INC     AL
14EB:0105 FEC0            INC     AL
14EB:0107 FEC0            INC     AL
```

We load a −2 into AL:

AX=00FE   BX=0070   CX=0000   DX=FFFF   SP=EA04   BP=0000

SI=0000   DI=0000   DS=14EB   ES=14EB   SS=14EB   CS=14EB
IP=0103

                                      NV UP EI NG NZ AC PO NC

14EB:0103 FEC0   INC AL

AX=00FF   BX=0070   CX=0000   DX=FFFF   SP=EA04   BP=0000
SI=0000   DI=0000   DS=14EB   ES=14EB   SS=14EB   CS=14EB
IP=0105

                                      NV UP EI NG NZ NA PE NC
                                                   *   *   *

We increment AL to −1. Note that the flags normally affected by an arithmetic instruction are also affected by INC.

14EB:0105 FEC0   INC AL

AX=0000   BX=0070   CX=0000   DX=FFFF   SP=EA04   BP=0000
SI=0000   DI=0000   DS=14EB   ES=14EB   SS=14EB   CS=14EB
IP=0107

                                      NV UP EI PL ZR AC PE NC
                                                *   *   *

In incrementing from −1 to zero we should have formed a carry. In this way—not affecting the carry flag—INC differs from normal arithmetic instructions.

14EB:0107 FEC0   INC AL

AX=0001   BX=0070   CX=0000   DX=FFFF   SP=EA04   BP=0000
SI=0000   DI=0000   DS=14EB   ES=14EB   SS=14EB   CS=14EB
IP=0109

                                      NV UP EI PL NZ NA PO NC
                                                *   *

In incrementing from zero to one, the flags reflect the change.

───

INS   **Input String from Port**
INSB   **Input Byte**
INSW   **Input Word**
INSD   **Input Doubleword**

INSTRUCTION	OPCODE	BINARY
INS r/m8,DX	6C	01101100
INS r/m16,DX	6D	01101101
INS r/m32,DX	6D	01101101

NOTE: INSB is a common assembler mnemonic for INS r/m8,DX
          INSW is a common assembler mnemonic for INS r/m16,DX
          INSD is a common assembler mnemonic for INS r/m32,DX

Purpose: These instructions allow a read from a device into memory, the input device being specified in the DX register. The data is read into the segment specified by ES and no segment override is possible. INS does *not* allow port number specification as an immediate value. The port must be addressed through DX.

These instructions normally use a REP prefix, to indicate the reading of the number of bytes as specified in CX.

Instruction Demonstration: The IN INS OUT OUTS instructions are demonstrated together because of their relationship with each other. See the IN instruction.

INT   Call to Interrupt Procedure
INTO   Interrupt on Overflow

INSTRUCTION	OPCODE	BINARY
INT 3	CC	11001100
INT imm8	CD ib	11001101
INTO	CE	11001110

Purpose: INT transfers control from one code segment location to another. These locations can be within the same code segment (*near*) or in different code segments (*far*). INT is a software-generated interrupt that allows a programmer to transfer control to an interrupt service routine from within a program.

INT*n* activates the interrupt service that corresponds to the number coded in the instruction. INT may specify any interrupt type. Note that Interrupts 0-31 are reserved by Intel. INT*n* returns control at the end of the service routine with an IRET.

INTO invokes Interrupt 4 if OF is set. Interrupt 4 is reserved for this purpose. OF is set by several arithmetic, logical, and string instructions.

Instruction Demonstration: The INT and IRET instructions are demonstrated together because of their interrelationship. This demonstrates the INT and IRET instructions.

The instruction sequence:

We legitimately take interrupt 42 from MS/DOS

```
14EB:0100 BA0002          MOV    DX,0200
14EB:0103 B042            MOV    AL,42
14EB:0105 B425            MOV    AH,25
14EB:0107 CD21            INT  21
```

and then use it as our interrupt.

```
14EB:0109 90              NOP
14EB:010A 90              NOP
14EB:010B CD42            INT  42
14EB:010D 90              NOP
```

Our interrupt handling routine:

```
14EB:0200 90              NOP
14EB:0201 CF              IRET
```

The registers and flags at the start:

```
AX=0000   BX=0000   CX=0008   DX=0000   SP=EA04   BP=0000
SI=0203   DI=0203   DS=14EB   ES=14EB   SS=14EB   CS=14EB
IP=0100
                                  NV UP EI PL NZ NA PO NC
```

```
14EB:0100 BA0002          MOV    DX,0200
```

```
AX=0000   BX=0000   CX=0008   DX=0200   SP=EA04   BP=0000
SI=0203   DI=0203   DS=14EB   ES=14EB   SS=14EB   CS=14EB
IP=0103
                                  NV UP EI PL NZ NA PO NC
```

We tell MS-DOS where our handler is located (DS:DX),

```
14EB:0103 B042            MOV    AL,42
```

```
AX=0042   BX=0000   CX=0008   DX=0200   SP=EA04   BP=0000
SI=0203   DI=0203   DS=14EB   ES=14EB   SS=14EB   CS=14EB
IP=0105
                                  NV UP EI PL NZ NA PO NC
```

which interrupt we want,

```
14EB:0105 B425            MOV    AH,25
```

```
AX=2542   BX=0000   CX=0008   DX−0200   SP=EA04   BP=0000
SI=0203   DI=0203   DS=14EB   ES=14EB   SS=14EB   CS=14EB
IP=0107
                                  NV UP EI PL NZ NA PO NC
```

and that we want a set vector operation.

```
14EB:0107 CD21            INT  21
```

AX=2542   BX=0000   CX=0008   DX=0200   SP=EA04   BP=0000
SI=0203   DI=0203   DS=14EB   ES=14EB   SS=14EB   CS=14EB
IP=0109

                                      NV UP EI PL NZ NA PO NC

We then call MS-DOS with a DOS CALL INT.

14EB:0109 90   NOP

AX=2542   BX=0000   CX=0008   DX=0200   SP=EA04   BP=0000
SI=0203   DI=0203   DS=14EB   ES=14EB   SS=14EB   CS=14EB
IP=010A

                                      NV UP EI PL NZ NA PO NC

The results:

        INT Vector 40   41   42   43
        0000:0100 59 EC 00 F0 20 00 3D 08-00 02 EB 14 FC 80 00 F0

14EB:010A 90   NOP

AX=2542   BX=0000   CX=0008   DX=0200   SP=EA04   BP=0000
SI=0203   DI=0203   DS=14EB   ES=14EB   SS=14EB   CS=14EB
IP=010B

                                      NV UP EI PL NZ NA PO NC

14EB:010B CD42   INT 42

AX=2542   BX=0000   CX=0008   DX=0200   SP=E9FE   BP=0000
SI=0203   DI=0203   DS=14EB   ES=14EB   SS=14EB   CS=14EB
IP=0200

                                      NV UP DI PL NZ NA PO NC

The INT places the flags, CS, and IP registers on the stack for use in returning.

14EB:E9FE 0D 01 EB 14 02 72

14EB:0200 90   NOP

AX=2542   BX=0000   CX=0008   DX=0200   SP=E9FE   BP=0000
SI=0203   DI=0203   DS=14EB   ES=14EB   SS=14EB   CS=14EB
IP=0201

                                      NV UP DI PL NZ NA PO NC

We handle the interrupt and

14EB:0201 CF   IRET

AX=2542   BX=0000   CX=0008   DX=0200   SP=EA04   BP=0000
SI=0203   DI=0203   DS=14EB   ES=14EB   SS=14EB   CS=14EB
IP=010D

                                   NV UP EI PL NZ NA PO NC

Return. Note that IP and SP have been adjusted.

IRET   **Return from Interrupt**
IRETD   **Return from Interrupt—32-bit Mode**

INSTRUCTION	OPCODE	BINARY
IRET	CF	11001111
IRETD	CF	11001111

Purpose: IRET returns control to an interrupted procedure. IRET differs from RET in that it also POPs the flags from the stack into the flags register. The flags are stored on the stack by the interrupt mechanism.

Note: In the case of IRET, the flags register is Flags. If, IRETD is used, then it's the EFLAGS register.

Instruction Demonstration: The INT and IRET instructions are demonstrated together because of their inter-relationship. See the INT instruction.

JMP   **Jump**
Jcc   **Jump on some Condition Code**

INSTRUCTION	OPCODE	BINARY
JA rel8	77 cb	01110111
JAE rel8	73 cb	01110011
JB rel8	72 cb	01110010
JBE rel8	76 cb	01110110
JC rel8	72 cb	01110010
JCXZ rel8	E3 cb	11100011
JECXZ rel8	E3 cb	11100011

JE rel8	74 cb	01110100	
JZ rel8	74 cb	01110100	
JG rel8	7F cb	01111111	
JGE rel88	7D cb	01111101	
JL rel8	7C cb	01111100	
JLE rel8	7E cb	01111110	
JNA rel8	76 cb	01110110	
JNAE rel8	72 cb	01110010	
JNB rel8	73 cb	01110011	
JNBE rel8	77 cb	01110111	
JNC rel8	73 cb	01110011	
JNE rel8	75 cb	01110101	
JNG rel8	7E cb	01111110	
JNGE rel8	7C cb	01111100	
JNL rel8	7D cb	01111101	
JNLE rel8	7F cb	01111111	
JNO rel8	71 cb	01110001	
JNP rel8	7B cb	01111011	
JNS rel8	79 cb	01111001	
JNZ rel8	75 cb	01110101	
JO rel8	70 cb	01110000	
JP rel8	7A cb	01111010	
JPE rel8	7A cb	01111010	
JPO rel8	7B cb	01111011	
JS rel8	78 cb	01111000	
JZ rel8	74 cb	01110100	
JA rel16/32	0F 87 cw/cd	00001111	10000111
JAE rel16/32	0F 83 cw/cd	00001111	10000011
JB rel16/32	0F 82 cw/cd	00001111	10000010
JBE rel16/32	0F 86 cw/cd	00001111	10000110
JC rel16/32	0F 82 cw/cd	00001111	10000010
JE rel16/32	0F 84 cw/cd	00001111	10000100
JZ rel16/32	0F 84 cw/cd	00001111	10000100
JG rel16/32	0F 8F cw/cd	00001111	10001111
JGE rel16/32	0F 8D cw/cd	00001111	10001101
JL rel16/32	0F 8C cw/cd	00001111	10001100
JLE rel16/32	0F 8E cw/cd	00001111	10001110
JNA rel16/32	0F 86 cw/cd	00001111	10000110
JNAE rel16/32	0F 82 cw/cd	00001111	10000010
JNB rel16/32	0F 83 cw/cd	00001111	10000011
JNBE rel16/32	0F 87 cw/cd	00001111	10000111
JNC rel16/32	0F 83 cw/cd	00001111	10000011
JNE rel16/32	0F 85 cw/cd	00001111	10000101
JNG rel16/32	0F 8E cw/cd	00001111	10001110
JNGE rel16/32	0F 8C cw/cd	00001111	10001100
JNL rel16/32	0F 8D cw/cd	00001111	10001101

JNLE rel16/32	0F 8F cw/cd	00001111	10001111
JNO rel16/32	0F 81 cw/cd	00001111	10000001
JNP rel16/32	0F 8B cw/cd	00001111	10001011
JNS rel16/32	0F 89 cw/cd	00001111	10001001
JNZ rel16/32	0F 85 cw/cd	00001111	10000101
JO rel16/32	0F 80 cw/cd	00001111	10000000
JP rel16/32	0F 8A cw/cd	00001111	10001010
JPE rel16/32	0F 8A cw/cd	00001111	10001010
JPO rel16/32	0F 8B cw/cd	00001111	10001011
JS rel16/32	0F 88 cw/cd	00001111	10001000
JZ rel16/32	0F 84 cw/cd	00001111	10000100

Purpose: JMP transfers control from one code segment location to another. These locations can be within the same code segment (*near*) or in different code segments (*far*). JMP unconditionally transfers control to the target location and is a one-way transfer. JMP does *not* save a return address on the stack.

JMP's implementation varies depending on whether the address is directly specified within the instruction or indirectly through a register or memory. A direct JMP includes the destination address as part of the instruction. An indirect JMP gets the destination address through a register or a pointer variable. An indirect JMP specifies an absolute address by one of the following ways: (1) a register modifies the address of the memory pointer to select a destination address; (2) the program can JMP to a location specified by a general register (EAX, EDX, ECS, EBX, EBP, ESI, or EDI)—the 80386 moves this 32-bit value into EIP and resumes execution; or (3) the 80386 obtains the destination address from a memory operand specified in the instruction.

The following are conditional transfer instructions that may or may not transfer control. It depends on the state of the CPU flags when the instruction executes:

JA/JNBE	Above, not below nor equal
JAE/JNB	Above or equal, not below
JB/NJAE	Below, not above nor equal
JBE/JNA	Below or equal, not above
JC	Carry
JE/JZ	Equal, zero
JNC	Not carry
JNE/JNZ	Not equal, not zero
JNP/JPO	Not parity, parity odd
JP/JPE	Parity, parity even

The following JMP instructions are signed control transfers:

JG/JNLE	Greater, not less nor equal
JGE/JNL	Greater or equal, not less
JL/JNGE	Less, not greater nor equal
JLE/JNG	Less or equal, not greater

JNO	Not overflow
JNS	Not sign (positive, including zero)
JO	Overflow
JS	Sign (negative)

JCXZ (Jump if ECX is zero) branches to the label specified in the instruction if it finds a value of zero in the ECX register. JCXZ is useful in that sometimes it is desirable to design a loop that executes zero times if the count variable in ECX is initialized to zero. When used with repeated string scan and compare instructions, JCXZ determines whether the repetitions ended due to a zero in ECX or to satisfaction of the scan or compare conditions.

Instruction Demonstration 1: This demonstrates the unconditional JMP instruction.

The instruction sequence:

```
14EB:0100 29C0        SUB    AX,AX
14EB:0102 750C        JNZ    0110
14EB:0104 EB0A        JMP    0110
```

The subtract has set the zero flag:

```
AX=0000  BX=0070  CX=0000  DX=FFFF  SP=EA04  BP=0000
SI=0000  DI=0000  DS=14EB  ES=14EB  SS=14EB  CS=14EB
IP=0102
                                   NV UP EI PL ZR NA PE NC
                                                    *
```

```
14EB:0102 750C              JNZ    0110
```

```
AX=0000  BX=0070  CX=0000  DX=FFFF  SP=EA04  BP=0000
SI=0000  DI=0000  DS=14EB  ES=14EB  SS=14EB  CS=14EB
IP=0104
                                   NV UP EI PL ZR NA PE NC
```

The JNZ tests for the condition NZ which is false. IP advances to the next sequential instruction.

```
14EB:0104 EB0A              JMP    0110
```

```
AX=0000  BX=0070  CX=0000  DX=FFFF  SP=EA04  BP=0000
SI=0000  DI=0000  DS=14EB  ES=14EB  SS=14EB  CS=14EB
IP=0110
                                   NV UP EI PL ZR NA PE NC
```

The JMP instruction alters program flow unconditionally. No flags or other conditions are tested.

Instruction Demonstration 2: This demonstrates the conditional jump instruction. The instruction sequence:

```
14EB:0100 29C0          SUB   AX,AX
14EB:0102 750C          JNZ   0110
14EB:0104 740A          JZ    0110
14EB:0106 90            NOP
```

Note that the subtract set the zero flag.

```
AX=0000  BX=0070  CX=0000  DX=FFFF  SP=EA04  BP=0000
SI=0000  DI=0000  DS=14EB  ES=14EB  SS=14EB  CS=14EB
IP=0102
                              NV UP EI PL ZR NA PE NC
                                               *
```

We encounter a conditional jump the JNZ.

```
14EB:0102 750C                JNZ   0110
```

```
AX=0000  BX=0070  CX=0000  DX=FFFF  SP=EA04  BP=0000
SI=0000  DI=0000  DS=14EB  ES=14EB  SS=14EB  CS=14EB
IP=0104
                              NV UP EI PL ZR NA PE NC
```

Note that the instruction pointer advances to the next sequential instruction because the tested condition is false. The condition tested by the JZ instruction is true, however. Note the resulting effect on the instruction pointer.

```
14EB:0104 740A                JZ   0110
```

```
AX-0000  BX=0070  CX-0000  DX-FFFF  SP=EA04  BP=0000
SI=0000  DI=0000  DS=14EB  ES=14EB  SS=14EB  CS=14EB
IP=0110
                              NV UP EI PL ZR NA PE NC
```

The sequential flow of instructions has been altered.

Instruction Demonstration 3: The JCXZ instruction tests the value in the CX register and jumps if the CX contains zeros. The importance of this instruction lies in the string REP instruction prefix and the LOOP instruction. Both use the CX register as a counter. The JCXZ provides a single instruction escape at the beginning of a sequence.

The instruction sequence:

```
14EB:0100 E302          JCXZ    0104
14EB:0102 EBFC          JMP     0100
14EB:0104 B90100        MOV     CX,0001
14EB:0107 E3FB          JCXZ    0104
```

The registers and flags at the start:

```
AX=0000   BX=0070   CX=0000   DX=FFFF   SP=EA04   BP=0000
SI=0000   DI=0000   DS=14EB   ES=14EB   SS=14EB   CS=14EB
IP=0100
                                        NV UP EI PL ZR NA PE NC
```

Note that CX is zero.

```
14EB:0100 E302             JCXZ    0104
```

```
AX=0000   BX=0070   CX=0000   DX=FFFF   SP=EA04   BP=0000
SI=0000   DI=0000   DS=14EB   ES=14EB   SS=14EB   CS=14EB
IP=0104
                                        NV UP EI PL ZR NA PE NC
```

The JCXZ instruction transfers to the MOV, bypassing the next instruction (the JMP to 100).

```
14EB:0104 B90100           MOV     CX,0001
```

```
AX=0000   BX=0070   CX=0001   DX=FFFF   SP=EA04   BP=0000
SI=0000   DI=0000   DS=14EB   ES=14EB   SS=14EB   CS=14EB
IP=0107
                                        NV UP EI PL ZR NA PE NC
```

The value in CX is set non zero.

```
14EB:0107 E3FB             JCXZ    0104
```

```
AX=0000   BX=0070   CX=0001   DX=FFFF   SP=EA04   BP=0000
SI=0000   DI=0000   DS=14EB   ES=14EB   SS=14EB   CS=14EB
IP=0109
                                        NV UP EI PL ZR NA PE NC
```

Because of this, the JCXZ allows sequential execution of the instructions that follow it.

LAHF   Load Flags into AH Register

Instruction	Opcode	Binary
LAHF	9F	10011111

Purpose: Though specific instructions exist to alter CF and DF, there is no direct way of altering the other applications-oriented flags. The flag transfer instructions (LAHF and SAHF) allow a program to alter the other flag bits with the bit manipulation instructions after transferring these flags to the stack or the AH register.

LAHF copies SF, ZF, AF, PF, and CF to AH bits 7, 6, 4, 2, and 0, respectively. The contents of the remaining bits (5, 3, and 1) are undefined. The flags remain unaffected.

Instruction Demonstration: The LAHF instruction copies the low byte of the flags word to AH.

The instruction sequence:

```
14EB:0100 29C0            SUB AX,AX
14EB:0102 9F              LAHF
```

The subtract sets the sign, zero, and parity flags:

```
AX=0000   BX=0070   CX=0001   DX=FFFF   SP=EA04   BP=0000
SI=0000   DI=0000   DS=14EB   ES=14EB   SS=14EB   CS=14EB
IP=0102
                                    NV UP EI PL ZR NA PE NC

14EB:0102 9F                    LAHF

AX=4600   BX=0070   CX=0001   DX=FFFF   SP=EA04   BP=0000
SI=0000   DI=0000   DS=14EB   ES=14EB   SS=14EB   CS=14EB
IP=0103
                                    NV UP EI PL ZR NA PE NC
```

The LAHF instruction copies the flags into AH. Note that 46 is 0 1 0 0 0 1 1 0 in binary and that the flags are: PL ZR xx NA xx PE xx NC.

LAR   Load Access Rights Byte

Instruction	Opcode	Binary		
LAR r16,r/m16	0F 02 /r	00001111 00000010	mm rrr r/m
LAR r32,r/m32	0F 02 /r	00001111 00000010	mm rrr r/m

Type	Name
1	Available 80286 TSS
2	LDT
3	Busy 80286 Call Gate
4	80286 Call Gate
5	80286/80386 Task Gate
6	80286 Trap Gate
7	80286 Interrupt Gate
9	Available 80386 TSS
B	Busy 80386 TSS
C	80386 Call Gate
E	80386 Trap Gate
F	80386 Interrupt Gate

Note: Types 0, 8, A, and D are invalid.

Fig. 10-3. Valid special segment and gate descriptor types.

Purpose: LAR reads a segment descriptor and puts the granularity (bit 23), programmer available (bit 20), Present (bit 15), DPL (bit 14), Type (bit 9-11), and accessed (bit 8) into a 32-bit register. If the user specifies a 16-bit register, the granularity, and programmer available bits are not moved.

Note: only the following are valid special segment and gate descriptor types:

Instruction Demonstration: The LAR instruction loads a masked image of the second doubleword of the descriptor selected by the second operand into the register specified by the first operand.

The instruction sequence:

0070:0100 6629C0   SUB   EAX,EAX

```
0070:0103 B84000              MOV    AX,0040
0070:0106 6689C3              MOV    EBX,EAX
0070:0109 660F02C3            LAR    EAX,EBX
0070:010D 90                  NOP
```

Because the 32 bit form of the registers destroy our normal format, thus only the registers affected are displayed.

EAX=00000000   EBX=00000000
IP=0070:0100

                                        NV UP EI PL NZ NA PE NC

0070:0100 6629C0   SUB   EAX,EAX

EAX=00000000   EBX=00000000
IP=0070:0103

                                        NV UP EI PL ZR NA PE NC

We set a selector into EAX.

0070:0103 B84000   MOV   AX,0040

EAX=00000400   EBX=00000000
IP=0070:0106

                                        NV UP EI PL ZR NA PE NC

and into EBX.

0070:0106 6689C3   MOV   EBX,EAX

EAX=00000040   EBX=00000040
IP=0070:0109

                                        NV UP EI PL ZR NA PE NC

We check the access rights for the descriptor thus selected.

Descriptor 0040 67 00 98 E8 00 8B 00 00
(Our active TSS segment)

0070:0109 660F02C3   LAR EAX,EBX

00FxFF00 is the mask

EAX=00008B00   EBX=00000040
IP=0070:010D

NV UP EI PL ZR NA PE NC

The zero flag is set. If the descriptor were not accessible either because of privilege or GDT or LDT limits, the access bytes are not loaded and the zero flag is reset.

0070:010D 90   NOP

LEA   Load Effective Address

INSTRUCTION	OPCODE	BINARY		
LEA r16,m	8D /r	10001101	mm rrr r/m	
LEA r32,m	8D /r	10001101	mm rrr r/m	

Purpose: LEA transfers the offset of the source operand, rather than its value, to the destination operand. The source operand must be a memory operand. The destination operand must be a general register. LEA is particularly useful for initializing registers before the execution of the string primitives or the XLAT.

Instruction Demonstration: The LEA instruction loads the offset portion of the address into the register specified.

The instruction:

14EB:0100 8D9C0402   LEA BX,[SI+0204]

The registers and flags at the start:

AX=4600   BX=0070   CX=0001   DX=FFFF   SP=EA04   BP=0000
SI=0100   DI=0000   DS=14EB   ES=14EB   SS=14EB   CS=14EB
IP=0100

NV UP EI PL ZR NA PE NC

14EB:0100 8D9C0402   LEA BX,[SI+0204]

AX=4600   BX=0304   CX=0001   DX=FFFF   SP=EA04   BP=0000
SI=0100   DI=0000   DS=14EB   ES=14EB   SS=14EB   CS=14EB
IP=0104

NV UP EI PL ZR NA PE NC

LEA loads the combined offset into the target register.

LEAVE   High Level Procedure Exit

INSTRUCTION	OPCODE	BINARY
LEAVE	C9	11001001

Purpose: LEAVE reverses the action of the previous ENTER. LEAVE does not use any operands. LEAVE copies EBP to ESP to release all stack space allocated to the procedure by the most recent ENTER. Then LEAVE pops the old value of EBP from the stack. A subsequent RET can then remove any arguments that were pushed on the stack by the calling program for use by the called procedure.

Instruction Demonstration: The CALL instruction, ENTER instruction, LEAVE instruction, and RET instruction are demonstrated together since they logically "fit" with each other and complement each other. See the CALL instruction.

LGDT   Load Global Descriptor Table Register
LIDT   Load Interrupt Descriptor Table Register

INSTRUCTION	OPCODE	BINARY
LGDT m16&32	0F 01 /2	00001111 00000001 mm 010 r/m
LIDT m16&32	0F 01 /3	00001111 00000001 mm 011 r/m

Purpose: LIDT tells the hardware where to go in case of interrupts. Both GDT and IDT are loaded at system reset (initialization of the operating system). This generally happens at the beginning of the work session.

Instruction Demonstration: See the program in Appendix 5.

LGS   Load Full Pointer
LSS   Load Pointer Using SS
LDS   Load Pointer Using DS
LES   Load Pointer Using ES
LFS   Load Pointer Using FS

INSTRUCTION	OPCODE	BINARY
LDS r16,m16:16	C5 /r	11000101 mm rrr r/m
LDS r32,m16:32	C5 /r	11000101 mm rrr r/m
LSS r16,m16:16	0F B2 /r	00001111 10110010 mm rrr r/m
LSS r32,m16:32	0F B2 /r	00001111 10110010 mm rrr r/m
LES r16,m16:16	C4 /r	11000100 mm rrr r/m
LES r32,m16:32	C4 /r	11000100 mm rrr r/m
LFS r16,m16:16	0F B4 /r	00001111 10110100 mm rrr r/m
LFS r32,m16:32	0F B4 /r	00001111 10110100 mm rrr r/m

| LGS r16,m16:16 | 0F B5 /r | 00001111 10110101 mm rrr r/m |
| LGS r32,m16:32 | 0F B5 /r | 00001111 10110101 mm rrr r/m |

Purpose: The data pointer instructions load a pointer which consists of a segment selector and an offset into a segment register and a general register.

LDS transfers a pointer variable from the source operand to DS and the destination register. The source operand must be a memory operand. The destination operand must be a general register. DS receives the segment-selector of the pointer. The destination register receives the offset part of the pointer, which points to a specific location within the segment.

The other instructions use the various registers, as noted in the instruction mnemonic.

LSS is particularly important because it allows the two registers that identify the stack (SS:ESP) to be changed in one uninterruptable operation.

Instruction Demonstration: The instruction group LGS/LSS/LDS/LES/LFS loads a full pointer into the indicated segment register and a specified pointer register. The value loaded is either a 16 or 32 bit pointer and a 16 bit selector. LGS/LDS/LES/LFS are convenient for loading full pointers. LSS is the only completely safe way of loading a stack pointer/stack segment descriptor pair. Even though the 8086-80286 automatically disable interrupts for one instruction following a MOV SS (as does the 80386), the use of two instructions on the 80386 could cause the two to be separated by a page fault. LSS maintains full stack integrity. The condition code is not changed.

```
14EB:0100 90C506          NOP
14EB:0101 C5065000         LDS    AX,[50]
14EB:0105 0FB2265000       LSS    SP,[54]
14EB:010A 90               NOP
```

The data to be loaded   DW   100H,1500H,200H,1580H

14EB:0050 00 01 00 15 00 02 80 15

The registers at the start.

```
AX=0000   BX=0000   CX=0000   DX=0000   SP=EA04   BP=0000
SI=0000   DI=0000   DS=14EB   ES=14EB   SS=14EB   CS=14EB
IP=0101
                                        NV UP EI PL ZR NA PE NC
```

Note the effect of LDS. Both AX and DS are changed in the one instruction.

14EB:0101 C5065000   LDS   AX,[0050]

```
AX=0100   BX=0000   CX=0000   DX=0000   SP=EA04   BP=0000
SI=0000   DI=0000   DS=1500   ES=14EB   SS=14EB   CS=14EB
IP=0105
                                        NV UP EI PL ZR NA PE NC
```

Note the effect of LSS. Not only convenience but integrity. Both SP and SS are changed in one instruction.

14EB:0105 0FB2265000   LSS   SP,[54]

AX=0100   BX=0000   CX=0000   DX=0000   SP=0000   BP=0000
SI=0000   DI=0000   DS=1500   ES=14EB   SS=0000   CS=14EB
IP=010A

                                        NV UP EI PL ZR NA PE NC

14EB:010A 90   NOP

═══

LLDT   Load Local Descriptor Table Register

INSTRUCTION	OPCODE	BINARY
LLDT r/m16	0F 00 /2	00001111 00000000 mm 010 r/m

Purpose: The Local Descriptor Table is loaded whenever a task or major subsystem gains or regains control of the system. LLDT loads the Local Descriptor Table Register (LDTR). The operand (memory or register) should hold a selector to the GDT. The descriptor registers are not affected and the LDT field in the task state segment does not change.

Instruction Demonstration: This instruction transfers the contents of a 16 bit register or memory word into the Local Descriptor Table Register. No flags are affected. The operand size attribute has no effect on the operation of LLDT.

        0070:0100 0F00D0   LLDT   AX
        0070:0103 90   NOP

The registers and flags at the start:

AX=0010   BX=0000   CX=0464   DX=0000   SP=0200   BP=0000
SI=0000   DI=0000   DS=0078   ES=0000   SS=0080   CS=0070
IP=0100

                                        NV UP EI PL NZ NA PO NC

We transfer the LDT selector from AX to the LDTR.

0070:0100 0F00D0   LLDT   AX

AX=0010   BX=0000   CX=0464   DX=0000   SP=0200   BP=0000
SI=0000   DI=0000   DS=0078   ES=0000   SS=0080   CS=0070
IP=0103

                                        NV UP EI PL NZ NA PO NC

0070:0103 90   NOP

LMSW   Load Machine Status Word

INSTRUCTION	OPCODE	BINARY
LMSW r/m16	0F 01 /6	00001111 00000001 mm 110 r/m

Purpose: LMSW loads the machine status word (MSW) into CR0 from the source as specified in the first operand. LMSW can be used to switch to Protected Mode. If so, the instruction queue must be flushed. LMSW will *not* switch back to Real address Mode.

Instruction Demonstration: This demonstrates the LMSW instruction by setting the machine status word part of CR0 from the specified source. AX is set using SMSW.

The Instruction sequence:

```
14EB:0101 0F01F0              LMSW   AX
14EB:0104 90                  NOP
```

The registers and flags at the start:

```
AX=FFE0  BX=0000  CX=0000  DX=0000  SP=EA04  BP=0000
SI=0000  DI=0000  DS=14EB  ES=14EB  SS=14EB  CS=14EB
IP=0101
                                NV UP EI PL NZ NA PO NC
```

```
14EB:0101 0F01F0              LMSW   AX

AX=FFE0  BX=0000  CX=0000  DX=0000  SP=EA04  BP=0000
SI=0000  DI=0000  DS=14EB  ES=14EB  SS=14EB  CS=14EB
IP=0104
                                NV UP EI PL NZ NA PO NC
```

The machine status word part of CR0 is set from the specified source. Note that AX was set using SMSW.

LOCK   Assert LOCK# Signal Prefix

INSTRUCTION	OPCODE	BINARY
LOCK	F0	11110000

Purpose: LOCK asserts a hold on shared memory so that the 80386 has exclusive use of it during the instruction which immediately follows the LOCK. LOCK's integrity is not affected by memory field alignment. LOCK will only work with:

```
BT, BTS, BTR, BTC                   memory, reg/imm
```

ADD, OR, ADC, SBB, AND, SUB, XOR memory, reg/imm
NOT, NEG, INC, DEC   memory
XCHG   reg, memory or memory, reg

An undefined opcode trap is generated if LOCK is used with any instruction not listed here. Note that XCHG always asserts LOCK# whether or not it has the LOCK prefix.

Note: LOCK is *not* assured if another 80386 is concurrently executing an instruction that has any of the following characteristics:

1. If it is not one of the instructions in the list above.
2. If it is not preceded by a LOCK prefix.
3. If it specifies a memory operand that does not *exactly* overlap the destination operand. LOCK is not guaranteed for partial overlap, even if one memory is contained wholly within the other.

Instruction Demonstration: Not demonstrated.

LODS   **Load String Operand**
LODSB **Load Byte**
LODSW **Load Word**
LODSD **Load Doubleword**

INSTRUCTION	OPCODE	BINARY
LODS m8	AC	10101100
LODS m16	AD	10101101
LODS m32	AD	10101101

Purpose: These instructions operate on strings rather than on logical or numeric values. They operate on one element of a string, which may be a byte, a word, or a doubleword. The string elements are addressed by the registers ESI and EDI. After each string operation, ESI and/or EDI are automatically updated to point to the next element of the string. If DF=0, the index registers are incremented. If DF=1, they are decremented. The amount incremented or decremented is 1, 2, or 4, depending on the size of the string element.

LODS places the source string element at ESI into AL for byte strings, AX for word strings, and in EAX for doubleword strings. LODS increments or decrements ESI according to DF.

Instruction Demonstration: This demonstration of the LODS instruction shows it in a loop where it might naturally reside.

The instruction sequence:

```
14EB:0100 B90500      MOV      CX,0005
14EB:0103 BE0002      MOV      SI,0200
14EB:0106 E307        JCXZ     010F
14EB:0108 AC          LODSB
14EB:0109 3C00        CMP      AL,00
14EB:010B E0FB        LOOPNZ   0108
```

```
          14EB:010D EBF7                    JMP      0106
```

The registers and flags after CX is set:

```
AX=FFA4  BX=0204   CX=0005   DX=FFB3   SP=EA04   BP=0000
SI=0205  DI=0000   DS=14EB   ES=14EB   SS=14EB   CS=14EB
IP=0103
                                    NV UP EI PL NZ NA PE CY
```

```
          14EB:0103 BE0002                  MOV      SI,0200
```

```
AX=FFA4  BX=0204   CX=0005   DX=FFB3   SP=EA04   BP=0000
SI=0200  DI=0000   DS=14EB   ES=14EB   SS=14EB   CS=14EB
IP=0106
                                    NV UP EI PL NZ NA PE CY
```

```
          14EB:0106 E307                    JCXZ     010F
```

```
AX=FFA4  BX=0204   CX=0005   DX=FFB3   SP=EA04   BP=0000
SI=0200  DI=0000   DS=14EB   ES=14EB   SS=14EB   CS=14EB
IP=0108
                                    NV UP EI PL NZ NA PE CY
```

Since CX is non zero, the jump is not taken.

```
          14EB:0108 AC                      LODSB
```

```
AX=FF41  BX=0204   CX=0005   DX=FFB3   SP=EA04   BP=0000
SI=0201  DI=0000   DS=14EB   ES=14EB   SS=14EB   CS=14EB
IP=0109
                                    NV UP EI PL NZ NA PE CY
```

A byte is loaded using SI and SI is incremented.

```
          14EB:0109 3C00                    CMP      AL,00
```

```
AX=FF41  BX=0204   CX=0005   DX=FFB3   SP=EA04   BP=0000
SI=0201  DI=0000   DS=14EB   ES=14EB   SS=14EB   CS=14EB
IP=010B
                                    NV UP EI PL NZ NA PE NC
```

We compare the byte for a null value. (A common end of string indicator.)

```
          14EB:010B E0FB                    LOOPNZ   0108
```

```
AX=FF00  BX=0204   CX=0001   DX=FFB3   SP=EA04   BP=0000
SI=0204  DI=0000   DS=14EB   ES=14EB   SS=14EB   CS=14EB
IP=010D
                                    NV UP EI PL ZR NA PE NC
                                               *
```

The LOOPNZ is executed 3 times with the NZ condition. It decrements the CX register each time and falls through on the fourth byte because of the condition code.

```
14EB:010D EBF7              JMP        0106
```

AX=FF00   BX=0204   CX=0001   DX=FFB3   SP=EA04   BP=0000
SI=0204   DI=0000   DS=14EB   ES=14EB   SS=14EB   CS=14EB
IP=0106

                                    NV UP EI PL ZR NA PE NC

For this demonstration we jump to extract the next string.

```
14EB:0106 E307              JCXZ       010F
```

AX=FF00   BX=0204   CX=0001   DX=FFB3   SP=EA04   BP=0000
SI=0204   DI=0000   DS=14EB   ES=14EB   SS=14EB   CS=14EB
IP=0108

                                    NV UP EI PL ZR NA PE NC

CX is not yet zero so we enter the loop again.

```
14EB:0108 AC               LODSB
```

AX=FF43   BX=0204   CX=0001   DX=FFB3   SP=EA04   BP=0000
SI=0205   DI=0000   DS=14EB   ES=14EB   SS=14EB   CS=14EB
IP=0109

                                    NV UP EI PL ZR NA PE NC

We load the byte which is not null.

```
14EB:0109 3C00             CMP        AL,00
```

AX=FF43   BX=0204   CX=0001   DX=FFB3   SP=EA04   BP=0000
SI=0205   DI=0000   DS=14EB   ES=14EB   SS=14EB   CS=14EB
IP=010B

                                    NV UP EI PL NZ NA PO NC
                                                  *

We compare to set a NZ condition code.

```
14EB:010B E0FB             LOOPNZ     0108
```

AX=FF43   BX=0204   CX=0000   DX=FFB3   SP=EA04   BP=0000
SI=0205   DI=0000   DS=14EB   ES=14EB   SS=14EB   CS=14EB
IP=010D

                                    NV UP EI PL NZ NA PO NC

We fall thru the LOOPNZ even though the condition code is NZ because the count in CX ran out. The NZ condition would normally be tested to determine the reason for the fall thru.

```
14EB:010D EBF7             JMP        0106
```

AX=FF43   BX=0204   CX=0000   DX=FFB3   SP=EA04   BP=0000
SI=0205   DI=0000   DS=14EB   ES=14EB   SS=14EB   CS=14EB
IP=0106

                                    NV UP EI PL NZ NA PO NC

We jump back to our guard instruction just before the loop.

14EB:0106 E307   JCXZ   010F

AX=FF43   BX=0204   CX=0000   DX=FFB3   SP=EA04   BP=0000
SI=0205   DI=0000   DS=14EB   ES=14EB   SS=14EB   CS=14EB
IP=010F

                                        NV UP EI PL NZ NA PO NC

It detects that the CX register is zero and bypasses the loop.
The data being tested:

    14EB:0200   41 42 43 00 43 42 41 00   ABC.CBA.

LOOP   **Loop Control while ECX Counter Not Zero**
LOOP *cond*
LOOPE   **Loop while Equal**
LOOPZ   **Loop while Zero**
LOOPNE   **Loop while Not Equal**
LOOPNZ   **Loop while Not Zero**

INSTRUCTION	OPCODE	BINARY
LOOP rel8	E2 cb	11100010
LOOPE rel8	E1 cb	11100001
LOOPNE rel8	E1 cb	11100001

NOTE: LOOPZ is an alternate mnemonic for LOOPE rel8
           LOOPNZ is an alternate mnemonic for LOOPNE rel8

Purpose: The LOOP instructions are conditional jumps that use a value stored in ECX to specify the number of times a section of software will loop. All LOOPs automatically decrement ECX and terminate when ECX=0.

LOOP first decrements ECX before testing ECX for the branch condition. If ECX is not zero, the program branches to the target label specified in the instruction. If ECX=0, control transfers to the instruction immediately following the LOOP. If ECX is initially zero, the LOOP executes 2^{32} times.

LOOPE and LOOPZ are synonymously the same instruction. These instructions decrement ECX before testing ECX and ZF for branch condition. If ECX is non-zero and ZF=1, the program branches to the target label as specified in the instruction. If LOOPE or LOOPZ finds ECX=0 *or* ZF=0, control transfers to the instruction immediately following the LOOPE or LOOPZ.

LOOPNE and LOOPNZ are synonymously the same instruction. These instructions decrement ECX before testing ECX or ZF for branch conditions. If ECX is non-zero and ZF=0, the program branches to the target label specified by the instruction. If ECX=0 or ZF=1, control transfers to the instruction immediately following LOOPNE or LOOPNZ.

Instruction Demonstration: Demonstrated with LODS.

======================================

LSL   Load Segment Limit

Instruction	OpcodeBinary	
LSL r16,r/m16	0F 03 /r	00001111 00000011 mm rrr r/m
LSL r32,r/m32	0F 03 /r	00001111 00000011 mm rrr r/m

Purpose: LSL loads a user-specified register with a segment limit. If the source selector is visible to the CPL and the descriptor is a type accepted by the LSL, LSL sets ZF to 1. Otherwise, LSL sets ZF to 0 and keeps the destination register unchanged.

The 32-bit forms of LSL store the 32-bit granular limit in the 16-bit destination register.

Note that this segment limit is a byte granular value. If the descriptor uses a page granular segment limit, LSL translates that value to a byte limit and then loads it into the destination register.

Instruction Demonstration:

The instruction sequence:

```
0070:0100 6629C0          SUB     EAX,EAX
0070:0103 6689C3          MOV     EBX,EAX
0070:0106 BB7800          MOV     BX,0078H
0070:0109 660F03C3        LSL     EAX,EBX
0070:010D 90              NOP
```

The registers displayed are again limited to those affected, because of the display of the 32 bit registers.

EAX=00000000   EBX=00000000
IP=0100

                                   NV UP EI PL NZ NA PO NC

0070:0100 6629C0   SUB   EAX,EAX

EAX=00000000   EBX=00000000
IP=0103

                                   NV UP EI PL ZR NA PO NC
                                            *

0070:0103 6689C3   MOV   EBX,EAX

EAX=00000000   EBX=00000000
IP=0106

                                   NV UP EI PL ZR NA PO NC

0070:0106 BB7800   MOV   BX,0078H

We now have the selector in EBX and EAX is cleared.

EAX=00000000   EBX=00000078
IP=0109
                                                NV UP EI PL ZR NA PO NC

0070:0109 660F03C3   LSL   EAX,EBX

   LSL loads the limit value from the selected descriptor. If we did not load the limit into a 32 bit register (i.e., into AX instead of EAX) the low order 16 bits of the limit would be loaded.

EAX=000FFFFF   EBX=00000078
IP=010D
                                                NV UP EI PL ZR NA PO NC

0070:010D 90   NOP

Descriptor 0078 = FF FF 00 AB 01 93 0F 00

LTR   Load Task Register

INSTRUCTION	OPCODE	BINARY
LTR r/m16	0F 00 /3	00001111 00000000 mm 011 r/m

Purpose: The first operand of LTR specifies the source register or memory location which contains information for the task register. LTR loads data from that location into the task register. The loaded TSS is marked busy; however, a task switch does *not* occur.

Instruction Demonstration: See the program listing in Appendix 5.

MOV   Move Data

INSTRUCTION	OPCODE	BINARY
MOV r/m8,r8	88 /r	10001000 mm rrr r/m
MOV r/m16,r16	89 /r	10001001 mm rrr r/m
MOV r/m32,r32	89 /r	10001001 mm rrr r/m
MOV r8,r/m8	8A /r	10001010 mm rrr r/m
MOV r16,r/m16	8B /r	10001011 mm rrr r/m
MOV r32,r/m 32	8B /r	10001011 mm rrr r/m

MOV r/m16,sreg	8C /r	10001100 mm rrr r/m
MOV Sreg,r/m16	8D /r	10001101 mm rrr r/m
MOV AL,moffs8	A0	10100000
MOV AX,moffs16	A1	10100001
MOV EAX,moffs32	A1	10100001
MOV moffs8,AL	A2	10100010
MOV moffs16,AX	A3	10100011
MOV moffs32,EAX	A3	10100011
MOV reg8,imm8	B0 + rb	10110rrr
MOV reg16,imm16	B8 + rw	10111rrr
MOV reg32,imm32	B8 + rd	10111rrr
MOV r/m8,imm8	C6	11000110 mm rrr r/m
MOV r/m16,imm16	C7	11000111 mm rrr r/m
MOV r/m32,imm32	C7	11000111 mm rrr r/m

Purpose: MOV transfers a byte, word, or doubleword from the source operand to the destination operand. MOV is useful for transferring data along these paths:

> Immediate data to a memory
> Immediate data to a register
> Between general registers
> To a register from memory
> To memory from a register

There are some variations of MOV that operate on segment registers.

Note: MOV cannot move from memory to memory or from segment register to segment register. Memory-to memory can be done with the string move MOVS.

Instruction Demonstration: See MOV To/From Special Registers and MOVS.

===

MOV   Move To/From Special Registers

INSTRUCTION	OPCODE	BINARY
MOV r32,CR0/CR2/CR3	0F 20 /r	00001111 00100000 mm ccc r/m
MOV CR0/CR2/CR3,r32	0F 22 /r	00001111 00100010 mm ccc r/m
MOV r32,TR6/TR7	0F 24 /r	00001111 00100100 mm +++ r/m
MOV TR6/TR7,r32	0F 26 /r	00001111 00100110 mm +++ r/m
MOV r32,DR0-3/6/7	0F 21 /r	00001111 00100001 mm ddd r/m
MOV DR3/6/7,r32	0F 23 /r	00001111 00100011

Purpose: These forms of MOV load or store special registers or from a general register. They are particularly designed for the Control Registers (CR0, CR2, CR3),

Test Registers (TR6 and TR7), and the Debug Registers (DR0, DR1, DR2, DR3, DR6, and DR7).

Instruction Demonstration 1: This demonstrates the movement of the control registers to first EAX then to memory. The values in the control registers are those for real address mode.

The instruction sequence:

```
14EB:0100 0F20C0          MOV     EAX,CR0
14EB:0103 66A30002        MOV     [0200],EAX
14EB:0107 0F20D0          MOV     EAX,CR2
14EB:010A 66A30402        MOV     [0204],EAX
14EB:010E 0F20D8          MOV     EAX,CR3
14EB:0111 66A30802        MOV     [0208],EAX
```

The registers and flags at the start:

```
AX=0000   BX=0204   CX=0000   DX=FE13   SP=EA04   BP=0000
SI=0206   DI=0000   DS=14EB   ES=14EB   SS=14EB   CS=14EB
IP=0100
                                        NV UP EI PL NZ NA PE CY
```

Get CR0 to EAX
14EB:0100 0F20C0   MOV   EAX,CR0

```
AX=FFE0   BX=0204   CX=0000   DX=FE13   SP=EA04   BP=0000
SI=0206   DI=0000   DS=14EB   ES=14EB   SS=14EB   CS=14EB
IP=0103
                                        NV UP EI PL NZ NA PE CY
```

Then to memory

14EB:0103 66A30002   MOV   [0200],EAX

```
AX=FFEO   BX=0204   CX=0000   DX=FE13   SP=EA04   BP=0000
SI=0206   DI=0000   DS=14EB   ES=14EB   SS=14EB   CS=14EB
IP=0107
                                        NV UP EI PL NZ NA PE CY
```

Now CR2

14EB:0107 0F20D0   MOV   EAX,CR2

```
AX=0000   BX=0204   CX=0000   DX=FE13   SP=EA04   BP=0000
SI=0206   DI=0000   DS=14EB   ES=14EB   SS=14EB   CS=14EB
IP=010A
                                        NV UP EI PL NZ NA PE CY
```

14EB:010A 66A30402   MOV   [0204],EAX

```
AX=0000   BX=0204   CX=0000   DX=FE13   SP=EA04   BP=0000
SI=0206   DI=0000   DS=14EB   ES=14EB   SS=14EB   CS=14EB
IP=010E
                                        NV UP EI PL NZ NA PE CY
```

and CR3

14EB:010E 0F20D8   MOV   EAX,CR3

AX=0000   BX=0204   CX=0000   DX=FE13   SP=EA04   BP=0000
SI=0206   DI=0000   DS=14EB   ES=14EB   SS=14EB   CS=14EB
IP=0111

                                    NV UP EI PL NZ NA PE CY

14EB:0111 66A30802   MOV   [0208],EAX

AX=0000   BX=0204   CX=0000   DX=FE13   SP=EA04   BP=0000
SI=0206   DI=0000   DS=14EB   ES=14EB   SS=14EB   CS=14EB
IP=0115

                                    NV UP EI PL NZ NA PE CY

14EB:0115 90   NOP

The resulting data:

14EB:0200 E0 FF FF 7F 00 00 00 00 00 00 00 00 ....
          CR0   CR2   CR3

Instruction Demonstration 2: This demonstrates the movement of the test registers
into memory via EAX.
    The instruction sequence:

            14EB:00FF 90   NOP
            14EB:0100 0F24F0   MOV   EAX,TR6
            14EB:0103 66A30002   MOV   [0200],EAX
            14EB:0107 0F24F8   MOV   EAX,TR7
            14EB:010A 66A30402   MOV   [0204],EAX

    The registers and flags at the start:

AX=F01C   BX=0000   CX=0000   DX=0000   SP=EA04   BP=0000
SI=0000   DI=0000   DS=14EB   ES=14EB   SS=14EB   CS=14EB
IP=0100

                                    NV UP DI PL NZ NA PO NC

    We move TR6 into EAX

14EB:0100 0F24F0   MOV   EAX,TR6

AX=FFFF   BX=0000   CX=0000   DX=0000   SP=EA04   BP=0000
SI=0000   DI=0000   DS=14EB   ES=14EB   SS=14EB   CS=14EB
IP=0103

                                    NV UP DI PL NZ NA PO NC

and then into memory.

14EB:0103 66A30002   MOV   [0200],EAX

AX=FFFF   BX=0000   CX=0000   DX=0000   SP=EA04   BP=0000
SI=0000   DI=0000   DS=14EB   ES=14EB   SS=14EB   CS=14EB
IP=0107

NV UP DI PL NZ NA PO NC

We move TR7 into EAX

14EB:0107 0F24F8   MOV   EAX,TR7

AX=F01C   BX=0000   CX=0000   DX=0000   SP=EA04   BP=0000
SI=0000   DI=0000   DS=14EB   ES=14EB   SS=14EB   CS=14EB
IP=010A

NV UP DI PL NZ NA PO NC

then into memory.

14EB:010A 66A30402   MOV   [0204],EAX

AX=F01C   BX=0000   CX=0000   DX=0000   SP=EA04   BP=0000
SI=0000   DI=0000   DS=14EB   ES=14EB   SS=14EB   CS=14EB
IP=010E

NV UP DI PL NZ NA PO NC

The contents of TR6 and TR7

14EB:0200 FF FF FF FF 1C F0 E7 02   .....pg.
           TR6   TR7

Instruction Demonstration 3: This demonstrates the movement of the debug registers into memory via EAX.

The instruction sequence:

```
14EB:00FF 90                    NOP
14EB:0100 0F21C0                MOV    EAX,DR0
14EB:0103 C066A30002            MOV    [0200],EAX
14EB:0107 0F21C8                MOV    EAX,DR1
14EB:010A 66A30402              MOV    [0204],EAX
14EB:010E 0F21D0                MOV    EAX,DR2
14EB:0111 66A30802              MOV    [0208],EAX
14EB:0115 0F21D8                MOV    EAX,DR3
14EB:0118 66A30C02              MOV    [020C],EAX
14EB:011C 0F21F0                MOV    EAX,DR6
14EB:011F 66A31002              MOV    [0210],EAX
14EB:0123 0F21F8                MOV    EAX,DR7
14EB:0126 66A31402              MOV    [0214],EAX
```

The registers and flags at the start:

AX=0000   BX=0000   CX=0000   DX=0000   SP=EA04   BP=0000
SI=0000   DI=0000   DS=14EB   ES=14EB   SS=14EB   CS=14EB
IP=0100

NV UP EI PL NZ NA PO NC

We move DR0 into EAX

14EB:0100 0F21C0   MOV   EAX,DR0

AX=0000   BX=0000   CX=0000   DX=0000   SP=EA04   BP=0000
SI=0000   DI=0000   DS=14EB   ES=14EB   SS=14EB   CS=14EB
IP=0103

                                  NV UP EI PL NZ NA PO NC

and then into memory.

14EB:0103 C066A30002   MOV   [0200],EAX

AX=0000   BX=0000   CX=0000   DX=0000   SP=EA04   BP=0000
SI=0000   DI=0000   DS=14EB   ES=14EB   SS=14EB   CS=14EB
IP=0107

                                  NV UP EI PL NZ NA PO NC

Same with DR1,

14EB:0107 0F21C8   MOV   EAX,DR1

AX=0000   BX=0000   CX=0000   DX=0000   SP=EA04   BP=0000
SI=0000   DI=0000   DS=14EB   ES=14EB   SS=14EB   CS=14EB
IP=010A

                                  NV UP EI PL NZ NA PO NC

14EB:010A 66A30402   MOV   [0204],EAX

AX=0000   BX=0000   CX=0000   DX=0000   SP=EA04   BP=0000
SI=0000   DI=0000   DS=14EB   ES=14EB   SS=14EB   CS=14EB
IP=010E

                                  NV UP EI PL NZ NA PO NC

DR2,

14EB:010E 0F21D0   MOV   EAX,DR2

AX=0000   BX=0000   CX=0000   DX=0000   SP=EA04   BP=0000
SI=0000   DI=0000   DS=14EB   ES=14EB   SS=14EB   CS=14EB
IP=0111

                              NV UP EI PL NZ NA PO NC

14EB:0111 66A30802   MOV   [0208],EAX

AX=0000   BX=0000   CX=0000   DX=0000   SP=EA04   BP=0000
SI=0000   DI=0000   DS=14EB   ES=14EB   SS=14EB   CS=14EB
IP=0115

                              NV UP EI PL NZ NA PO NC

DR3,

14EB:0115 0F21D8   MOV   EAX,DR3

AX=0000   BX=0000   CX=0000   DX=0000   SP=EA04   BP=0000
SI=0000   DI=0000   DS=14EB   ES=14EB   SS=14EB   CS=14EB
IP=0118

                              NV UP EI PL NZ NA PO NC

14EB:0118 66A30C02   MOV   [020C],EAX

AX=0000   BX=0000   CX=0000   DX=0000   SP=EA04   BP=0000
SI=0000   DI=0000   DS=14EB   ES=14EB   SS=14EB   CS=14EB

IP=011C

NV UP EI PL NZ NA PO NC

DR6,

14EB:011C 0F21F0   MOV   EAX,DR6

AX=4FF0   BX=0000   CX=0000   DX=0000   SP=EA04   BP=0000
SI=0000   DI=0000   DS=14EB   ES=14EB   SS=14EB   CS=14EB
IP=011F

NV UP EI PL NZ NA PO NC

and DR7.

14EB:011F 66A31002   MOV   [0210],EAX

AX=4FF0   BX=0000   CX=0000   DX=0000   SP=EA04   BP=0000
SI=0000   DI=0000   DS=14EB   ES=14EB   SS=14EB   CS=14EB
IP=0123

NV UP EI PL NZ NA PO NC

14EB:0123 0F21F8   MOV   EAX,DR7

AX=0400   BX=0000   CX=0000   DX=0000   SP=EA04   BP=0000
SI=0000   DI=0000   DS=14EB   ES=14EB   SS=14EB   CS=14EB
IP=0126

NV UP EI PL NZ NA PO NC

14EB:0126 66A31402   MOV   [0214],EAX

AX=0400   BX=0000   CX=0000   DX=0000   SP=EA04   BP=0000
SI=0000   DI=0000   DS=14EB   ES=14EB   SS=14EB   CS=14EB
IP=012A

NV UP EI PL NZ NA PO NC

The data stored:
```
14EB:0200   00 00 00 00 00 00 00 00 00 00 00 00 00 00 00 00
............... DR0        DR1        DR2        DR3
14EB:0210   F0 4F FF FF 00 04 00 00
p0......    DR6        DR7
```

MOVS	Move Data from String to String
MOVSB	**Move String Byte**
MOVSW	**Move String Word**
MOVSD	**Move String Doubleword**

INSTRUCTION	OPCODE	BINARY
MOVS m8,m8	A4	10100100
MOVS m16,m16	A5	10100101
MOVS m32,m32	A5	10100101

NOTE: MOVSB is a common assembler mnemonic for MOVS m8,m8
MOVSW is a common assembler mnemonic for MOVS m16,m16
MOVSD is a common assembler mnemonic for MOVS m32,m32

Purpose: These instructions operate on strings rather than on logical or numeric values. They operate on one element of a string, which may be a byte, a word, or a doubleword. The string elements are addressed by the registers ESI and EDI. After each string operation, ESI and/or EDI are automatically updated to point to the next element of the string. If DF=0, the index registers are incremented. If DF=1, they are decremented. The amount incremented or decremented is 1, 2, or 4, depending on the size of the string element.

MOVS moves the string element pointed to by ESI to the location pointed to by EDI. When accompanied by an REP prefix, MOVS operates as a memory-to-memory block transfer. To set this up, the program must first initialize ECX and the register pairs ESI and EDI. ECX specifies the number of bytes, words or doublewords in the block. If DF=0, the program must point ESI to the first element of the source string and point EDI to the destination address for the first element. If DF=1, the program points these two registers to the last element of the source string and to the destination address for the last element, respectively.

MOVSB operates on bytes. MOVSW operates on words. MOVSD operates on doublewords.

Instruction Demonstration: This demonstrates the string move instruction. The instruction can move a byte, word or doubleword at a time. This demonstration uses the word width movement.

The instruction sequence:

```
14EB:0100 90          NOP
14EB:0101 BE0002       MOV   SI,0200
14EB:0104 BF0003       MOV   DI,0300
14EB:0107 B92000       MOV   CX,0020
14EB:010A E302         JCXZ  010E
14EB:010C F3           REPZ
14EB:010D A5           MOVSW
14EB:010E 90          NOP
```

The data at SI:

```
14EB:0200  01 00 01 00 01 00 01 00-01 00 01 00 01 00 01 00
. . . . . . . . . . . . . . .
14EB:0210  01 00 01 00 01 00 01 00-01 00 01 00 01 00 01 00
. . . . . . . . . . . . . . .
14EB:0220  01 00 01 00 01 00 01 00-01 00 01 00 01 00 01 00
. . . . . . . . . . . . . . .
14EB:0230  01 00 01 00 01 00 01 00-01 00 01 00 01 00 01 00
. . . . . . . . . . . . . . .
```

The data at DI:

```
14EB:0300  00 00 00 00 00 00 00 00-00 00 00 00 00 00 00 00
...............
14EB:0310  00 00 00 00 00 00 00 00-00 00 00 00 00 00 00 00
...............
14EB:0320  00 00 00 00 00 00 00 00-00 00 00 00 00 00 00 00
...............
14EB:0330  00 00 00 00 00 00 00 00-00 00 00 00 00 00 00 00
...............
```

The registers and flags at the start:

```
AX=0000   BX=0000   CX=0000   DX=0000   SP=EA04   BP=0000
SI=0000   DI=0000   DS=14EB   ES=14EB   SS=14EB   CS=14EB
IP=0101
                              NV UP EI PL NZ NA PO NC
```

Note that the direction flag is UP.

```
14EB:0101 BE0002              MOV   SI,0200

AX=0000   BX=0000   CX=0000   DX=0000   SP=EA04   BP=0000
SI=0200   DI=0000   DS=14EB   ES=14EB   SS=14EB   CS=14EB
IP=0104
                              NV UP EI PL NZ NA PO NC


14EB:0104 BF0003              MOV   DI,0300

AX=0000   BX=0000   CX=0000   DX=0000   SP=EA04   BP=0000
SI=0200   DI=0300   DS=14EB   ES=14EB   SS=14EB   CS=14EB
IP=0107
                              NV UP EI PL NZ NA PO NC


14EB:0107 B92000              MOV   CX,0020

AX=0000   BX=0000   CX=0020   DX=0000   SP=EA04   BP=0000
SI=0200   DI=0300   DS=14EB   ES=14EB   SS=14EB   CS=14EB
IP=010A
                              NV UP EI PL NZ NA PO NC
```

The registers are now set. The JCXZ is included as it normally would be if the count in CX had been loaded from a variable.

```
14EB:010A E302               JCXZ   010E

AX=0000   BX=0000   CX=0020   DX=0000   SP=EA04   BP=0000
SI=0200   DI=0300   DS=14EB   ES=14EB   SS=14EB   CS=14EB
IP=010C
                              NV UP EI PL NZ NA PO NC


14EB:010C F3                 REPZ
14EB:010D A5                 MOVSW
```

The repeated move continues until CX words are moved.

AX=0000   BX=0000   CX=0000   DX=0000   SP=EA04   BP=0000
SI=0240   DI=0340   DS=14EB   ES=14EB   SS=14EB   CS=14EB
IP=010E

                                        NV UP EI PL NZ NA PO NC

The data at SI

14EB:0200 01 00 01 00 01 00 01 00-01 00 01 00 01 00 01 00
....

14EB:0210 01 00 01 00 01 00 01 00-01 00 01 00 01 00 01 00
....

14EB:0220 01 00 01 00 01 00 01 00-01 00 01 00 01 00 01 00
....

14EB:0230 01 00 01 00 01 00 01 00-01 00 01 00 01 00 01 00
....

has been moved to DI without change to the source.

14EB:0300 01 00 01 00 01 00 01 00-01 00 01 00 01 00 01 00
....

14EB:0310 01 00 01 00 01 00 01 00-01 00 01 00 01 00 01 00
....

14EB:0320 01 00 01 00 01 00 01 00-01 00 01 00 01 00 01 00
....

14EB:0330 01 00 01 00 01 00 01 00-01 00 01 00 01 00 01 00
....

MOVSX Move with Sign Extension

INSTRUCTION	OPCODE	BINARY
MOVSX r16,r/m8	0F BE /r	00001111 10111110 mm rrr r/m
MOVSX r32,r/m8	0F BE /r	00001111 10111110 mm rrr r/m
MOVSX r32,r/m16	0F BF /r	00001111 10111111 mm rrr r/m

Purpose: MOVSX sign-extends an 8-bit value to a 16-bit value and an 8-bit or 16-bit value to 32-bit value.

Instruction Demonstration: This instruction moves a byte to a word or doubleword or a word to a doubleword with sign extension. The demonstration moves a byte from BL to AX extending the sign.

The instruction sequence:

```
14EB:0100 B3F0              MOV       BL,F0
14EB:0102 0FBEC3            MOVXS     AX,BL
```

                14EB:0105 90   NOP

The registers and flags at the start:

AX=0000   BX=00F0   CX=0000   DX=0000   SP=EA04   BP=0000
SI=0240   DI=0340   DS=14EB   ES=14EB   SS=14EB   CS=14EB
IP=0102

                                        NV UP EI PL NZ NA PO NC

14EB:0102 0FBEC3   MOVSX   AX,BL

AX=FFF0   BX=00F0   CX=0000   DX=0000   SP=EA04   BP=0000
SI=0240   DI=0340   DS=14EB   ES=14EB   SS=14EB   CS=14EB
IP=0105

                                        NV UP EI PL NZ NA PO NC

The sign is extended into AH. No flags are affected.

MOVZX   Move with Zero Extension

INSTRUCTION	OPCODE	BINARY
MOVZX r16,r/m8	0F B6 /r	00001111 10110110 mm rrr r/m
MOVZX r32,r/m8	0F B6 /r	00001111 10110110 mm rrr r/m
MOVZX r32,r/m16	0F B7 /r	00001111 10110111 mm rrr r/m

Purpose: MOVZX extends an 8-bit value to a 16-bit value and an 8- or 16-bit value to 32-bit value by padding with high-order zeros.

Instruction Demonstration: This instruction moves a byte to a word or doubleword, or a word to a doubleword, with zero extension. The demonstration moves a byte from BL to AX extending with zeros.

The instruction sequence:

            14EB:0100 B3F0   MOV   BL,F0
            14EB:0102 0FB6C3   MOVZS   AX,BL
            14EB:0105 90   NOP

The registers and flags at the start:

AX=FFF0   BX=00F0   CX=0000   DX=0000   SP=EA04   BP=0000
SI=0240   DI=0340   DS=14EB   ES=14EB   SS=14EB   CS=14EB
IP=0102

                                        NV UP EI PL NZ NA PO NC

14EB:0102 0FB6C3   MOVZX   AX,BL

AX=00F0   BX=00F0   CX=0000   DX=0000   SP=EA04   BP=0000
SI=0240   DI=0340   DS=14EB   ES=14EB   SS=14EB   CS=14EB
IP=0105

NV UP EI PL NZ NA PO NC

Zeros are extended into AH. No flags are affected.

MUL   Unsigned Integer Multiply of AL Register or AX Register

INSTRUCTION	OPCODE	BINARY
MUL AL,r/m8	F6 /4	11110110 mm 100 r/m
MUL AX,r/m16	F7 /4	11110111 mm 100 r/m
MUL EAX,r/m32	F7 /4	11110111 mm 100 r/m

Purpose: MUL multiplies the numbers in the source operand and the accumulator. If the source is a byte, the 80386 multiplies it by the contents of AL and returns the double-length result in AH and AL. If the source operand is a word, the 80386 multiplies it by the contents of AX and returns the double-length result to DX and AX. If the source is a doubleword, the processor multiplies it by the contents of EAX and returns the 64-bit result in EDX and EAX. MUL sets CF and OF when the upper half of the result is non-zero. Otherwise CF and OF are cleared.

Instruction Demonstration: This demonstration shows how MUL works. Compare it with the IMUL instruction.

The instruction sequence:

```
14EB:0100 90            NOP
14EB:0101 B033          MOV    AL,33
14EB:0103 B381          MOV    BL,81
14EB:0105 F6E3          MUL    BL
```

The registers and flags at the start:

AX=0D8C BX=0044 CX=0000 DX=0000 SP=EA04 BP=0000
SI=0240 DI=0340 DS=14EB ES=14EB SS=14EB CS=14EB
IP=0101

OV UP EI PL NZ NA PE CY

We load AL with hex 33 (51 decimal).

14EB:0101 B033   MOV   AL,33

AX=0D33 BX=0044 CX=0000 DX−0000 SP=EA04 BP=0000
SI=0240 DI=0340 DS=14EB ES=14EB SS=14EB CS=14EB
IP=0103

OV UP EI PL NZ NA PE CY

Then we load BL with hex 81 (129 decimal).

14EB:0103 B381   MOV   BL,81

```
AX=0D33   BX=0081   CX=0000   DX=0000   SP=EA04   BP=0000
SI=0240   DI=0340   DS=14EB   ES=14EB   SS=14EB   CS=14EB
IP=0105
                                    OV UP EI PL NZ NA PE CY
```

The unsigned multiply produces the product 19B3 hex (6579 decimal) treating BL as an unsigned 8 bit value.

```
14EB:0105 F6E3              MUL  BL
```

```
AX=19B3   BX=0081   CX=0000   DX=0000   SP=EA04   BP=0000
SI=0240   DI=0340   DS=14EB   ES=14EB   SS=14EB   CS=14EB
IP=0107
                                    OV UP EI PL NZ NA PE CY
```

NEG   Negate (Two's Complement)

INSTRUCTION	OPCODE	BINARY		
NEG r/m8	F6 /3	11110110	mm 011 r/m	
NEG r/m16	F7 /3	11110111	mm 011 r/m	
NEG r/m32	F7 /3	11110111	mm 011 r/m	

Purpose: NEG subtracts a signed integer operand from zero. Its effect is to make a positive into a negative or vice versa.

Instruction Demonstration: This demonstrates the action of the NEG instruction. It takes the twos complement of the value being acted on.

The instruction sequence:

```
14EB:0100  B80002                  MOV  AX,0200
14EB:0103  F7D8                    NEG  AX
```

The registers and flags after setting AX:

```
AX=0200   BX=0044   CX=0000   DX=0000   SP=EA04   BP=0000
SI=0240   DI=0340   DS=14EB   ES=14EB   SS=14EB   CS=14EB
IP=0103
                                    OV UP EI PL NZ NA PE NC
```

The value in AX is replaced with its two's complement.

```
14EB:0103         F7D8         NEG     AX
```

```
AX=FE00    BX=0044    CX=0000    DX=0000    SP=EA04    BP=0000
```

SI=0240   DI=0340   DS=14EB   ES=14EB   SS=14EB   CS=14EB
IP=0105

NV UP EI NG NZ NA PE CY
       *   *   *

The flags are set according to the result of the negation. Carry is set unless the operand is zero in which case it is reset.

NOP   No Operation

INSTRUCTION	OPCODE	BINARY
NOP	90	10010000

Purpose: NOP occupies a byte of storage. It affects nothing but the instruction pointer, EIP. NOP is useful for providing space in 'fixing up' branch addresses, i.e., the address may require an 8- or 16-bit displacement—if 16 bits are reserved, an 8-bit displacement and a NOP can be used to fill the 16 bits.

Instruction Demonstration: NOP is demonstrated with several instructions. See MUL for example.

NOT   Negate (One's Complement)

INSTRUCTION	OPCODE	BINARY		
NOT r/m8	F6 /2	11110110	mm 010 r/m
NOT r/m16	F7 /2	11110111	mm 010 r/m
NOT r/m32	F7 /2	11110111	mm 010 r/m

Purpose: NOT inverts the bits in the specified operand to form a one's complement of the operand. NOT is a unary operation (refers to an arithmetic operator having only one term) that uses a single operand in a register or memory. NOT has no effect on flags.

Instruction Demonstration: This demonstrates the NOT instruction. This instruction takes the ones complement of its operand.

The instruction sequence:

```
14EB:0100  B80002              MOV  AX,0200
14EB:0103  F7D0                NOT  AX
```

The registers and flags after setting AX:

AX=0200   BX=0044   CX=0000   DX=0000   SP=EA04   BP=0000

SI=0240   DI=0340   DS=14EB   ES=14EB   SS=14EB   CS=14EB
IP=0103

NV UP EI NG NZ NA PE CY

14EB:0103 F7D0   NOT AX

AX=FDFF BX=0044 CX=0000 DX=0000 SP=EA04 BP=0000
SI=0240 DI=0340 DS=14EB ES=14EB SS=14EB CS=14EB
IP=0105

NV UP EI NG NZ NA PE CY

The NOT instruction inverts each bit of its operand. No flags are affected.

OR   Logical Inclusive OR

Instruction	Opcode	Binary			
OR AL,imm8	0C ib	00001100			
OR AX,imm16	0D iw	00001101			
OR EAX,imm32	0D id	00001101			
OR r/m8,imm8	80 /1 ib	10000000	mm	001	r/m
OR r/m16,imm16	81 /1 i2	10000001	mm	001	r/m
OR r/m32,imm32	81 /1 id	10000001	mm	001	r/m
OR r/m16,imm8	83 /1 ib	10000011	mm	001	r/m
OR r/m32,imm8	83 /1 ib	10000011	mm	001	r/m
OR r/m8,r8	08 /r	00001000	mm	001	r/m
OR r/m16,r16	09 /r	00001001	mm	001	r/m
OR r/m32,r32	09 /r	00001001	mm	001	r/m
OR r8,r/m8	0A /r	00001010	mm	rrr	r/m
OR r16,r/m16	0B /r	00001011	mm	rrr	r/m
OR r32,r/m32	0B /r	00001011	mm	rrr	r/m

Purpose: OR compares its two operands and computes the following. If each corresponding bit in the the operands are zeros, the result is a zero; otherwise, the result is a 1.

Operand 1	0	0	1	1
Operand 2	0	1	1	0
Result	0	1	1	1

Instruction Demonstration: The OR instruction combines two values bit by bit. If a bit is on in either or both of the operands it is set on in the result.

The instruction sequence:

14EB:0100 B80002   MOV AX,0200

14EB:0103 0C3F   OR   AL,3F
14EB:0105 0D000A   OR   AX,0A00

The registers and flags after setting AX:

AX=0200   BX=0044   CX=0000   DX=0000   SP=EA04   BP=0000
SI=0240   DI=0340   DS=14EB   ES=14EB   SS=14EB   CS=14EB
IP=0103

NV UP EI PL NZ NA PE NC

The overflow and carry flags are forced to zero by the OR instruction. Note that oring one bits against zero bits sets the bits in the result and that zero bits against zero bits leave the bits zero.

14EB:0103 0C3F   OR   AL,3F

AX=023F   BX=0044   CX=0000   DX=0000   SP=EA04   BP=0000
SI=0240   DI=0340   DS=14EB   ES=14EB   SS=14EB   CS=14EB
IP=0105

NV UP EI PL NZ NA PE NC

ORing bits which were on against bits which were on doesn't change their value.

14EB:0105 0D000A   OR   AX,0A00

AX=0A3F   BX=0044   CX=0000   DX=0000   SP=EA04   BP=0000
SI=0240   DI=0340   DS=14EB   ES=14EB   SS=14EB   CS=14EB
IP=0108

NV UP EI PL NZ NA PE NC

OUT   Output to Port

Instruction	Opcode	Binary
OUT imm8,AL	E6 ib	11100110
OUT imm8,AX	E7 ib	11100111
OUT imm8,EAX	E7 ib	11100111
OUT DX,AL	EE	11101110
OUT DX,AX	EF	11101111
OUT DX,EAX	EF	11101111

Purpose: OUT transfers data from a register to an output port. The source is a register (AL, AX, or EAX) and is given as the second operand. The output port is numbered in the first operand. To output data to any port from 0 to 65536, the port number is placed in the DX register. OUT is then used with DX as the first operand. If the instruction contains an 8-bit port ID, the value is zero-extended to 16 bits.

Instruction Demonstration: The IN, INS, OUT, and OUTS instructions are demonstrated together because of their relationship with each other. See the IN instruction.

OUTS   **Output String to Port**
OUTSB   **Output Byte**
OUTSW   **Output Word**
OUTSD   **Output Doubleword**

INSTRUCTION	OPCODE	BINARY
OUTS DX,r/m8	6E	01101110
OUTS DX,r/m16	6F	01101111
OUTS DX,r/m32	6F	01101111

NOTE: OUTSB is a common assembler mnemonic for OUTS DX,r/m8
OUTSW is a common assembler mnemonic for OUTS DX,r/m16
OUTSD is a common assembler mnemonic for OUTS DX,r/m32

Purpose: OUTS operates much like OUT, in that it transfers data (memory byte, word, or doubleword) at the source-index register to the output port addressed by the DX register. After the data transfer, the source-index register (SI or ESI, see below) is advanced; that is, it is either incremented or decremented. If the DF is 0 (CLD was executed), the index is incremented. If DF is 1 (STD was executed), it is decremented. The amount it is changed depends on the size of the output: a 1 if it is a byte, a 2 if a word, or 4 if a double-word.

The source data address is determined by the contents of a source-index register. The correct index value must be loaded into either SI or ESI prior to executing these instructions. SI is used for the source-index register if the address size attribute for these instructions is 16 bits. Otherwise, ESI is used and the address size attribute is 32 bits.

The port must be addressed through the DX register value. OUTS does *not* allow specification of the port number as an immediate value.

Instruction Demonstration: The IN, INS, OUT, and OUTS instructions are demonstrated together because of their relationship with each other. See the IN instruction.

POP   **Pop a Word from the Stack**

INSTRUCTION	OPCODE	BINARY		
POP m16	8F /0	10001111	mm 000 r/m
POP m32	8F /0	10001111	mm 000 r/m

POP r16	58 + rw	01011rrr
POP r32	58 + rd	01011rrr
POP DS	1F	00011111
POP ES	07	00000111
POP SS	17	00010111
POP FS	0F A1	00001111 10100001
POP GS	0F A9	00001111 10101001

Purpose: POP transfers the word or doubleword at the current top of stack (indicated by ESP) to the destination operand. It then increments ESP to point to the new top of stack.

Instruction Demonstration: This demonstration shows the action of the PUSH and POP instructions. They are demonstrated together because of their logical interaction.

The instruction sequence:

14EB:0100 50		PUSH AX
14EB:0101 5B		POP BX

The registers and flags at the start:

AX=0101 BX=0202 CX=0303 DX=0404 SP=E9A4 BP=0505
SI=0606 DI=0707 DS=14EB ES=14EB SS=14EB CS=14EB
IP=0100

                                NV UP EI PL NZ NA PO NC

14EB:0100 50   PUSH   AX

AX=0101 BX=0202 CX=0303 DX=0404 SP=E9A2 BP=0505
SI=0606 DI=0707 DS=14EB ES=14EB SS=14EB CS=14EB
IP=0101

                                NV UP EI PL NZ NA PO NC

Note that PUSH decrements the stack pointer as it places the register on the stack. Only the stack is changed.

14EB:0101 5B   POP   BX

AX=0101 BX=0101 CX=0303 DX=0404 SP=E9A4 BP=0505
SI=0606 DI=0707 DS=14EB ES=14EB SS=14EB CS=14EB
IP=0102

                                NV UP EI PL NZ NA PO NC

POP removes a word from the stack. SP is incremented and the destination register receives the data.

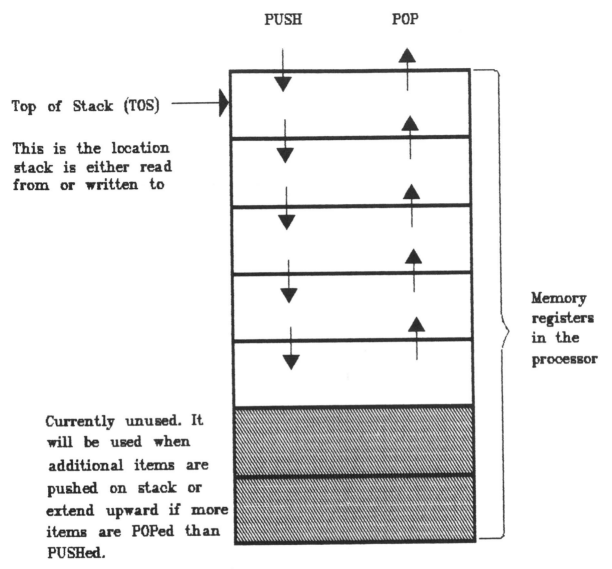

Fig. 10-4. Representation of stack processing.

POPA   Pop All Registers
POPAD   Pop All Registers—32-bit Mode

INSTRUCTION	OPCODE	BINARY
POPA	61	01100001
POPAD	61	01100001

Purpose: POPA restores the registers saved on the stack by PUSHA. It ignores the saved value of ESP.

Instruction Demonstration: This demonstrates the action of the POPA instruction. All the general registers are restored off the stack, either the double word or the single word registers are restored.

The instruction sequence:

```
14EB:010E  6661          POPAD
14EB:0110  61            POPA
```

The data at SP at the start:

```
14EB:E9A0                    07 07 00 00-06 06 00 00 05 05 00 00
............
14EB:E9B0        C4 E9 00 00 02 02 00 00-04 04 00 00 03 03 00 00
Di.............
14EB:E9C0        01 01 DC 3D 07 07 06 06-05 05 D4 E9 02 02 04 04
.. \ =......Ti....
14EB:E9D0        03 03 01 01
....
```

The registers and flags at the start:

```
AX=0000   BX=0000   CX=0000   DX=0000   SP=E9A4   BP=0000
SI=0000   DI=0000   DS=14EB   ES=14EB   SS=14EB   CS=14EB
IP=010E
                                NV UP EI PL ZR NA PE NC


14EB:010E  6661          POPAD


AX=0101   BX=0202   CX=0303   DX=0404   SP=E9C4   BP=0505
SI=0606   DI=0707   DS=14EB   ES=14EB   SS=14EB   CS=14EB
IP=0110
                                NV UP EI PL ZR NA PE NC
```

Note that the width override caused the doubleword registers to be POPed. The value of SP has been decreased by 32.

```
14EB:0110  61           POPA


AX=0101   BX=0202   CX=0303   DX=0404   SP=E9D4   BP=0505
SI=0606   DI=0707   DS=14EB   ES=14EB   SS=14EB   CS=14EB
IP=0111
                                NV UP EI PL ZR NA PE NC
```

The single word registers have been POPed. SP has been reduced by 16. Note that the flags are unchanged.

POPF   Pop Stack into FLAGS or EFLAGS Register
POPFD   Pop Stack—32-bit Mode

INSTRUCTION	OPCODE	BINARY
POPF	9D	10011101
POPFD	9D	10011101

Purpose: POPF transfers specific bits from the word at the top of stack into the low-order byte of EFLAGS. Then POPF encrements ESP by two. POPFD transfers the bits and encrements ESP by four. The RF and VM flags are not changed by either POPF or POPFD.

PUSHF and POPF are useful for storing the flags in memory where they can be examined and modified. They are useful also for preserving the state of the flags register while executing a procedure.

Instruction Demonstration: This demonstrates the effects of the PUSHF and POPF instructions. The flags are PUSHed twice, POPed into AX and inverted. Then AX is PUSHed and the value POPed into the flags. Then the original flags are restored.

The instruction sequence:

```
14EB:0100  90      NOP
14EB:0101  9C      PUSHF
14EB:0102  9C      PUSHF
14EB:0103  58      POP    AX
14EB:0104  F7D0    NOT    AX
14EB:0106  50      PUSH   AX
14EB:0107  9D      POPF
14EB:0108  9D      POPF
```

The registers and flags at the start:

```
AX=8DB9   BX=0000   CX=0000   DX=0000   SP=EA04   BP=0000
SI=0000   DI=0000   DS=14EB   ES=14EB   SS=14EB   CS=14EB
IP=0101
                                 NV UP EI PL ZR NA PE NC
```

14EB:0101 9C   PUSHF

```
AX=8DB9   BX=0000   CX=0000   DX=0000   SP=EA02   BP=0000
SI=0000   DI=0000   DS=14EB   ES=14EB   SS=14EB   CS=14EB
IP=0102
                                 NV UP EI PL ZR NA PE NC
```

14EB:0102 9C   PUSHF

```
AX=8DB9    BX=0000    CX=0000    DX=0000    SP=EA00    BP=0000
SI=0000    DI=0000    DS=14EB    ES=14EB    SS=14EB    CS=14EB
IP=0103
                                    NV UP EI PL ZR NA PE NC
```

The flags have been PUSHed twice.

14EB:0103 58   POP   AX

```
AX=7246    BX=0000    CX=0000    DX=0000    SP=EA02    BP=0000
SI=0000    DI=0000    DS=14EB    ES=14EB    SS=14EB    CS=14EB
IP=0104
                                    NV UP EI PL ZR NA PE NC
```

We get one copy off the stack into AX.

14EB:0104 F7D0   NOT   AX

```
AX=8DB9    BX=0000    CX=0000    DX=0000    SP=EA02    BP=0000
SI=0000    DI=0000    DS=14EB    ES=14EB    SS=14EB    CS=14EB
IP=0106
                                    NV UP EI PL ZR NA PE NC
```

Flip all the bits.

14EB:0106 50   PUSH   AX

```
AX=8DB9    BX=0000    CX=0000    DX=0000    SP=EA00    BP=0000
SI=0000    DI=0000    DS=14EB    ES=14EB    SS=14EB    CS=14EB
IP=0107
                                    NV UP EI PL ZR NA PE NC
```

We put the inverted bits on the stack.

14EB:0107 9D   POPF

```
AX=8DB9    BX=0000    CX=0000    DX=0000    SP=EA02    BP=0000
SI=0000    DI=0000    DS=14EB    ES=14EB    SS−14EB    CS=14EB
IP=0108
                                    OV DN DI NG NZ AC PO CY
                                     *  *  *  *  *  *  *  *
```

Then we put them into the flag register. Note that all are changed.

14EB:0108 9D   POPF

AX=8DB9	BX=0000	CX=0000	DX=0000	SP=EA04	BP=0000
SI=0000	DI=0000	DS=14EB	ES=14EB	SS=14EB	CS=14EB
IP=0109					

NV UP EI PL ZR NA PE NC

Then we restore the original flags.

PUSH   Push Operand onto the Stack

INSTRUCTION	OPCODE	BINARY	
PUSH m16	FF /6	11111111	mm 110 r/m
PUSH m32	FF /6	11111111	mm 110 r/m
PUSH r16	50 + /r	01010rrr	
PUSH r32	50 + /r	01010rrr	
PUSH imm8	6A	01101010	
PUSH imm16	68	01101000	
PUSH imm32	68	01101000	
PUSH CS	0E	00001110	
PUSH SS	16	00010110	
PUSH DS	1E	00011110	
PUSH ES	06	00000110	
PUSH FS	0F A0	00001111	10100000
PUSH GS	0F A8	00001111	10101000

Purpose: PUSH decrements the stack pointer (ESP) then transfers the source operand to the top of stack (TOS) indicated by ESP. PUSH is often used to place parameters on the stack before calling a procedure. It is also the means of storing temporary variables on the stack. PUSH operates on memory operands, register operands (including segment registers) and immediate operands.

Instruction Demonstration: PUSH is demonstrated with the POP instruction.

PUSHA   Push All General Registers

PUSHAD

INSTRUCTION	OPCODE	BINARY
PUSHA	60	01100000
PUSHAD	60	01100000

Purpose: PUSHA saves the contents of the eight general registers on the stack.

PUSHA simplifies procedure calls by reducing the number of instructions required to retain the contents of the general registers for use in a procedure. The general registers are pushed onto the stack in the following order: EAX, ECX, EDX, EBX, the initial value of ESP (Stack Pointer) before EAX was pushed, EBP, ESI, and EDI.

Instruction Demonstration: This demonstration shows the effect of the PUSHA instruction. The operand size override is used to save the doubleword registers because the demonstration was executed with a default width of 16 bits. If the default width were set to 32 bits, the override would cause the instruction to use the 16 bit width.

The instruction sequence:

```
14EB:0115  60              PUSHA
14EB:0116  6660            PUSHAD
```

The registers and flags at the start:

```
AX=0101    BX=0202    CX=0303    DX=0404    SP=E9D4    BP=0505
SI=0606    DI=0707    DS=14EB    ES=14EB    SS=14EB    CS=14EB
IP=0115
```

                              NV UP EI PL NZ NA PE NC

```
14EB:0115  60              PUSHA
```

```
AX=0101    BX=0202    CX=0303    DX=0404    SP=E9C4    BP=0505
SI=0606    DI=0707    DS=14EB    ES=14EB    SS=14EB    CS=14EB
IP=0116
```

                              NV UP EI PL NZ NA PE NC

Note that the only change is in SP.

```
14EB:0116  6660            PUSHAD
```

```
AX=0101    BX=0202    CX=0303    DX=0404    SP=E9A4    BP=0505
SI=0606    DI=0707    DS=14EB    ES=14EB    SS=14EB    CS=14EB
IP=0118
```

                              NV UP EI PL NZ NA PE NC

The same is true for the double word version.
The data at SP showing the result of the double word PUSHA.

```
                            EDI         ESI         EBP
14EB:E9A0                   07 07 00 00-06 06 00 00 05 05 00 00
                  ESP            EBX         EDX         ECX
14EB:E9B0         C4 E9 00 00 02 02 00 00-04 04 00 00 03 03 00 00
                            Also the results of the word sized
PUSHA.
```

	EAX	DI	SI	BP	SP	BX	DX
14EB:E9C0	01 01 DC 3D	07 07	06 06-05	05	D4 E9	02 02	04 04

.. \ =......Ti....

	CX	AX
14EB:E9D0	03 03	01 01

....

PUSHF   Push Flags Register EFLAGS onto the Stack
PUSHFD

INSTRUCTION	OPCODE	BINARY
PUSHF	9C	10011100
PUSHFD	9C	10011100

Purpose: PUSHF decrements ESP (Stack Pointer) by two and then transfers the low-order word of EFLAGS to the word at the top of stack pointed to by ESP. PUSHFD decrements ESP by four then transfers both words of the EFLAGS to the top of stack pointed to by ESP. Note the VM and RF flags are not moved.

PUSHF and POPF are useful for storing the flags in memory where they can be examined and modified. They are useful also for preserving the state of the flags register while executing a procedure.

Instruction Demonstration: PUSHF is demonstrated with the POPF instruction.

RCL   Rotate Left through Carry—Uses CF for extension
RCR   Rotate Right through Carry—Uses CF for extension
ROL   Rotate Left—Wrap bits around
ROR   Rotate Right—Wrap bits around

INSTRUCTION	OPCODE	BINARY		
RCL r/m8,1	D0 /2	11010000	mm 010 r/m
RCL r/m8,CL	D2 /2	11010010	mm 010 r/m
RCL r/m8,imm8	C0 /2 ib	11000000	mm 010 r/m
RCL r/m16,1	D1 /2	11010001	mm 010 r/m
RCL r/m16,CL	D3 /2	11010011	mm 010 r/m
RCL r/m16,imm8	C1 /2 ib	11000001	mm 010 r/m
RCL r/m32,1	D1 /2	11010001	mm 010 r/m
RCL r/m32,CL	D3 /2	11010011	mm 010 r/m
RCL r/m32,imm8	C1 /2 ib	11000001	mm 010 r/m
RCR r/m8,1	D0 /3	11010000	mm 011 r/m

RCR r/m8,CL	D2 /3	11010010	mm 011	r/m
RCR r/m8,imm8	C0 /3 ib	11000000	mm 011	r/m
RCR r/m16,1	D1 /3	11010001	mm 011	r/m
RCR r/m16,CL	D3 /3	11010011	mm 011	r/m
RCR r/m16,imm8	C1 /3 ib	11000001	mm 011	r/m
RCR r/m32,1	D1 /3	11010001	mm 011	r/m
RCR r/m32,CL	D3 /3	11010011	mm 011	r/m
RCR r/m32,imm8	C1 /3 ib	11000001	mm 011	r/m
ROL r/m8,1	D0 /0	11010000	mm 000	r/m
ROL r/m8,CL	D2 /0	11010010	mm 000	r/m
ROL r/m8,imm8	C0 /0 ib	11000000	mm 000	r/m
ROL r/m16,1	D1 /0	11010001	mm 000	r/m
ROL r/m16,CL	D3 /0	11010011	mm 000	r/m
ROL r/m16,imm8	C1 /0 ib	11000001	mm 000	r/m
ROL r/m32,1	D1 /0	11010001	mm 000	r/m
ROL r/m32,CL	D3 /0	11010011	mm 000	r/m
ROL r/m32,imm8	C1 /0 ib	11000001	mm 000	r/m
ROR r/m8,1	C0 /1	11000000	mm 001	r/m
ROR r/m8,CL	D2 /1	11010010	mm 001	r/m
ROR r/m8,imm8	C0 /1 ib	11000000	mm 001	r/m
ROR r/m16,1	D1 /1	11010001	mm 001	r/m
ROR r/m16,CL	D3 /1	11010011	mm 001	r/m
ROR r/m16,imm8	C1 /1 ib	11000001	mm 001	r/m
ROR r/m32,1	D1 /1	11010001	mm 001	r/m
ROR r/m32,CL	D3 /1	11010011	mm 001	r/m
ROR r/m32,imm8	C1 /1 ib	11000001	mm 001	r/m

Purpose: Rotate instructions allow bits in bytes, words and doublewords to be rotated. Bits rotated out of an operand are not lost as in a shift but are "circled back" into the other "end" of the operand. Rotates affect only the carry and overflow flags. CF may act as an extension of the operand in two of the rotate instructions. This allows a bit to be isolated and then tested by a conditional jump instruction (JC or JNC). CF always contains the value of the last bit rotated out, even if the instruction does not use this bit as an extension of the rotated operand.

In single-bit rotates, OF is set if the operation changes the high-order (sign) bit of the destination operand. If the sign bit retains its original value, OF is cleared. On multi-bit rotates, the value of OF is *always* undefined.

RCL rotates bits in the byte, word, or doubleword destination operand *left* by one or by the number of bits specified in the count operand. RCL differs from ROL in that it treats CF as a high-order one-bit extension of the destination operand. Each high-order bit that exits from the left side of the operand moves to CF before it returns to the operand as the low-order bit on the next rotation cycle.

RCR rotates bits in the byte, word, or doubleword destination *right* by one or by the number of bits specified in the count operand. RCR differs from ROR in that it treats CF as a low-order one-bit extension of the destination operand. Each low-order bit that exits from the right side of the operand moves to CF before it returns to the operand as the high-order bit on the next rotation cycle.

ROL rotates the byte, word, or doubleword destination operand *left* by one or by the number of bits specified in the count operand. For each rotation specified, the high-order bit that exits from the left of the operand returns at the right to become the new low-order bit of the operand.

ROR rotates the byte, word, or doubleword destination operand *right* by one or by the number of bits specified in the count operand. For each rotation, the low-order bit that exits from the right of the operand returns at the left to become the new high-order bit of the operand.

Instruction Demonstration: RCL ROL RCR ROR instructions

This demonstrates the action of the rotate instructions. The rotate thru carry (RCx) which includes the carry as one of the bits rotated is demonstrated first. The rotate only (ROx) is demonstrated and contrasted with the RCx.

The instruction sequence:

```
14EB:0100   F8              CLC
14EB:0101   B081            MOV  AL,81
14EB:0103   B102            MOV  CL,02
14EB:0105   D0D0            RCL  AL,1
14EB:0107   D0D0            RCL  AL,1
14EB:0109   D0D8            RCR  AL,1
14EB:010B   D0D8            RCR  AL,1
14EB:010D   D2D0            RCL  AL,CL
14EB:010F   D2D8            RCR  AL,CL
14EB:0111   90              NOP
14EB:0112   B081            MOV  AL,81
14EB:0114   D0C0            ROL  AL,1
14EB:0116   D0C0            ROL  AL,1
14EB:0118   D0C8            ROR  AL,1
14EB:011A   D0C8            ROR  AL,1
14EB:011C   D2C0            ROL  AL,CL
14EB:011E   D2C8            ROR  AL,CL
```

The registers and flags at the start:

```
AX=0081   BX=0000   CX=0002   DX=0000   SP=EA04   BP=0000
SI=0000   DI=0000   DS=14EB   ES=14EB   SS=14EB   CS=14EB
IP=0105
                                  OV UP EI PL NZ NA PO NC
```

We have forced the carry to zero, loaded a count of 2 into CL and a value of hex 81 into AL. The bits to be rotated are:

1000 0001 0

14EB:0105 D0D0   RCL AL,1

AX=0002	BX=0000	CX=0002	DX=0000	SP=EA04	BP=0000
SI=0000	DI=0000	DS=14EB	ES=14EB	SS=14EB	CS=14EB
IP=0107					

OV UP EI PL NZ NA PO CY
          *   *

The first rotate has changed the bits to: 0000 0010 1 Note that the carry has been set as is the overflow flag.

14EB:0107 D0D0   RCL   AL,1

AX=0005	BX=0000	CX=0002	DX=0000	SP=EA04	BP=0000
SI=0000	DI=0000	DS=14EB	ES=14EB	SS=14EB	CS=14EB
IP=0109					

NV UP EI PL NZ NA PO NC
          *   *

The second rotate changes the bits to: 0000 0101 0. Note that the carry is zero and the overflow flag is off.

14EB:0109 D0D8   RCR   AL,1

AX=0002	BX=0000	CX=0002	DX=0000	SP=EA04	BP=0000
SI=0000	DI=0000	DS=14EB	ES=14EB	SS=14EB	CS=14EB
IP=010B					

NV UP EI PL NZ NA PO CY
                                       *

The rotate right brings the bits back to: 0000 0010 1 The carry is on and the overflow flag is off.

14EB:010B D0D8   RCR   AL,1

AX=0081	BX=0000	CX=0002	DX=0000	SP=EA04	BP=0000
SI=0000	DI=0000	DS=14EB	ES=14EB	SS=14EB	CS=14EB
IP=010D					

OV UP EI PL NZ NA PO NC
                                       *

The bits are rotated back to their original values.

14EB:010D D2D0   RCL   AL,CL

AX=0005	BX=0000	CX=0002	DX=0000	SP=EA04	BP=0000
SI=0000	DI=0000	DS=14EB	ES=14EB	SS=14EB	CS=14EB

IP=010F

NV UP EI PL NZ NA PO NC

The two bit rotate has included the carry flag. The overflow flag is changed but is undefined. Therefore it should not be used after a multiple bit rotate. Note that the bits are: 0000 0101 0 after the two rotates. Also the count is unchanged in CL.

14EB:010F D2D8   RCR   AL,CL

AX=0081   BX=0000   CX=0002   DX=0000   SP=EA04   BP=0000
SI=0000   DI=0000   DS=14EB   ES=14EB   SS=14EB   CS=14EB
IP=0111

OV UP EI PL NZ NA PO NC

The two bit rotate right returns the value to 1000 0001 0

14EB:0111 90   NOP

AX=0081   BX=0000   CX=0002   DX=0000   SP=EA04   BP=0000
SI=0000   DI=0000   DS=14EB   ES=14EB   SS=14EB   CS=14EB
IP=0112

OV UP EI PL NZ NA PO NC

14EB:0112 B081   MOV   AL,81

AX=0081   BX=0000   CX=0002   DX=0000   SP=EA04   BP=0000
SI=0000   DI=0000   DS=14EB   ES=14EB   SS=14EB   CS=14EB
IP=0114

OV UP EI PL NZ NA PO NC

14EB:0114 D0C0   ROL   AL,1

AX=0003   BX=0000   CX=0002   DX=0000   SP=EA04   BP=0000
SI=0000   DI=0000   DS=14EB   ES=14EB   SS=14EB   CS=14EB
IP=0116

OV UP EI PL NZ NA PO CY
   *   *

The rotate only has rotated the bits to: 0000 0011 1. Note that the carry and over-flow flags are set but that the carry does not move into the rotated value.

14EB:0116 D0C0   ROL   AL,1

AX=0006   BX=0000   CX=0002   DX=0000   SP=EA04   BP=0000
SI=0000   DI=0000   DS=14EB   ES=14EB   SS=14EB   CS=14EB
IP=0118

NV UP EI PL NZ NA PO NC
   *   *

Again the rotate does not include the carry but does set it to zero, the value of the bit rotated out of the high order position. The result: 0000 0110 0

14EB:0118 D0C8   ROR   AL,1

AX=0003   BX=0000   CX=0002   DX=0000   SP=EA04   BP=0000
SI=0000   DI=0000   DS=14EB   ES=14EB   SS=14EB   CS=14EB
IP=011A

                              NV UP EI PL NZ NA PO NC

The right rotate brings us back to a value of: 0000 0011 0

14EB:011A D0C8   ROR   AL,1

AX=0081   BX=0000   CX=0002   DX=0000   SP=EA04   BP=0000
SI=0000   DI=0000   DS=14EB   ES=14EB   SS=14EB   CS=14EB
IP=011C

                              OV UP EI PL NZ NA PO CY
                                 *   *

The second right rotate brings us back to the original value of: 1000 0001 1. The carry flag is set on a right rotate when a bit is rotated into the high order bit. The overflow is set on a single right rotate of 1 when the result shows the carry has changed.

14EB:011C D2C0   ROL   AL,CL

AX=0006   BX=0000   CX=0002   DX=0000   SP=EA04   BP=0000
SI=0000   DI=0000   DS=14EB   ES=14EB   SS=14EB   CS=14EB
IP=011E

                              NV UP EI PL NZ NA PO NC
                                                     *

The two bit left rotate results in a value of: 0000 0110 0. The carry is reset because the last bit rotated out of the high order position was zero.

14EB:011E D2C8   ROR   AL,CL

AX=0081   BX=0000   CX=0002   DX=0000   SP=EA04   BP=0000
SI=0000   DI=0000   DS=14EB   ES=14EB   SS=14EB   CS=14EB
IP=0120

                              OV UP EI PL NZ NA PO CY
                                                     *

The two bit right rotate returns the original value and sets the carry because the last bit rotated into the high order position was a one.

REP **Repeat Following String Operation**

REPE **Repeat while Equal**

REPZ **Repeat while Zero**

REPNE **Repeat while Not Equal**

REPNZ **Repeat while Not Zero**

INSTRUCTION	OPCODE	BINARY
REP INS r/m8,DX	F3 6C	11110011 01101100
REP INS r/m16,DX	F3 6D	11110011 01101101
REP INS r/m32,DX	F3 6D	11110011 01101101
REP MOVS m8,m8	F3 A4	11110011 10100100
REP MOVS m16,m16	F3 A5	11110011 10100101
REP MOVS m32,m32	F3 A5	11110011 10100101
REP OUTS DX,r/m8	F3 6E	11110011 01101110
REP OUTS DX,r/m16	F3 6F	11110011 01101111
REP OUTS DX,r/m32	F3 6F	11110011 01101111
REP STOS m8	F3 AA	11110011 10101010
REP STOS m16	F3 AB	11110011 10101011
REP STOS m32	F3 AB	11110011 10101011
REPE CMPS m8,m8	F3 A6	11110011 10100110
REPE CMPS m16,m16	F3 A7	11110011 10100111
REPE CMPS m32,m32	F3 A7	11110011 10100111
REPE SCAS m8	F3 AE	11110011 10101110
REPE SCAS m16	F3 AF	11110011 10101111
REPE SCAS m32	F3 AF	11110011 10101111
REPNE CMPS m8,m8	F2 A6	11110010 10100110
REPNE CMPS m16,m16	F2 A7	11110010 10100111
REPNE CMPS m32,m32	F2 A7	11110010 10100111
REPNE SCAS m8	F2 AE	11110010 10101110
REPNE SCAS m16	F2 AF	11110010 10101111
REPNE SCAS m32	F2 AF	11110010 10101111

Purpose: The REP prefixes specify repeated operation of a string, which enables the 80386 to process strings much faster than with a regular software loop. When a string operation has one of these repeat prefixes, the operation is executed repeatedly. Each time, the operation uses a different element of the string. The repetition ends when one of the conditions specified by the prefix is satisfied.

At the repetition of the instruction, the string operation can be suspended temporarily to handle an external interrupt or exception. After that interrupt has been handled, the string operation begins where it left off.

Instruction Demonstration: Demonstrated with MOVS.

RET   Return from Procedure

INSTRUCTION	OPCODE	BINARY
RET	C3	11000011
RET imm16	CA /w	11001010

Purpose: RET ends the execution of a CALLed procedure and transfers control through the back-link on the stack. The back-link points to the program that originally invoked the procedure. RET restores the value of EIP (instruction pointer) that was saved on the stack by the previous CALL instruction.

RET can optionally specify an immediate operand. By adding this constant to the new top-of-stack pointer, RET removes any arguments that the CALLing program pushed onto the stack before the CALL executed.

Instruction Demonstration: The CALL instruction, ENTER instruction, LEAVE instruction, and RET instruction are demonstrated together since they logically "fit" with each other and complement each other. See the CALL instruction.

SAHF   Store AH into Flags

INSTRUCTION	OPCODE	BINARY
SAHF	9E	10011110

Purpose: Though specific instructions exist to alter CF and DF, there is no direct way of altering the other applications-oriented flags. The flag transfer instructions (LAHF and SAHF) allow a program to alter the other flag bits with the bit manipulation instructions after transferring these flags to the stack or the AH register.

Instruction Demonstration: This demonstrates the movement of the AH register value into the flags register.

The instruction sequence:

```
14EB:0100    B80000    MOV    AX,0000
14EB:0103    9E        SAHF
14EB:0104    F6D4      NOT    AH
14EB:0106    9E        SAHF
```

The registers and flags at the start:

```
AX=0000   BX=0000   CX=0002   DX=0000   SP=EA04   BP=0000
SI=0000   DI=0000   DS=14EB   ES=14EB   SS=14EB   CS=14EB
IP=0103
                              OV UP EI PL NZ NA PO CY
```

First we set the flags to zero. (The value in AH)

14EB:0103   9E   SAHF

AX=0000   BX=0000   CX=0002   DX=0000   SP=EA04   BP=0000
SI=0000   DI=0000   DS=14EB   ES=14EB   SS=14EB   CS=14EB
IP=0104

                                               OV UP EI PL NZ NA PO NC
                                                           *

We invert all the bits of AH.

14EB:0104   F6D4   NOT   AH

AX=FF00   BX=0000   CX=0002   DX=0000   SP=EA04   BP=0000
SI=0000   DI=0000   DS=14EB   ES=14EB   SS=14EB   CS=14EB
IP=0106

                                               OV UP EI PL NZ NA PO NC

Then set the flags to ones.

14EB:0106   9E   SAHF

AX=FF00   BX=0000   CX=0002   DX=0000   SP=EA04   BP=0000
SI=0000   DI=0000   DS=14EB   ES=14EB   SS=14EB   CS=14EB
IP=0107

                                               OV UP EI NG ZR AC PE CY
                                                              *   *   *   *   *

SAL   Shift Instructions
SAR
SHL
SHR

INSTRUCTION	OPCODE	BINARY		
SAL r/m8,1	D0 /4	11010000	mm 100 r/m	
SAL r/m8,CL	D2 /4	11010010	mm 100 r/m	
SAL r/m8,imm8	C0 /4 ib	11000000	mm 100 r/m	
SAL r/m16,1	D1 /4	11010001	mm 100 r/m	
SAL r/m16,CL	D3 /4	11010011	mm 100 r/m	
SAL r/m16,imm8	C1 /4 ib	11000001	mm 100 r/m	
SAL r/m32,1	D1 /4	11010001	mm 100 r/m	
SAL r/m32,CL	D3 /4	11010011	mm 100 r/m	
SAL r/m32,imm8	C1 /4 ib	11000001	mm 100 r/m	

SAR r/m8,1	D0	/7		11010000	mm	111	r/m
SAR r/m8,CL	D2	/7		11010010	mm	111	r/m
SAR r/m8,imm8	C0	/7	ib	11000000	mm	111	r/m
SAR r/m16,1	C1	/7		11000001	mm	111	r/m
SAR r/m16,CL	D3	/7		11010011	mm	111	r/m
SAR r/m16,imm8	C1	/7	ib	11000001	mm	111	r/m
SAR r/m32,1	D1	/7		11010001	mm	111	r/m
SAR r/m32,CL	D3	/7		11010011	mm	111	r/m
SAR r/m32,imm8	C1	/7	ib	11000001	mm	111	r/m
SHR r/m8,1	D0	/5		11010000	mm	101	r/m
SHR r/m8,CL	C2	/5		11000010	mm	101	r/m
SHR r/m8,imm8	C0	/5	ib	11000000	mm	101	r/m
SHR r/m16,1	D1	/5		11010001	mm	101	r/m
SHR r/m16,CL	D3	/5		11010011	mm	101	r/m
SHR r/m16,imm8	C1	/5	ib	11000001	mm	101	r/m
SHR r/m32,1	D1	/5		11010001	mm	101	r/m
SHR r/m32,CL	D3	/5		11010011	mm	101	r/m
SHR r/m32,imm8	C1	/5	ib	11000001	mm	101	r/m

NOTE: SHL is an alternate assembler opcode for SAL.

Purpose: The bits in bytes, words and doublewords can be shifted logically or arithmetically. Bits can be shifted up to 31 places, depending on a specified count. Shift instructions specify the count in one of three ways: (1) implicitly by specifying the count as a single shift; (2) specifying the count as an immediate value; or (3) specifying the count as the value contained in CL.

The shift instructions provide a convenient way to do multiplication or division by binary. The division of signed numbers by shifting right is *not* the same kind of division performed by IDIV.

CF always contains the value of the last bit shifted out of the destination operand. In a single-bit shift, OF is set if the value of the high-order (sign) bit was changed by the operation. If the sign bit was not changed, OF is cleared. After a multibit shift, the contents of OF is *always* undefined.

SAL shifts the destination byte, word or doubleword operand left by one or by the number of bits specified in the count register. The processor shifts zeros in from the right (low-order) side of the operand as bits exit from the left (high-order) side.

SAR shifts the destination byte, word, or doubleword operand to the right by one or by the number of bits specified in the count operand. The processor preserves the sign of the operand by shifting in zeros on the lift (high-order) side if the value is positive or by shifting by ones if the value is negative.

SHL is a synonym for SAL.

SHR shifts the destination byte, word, or doubleword operand right by one or by the number of bits specified in the count operand. The processor shifts zeros in from the left (high-order) side of the operand as bits exit from the right (low-order) side.

Instruction Demonstration: This demonstrates the arithmetic and logical shift instructions.

The instruction sequence:

```
14EB:0100    B88100    MOV    AX,0081
14EB:0103    F8        CLC
14EB:0104    B103      MOV    CL,03
14EB:0106    D0F8      SAR    AL,1
14EB:0108    D0F0      SAL    AL,1
14EB:010A    D0E8      SHR    AL,1
14EB:010C    D0E0      SHL    AL,1
14EB:010E    B081      MOV    AL,81
14EB:0110    D2F8      SAR    AL,CL
14EB:0112    D2F0      SAL    AL,CL
14EB:0114    D2E8      SHR    AL,CL
14EB:0116    D2E0      SHL    AL,CL
```

The registers and flags at the start:

```
AX=0081  BX=0000  CX=0003  DX=0000  SP=EA04  BP=0000
SI=0000  DI=0000  DS=14EB  ES=14EB  SS=14EB  CS=14EB
IP=0106

                          NV UP EI PL ZR AC PO NC
```

```
14EB:0106    D0F8    SAR    AL,1
```

```
AX=00C0  BX=0000  CX=0003  DX=0000  SP=EA04  BP=0000
SI=0000  DI=0000  DS=14EB  ES=14EB  SS=14EB  CS=14EB
IP=0108

                          NV UP EI NG NZ AC PE CY
                                   *  *     *  *
```

The arithmetic right shift extends the sign to the right. No rotation occurs. This can be considered a signed integer divide by two without rounding.

```
14EB:0108    D0F0    SAL    AL,1
```

```
AX=0080  BX=0000  CX=0003  DX=0000  SP=EA04  BP=0000
SI=0000  DI=0000  DS=14EB  ES=14EB  SS=14EB  CS=14EB
IP=010A

                          NV UP EI NG NZ AC PO CY
                                               *
```

The arithmetic left shift multiplies the shifted value by two. Carry is set because the high order bit shifted out was a one.

```
14EB:010A D0E8           SHR    AL,1
```

```
AX=0040  BX=0000  CX=0003  DX=0000  SP=EA04  BP=0000
```

SI=0000   DI=0000   DS=14EB   ES=14EB   SS=14EB   CS=14EB
IP=010C

                                        OV UP EI PL NZ AC PO NC
                                           *   *   *

The logical right shift fills zeros into the sign position. OV is set because the high bit of the original value of AL was one. The low order bit was zero and was shifted into the carry.

14EB:010C D0E0   SHL   AL,1

AX=0080   BX=0000   CX=0003   DX=0000   SP=EA04   BP=0000
SI=0000   DI=0000   DS=14EB   ES=14EB   SS=14EB   CS=14EB
IP=010E

                                        OV UP EI NG NZ AC PO NC
                                           *

The logical left shift performs an unsigned multiply by two. The negative flag is set because the high bit of the operand is now set. OV remains set because the high bit of the result is different from the carry flag. OV records the fact that a left shift changed the sign bit.

14EB:010E B081   MOV   AL,81

AX=0081   BX=0000   CX=0003   DX=0000   SP=EA04   BP=0000
SI=0000   DI=0000   DS=14EB   ES=14EB   SS=14EB   CS=14EB
IP=0110

                                        OV UP EI NG NZ AC PO NC

14EB:0110 D2F8   SAR   AL,CL

AX=00F0   BX=0000   CX=0003   DX=0000   SP=EA04   BP=0000
SI=0000   DI=0000   DS=14EB   ES=14EB   SS=14EB   CS=14EB
IP=0112

                                        NV UP EI NG NZ AC PE NC
                                           *   *

The shift of three bits (the value in CL is ANDed against hex 1F to limit the shift count to 31 bits maximum) caused the sign to be propagated into AL. The parity flag is set as are other arithmetic flags. The OV flag is changed but its value in multiple bit shifts is undefined.

14EB:0112 D2F0   SAL   AL,CL

AX=0080   BX=0000   CX=0003   DX=0000   SP=EA04   BP=0000

SI=0000   DI=0000   DS=14EB   ES=14EB   SS=14EB   CS=14EB
IP=0114

NV UP EI NG NZ AC PO CY
* *

The left shift of three bits sets the carry because a one bit was shifted out of AL on the last shift of the count. Zeros are filled from the right.

14EB:0114 D2E8   SHR   AL,CL

AX=0010   BX=0000   CX=0003   DX=0000   SP=EA04   BP=0000
SI=0000   DI=0000   DS=14EB   ES=14EB   SS=14EB   CS=14EB
IP=0116

NV UP EI PL NZ AC PO NC
*

The logical shift right fills the left bits with zeros. Note that the sign bit has no special significance and is just another bit to be shifted.

14EB:0116 D2E0   SHL   AL,CL

AX=0080   BX=0000   CX=0003   DX=0000   SP=EA04   BP=0000
SI=0000   DI=0000   DS=14EB   ES=14EB   SS=14EB   CS=14EB
IP=0118

OV UP EI NG NZ AC PO NC
*   *

The left logical shift again fills zeros on the right. No carry is set because the last bit shifted out of the register was a zero. OV is changed but is undefined.

SBB   Subtract Integers with Borrow

INSTRUCTION	OPCODE	BINARY
SBB AL,imm8	1C ib	00011100
SBB AX,imm16	1D iw	00011101
SBB EAX,imm32	1D id	00011101
SBB r/m8,imm8	80 /3 ib	10000000 mm 011 r/m
SBB r/m16,imm16	81 /3 iw	10000001 mm 011 r/m
SBB r/m32,imm32	81 /3 id	10000001 mm 011 r/m
SBB r/m16,imm8	83 /3 ib	10000011 mm 011 r/m
SBB r/m32,imm8	83 /3 ib	10000011 mm 011 r/m

SBB r/m8,r8	18 /r	00011000 mm rrr r/m
SBB r/m16,r16	19 /r	00011001 mm rrr r/m
SBB r/m32,r32	19 /r	00011001 mm rrr r/m
SBB r8,r/m8	1A /r	00011010 mm rrr r/m
SBB r16,r/m16	1B /r	00011011 mm rrr r/m
SBB r32,r/m32	1B /r	00011011 mm rrr r/m

Purpose: SBB subtracts the source operand from the destination operand. It subtracts 1 if CF is set. It then returns the results to the destination operand. If CF is cleared, SBB performs the same operation as does SUB. SUB followed by multiple SBB instructions may be used to subtract numbers longer than 32 bits.

Instruction Demonstration: This demonstrates the action of the SBB instruction. The instruction sequence:

```
14EB:0100 F8               CLC
14EB:0101 B80100           MOV      AX,0001
14EB:0104 1D0100           SBB      AX,0001
14EB:0107 1D0100           SBB      AX,0001
14EB:010A 1D0100           SBB      AX,0001
```

The registers and flags at the start:

```
AX=0001   BX=0000   CX=0003   DX=0000   SP=EA04   BP=0000
SI=0000   DI=0000   DS=14EB   ES=14EB   SS=14EB   CS=14EB
IP=0104
                                       NV UP EI NG NZ NA PO NC

14EB:0104 1D0100           SBB      AX,0001


AX=0000   BX=0000   CX=0003   DX=0000   SP=EA04   BP=0000
SI=0000   DI=0000   DS=14EB   ES=14EB   SS=14EB   CS=14EB
IP=0107
                                       NV UP EI PL ZR NA PE NC
                                              *  *        *
```

The result of the first SBB is to set the flags according to the result of the subtraction. $(1-1=0)$

```
14EB:0107 1D0100           SBB      AX,0001


AX=FFFF   BX=0000   CX=0003   DX=0000   SP=EA04   BP=0000
SI=0000   DI=0000   DS=14EB   ES=14EB   SS=14EB   CS=14EB
IP=010A
                                       NV UP EI NG NZ AC PE CY
                                              *  *  *     *
```

This subtraction causes a borrow (The result is as if a high order bit were available just beyond the register). This sets the carry flag in addition to the sign and non zero flags. $(0 - 1 = -1)$

14EB:010A 1D0100   SBB   AX,0001

AX=FFFD BX=0000 CX=0003 DX=0000 SP=EA04 BP=0000
SI=0000 DI=0000 DS=14EB ES=14EB SS=14EB CS=14EB
IP=010D

NV UP EI NG NZ NA PO NC
                           *   *   *

This SBB subtracts the immediate value from the register but also subtracts one for the previous borrow as 'remembered' in the carry flag. $(-1 - 1 - 1 = -3)$

SCAS   Compare String Data
SCASB
SCASW
SCASD

INSTRUCTION	OPCODE	BINARY
SCAS m8	AE	10101110
SCAS m16	AF	10101111
SCAS m32	AF	10101111

NOTE: SCASB is a common assembler mnemonic for SCAS m8
                 SCASW is a common assembler mnemonic for SCAS m16
                 SCASD is a common assembler mnemonic for SCAS m32

Purpose: These instructions operate on strings rather than on logical or numeric values. They operate on one element of a string, which may be a byte, a word, or a doubleword. The string elements are addressed by the registers ESI and EDI. After each string operation, ESI and/or EDI are updated to point to the next element of the string. If the DF=0, the index registers are incremented. If DF=1, they are decremented. The amount incremented or decremented is 1, 2, or 4, depending on the size of the string element.

SCAS subtracts the destination string element at ES:EDI from EAX, AX or AL and updates the flags: AF, SF, ZF, PF, CF, and OF. If the values are equal, ZF=1. Otherwise, ZF=0. If DF=0, the 80386 increments the memory pointer (EDI) for the string. The destination segment register (ES) cannot be overridden.

SCASB scans bytes. SCASW scans words. SCASD scans doublewords.

If the REPE or REPNE prefix modifies this instruction, the 80386 compares the value of the current string element with the value in AL for byte elements, in AX for word elements, and in EAX for doubleword elements. Termination of the repeated operation depends on the resulting state of ZF as well as on the value in ECX.

Instruction Demonstration: This demonstrates the use of SCAS instruction in searching for a particular byte in a string.

The instruction sequence:

```
14EB:0100 B90400          MOV    CX,0004
14EB:0103 BF0002          MOV    DI,0200
14EB:0106 B84300          MOV    AX,0043
14EB:0109 F2              REPNZ
14EB:010A AE              SCASB
```

The data to be scanned:

14EB:0200   41 42 43 44

The registers and flags at the start:

```
AX=0043    BX=0000    CX=0004    DX=0000    SP=EA04    BP=0000
SI=0300    DI=0203    DS=14EB    ES=14EB    SS=14EB    CS=14EB
IP=0103
                                    NV UP EI PL NZ NA PE NC
```

The count is in CX.

14EB:0103 BF0002   MOV   DI,0200

```
AX=0043    BX=0000    CX=0004    DX=0000    SP=EA04    BP=0000
SI=0300    DI=0200    DS=14EB    ES=14EB    SS=14EB    CS=14EB
IP=0106
                                    NV UP EI PL NZ NA PE NC
```

DI is now set to the string to be scanned.

14EB:0106 B84300   MOV   AX,0043

```
AX=0043    BX=0000    CX=0004    DX=0000    SP=EA04    BP=0000
SI=0300    DI=0200    DS=14EB    ES=14EB    SS=14EB    CS=14EB
IP=0109
                                    NV UP EI PL NZ NA PE NC
```

The value to be searched for is set in AL. Note that a REPNZ prefix is used to skip unmatching characters. If we wanted to skip matching characters such as spaces we would use the REPZ prefix.

```
14EB:0109 F2              REPNZ
14EB:010A AE              SCASB
```

AX=0043	BX=0000	CX=0001	DX=0000	SP=EA04	BP=0000
SI=0300	DI=0203	DS=14EB	ES=14EB	SS=14EB	CS=14EB
IP=010B

NV UP EI PL ZR NA PE NC

                                             *

Note that the zero flag is set. This indicates that a match was found in the string. Note that CX could be zero if we matched on the last byte. DI points to the position following the position which matched.

SETcc   **Set Byte on Condition**

INSTRUCTION	OPCODE	BINARY
SETA r/m8	0F 97	00001111 10010111 mm rrr r/m
SETAE r/m8	0F 93	00001111 10010011 mm rrr r/m
SETB r/m8	0F 92	00001111 10010010 mm rrr r/m
SETBE r/m8	0F 96	00001111 10010110 mm rrr r/m
SETC r/m8	0F 92	00001111 10010010 mm rrr r/m
SETE r/m8	0F 94	00001111 10010100 mm rrr r/m
SETG r/m8	0F 9F	00001111 10011111 mm rrr r/m
SETGE r/m8	0F 9D	00001111 10011101 mm rrr r/m
SETL r/m8	0F 9C	00001111 10011100 mm rrr r/m
SETLE r/m8	0F 9E	00001111 10011110 mm rrr r/m
SETNA r/m8	0F 96	00001111 10010110 mm rrr r/m
SETNAE r/m8	0F 92	00001111 10010010 mm rrr r/m
SETNB r/m8	0F 93	00001111 10010011 mm rrr r/m
SETNBE r/m8	0F 97	00001111 10010111 mm rrr r/m
SETNC r/m8	0F 93	00001111 10010011 mm rrr r/m
SETNE r/m8	0F 95	00001111 10010101 mm rrr r/m
SETNG r/m8	0F 9E	00001111 10011110 mm rrr r/m
SETNGE r/m8	0F 9C	00001111 10011100 mm rrr r/m
SETNL r/m8	0F 9D	00001111 10011101 mm rrr r/m
SETNLE r/m8	0F 9F	00001111 10011111 mm rrr r/m
SETNO r/m8	0F 91	00001111 10010001 mm rrr r/m
SETNP r/m8	0F 9B	00001111 10011011 mm rrr r/m
SETNS r/m8	0F 99	00001111 10011001 mm rrr r/m
SETNZ r/m8	0F 95	00001111 10010101 mm rrr r/m
SETO r/m8	0F 90	00001111 10010000 mm rrr r/m
SETP r/m8	0F 9A	00001111 10011010 mm rrr r/m
SETPE r/m8	0F 9A	00001111 10011010 mm rrr r/m
SETPO r/m8	0F 9B	00001111 10011011 mm rrr r/m
SETS r/m8	0F 98	00001111 10011000 mm rrr r/m
SETZ r/m8	0F 94	00001111 10010100 mm rrr r/m

Purpose: SETcc sets a byte to zero or one depending on any of the 16 conditions defined by the status flags. The byte may be in memory or may be a one-byte general register. SETcc sets the byte to one if the condition cc is true; otherwise, it sets the byte to zero.

Instruction Demonstration: This demonstrates the action of the SETcc instruction. The instruction sequence:

```
14EB:0100 0F95C0          SETNZ  AL
14EB:0103 0F94C0          SETZ   AL
14EB:0106 90              NOP
```

The registers and flags at the start:

```
AX=0001   BX=0000   CX=0001   DX=0000   SP=EA04   BP=0000
SI=0300   DI=0203   DS=14EB   ES=14EB   SS=14EB   CS=14EB
IP=0100
                                        NV UP EI PL ZR NA PE NC
```

```
14EB:0100 0F95C0          SETNZ  AL
```

```
AX=0000   BX=0000   CX=0001   DX=0000   SP=EA04   BP=0000
SI=0300   DI=0203   DS=14EB   ES=14EB   SS=14EB   CS=14EB
IP=0103
                                        NV UP EI PL ZR NA PE NC
```

Because the zero flag is set, the SETcc instruction places a byte of zero into AL showing that the condition checked for was false.

```
14EB:0103 0F94C0          SETZ   AL
```

```
AX=0001   BX=0000   CX=0001   DX=0000   SP=EA04   BP=0000
SI=0300   DI=0203   DS=14EB   ES=14EB   SS=14EB   CS=14EB
IP=0106
                                        NV UP EI PL ZR NA PE NC
```

In this case, a byte of hex 01 is placed in AL because the condition tested for was true.

SGDT   Store Global Descriptor Table Register
SIDT   Store Interrupt Descriptor Table Register

INSTRUCTION	OPCODE	BINARY
SGDT m	0F 01 /0	00001111 00000001 mm 000 r/m
SIDT m	0F 01 /1	00001111 00000001 mm 001 r/m

Purpose: These instructions copy the contents of the descriptor table register the 6 bytes indicated by the operand. The 16-bit forms of the SGDT/SIDT instructions are compatible with the 80286, but only if the value in the upper 8 bits is not referenced. The 80286 stores "1's" in these bits while the 80386 stores "0's."

Instruction Demonstration 1: This demonstrates the storing of the global descriptor table register.

```
14EB:0100 660F0105          SGDT    [DI]
14EB:0104 90                NOP
```

The data at ES:DI

```
14EB:0200   01 01 01 01 01 01 01 01        ........
```

The registers and flags at the start:

```
AX=0000   BX=0000   CX=0000   DX=0000   SP=EA04   BP=0000
SI=0000   DI=0200   DS=14EB   ES=14EB   SS=14EB   CS=14EB
IP=0100
                                    NV UP EI NG NZ NA PO NC
```

Note the operand width modifier.

```
14EB:0100 660F0105          SGDT    [DI]
```

```
AX=0000   BX=0000   CX=0000   DX=0000   SP=EA04   BP=0000
SI=0000   DI=0200   DS=14EB   ES=14EB   SS=14EB   CS=14EB
IP=0104
                                    NV UP EI NG NZ NA PO NC
```

The resulting 48 bit register.

```
14EB:0200   FF FF 00 00 00 00 01 01        ........
```

Instruction Demonstration 2: This demonstrates the action of the SIDT instruction.

The instruction sequence:

```
14EB:0100 660F010D          SIDT   [DI]
14EB:0104 90                NOP
```

The data at ES:DI

```
14EB:0200   01 01 01 01 01 01 01 01        ........
```

The registers and flags at the start:

```
AX=0000   BX=0000   CX=0000   DX=0000   SP=EA04   BP=0000
```

SI=0000   DI=0200   DS=14EB   ES=14EB   SS=14EB   CS=14EB
IP=0100

                                       NV UP EI NG NZ NA PO NC

Note the operand width override prefix.

14EB:0100 660F010D   SIDT   [DI]

AX=0000   BX=0000   CX=0000   DX=0000   SP=EA04   BP=0000
SI=0000   DI=0200   DS=14EB   ES=14EB   SS=14EB   CS=14EB
IP=0104

                                       NV UP EI NG NZ NA PO NC

The resulting 48 bit value:

        14EB:0200   FF FF 00 00 00 00 01 01   ....

SHLD   **Double Precision Shift Left**
SHRD   **Double Precision Shift Right**

INSTRUCTION	OPCODE	BINARY
SHLD r/m16,r16,imm8	0F A4	00001111 10100100 mm rrr r/m
SHLD r/m32,r32,imm8	0F A4	00001111 10100100 mm rrr r/m
SHLD r/m16,r16,CL	0F A5	00001111 10100101 mm rrr r/m
SHLD r/m32,r32,CL	0F A5	00001111 10100101 mm rrr r/m
SHRD r/m16,r16,imm8	0F AC	00001111 10101100 mm rrr r/m
SHRD r/m32,r32,imm8	0F AC	00001111 10101100 mm rrr r/m
SHRD r/m16,r16,CL	0F AD	00001111 10101101 mm rrr r/m
SHRD r/m32,r32,CL	0F AD	00001111 10101101 mm rrr r/m

Purpose: SHLD and SHRD provide the basic operations needed to implement operations on long unaligned bit strings. The double shifts either (1) take two word operands as input and produce a one-word output, or (2) take two doubleword operands as input and produce a doubleword output.

One of the two input operands may either be in a general register or in memory; the other may only be in a general register. The results replace the memory or register operand. The number of bits to be shifted is specified either in the CL register or in an immediate byte of the instruction. CF is set to the value of the last bit shifted ·out of the destination operand. SF, ZF, and PF are set according to the value of the result. OF and AF are left undefined.

Instruction Demonstration 1: This demonstrates the effects of the SHLD instruction.

The instruction sequence:

```
14EB:0100 B80000          MOV     AX,0000
14EB:0103 BB3412          MOV     BX,1234
14EB:0106 0FA4D808        SHLD    AX,BX,8
14EB:010A 6650            PUSH    EAX
14EB:010C B10C            MOV     CL,0C
14EB:010E 0FA5D8          SHLD    AX,BX,CL
```

The registers and flags at the start:

```
AX=2123   BX=1234   CX=000C   DX=5555   SP=EA00   BP=0000
SI=0000   DI=0200   DS=14EB   ES=14EB   SS=14EB   CS=14EB
IP=0100
                                 OV UP EI PL NZ AC PO CY
```

```
14EB:0100 B80000            MOV     AX,0000
```

```
AX=0000   BX=1234   CX=000C   DX=5555   SP=EA00   BP=0000
SI=0000   DI=0200   DS=14EB   ES=14EB   SS=14EB   CS=14EB
IP=0103
                                 OV UP EI PL NZ AC PO CY
```

```
14EB:0103 BB3412            MOV     BX,1234
```

```
AX=0000   BX=1234   CX=000C   DX=5555   SP=EA00   BP=0000
SI=0000   DI=0200   DS=14EB   ES=14EB   SS=14EB   CS=14EB
IP=0106
                                 OV UP EI PL NZ AC PO CY
```

```
14EB:0106 0FA4D808          SHLD    AX,BX,8
```

```
AX=0012   BX=1234   CX=000C   DX=5555   SP=EA00   BP=0000
SI=0000   DI=0200   DS=14EB   ES=14EB   SS=14EB   CS=14EB
IP=010A
                                 NV UP EI PL NZ AC PE NC
                                                 *    *
```

The double shift uses the third operand for the count of bits to shift. The first operand is shifted in conjunction with a copy of the second operand the number of bits specified. The count may be immediate as in this example, or contained in CL. Note that the second operand is unchanged. The sign, zero and parity flags are set according to the result in the first operand. Carry is set to the value of the last bit shifted out of operand one. The adjust and overflow flags are undefined.

```
14EB:010A 6650              PUSH    EAX
```

AX=0012   BX=1234   CX=000C   DX=5555   SP=E9FC   BP=0000
SI=0000   DI=0200   DS=14EB   ES=14EB   SS=14EB   CS=14EB
IP=010C

                                    NV UP EI PL NZ AC PE NC

    We save EAX on the stack to show that with an operand width of 16 bits, the upper half is undisturbed.

14EB:010C B10C   MOV   CL,0C

AX=0012   BX=1234   CX=000C   DX=5555   SP=E9FC   BP=0000
SI=0000   DI=0200   DS=14EB   ES=14EB   SS=14EB   CS=14EB
IP=010E

                                      NV UP EI PL NZ AC PE NC

14EB:010E 0FA5D8   SHLD   AX,BX,CL

AX=2123   BX=1234   CX=000C   DX=5555   SP=E9FC   BP=0000
SI=0000   DI=0200   DS=14EB   ES=14EB   SS=14EB   CS=14EB
IP=0111

                                  OV UP EI PL NZ AC PO CY
                                           *   *

    This 12 bit shift results in a carry because the last bit shifted out of the AX register was a one.
    The saved EAX register:

                      14EB:E9FC   12 00 DC 3D

    Instruction Demonstration 2: This demonstrates the action of the SHRD instruction.
    The instruction sequence:

        14EB:0100 B80000   MOV   AX,0000
        14EB:0103 BB3412   MOV   BX,1234
        14EB:0106 0FACD808   SHRD   AX,BX,8
        14EB:010A 6650   PUSH   EAX
        14EB:010C B10C   MOV   CL,0C
        14EB:010E 0FADD8   SHRD   AX,BX,CL
        14EB:0111 90   NOP

    The registers and flags at the start:

AX=2123   BX=1234   CX=000C   DX=5555   SP=E9FC   BP=0000
SI=0000   DI=0200   DS=14EB   ES=14EB   SS=14EB   CS=14EB
IP=0100

                                      OV UP EI PL NZ AC PO CY

14EB:0100 B80000   MOV   AX,0000

AX=0000   BX=1234   CX=000C   DX=5555   SP=E9FC   BP=0000
SI=0000   DI=0200   DS=14EB   ES=14EB   SS=14EB   CS=14EB
IP=0103
                                    OV UP EI PL NZ AC PO CY

14EB:0103 BB3412   MOV   BX,1234

AX=0000   BX=1234   CX=000C   DX=5555   SP=E9FC   BP=0000
SI=0000   DI=0200   DS=14EB   ES=14EB   SS=14EB   CS=14EB
IP=0106
                                    OV UP EI PL NZ AC PO CY

14EB:0106 0FACD808   SHRD   AX,BX,8

AX=3400   BX=1234   CX=000C   DX=5555   SP=E9FC   BP=0000
SI=0000   DI=0200   DS=14EB   ES=14EB   SS=14EB   CS=14EB
IP=010A
                                    NV UP EI PL NZ AC PE NC
                                                     *   *

The 8 bit right double shift has shifted the right 8 bits of the second operand's copy into the first operand. The carry flag is set to reflect the value of the last bit shifted out of the first operand. The sign, zero and parity flags are set according to the result in the first operand. Overflow and adjust are undefined.

14EB:010A 6650   PUSH   EAX

AX=3400   BX=1234   CX=000C   DX=5555   SP=E9F8   BP=0000
SI=0000   DI=0200   DS=14EB   ES=14EB   SS=14EB   CS=14EB
IP=010C
                                    NV UP EI PL NZ AC PE NC

14EB:010C B10C   MOV   CL,0C

AX=3400   BX=1234   CX=000C   DX=5555   SP=E9F8   BP=0000
SI=0000   DI=0200   DS=14EB   ES=14EB   SS=14EB   CS=14EB
IP=010E
                                    NV UP EI PL NZ AC PE NC

14EB:010E 0FADD8   SHRD   AX,BX,CL

AX=2343   BX=1234   CX=000C   DX=5555   SP=E9F8   BP=0000
SI=0000   DI=0200   DS=14EB   ES=14EB   SS=14EB   CS=14EB
IP=0111

                                    NV UP EI PL NZ AC PO NC
                                                        *

The 12 bit right shift from the copy of BX into AX is now completed. Flags are set as indicated above.

The saved EAX value:

                    14EB:E9F8   00 34 DC 3D

SLDT   Store Local Descriptor Table Register

Instruction	Opcode	Binary
SLDT r/m16	0F 00 /0	00001111 00000000 mm 000 r/m

Purpose: The LDT is pointed to by a selector that resides in the LDT Register. SLDT stores the LDTR in the register or memory location indicated by the effective address operand.

Note: The operand-size attribute has no effect on the operation of SLDT.

Instruction Demonstration: This instruction transfers the content of the local descriptor table selector register into memory or a 16 bit register. No flags are affected.

        0070:0100 0F00C0   SLDT   AX
        0070:0103 90   NOP

The registers and flags at the start.

AX=0000   BX=0000   CX=0464   DX=0000   SP=0200   BP=0000
SI=0000   DI=0000   DS=0078   ES=0000   SS=0080   CS=0070
IP=0100

                                    NV UP EI PL NZ NA PO NC

We transfer the LDT selector to AX.

0070:0100 0F00C0   SLDT   AX

AX=0010   BX=0000   CX=0464   DX=0000   SP=0200   BP=0000
SI=0000   DI=0000   DS=0078   ES=0000   SS=0080   CS=0070
IP=0103

                                    NV UP EI PL NZ NA PO NC

Note that the selector value is in AX.

        0070:0103 90   NOP

SMSW   Store Machine Status Word

INSTRUCTION	OPCODE	BINARY
SMSW r/m16	0F 01 /4	00001111 00000001 mm 100 r/m

Purpose: The Machine Status Word is part of Control Register Zero (CR0). SMSW stores this word in the 2-byte register or memory location indicated by the effective address operand. SMSW provides compatibility with the 80286. 80386 programs should use MOV ... CR0.

Instruction Demonstration: This demonstration shows how to store the Machine Status Word.

The Instruction sequence:

```
14EB:0101 0F01E0          SMSW   AX
14EB:0104 90              NOP
```

The registers and flags at the start:

```
AX=0000   BX=0000   CX=0000   DX=0000   SP=EA04   BP=0000
SI=0000   DI=0000   DS=14EB   ES=14EB   SS=14EB   CS=14EB
IP=0101
                                   NV UP EI PL NZ NA PO NC
```

```
14EB:0101 0F01E0          SMSW   AX
```

```
AX=FFE0   BX=0000   CX=0000   DX=0000   SP=EA04   BP=0000
SI=0000   DI=0000   DS=14EB   ES=14EB   SS=14EB   CS=14EB
IP=0104
                                   NV UP EI PL NZ NA PO NC
```

The machine status word part of CR0 is stored in the destination.

STC   Set Carry Flag (CF)

INSTRUCTION	OPCODE	BINARY
STC	F9	11111001

Purpose: STC sets CF to 1.

Instruction Demonstration: This demonstrates the action of the STC instruction.

The instruction sequence:

```
14EB:0100 F8                       CLC
```

```
                    14EB:0101 F9                    STC
                    14EB:0102 90                    NOP
```

The registers and flags at the start:

```
AX=FFF1  BX=0000   CX=0000   DX=0000   SP=EA04   BP=0000
SI=0000  DI=0000   DS=14EB   ES=14EB   SS=14EB   CS=14EB
IP=0101
                                    NV UP EI PL NZ NA PO NC
                                                          *
```

Note that the carry is reset.

```
14EB:0101 F9                    STC
```

```
AX=FFF1  BX=0000   CX=0000   DX=0000   SP=EA04   BP=0000
SI=0000  DI=0000   DS=14EB   ES=14EB   SS=14EB   CS=14EB
IP=0102
                                    NV UP EI PL NZ NA PO CY
                                                          *
```

After the STC, the carry is set to one.

STD   Set Direction Flag (DF)

Instruction	Opcode	Binary
STD	FD	11111101

Purpose: STD sets DF to 1. This causes all subsequent string operations to decrement the index register(s) SI (or ESI), DI (or EDI).

Instruction Demonstration: This demonstrates the STD instruction's action. The instruction sequence:

```
            14EB:0100 FC                    CLD
            14EB:0101 FD                    STD
```

The registers and flags prior to the STD:

```
AX=FFF1  BX=0000   CX=0000   DX=0000   SP=EA04   BP=0000
SI=0000  DI=0000   DS=14EB   ES-14EB   SS=14EB   CS=14EB
IP=0101
                                    NV UP EI PL NZ NA PO NC
                                                  *
```

Note that the direction flag is set to 'up' (zero).

```
14EB:0101 FD                    STD
```

AX=FFF1 BX=0000 CX=0000 DX=0000 SP=EA04 BP=0000
SI=0000   DI=0000 DS=14EB ES=14EB SS=14EB CS=14EB
IP=0102

                                       NV DN EI PL NZ NA PO NC
                                               *

Now the direction flag is set to 'down' (one), the IP register is advanced and that no other registers or flags are affected.

STI   Set Interrupt Flag (IF)

INSTRUCTION	OPCODE	BINARY
STI	FB	11111011

Purpose: STI sets IF to 1. After executing the next operation, the 80386 responds to external interrupts—if the next instruction allows the interrupt flag to remain enabled. However, if external interrupts are disabled, code STI, RET (like at the end of a subroutine) and RET is allowed to execute before external interrupts are recognized. Also, if external interrupts are disabled, and STI, CLI are coded, the interrupts *are not* recognized because CLI clears the interrupt flag during its execution.

Instruction Demonstration: This demonstrates the action of the STI instruction.
The instruction sequence:

```
14EB:0100 FA              CLI
14EB:0101 FB              STI
14EB:0102 FA              CLI
```

The registers prior to the STI instruction:

AX=FFF1 BX=0000 CX=0000 DX=0000 SP=EA04 BP=0000
SI=0000   DI=0000 DS=14EB ES=14EB SS=14EB CS=14EB
IP=0101

                                       NV UP DI PL NZ NA PO NC
                                               *

Note that the interrupt flag is reset (disabled).

14EB:0101 FB   STI

AX=FFF1 BX=0000 CX=0000 DX=0000 SP=EA04 BP=0000
SI=0000   DI=0000 DS=14EB ES=14EB SS=14EB CS=14EB
IP=0102

                                       NV UP EI PL NZ NA PO NC
                                             *

The interrupt flag is set (enabled) and the IP register is advanced. No other registers or flags are affected.

STOS **Store String Data**
STOSB **Store Byte**
STOSW **Store Word**
STOSD **Store Doubleword**

Instruction	Opcode	Binary
STOS m8	AA	10101010
STOS m16	AB	10101011
STOS m32	AB	10101011

Purpose: These instructions operate on strings rather than on logical or numeric values. They operate on one element of a string, which may be a byte, a word, or a doubleword. The string elements are addressed by the registers ESI and EDI. After each string operation, ESI and/or EDI are automatically updated to point to the next element of the string. If DF=0, the index registers are incremented. If DF=1, they are decremented. The amount incremented or decremented is 1, 2, or 4, depending on the size of the string element.

Instruction Demonstration: This demonstrates the STOS instruction as used to initialize a memory area to a fixed value.

The instruction sequence:

```
14EB:0100 BF0002        MOV    DI,0200
14EB:0103 B8FF00        MOV    AX,00FF
14EB:0106 B90800        MOV    CX,0008
14EB:0109 F3            REP
14EB:010A AB            STOSW
```

The original value in memory:

```
14EB:0200   00 00 00 00 00 00 00 00-00 00 00 00 00 00 00 00
. . . . . . . . . . . . . . .
```

The registers and flags at the start:

```
AX=0000   BX=0000   CX=0000   DX=0000   SP=EA04   BP=0000
SI=0000   DI=0000   DS=14EB   ES=14EB   SS=14EB   CS=14EB
IP=0100
```

                              NV UP EI NG NZ NA PO NC

```
14EB:0100 BF0002              MOV    DI,0200
```

```
AX=0000   BX=0000   CX=0000   DX=0000   SP=EA04   BP=0000
```

SI=0000   DI=0200   DS=14EB   ES=14EB   SS=14EB   CS=14EB
IP=0103
                                                NV UP EI NG NZ NA PO NC

14EB:0103 B8FF00   MOV   AX,00FF

AX=00FF   BX=0000   CX=0000   DX=0000   SP=EA04   BP=0000
SI=0000   DI=0200   DS=14EB   ES=14EB   SS=14EB   CS=14EB
IP=0106
                                                NV UP EI NG NZ NA PO NC

14EB:0106 B90800   MOV   CX,0008

AX=00FF   BX=0000   CX=0008   DX=0000   SP=EA04   BP=0000
SI=0000   DI=0200   DS=14EB   ES=14EB   SS=14EB   CS=14EB
IP=0109
                                                NV UP EI NG NZ NA PO NC

The REP prefix continues the store process until the count of items in CX has been stored. In this case the default buss width is 16 bits so the AF register is stored in 8 sequential word locations.

14EB:0109 F3   REP
14EB:010A AB   STOSW

AX=00FF   BX=0000   CX=0000   DX=0000   SP=EA04   BP=0000
SI=0000   DI=0210   DS=14EB   ES=14EB   SS=14EB   CS=14EB
IP=010B
                                                NV UP EI NG NZ NA PO NC

The results in memory:

   14EB:0200   FF 00 FF 00 FF 00 FF 00-FF 00 FF 00 FF 00 FF 00

   ....

STR   Store Task Register

INSTRUCTION	OPCODE	BINARY
STR r/m16	0F 00 /1	00001111 00000000 mm 001 r/m

Purpose: STR copies the contents of the Task Register to the 2-byte register or memory location specified in the effective address operand. The operand-size attribute has no effect on STR.

Instruction Demonstration: This instruction transfers the content of the task register into memory or a 16 bit register. No flags are affected. The operand size attribute has no effect on the operation of STR.

0070:0100 0F00C8	STR	AX
0070:0103 90	NOP	

The registers and flags at the start:

AX=0000   BX=0000   CX=0464   DX=0000   SP=0200   BP=0000
SI=0000   DI=0000   DS=0078   ES=0000   SS=0080   CS=0070
IP=0100

                                      NV UP EI PL NZ NA PO NC

We transfer the TSS selector to AX.

0070:0100 0F00C8   STR   AX

AX=0040   BX=0000   CX=0464   DX=0000   SP=0200   BP=0000
SI=0000   DI=0000   DS=0078   ES=0000   SS=0080   CS=0070
IP=0103

                                      NV UP EI PL NZ NA PO NC

Note that the selector value is in AX.

0070:0103 90   NOP

SUB   Subtract Integers

INSTRUCTION	OPCODE	BINARY
SUB AL,imm8	2C ib	00101100
SUB AX,imm16	2D iw	00101101
SUB EAX,imm32	2D id	00101101
SUB r/m8,imm8	80 /5 ib	10000000 mm 101 r/m
SUB r/m16,imm16	81 /5 iw	10000001 mm 101 r/m
SUB r/m32,imm32	81 /5 id	10000001 mm 101 r/m
SUB r/m16,imm8	83 /5 ib	10000011 mm 101 r/m
SUB r/m32,imm8	83 /5 ib	10000011 mm 101 r/m
SUB r/m8,r8	28 /r	00101000 mm rrr r/m
SUB r/m16,r16	29 /r	00101001 mm rrr r/m
SUB r/m32,r32	29 /r	00101001 mm rrr r/m
SUB r8,r/m8	2A /r	00101010 mm rrr r/m
SUB r16,r/m16	2B /r	00101011 mm rrr r/m
SUB r32,r/m32	2B /r	00101011 mm rrr r/m

Purpose: SUB subtracts the source operand from the destination operand and then replaces the destination operand with the result. If a borrow is required, CF is set. The operands may be signed or unsigned bytes, words or doublewords.

Instruction Demonstration: This demonstrates the action of the integer subtract instruction. The SUB instruction is to the SBB instruction as ADD is to ADC. It ignores the value of the borrow.

The instruction sequence:

```
14EB:0100 B80100          MOV     AX,0001
14EB:0103 89C3            MOV     BX,AX
14EB:0105 29D8            SUB     AX,BX
14EB:0107 29D8            SUB     AX,BX
14EB:0109 29D8            SUB     AX,BX
14EB:010B 29D8            SUB     AX,BX
```

The registers and flags at the start:

```
AX=FFFF  BX=0001  CX=0000  DX=0000  SP=EA04  BP=0000
SI=0000  DI=0210  DS=14EB  ES=14EB  SS=14EB  CS=14EB
IP=0100
                              NV UP EI NG NZ AC PE CY
```

```
14EB:0100 B80100          MOV     AX,0001
```

```
AX=0001  BX=0001  CX=0000  DX=0000  SP=EA04  BP=0000
SI=0000  DI=0210  DS=14EB  ES=14EB  SS=14EB  CS=14EB
IP=0103
                              NV UP EI NG NZ AC PE CY
```

```
14EB:0103 89C3            MOV     BX,AX
```

```
AX=0001  BX=0001  CX=0000  DX=0000  SP=EA04  BP=0000
SI=0000  DI=0210  DS=14EB  ES=14EB  SS=14EB  CS=14EB
IP=0105
                              NV UP EI NG NZ AC PE CY
```

We start with a one in AX and in BX.

```
14EB:0105 29D8            SUB     AX,BX
```

```
AX=0000  BX=0001  CX=0000  DX=0000  SP=EA04  BP=0000
SI=0000  DI=0210  DS=14EB  ES=14EB  SS=14EB  CS=14EB
IP=0107
                              NV UP EI PL ZR NA PE NC
                                      *  *  *     *
```

The first subtract results in a zero in AX. The flags are set according to the result.

14EB:0107 29D8   SUB   AX,BX

AX=FFFF   BX=0001   CX=0000   DX=0000   SP=EA04   BP=0000
SI=0000   DI=0210   DS=14EB   ES=14EB   SS=14EB   CS=14EB
IP=0109

                NV UP EI NG NZ AC PE CY
                             *   *   *   *

The result is −1. The carry flag is set because a borrow was needed. The other flags are set according to the result. AC is set because a borrow was taken from the high 4 bits of AL to the low 4.

14EB:0109 29D8   SUB   AX,BX

AX=FFFE   BX=0001   CX=0000   DX=0000   SP=EA04   BP=0000
SI=0000   DI=0210   DS=14EB   ES=14EB   SS=14EB   CS=14EB
IP=010B

                NV UP EI NG NZ NA PO NC
                             *   *   *

The result is −2. The carry flag was not included in the operation. No borrow was required so the carry flag is reset.

TEST   Logical Compare

Instruction	Opcode	Binary
TEST AL,imm8	A8 ib	10101000
TEST AX,imm16	A9 iw	10101001
TEST EAX,imm32	A9 id	10101001
TEST r/m8,imm8	F6 /0 ib	11110110 mm 000 r/m
TEST r/m16,imm16	F7 /0 iw	11110111 mm 000 r/m
TEST r/m32,imm32	F7 /0 id	11110111 mm 000 r/m
TEST r/m8,r8	84 /r	10000100 mm rrr r/m
TEST r/m16,r16	85 /r	10000101 mm rrr r/m
TEST r/m32,r32	85 /r	10000101 mm rrr r/m

Purpose: TEST "ANDs" two operands. It then clears OF and CF, leaves AF undefined and updates SF, ZF, and PF. The flags can be tested by conditional control transfer instructions or by the byte-set-on-condition instructions.

The difference between TEST and AND is that TEST does *not* alter the destination operand. TEST differs from BT (Bit Test) in that TEST tests the value of multi-

ple bits in one operation, while BT tests a single bit.
Instruction Demonstration: This demonstrates the TEST instruction.

The instruction sequence:

```
14EB:0100 B80F0F          MOV     AX,0F0F
14EB:0103 BE0002          MOV     SI,0200
14EB:0106 29DB            SUB     BX,BX
14EB:0108 A90F00          TEST    AX,000F
14EB:010B 8504            TEST    [SI],AX
14EB:010D F7C71000        TEST    DI,0010
```

The data at SI.

```
14EB:0200   F0 F0
```

The registers and flags at the start:

```
AX=0F0F   BX=0000   CX=0000   DX=0000   SP=EA04   BP=0000
SI=0200   DI=0210   DS=14EB   ES=14EB   SS=14EB   CS=14EB
IP=0103
                              NV UP EI PL NZ NA PO NC
```

```
14EB:0103 BE0002            MOV     SI,0200
```

```
AX=0F0F   BX=0000   CX−0000   DX=0000   SP=EA04   BP=0000
SI=0200   DI=0210   DS=14EB   ES=14EB   SS=14EB   CS=14EB
IP=0106
                              NV UP EI PL NZ NA PO NC
```

```
14EB:0106 29DB             SUB     BX,BX
```

```
AX=0F0F   BX=0000   CX=0000   DX=0000   SP=EA04   BP=0000
SI=0200   DI=0210   DS=14EB   ES=14EB   SS=14EB   CS=14EB
IP=0108
                              NV UP EI PL ZR NA PE NC
                                          *        *
```

```
14EB:0108 A90F00            TEST    AX,000F
```

```
AX=0F0F   BX=0000   CX=0000   DX=0000   SP=EA04   BP=0000
SI=0200   DI=0210   DS=14EB   ES=14EB   SS=14EB   CS=14EB
IP=010B
                              NV UP EI PL NZ NA PE NC
                                                *
```

This TEST 'AND's the immediate value 000F against the value in the AX register (0F0F) to get a result of 000F which is non-zero. The flags are set according to the temporary result which is then discarded. The result is positive, non-zero and its low byte has even parity. In all cases the carry and overflow flags are forced to zero.

```
14EB:010B 8504              TEST    [SI],AX
DS:0200=F0F0
```

```
AX=0F0F   BX=0000   CX=0000   DX=0000   SP=EA04   BP=0000
SI=0200   DI=0210   DS=14EB   ES=14EB   SS=14EB   CS=14EB
IP=010D
                            NV UP EI PL ZR NA PE NC
                                             *
```

This TEST 'AND's the value at [SI] (F0F0) against the value in AX (0F0F) to get a zero result. The flags are set accordingly.

```
14EB:010D F7C71000          TEST    DI,0010
```

```
AX=0F0F   BX=0000   CX=0000   DX=0000   SP=EA04   BP=0000
SI=0200   DI=0210   DS=14EB   ES=14EB   SS=14EB   CS=14EB
IP=0111
                            NV UP EI PL NZ NA PO NC
                                       *        *
```

This TEST 'AND's the value in DI (0210) against the immediate value (0010) to get a result of 0010. The flags are set according to the temporary result.

VERR	Verify a Segment for Reading
VERW	Verify a Segment for Writing

INSTRUCTION	OPCODE	BINARY
VERR r/m16	0F 00 /4	00001111 00000000 mm 100 r/m
VERW r/m16	0F 00 /5	00001111 00000000 mm 101 r/m

Purpose: These instructions verify whether a segment noted by the selector is reachable with the current privilege level and if the segment is readable or writeable. If the segment is accessible, ZF is set to 1. If not, ZF is set to 0. The validation done is the same as if the segment were loaded into DS, ES, FS or GS and the indicated read or write were performed.

Since ZF receives the result of the validation, the selector's value does not result in a protection exception. This allows software to anticipate possible segment access problems.

Instruction Demonstration: These instructions test whether the issuing program can use the descriptor for the indicated selector for reading or writing data respectively. If the tested access is valid, the zero flag is set, otherwise it is reset.

```
0070:0100 B87000          MOV     AX,0070
0070:0103 09C0            OR      AX,AX
0070:0105 0F00E0          VERR    AX
0070:0108 0F00E8          VERW    AX
```

```
AX=0000   BX=0000   CX=0464   DX=0000   SP=0200   BP=0000
SI=0000   DI=0000   DS=0078   ES=0000   SS=0080   CS=0070
IP=0100
                                        NV UP EI PL NZ NA PO NC
```

We load a selector in to AX for testing. (The selector could also reside in memory.)

```
0070:0100 B87000          MOV     AX,0070
```

```
AX=0070   BX=0000   CX=0464   DX=0000   SP=0200   BP=0000
SI=0000   DI=0000   DS=0078   ES=0000   SS=0080   CS=0070
IP=0103
                                        NV UP EI PL NZ NA PO NC
```

```
0070:0103 09C0                    OR      AX,AX
```

The OR ensures that the zero flag is not set.

```
AX=0070   BX=0000   CX=0464   DX=0000   SP=0200   BP=0000
SI=0000   DI=0000   DS=0078   ES=0000   SS=0080   CS=0070
IP=0100
                                        NV UP EI PL NZ NA PO NC
```

We use the VERR to check if we have authority to read the segment.

```
0070:0105 0F00E0          VERR    AX
```

```
AX=0070   BX=0000   CX=0464   DX=0000   SP=0200   BP=0000
SI=0000   DI=0000   DS=0078   ES=0000   SS=0080   CS=0070
IP=0100
                                        NV UP EI PL ZR NA PO NC
                                                    *
```

The resulting setting of the zero flag indicates that we are allowed to read the segment (our code segment). We use the VERW to check if we have authority to write the segment.

```
0070:0108 0F00E8          VERW    AX
```

AX=0070 BX=0000 CX=0464 DX=0000 SP=0200 BP=0000
SI=0000 DI=0000 DS=0078 ES=0000 SS=0080 CS=0070
IP=0100

NV UP EI PL NZ NA PO NC
*

The resulting setting of the zero flag (NZ) indicates that we are not allowed to write the segment (our code segment).

xx (access flag)
Descriptor 0070 = FF FF 00 AB 01 9B 0F 00

The access flag indicates present, code, readable, non-conforming and accessed.

WAIT   Wait until BUSY# Pin is Inactive (High)

INSTRUCTION	OPCODE	BINARY
WAIT	9B	10011011

Purpose: A numeric coprocessor provides an extension to the instruction set of the 80386. The coprocessor supports high-precision integer and floating-point calculations, in addition to containing a set of useful constants to enhance the speed of numeric calculations. The coprocessor operates in parallel with the CPU to provide maximum instruction throughput.

A program contains coprocessor instructions in the same instruction stream with the 80386 instructions. The system executes the coprocessor set in the same order as they appear in the stream.

WAIT suspends 80386 program execution until the 80386 CPU detects that the BUSY pin is inactive. This indicates that the coprocessor has completed its processing task and that the CPU can now obtain the results.

Instruction Demonstration: Not demonstrated.

XCHG   Exchange Register/Memory with Register

INSTRUCTION	OPCODE	BINARY
XCHG AX,r16	90 + r	10010rrr
XCHG r16,AX	90 + r	10010rrr
XCHG EAX,r32	90 + r	10010rrr
XCHG r32,EAX	90 + r	10010rrr
XCHG r/m8,r8	86 /r	10000110 mm rrr r/m
XCHG r8,r/m8	86 /r	10000110 mm rrr r/m
XCHG r/m16,r16	87 /r	10000111 mm rrr r/m
XCHG r16,r/m16	87 /r	10000111 mm rrr r/m
XCHG r/m32,r32	87 /r	10000111 mm rrr r/m
XCHG r32,r/m32	87 /r	10000111 mm rrr r/m

Note that "XCHG, AX,AX" is a NOP.

Purpose: XCHG swaps the contents of two operands and takes the place of three MOV instructions. It does not require a temporary location to save the contents of one operand while loading the other. XCHG is useful for implementing semaphores or similar data structures for process synchronization.

Instruction Demonstration: This demonstrates the exchange instruction. The instruction sequence:

14EB:0100 93	XCHG	AX,BX
14EB:0101 87F0	XCHG	SI,AX
14EB:0103 871E0002	XCHG	BX,[0200]
14EB:0107 871E0002	XCHG	BX,[0200]

The registers and flags at the start:

AX=0200   BX=0F0F   CX=0000   DX=0000   SP=EA04   BP=0000
SI=0000   DI=0210   DS=14EB   ES=14EB   SS=14EB   CS=14EB
IP=0100   NV UP EI PL NZ NA PO NC

14EB:0100 93   XCHG   AX,BX

AX=0F0F   BX=0200   CX=0000   DX=0000   SP=EA04   BP=0000
SI=0000   DI=0210   DS=14EB   ES=14EB   SS=14EB   CS=14EB
IP=0101   NV UP EI PL NZ NA PO NC

The values in AX and BX have been exchanged.

14EB:0101 87F0   XCHG   SI,AX

AX=0000   BX=0200   CX=0000   DX=0000   SP=EA04   BP=0000
SI=0F0F   DI=0210   DS=14EB   ES=14EB   SS=14EB   CS=14EB
IP=0103   NV UP EI PL NZ NA PO NC

The values in SI and AX are exchanged.

14EB:0103 871E0002   XCHG   BX,[0200]
DS:0200=0000

AX=0000   BX=0000   CX=0000   DX=0000   SP=EA04   BP=0000
SI=0F0F   DI=0210   DS=14EB   ES=14EB   SS=14EB   CS=14EB
IP=0107   NV UP EI PL NZ NA PO NC

The value in BX is exchanged with the value at DS:0200.

14EB:0107 871E0002   XCHG   BX,[0200]
DS:0200=0200

```
AX=0000   BX=0200   CX=0000   DX=0000   SP=EA04   BP=0000
SI=0F0F   DI=0210   DS=14EB   ES=14EB   SS=14EB   CS=14EB
IP=010B
```
                                        NV UP EI PL NZ NA PO NC

We exchange again and the BX value is restored. Note that the exchange instruction does not affect the flags.

═══

XLAT   Table Look-up Translation
XLATB

INSTRUCTION	OPCODE	BINARY
XLAT m8	D7	11010111

Purpose: XLAT is useful for translating from one coding system to another, such as from EBCDIC to ASCII. The translate table can be up to 256 bytes long. The value placed in AL serves as an index to the location of the corresponding translation value.

XLAT replaces a byte in AL with a byte from a user-coded translation table. When XLAT is executed, AL should have the unsigned index to the table addressed by EBX. XLAT changes the contents of AL from the table index to the table entry. EBX in unchanged.

Instruction Demonstration: This demonstrates the XLAT instruction.

The instruction sequence:

```
14EB:0100 BB0002          MOV    BX,0200
14EB:0103 B80500          MOV    AX,0005
14EB:0106 D7              XLAT
14EB:0107 D7              XLAT
```

The data at DS:0200

    14EB:0200   FF FF FF 0F 04 03 02 01-00 00 FF 00 FF 00 FF 00

    ....

The registers and flags at the start:

```
AX=00FF   BX=0000   CX=0000   DX=0000   SP=EA04   BP=0000
SI=0F0F   DI=0210   DS=14EB   ES=14EB   SS=14EB   CS=14EB
IP=0100
```
                                        NV UP EI PL NZ NA PO NC

We must set the address displacement of our translate table into BX.

```
14EB:0100 BB0002              MOV    BX,0200
```

```
AX=00FF   BX=0200   CX=0000   DX=0000   SP=EA04   BP=0000
```

SI=0F0F   DI=0210   DS=14EB   ES=14EB   SS=14EB   CS=14EB
IP=0103

NV UP EI PL NZ NA PO NC

The byte to translate must be in AL.

14EB:0103 B80500   MOV   AX,0005

AX=0005   BX=0200   CX=0000   DX=0000   SP=EA04   BP=0000
SI=0F0F   DI=0210   DS=14EB   ES=14EB   SS=14EB   CS=14EB
IP=0106

NV UP EI PL NZ NA PO NC

14EB:0106 D7   XLAT

AX=0003   BX=0200   CX=0000   DX=0000   SP=EA04   BP=0000
SI=0F0F   DI=0210   DS=14EB   ES=14EB   SS=14EB   CS=14EB
IP=0107

NV UP EI PL NZ NA PO NC

The XLAT instruction replaces the byte in AL with the byte fetched from DS:BX+AL. In this case the byte at 205 which was 03.

14EB:0107 D7   XLAT

AX=000F   BX=0200   CX=0000   DX=0000   SP=EA04   BP=0000
SI=0F0F   DI=0210   DS=14EB   ES=14EB   SS-14EB   CS=14EB
IP=0108

NV UP EI PL NZ NA PO NC

This execution of the XLAT computes the address 203 as the source for the byte to be fetched. No flags arc affected.

XOR   Logical, Exclusive OR

INSTRUCTION	OPCODE	BINARY
XOR AL,imm8	34 ib	00110100
XOR AX,imm16	35 iw	00110101
XOR EAX,imm32	35 id	00110101
XOR r/m8,imm8	80 /6 ib	10000000 mm 110 r/m
XOR r/m16,imm16	81 /6 iw	10000001 mm 110 r/m
XOR r/m32,imm32	81 /6 id	10000001 mm 110 r/m
XOR r/m16,imm8	83 /6 ib	10000011 mm 110 r/m
XOR r/m32,imm8	83 /6 ib	10000011 mm 110 r/m
XOR r/m8,r8	30 /r	00110000 mm rrr r/m
XOR r/m16,r16	31 /r	00110001 mm rrr r/m

```
XOR  r/m32,r32        31 /r       00110001 mm rrr r/m
XOR  r8,r/m8          32 /r       00110010 mm rrr r/m
XOR  r16,r/m16        33 /r       00110011 mm rrr r/m
XOR  r32,r/m32        33 /r       00110011 mm rrr r/m
```

Purpose: XOR compares the bits in its two operands. Each bit of the result is 1 if the corresponding bits in the operands are *different*. Each bit is 0 if the corresponding bits are the same. The result replaces the first operand.

```
Operand 1       110001
Operand 2       001101
Result          111100
```

Instruction Demonstration: This demonstrates the XOR instruction. The XOR instruction computes the exclusive OR of the two operands. On a bit by bit basis the result is computed as R = (A or B) and not(A and B).

The instruction sequence:

```
14EB:0100 B8FF0F            MOV    AX,0FFF
14EB:0103 350FF0            XOR    AX,F00F
```

The registers and flags at the start:

```
AX=000F  BX=0200  CX=0000  DX=0000  SP=EA04  BP=0000
SI=0F0F  DI=0210  DS=14EB  ES=14EB  SS=14EB  CS=14EB
IP=0100
                            NV UP EI PL NZ NA PO NC
```

```
14EB:0100 B8FF0F            MOV    AX,0FFF
```

```
AX=0FFF  BX=0200  CX=0000  DX=0000  SP=EA04  BP=0000
SI=0F0F  DI=0210  DS=14EB  ES=14EB  SS=14EB  CS=14EB
IP=0103
                            NV UP EI PL NZ NA PO NC
```

```
14EB:0103 350FF0            XOR    AX,F00F
```

```
AX=FFF0  BX=0200  CX=0000  DX=0000  SP=EA04  BP=0000
SI=0F0F  DI=0210  DS=14EB  ES=14EB  SS=14EB  CS=14EB
IP=0106
                            NV UP EI NG NZ NA PE NC
                                    *   *      *
```

The XOR produces the exclusive or in the destination. The flags are set according to the result for the sign, zero and parity. Carry and overflow are forced to zeros. The adjust flag is undefined.

11

Introduction to Integrated Circuits

The electronics industry created another major evolution with the introduction of a 32-bit chip that enables desktop computers to enter the virtual system world. And in no other industry is the maxim "the future depends on the past" as much a keystone as in the data processing and electronics industries. To understand where it's all going, let's first take a look at what's already been done in the general electronics and integrated circuit technology.

To be a useful system, microprocessors interconnect with the various components that make up a microcomputer. This interconnection has to take into account the nature and timing of the signals generated and expected by each component. There are three classes of signals: data, address, and control. Obviously, those signals must travel from one component to another. That process is called *interfacing*. Chapter 12 overviews the processes of interfacing.

Information can be saved in various ways, but think of memory as the channel that allows data to be retained for future use. Thousands of 1-bit registers can be incorporated into a single integrated circuit, an IC, and share a common set of inputs, a common set of outputs and a single clock line. This entity is referred to as a *memory* chip. Chapter 13 details memory and its management and Chapter 4 discusses how the 80386 handles memory.

Computer speeds are determined by three basic limitations. One concerns hardware; that is, how fast gates switch and how many inches of wire or board must a signal traverse. The second limitation concerns the logic of the interaction of machine design and organization. The third looks at how effectively the operating system uses the hardware design. Chapter 14 addresses these last two.

To better understand the current generation of Intel chips, take a look at Appendix 1 which discusses the previous Intel chips—in the same family—to determine what design decisions and directions influenced the basic design of the new 80386.

IN THE BEGINNING

The leap-forward progress in electronics was made possible when early researchers built upon Thomas Edison's discoveries. Edison noticed that when he placed an isolated metal plate in his evacuated light bulb, he got a shock when he then touched a wire lead that was attached to it. This shock occurred because the metal plate was collecting electrons being emitted by the lamp filament. Edison's discovery was important for the later development of vacuum tubes.

Around 1904, J. Ambrose Flemming expanded on Edison's concept and discovered the two-element vacuum tube: the diode. The vacuum tubes were about 6 inches long and 1.5 inches in diameter. These high-cost tubes were inefficient glass bottles and were used in early radio receivers to introduce the age of radio.

In 1948, J. Bardeen and W.H. Brattain of the Bell Telephone Laboratories invented the transistor. The name *transistor* is derived from *tran*sfer re*sistor*. That first transistor came to life when two sharply-pointed metal needles were placed in contact with the surface of a piece of germanium. When one of these needles was forward biased with respect to the germanium n-type *base* wafer, holes were injected into the wafer. The name *base* remains for this transistor lead. The second needle was spaced close to the first and was reverse biased with respect to the base wafer. This second needle collected a large portion of the injected holes: this is transistor action.

These original needles were too fragile for high-quantity commercial manufacture and use. In 1949, William Shockley, also of Bell Laboratories, introduced the idea for the completely solid structure of the junction transistor. This breakthrough began the transistor era, in the 1950s.

The transistor is small and energy efficient. Nothing has to be heated to provide a source of current carriers. In addition, high voltages that were once required to drive the huge vacuum tubes are no longer needed. Relatively small voltages can be used because of the extremely small spacings between the different regions of a transistor; that is, the short travel distance. The continued reduction in spacing is the reason that the industry is expected to reduce the value of the present, standard, logic 5-volt power supply voltage. Even 5V is too high for the small transistors in the upcoming VLSIs.

As a historical note: to emphasize the low power requirements of the early transistors, a couple of wires were stuck into a lemon to demonstrate the simplest germanium transistor circuits. The electrolysis taking place created enough electrical power for the circuit to operate.

The early transistors were the point-contact type, with two thin wires or "whiskers" welded on a semiconductor block to form two junctions. This construction had good response for high frequencies but was limited in power dissipation. Practical, consumer usage came next.

The first electronic calculator was introduced in 1963 by a British firm, the Bell Punch Company. That calculator was made of discrete transistors and was about the size of a cash register. Four years later, Texas Instruments came out with their first *integrated circuits* (IC) calculator and the rush to miniaturization was on.

What is an IC Made Of?

All the materials we know contain two basic particles of electric charge, the *electron* and the *proton*. An electron is the smallest amount of electrical charge having the characteristic called *negative polarity*. The proton has a *positive polarity*. It is the arrangement of electrons and protons as basic particles that determines the electrical characteristics of a substance.

When electrons move easily from atom to atom within a substance, that substance is called a *conductor*. In general, metals are good conductors, with silver the best and copper second, because metal's atomic structure allows free movement of the electrons.

An IC is a small piece of silicon engineered, by a process like contact printing, to manipulate the positive and negative electrical signals. The IC generally looks like a dull fleck of aluminum, and is about the size of a baby's fingernail.

The major physical ingredient of an IC is silicon, the second most abundant substance on earth. As another historical note, the element *Si* (silicon) was discovered in 1823. Silicon is a *semiconductor*. That is, it is a type of solid whose ability to conduct electricity is reasonably good, somewhere between copper (good) and rubber (poor). A semiconductor's ability to conduct electricity can be increased by adding impurity elements, a process called *doping*.

The purpose of doping is to inject free charges that can be moved easily by an applied voltage. These added charge carriers can be either negative or positive, depending on the doping. When electrons are added, the doped semiconductor is negative, or *N-Type*. A lack of electrons makes the material positive, or *P-Type*. Doping increases the conductance of the material by a factor of 10 to 50 times. Pure semiconductor without doping is *intrinsic*. The doping results in *extrinsic* semiconductor.

The IC is fabricated by extending previous semiconductor manufacturing processes to include a large number of transistors, diodes, and resistors on a common substrate. The circuit elements arc formed on a single substrate of silicon by a technique which involves a combination of photolithography, diffusion, heating and baking, vaporizing and depositing, and ion implantation. On each silicon slice, the same circuits may be repeated a large number of times, a definite saving in manufacturing costs and processing. For instance, a silicon-substrate chip less than a quarter of an inch on an edge can contain well over 250,000 semiconductor components. See Fig. 11-1.

To reduce the handling costs of each IC chip, the original 3/4 inch (19 mm) diameter wafers that were used for the early ICs were quickly increased to 1.5 inches (38 mm). In 1971, 3 inch (76 mm) wafers were introduced to the IC fabrication lines. The 3 inch wafers continued in high volume production until the first part of 1980, when 4 inch (100 mm) wafers took over. Then, late 1982, 5 inch (125 mm) wafers went into production.

By the end of 1983, 6 inch wafers (150 mm) were rolling off the production lines and 8 inch were coming fast. The 8 inch wafers are so large that holes had to be drilled in the center to relieve film stresses created during fabrication. The consumption of silicon wafers in the United States alone exceeds 70 million per year. Piled on top of each other, they'd make a stack some 15 miles high.

An integrated circuit is made up of transistors. In general, transistors have two different applications. The first is in analog devices such as radios, televisions, and the like. In this application, the transistor serves primarily as an amplifier. The second application is in digital usages, such as computers, calculators, and such units.

X-RAY Lithography   Electron-beam Lithography

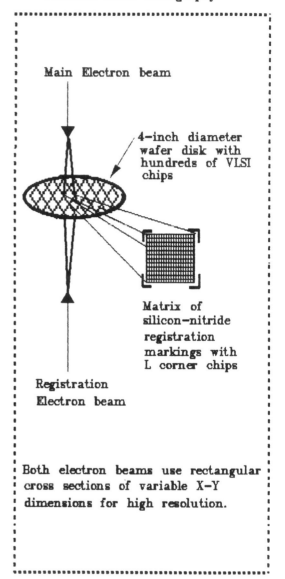

Vacuum chamber
with rotating
anode electron
gun

X-RAY source
A thin window

X-RAYS

Wafer
allignment
mount
(or table)

Disk
thickness
out of
scale

Mask substrate

XRAY absorber

Space

Photo-resist

Wafer disk
(Silicon
substrate)

Main Electron beam

4-inch diameter
wafer disk with
hundreds of VLSI
chips

Matrix of
silicon-nitride
registration
markings with
L corner chips

Registration
Electron beam

Both electron beams use rectangular
cross sections of variable X-Y
dimensions for high resolution.

Fig. 11-1. Forming a silicon chip.

The transistors function here as switches, turning on and off millions of times a second.

A *field-effect transistor* (FET) is a semiconductor device in which the resistance between two terminals is controlled by the voltage on a third terminal. One form of FET, referred to as a *metal oxide semiconductor field-effect transistor* (MOSFET) is constructed from a piece of lightly doped semiconductor material, called a substrate, upon which are formed two regions of the opposite type of semiconductor material. One of these regions is called a *source* since charge carriers originate from it. The other region is called a *drain* since charge carriers terminate at it.

The region of semiconductor material lying between the source and the drain is called the *channel.* Above the channel is a metal electrode, called the *gate,* lying along the entire length of the channel and separated from it by a layer of insulation. The name for this type of FET comes from the metal gate, oxide insulation, and semiconductor substrate.

PMOS and NMOS

There are several logic families based on the field-effect transistor. Two well-known ones are NMOS, which designates that the N-channel MOSFETs are used, and PMOS, which says that P-channel MOSFETs are used. MOS material is doped so that it is either N-type or P-type. To obtain the N-type, the doping elements of arsenic, antimony, and phosphorous are used. For the P-type, aluminum, gallium, boron, and iridium are used.

A bipolar device is a semiconductor in which there are both minority and majority carriers present; that is, it is a current-driven device. Bipolar fabrication generally requires 12 masking steps and 4 diffusion steps. The early PMOS wafers required fewer processing steps than were needed for bipolar fabrication. This simplicity allowed acceptable yields for more complex logic chips. Thus, it was PMOS that allowed the LSI circuit chips to be brought to the marketplace in the early to mid-1970's. Today, PMOS is essentially obsolete and few products are kept in production.

During this time, the technologists learned more about the physics of the silicon surface and there was now strong motivation to develop the NMOS process to take advantage of the 3:1 performance benefits of the N-channel transistor over the P-channel transistor.

The NMOS circuits are faster than the PMOS, in addition to containing more transistors. Both PMOS and NMOS operate in enhancement-mode. Enhancement mode simply means than an applied voltage enhances the number of charge carriers in the channel between the source and drain.

CMOS

A third, well-known MOSFET is *complementary metal oxide semiconductor,* CMOS. The CMOS has both P-channel and N-channel MOSFETs in the same circuit. A CMOS logic gate consists of two portions, one pulls down the gate output for the correct input conditions and the other pulls up the gate output for other input conditions.

CMOS logic is more complex than either NMOS or PMOS, and is, therefore, not capable of achieving gate densities as high as the other two. Its structure, however, does offer an advantage over all other common forms of logic. There is never a conductive path in the steady state between ground and power-supply voltage. Therefore, no discernible power is consumed during times in which the inputs are constant.

This different handling of power consumption is of great importance for applications that involve power supplied from batteries. Power is consumed during switching for two major reasons. The first is that there are capacitances throughout the circuit, primarily between the electrodes of the MOSFETs. A capacitance is the property which allows the storage of electrically separate charges when a potential difference exists between conductors. This capacitance must be charged each time a gate is switched.

The second reason is that both the pull-up and pull-down portions of a logic gate are partially on during the transition from input signals. As a result, current momentarily flows from the power-supply voltage to ground.

The added processing steps that were required for a CMOS IC raised the fabricating cost of the CMOS wafer. The cost was passed along to users.

Very Large Scale Integration (VLSI)

When looking at gates on a chip, the number of gates fall into four categories: *small-scale integration* (SSI), *medium-scale integration* (MSI), *large-scale integration* (LSI), and *very large-scale integration* (VLSI). From one to four gates, the IC is called an SSI. From four to 100 gates, it's called an MSI. At the 100-gate threshold, the chip is called LSI. Once the number of gates soars past 20,000, it's called a VLSI chip. Some VLSI chips hold as many as 250,000 gates.

Advanced high-density N-channel silicon-gate MOS technology (HMOS) has a potential of getting more and more gates onto a single chip. This shrinking of IC patterns brings forward the possibility of increasing switching speeds and reducing the chip's power consumption.

VLSI technology became established because of the capability of IC manufacturers to make uncontaminated and accurate exposures of high-resolution circuit patterns on resist-covered silicon wafers. High resolution of these patterns extend to the minimum line-widths of 2 microns to 1 micron, due to a wide variety of lithographic techniques such as contact, proximity, 1:1 projection, step-and-repeat projection, X-ray, and electron-beam projections.

Industry experts now estimate that VLSI technology will soon extend the fabrication densities to a million logic gates per chip. A serious problem in designing VLSI chips is the large commitment of resources that is required to develop the internal logic. It becomes easier to miss the market because the market may not agree with the basic design choices that must be made at each major design step.

To avoid this missed-market trap, semiconductor companies had to learn to do business in a new way. No longer could engineers and design technicians use manual processes to think through, design, and then test a possible chip—that takes too long. The complex over-all design is broken into a series of tasks, each of which can be programmed into computers.

First comes the functional design—the synthesis, verification, simulation and testing done at the architectural, system, logic, circuit, device and process levels. Next comes the physical design—the partitioning, layout, and topological analysis. At both of these two phases, functionality, testability and physical design factors must be considered in parallel with design.

Computer-aided design (CAD) requires large memory resources and many hours of CPU time to solve the problems associated with complex chip layout. In addition, the computer programs are not advanced to the state that they can make better decisions than experienced human designers, so each step must be cross-checked and verified before going on. Regardless, CAD has sped chip development.

IC PACKAGING

One of the main constraints imposed on IC design is the package the IC resides

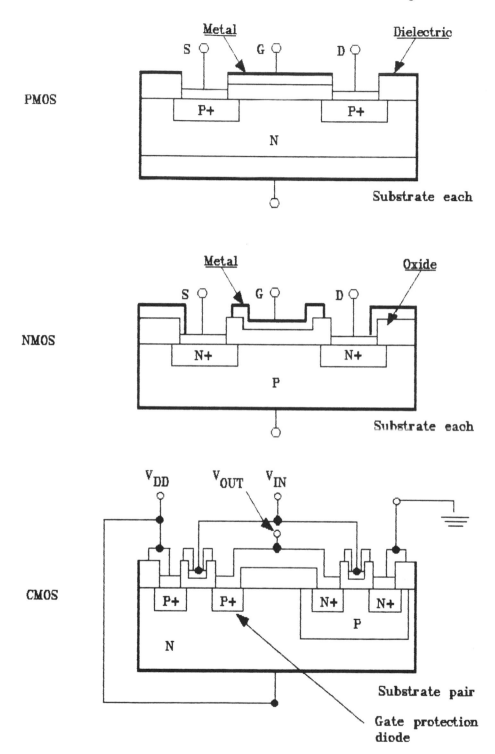

Fig. 11-2. Comparison of PMOS, NMOS, and CMOS.

in. Some of the things that limit designers are:

- The processor must be equipped with a data bus. This bus requires the number of pins that is the width of the bus (16 for the 8086 and 80286, 32 for the 80386).
- Then additional pins are required for the address bus, again the number of bits that is the full width of the address.
- Two pins are needed for power and ground.
- Tradeoff the number of pins for complexity like memory chips RAS/CAS.
- Finally, it requires at least two pins, sometimes four, for connection to an external clock.

In addition to those five points, some number of pins are an absolute minimum for synchronization with external events. In practice, this means that 32-bit microproces-

Pin Position

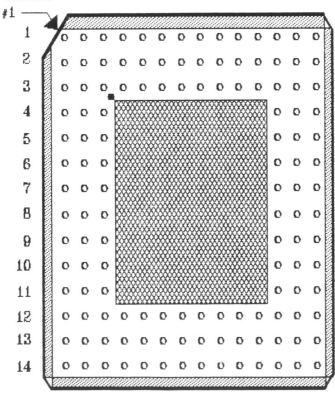
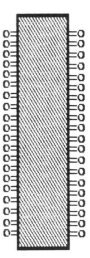

80386 Pin Grid Array (PGA)   Dual Inline Pin (DIP)

Fig. 11-3. 80386 PGA and a DIP.

sors *cannot* be implemented in 40-pin packages. Note the pin layout of the 80386 as shown early in this chapter.

Another constraint is due to the technological limitation of the amount of chip area (or real estate as it's often called) that can be economically implemented at any time. Designers realize they want to implement as many functions as possible.

The new gate array products have forced the IC industry to find ways to package high lead count, 68 and greater. A combination of both insertion and surface mount packages are appearing and both are available in ceramic for military applications and plastic for industrial and consumer applications.

A high density package is the *pin grid array* (PGA). The PGA looks like a square bed of nails. It uses a ceramic substrate, has 0.100 inch pin spacings, excellent thermal characteristics, and provides for very high density. This was the design chosen for the 80386 microprocessor. Figure 11-3 illustrates the quantum difference between the newer PGA design over the traditional dual in-line package (DIP).

Traditional silicon processing is racing to its final, physical limits. Practical reconsiderations are needed, for instance, in the reduced reliability that results from extensive device size reduction. There's also the limited economic resources that are made available to provide the necessary computer-based tools; there is an extremely limited number of programmers who understand the CAD requirements thoroughly enough to program solutions. Also, there's the increased cost and reduced throughput of the new VLSI fabrication equipment.

Many observers are concerned that a move away from the 5V standard power supply voltage will meet with stiff opposition—even though this change is necessary if the smallest channel-length transistors are to be used. Too much, they feel, has been designed around 5V for either an easy or a quick change.

We are progressing to the SLSI (Super-Large-Scale Integration). We are also entering the era of distributed processing. Within the microprocessor itself, each of the input/output and peripheral chips will become processor-equipped.

From a human and social standpoint, it is predicted that multi-function microprocessors with built-in intelligence will become as common as the electric motor is today.

12

Interfacing Concepts

To be a useful system, a microprocessor must connect with the various components that make up a microcomputer. This interconnection has to take into account the nature and timing of signals generated and expected by each component.

There are three classes of signals: data, address, and control. From the viewpoint of the CPU, the signals are bidirectional (both input and output) for data and control, and output only for addresses. Obviously, those signals must travel from one component to another and exchange information and data. That process is called *interfacing*.

To get signals from one component to another, it's necessary to design supplementary circuits and to choose appropriate components.

INTERFACING

In computers, there are two basic interface methods: hardware and software. In practice, most designers use a combination of the two. A software interface has two major parameters: the time required for its execution and the memory required to store it. Take care to avoid creating software bottlenecks. For instance, if a software interface spends too much time executing a complex I/O routine, the I/O routine may leave too little time for another necessary computation.

Hardware is suited to interface those signals sent and received for control of time-critical, fixed-logic operations such as collecting bit strings from serial devices. Instead of looping to collect and shift each bit to form a byte, the system program can handle interrupt requests which come from hardware signals to read a byte at a time. However, remember that hardware is more difficult to design and check than software. Figure 12-1 shows a block diagram of a typical interface between a processor and a peripheral controller.

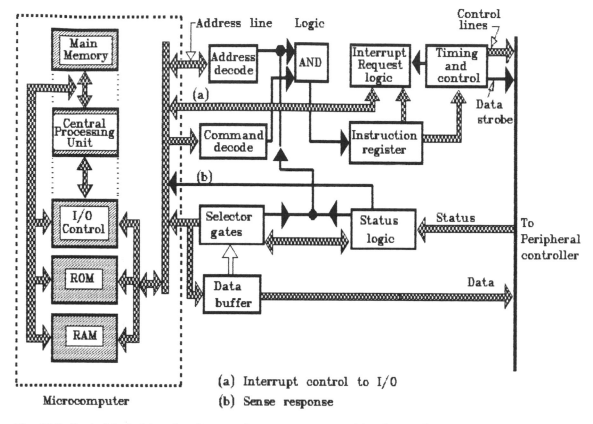

Fig. 12-1. Typical logical interface from a microcomputer to a peripheral controller.

Levels

Interfacing can be described at several levels: mechanical, electrical, functional (processor to peripheral), and user (peripheral to processor).

The mechanical interface concerns the physical characteristics of the connection between two devices or subsystems. This may take the form of a connector plug having a certain size and shape with a given number of pins. Electrical interfacing refers to the definition of the electrical signals on each of the pins. This includes the voltage level and the specific function of the electrical signal on the pins.

Functional interfacing refers to the rules or protocol for sending signals over the connection, including the specific sequence of signals generated by both devices that define the purpose of the communication.

The user interface level involves the meaning of the information or data being conveyed from one device to another. This meaning may be defined within the context of a particular operating system or application program. An example is a series of bits that is interpreted as "job is finished." The meaning may be defined by the device, such as a bit pattern indicating I/O error types.

Register

An essential component of any processor/device interface is a register to store data being transmitted to or from the processor. The register acts as temporary or buffer store so that information can be interchanged efficiently between the processor and devices which may have very different rates of information flow. Without this temporary storage, the faster of the two (usually the processor) would spend most of its time waiting until the slow one finishes.

Information may be stored as a byte, a word, a doubleword, or a number of words. The largest amount is probably that incorporated in some visual display units. Because the picture must be "refreshed" or re-presented on the Video Display Unit (VDU) 10 to 20 times each second, the entire body of information presented must be read out at the same rate. Often, to avoid monopolizing the processor, display units incorporate a store holding several thousand bytes which contain the display information.

A frequent requirement in interfacing design is a register with interstage connections arranged so that an external pulse can increase or decrease the register contents by one; that is, a *counter*. A typical application for a counter is in the interface for a block data transfer where it checks the progress of the transfer. The counter is first loaded with the number of words to be transferred. A pulse is fed to it for each word transferred, thus decreasing the contents by one. The transfer operation is complete when the number stored in the counter falls to zero.

Another use for a counter is as an interval timer. The counter is decremented by the system clock. This allows a program to load an interval to be counted down.

Buffer

An issue in buffer interfacing is optimizing buffer space to keep the system coordinated. That is, the CPU and the rest of the circuitry must be balanced so that the best throughput is achieved. For example, interrupts should be trapped and prioritized before being allowed to stop CPU processing; then the CPU should turn to interrupt handling software that needs to be quickly available.

To eliminate interface problems, many manufacturers developed special interfacing chips that correspond to individual devices. These interface chips provide all necessary logic circuits for a general-purpose interface. These chips are identified to the processor by use of address select lines externally wired to specify the address of the subject chip.

Peripherals

Special instructions and control signals are provided for testing the status of peripheral devices and for transferring data to and from these devices. To handle this testing and transfer, there are three basic forms of communication between processors and their outside world: programmed data transfers, direct memory access (DMA), and interrupts.

Peripherals may be wired to the computer's buses using the same control signals that are used to control memory. By using these signals, the peripheral is interfaced to the processor using *memory-mapped I/O* techniques. To communicate with the peripheral, the processor executes a memory-reference instruction so that the memory control signals are generated.

If the processor needs the data, the peripheral places information onto the data bus so that the processor can read it. If the processor is writing data, the peripheral takes the information off the bus. Peripherals may also be addressed using an address space set aside for that purpose. The addresses in this I/O space are known as I/O ports. There are special IN and OUT instructions for communicating with I/O ports.

Memory

Memory in a microcomputer is an array of storage locations for data and program instructions. There are many possible memory devices. There is a mixture of random-access memory (RAM), or certain memory-mapped devices such as I/O ports, digital-to-analog (D/A) devices, analog-to-digital (A/D) converters, and so on. The basic control signals that apply to memory operations are some form of memory request, memory write, and memory read.

The simplest arrangement is a single digital output which switches some device on or off. This consists of a single-digit store which is set or cleared by programs. Since it is usually a matter of chance how one of these stores settles when the power is first switched on, the computer usually sets all such circuits, internal and external, to a known state before starting computation.

A slightly more complex interface is used for a digital-to-analog converter. In its simplest form, this arrangement produces an output which varies in voltage, depending on what number is sent to it. Each output voltage remains until a different number is received by the device. For this interface, data is gated from the data lines into an interface register under program control. The register holds the number until the next one overwrites it. If several analog outputs are required, a multiplexer may be connected to the converter output to enable it to energize several different circuits.

Often, a computer requires an analog-to-digital process. That is, the computer samples an analog voltage that occurs outside the computer and converts its value to a digital representation. Some care is required when doing this. The time taken to do the conversion with an accuracy of 10-12 binary digits may be many machine cycles, say 30 to 50 microseconds, or on a 16 MHz 80386, 480 to 800 cycles. Thus, once having started the process of conversion, it is essential to wait before trying to transfer the contents of the converter buffer register into the accumulator.

Some analog-to-digital converters can be switched to provide a range of different output word sizes, the smaller sizes giving a less accurate but quicker result. Thus, it is possible to program or manually select the most suitable combination of speed and accuracy for each application. In such cases, no advantage is obtained unless the program delay is adjusted automatically to be just in excess of the conversion time. Generally, some single-digit flag bit is set to signal the end of the conversion.

BUSES

A *bus* is a data path that is shared by the units of a system. A bus may be a number of lines etched on a printed circuit board, soldered wires between connectors into which circuit board modules are placed, or ribbon cable. The components of the computer system are physically packaged on one or more printed circuit boards, the number and type of functions supplied vary with the system, the manufacturer, and often by the generation of the chip.

Information travels over the bus in the form of groups of bits. A bus may have a separate line to accommodate each bit of a word (a parallel bus) or it may have a single line that is shared in time by all bits of a word (a serial bus). Figure 12-2 shows a typical data bus arrangement.

Three-State Bus

A three-state bus is like a telephone party line, with many callers connected. The three states are High, Low, and High Impedance, which prevents the device/chip from affecting the state being presented by other devices/chips connected to the bus. Thus, only one device drives the bus. The control logic chooses only one driver (talker) to be active at any one time. When the driver is enabled, its data is placed on the bus and all other drivers are disabled.

There can be many listeners on the bus. In general, data on the bus is intended for only one of them. A combination of control and address signals identify which one. The control logic generates signals (data strobes) to tell the listener when to receive the data. The talkers/listeners can be either unidirectional (able to be talker *or* listener) or bi-directional (able to be both). Figure 12-3 shows bi-directional talkers/listeners connected to bus lines.

The bus structure approach to design is popular because it uses a standard inter-

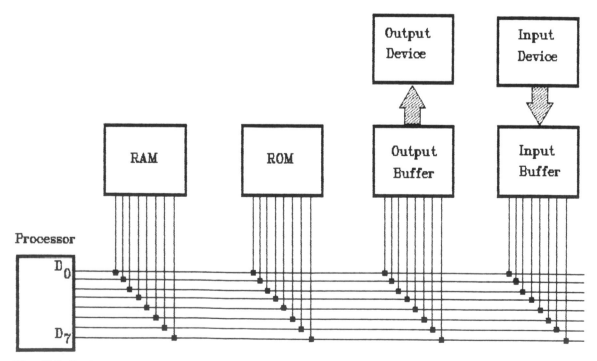

Fig. 12-2. Typical data bus arrangement.

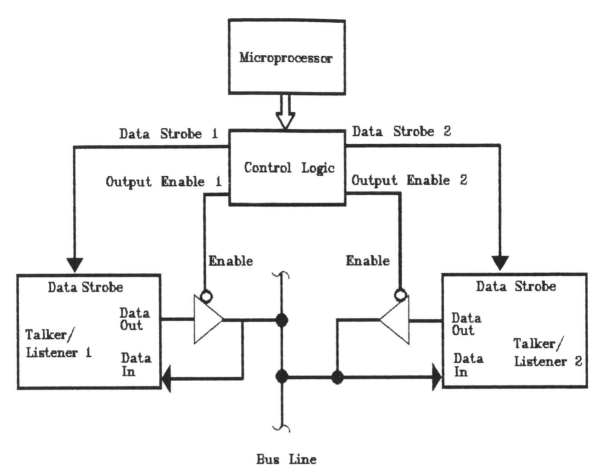

Bus Line

Fig. 12-3. Bidirectional talker/listener connected to bus lines.

facing discipline for all devices. In general, standard architecture design calls for connecting the CPU modules and I/O through a set of three buses.

Bus Types

The three buses that interface to the CPU are: the *data bus,* the *address bus,* and the *control bus.* Data travels over the data bus between the CPU and memory, or CPU and I/O devices. This data can be either instructions for the CPU or information that the CPU is passing to or from I/O ports. In the 8088, the data bus is 8 bits wide. In the 8086, 80186, and 80286, it is 16 bits wide; in the 80386, it is 32 bits wide.

The CPU uses the address bus to select the desired memory or I/O device by providing a unique address that corresponds to one of the memory locations or I/O elements of the system. Finally, the control bus carries control signals to the memory and I/O devices, specifying whether data is to go into or out of the CPU, and exactly when the data is being transferred.

Most buses have a control module that acts as traffic director in the data exchange.

The main purpose of the control module is to cause a word to be transferred between two other modules.

General Operation

A bus system begins operating when the control module places a sending module's code word onto the bus and activates the Sender strobe line. This causes the module whose code word is on the bus to realize that it is the sender. The control module then places the receiving module's code word onto the bus and activates the Receiver strobe line. This causes the module whose code word is now on the bus to realize that it is the receiver.

The control module then activates the data strobe line, causing the contents of the sender's register to be transferred to the receiver's register. This step can be repeated for any additional data words to be transferred between the two modules.

Data is transferred between the sender and receiver in response to a pulse on the appropriate strobe line from the control module. This requires that, at the time of the strobe pulse, the sender module has data available and the receiver module is ready to accept the data. This is called *synchronous* (synchronized) transfer of data.

What happens if one or both the sender and receiver modules sends/accepts data only under certain conditions? The bus can be operated in asynchronous (unsynchronized) fashion. The transfer of data between a sender and receiver module could be coordinated with the use of status lines that reflect the condition of the two modules. Once a sender is designated, it controls the Sender Ready line, indicating when it is ready to send. The designated receiver controls the Receiver Ready line, indicating when it will accept data.

Two objectives must to be met to coordinate data transfers. First, the transfer should occur as soon as both the sender and receiver are ready. Second, each data word should be transferred only once. To ensure that these objectives are met, a sequence is prescribed for data transfer. This sequence is referred to as *protocol*.

With protocols, the receiver is informed when a new word is available at the sender and the sender is informed when a data word has been accepted by the receiver. The state of the ready lines at any point in time determines the appropriate action to be taken by each of the two modules.

Each instant of data transfer from one part of the system to another is called a *bus cycle* (or often, a *machine cycle*.). The timing of these cycles depends on the CPU clock signal. The length of bus cycles is based on the frequency of a clock signal. Typical clock rates are 5, 8, 10, and 16 MHz (megahertz or millions of cycles per second). The newer clocks send up to 24 MHz.

INPUT/OUTPUT PORTS

Computer input/output (I/O) address space is organized into ports. A port is a group of I/O lines that are read or written in parallel between the CPU and the I/O unit, generally one line per bit. The number of lines in a port is usually the same as in the word-size of the processor. For inputs, ports are usually sets of logic gates that route input signals to the system's data bus. For outputs, ports are sets of latches into which signals from the data bus are stored.

By use and convention, the direction of input and output information flow that involves the microprocessor is regarded relative to the processor itself. An *input port* is any source of data (such as a register) that connects in a selectable manner to the processor data bus and that sends a data word *to* the processor. Conversely, an *output port* is a receptacle of data (such as a register) that connects in a selectable manner to the processor data bus. When selected, it receives a data word *from* the microprocessor.

A processor needs a means of coordinating its timing to that of an external device with which it wants to exchange information. Otherwise, a data transfer from a given input port might be performed before it was required, thus stepping on some process within the CPU. As noted above, this coordination of timing is called handshaking.

I/O Port Techniques

There are three types of I/O techniques by which a processor communicates: programmed I/O, interrupt I/O, and direct memory access (DMA).

Programmed I/O is a processor-initiated I/O transfer where the processor executes a program to accomplish the I/O. Interrupt I/O is a device-initiated technique. Generally, an external device connected to the processor interrupt pin raises the signal of the interrupt pin. (Or lowers the signal, depending on the processor.) In response, the processor completes the execution of the current instruction, saves the program counter onto the correct stack, and executes a program called the Interrupt Service Routine to complete the transfer.

Direct memory access is also device-initiated. Data transfer between memory and the I/O device occurs without processor involvement. Typically, DMA controller chips are required to complete the transfer.

UNIVERSAL SYNCHRONOUS/ASYNCHRONOUS RECEIVER/TRANSMITTER

A microprocessor communicates with peripheral devices that receive and transmit data serially. The processor must go through a parallel-to-serial and then a serial-to-parallel conversion during this communication.

Most serial data transfers between the processor and peripheral devices are carried out asynchronously. That is, the device may transmit at any point in time. When no data is being sent, the device sends a simple mark bit, generally a high signal value so that any break in the transmission circuit will be known immediately. When the device is ready to transmit data, the transmitter sends a zero bit to show the start of transmission. This start bit is followed by the data, then a parity bit, and one or two stop bits. At the end of transmission, the sender continues to send the high signal value as the ''no data coming'' mark.

To simplify interface design between processors and both synchronous and asynchronous serial devices, universal synchronous/asynchronous receiver/transmitter chips, called USARTs, are designed. USARTs consist of a receiver and a transmitter and each section can operate independently. Figure 12-4 shows a typical USART.

The USART is a full-duplex device (it can send and receive at the same time) in a 40-pin package. It supplies logical formatting. Additional circuitry may be re-

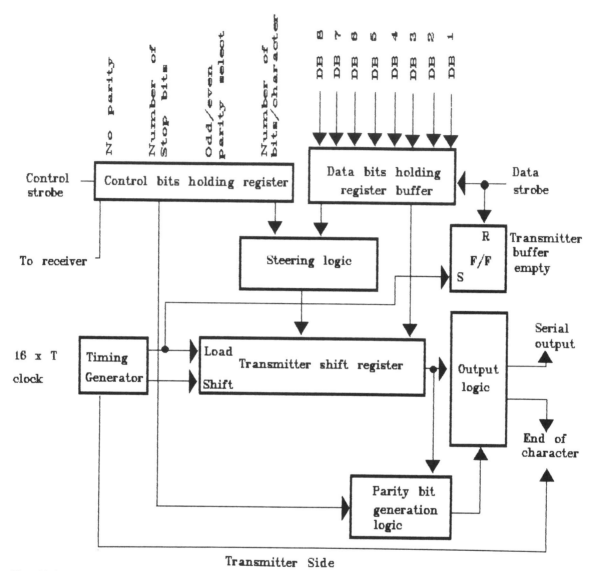

Fig. 12-4A. Typical transmitter sections of an USART.

quired for the electrical interface, but no common clock signal is required between the USART and the device with which it communicates. USART transmitters are double-buffered, so that the next data byte can be accepted as soon as the current byte is ready for transmission.

USARTs that operate at rates up to 200K baud are available. The baud rate can be different for the receiver and transmitter and is set by external clocks which run at 16 times the desired baud rate and which are connected to the separate receiver and transmitter clock signals.

Typically, both the microprocessor and the I/O devices are connected in parallel to their USART with a serial connection (e.g., RS-232C) between them.

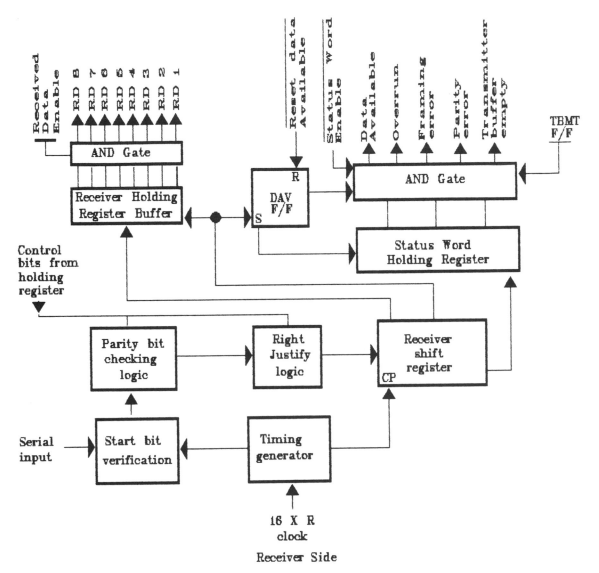

Fig. 12-4B. Receiver sections of an USART.

MULTIBUS

The bus structure that supplies the interface for all the hardware connections is one of the most important elements in a computer system. This structure allows the various system components to interact with each other. In addition, it allows generation of interrupts, direct memory access, memory and I/O data transfers, and so on.

As one sample of a general bus, the Intel MULTIBUS® architecture provides a communications channel that can be used to coordinate a wide variety of computing modules. (For more information on 80386 and MULTIBUS® I and II, see Appendix 4.) To do this, the various modules in a MULTIBUS® system are designated as *masters* or *slaves*.

Masters

A master is any module that has the ability to control the bus. It obtains control of the bus through bus exchange logic and initiates data transfers on it using either built-in processors or dedicated logic. Masters generate command signals, address signals, and memory or I/O addresses.

A master operates in one of two modes: Mode 1 or Mode 2. In Mode 1, masters are limited to a single bus transfer per bus connect. If all masters in the system are operating in Mode 1, then system timing is limited by a maximum bus busy period. This mode allows system designers to predict the overall performance of their system.

In Mode 2, masters are not limited in bus control and can invoke bus override. In this mode, bus time-outs are allowed and masters are not required to operate within the maximum busy period. This mode allows a broad class of operations, which gives users flexibility in meeting their applications' needs.

Slaves

Slaves, on the other hand, are recipients of data transfer requests only. They decode the address lines and act on the command signals of masters. Figure 12-5 shows a block diagram of a MULTIBUS® Master and Slave examples.

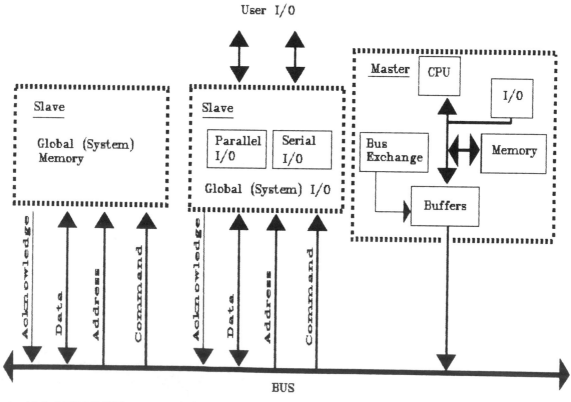

Fig. 12-5. MULTIBUS® master and slave examples.

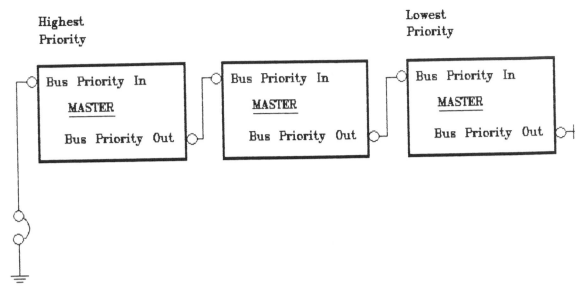

Fig. 12-6. Serial priority technique.

Bus Operation

MULTIBUS® accommodates several bus masters on the same system, each taking control as it needs to transfer data. The masters request bus control through a bus exchange sequence. This sequence uses a set of six signals that test whether the bus is currently in use, check that no other master with a higher priority is requesting the bus, request the bus, and release it.

Priority Techniques. There are two bus priority techniques: serial and parallel. In the serial scheme, master priority is resolved via a daisy-chain technique. That is, the bus priority of one master is connected to the bus priority of the next lower master. The highest priority is on one end of the chain and the lowest on the other end.

Serial priority is determined as each master requests the bus. If no other master of higher or equal priority is controlling the bus, then the requesting master takes control. The number of masters that can be linked in a serial chain is limited by the fact that the priority signal must propagate through the entire chain within one bus cycle. If 10 MHz is used, then the number of masters in a serial chain is limited to three. Figure 12-6 shows a serial priority technique.

In a parallel scheme, a Bus Arbiter determines allocation. This may be done with a priority scheme which determines the next master by a fixed priority list or other method as defined by the system. Figure 12-7 shows one parallel priority scheme.

Bus Design

MULTIBUS® has 16 data lines, 20 address lines, 8 multilevel interrupt lines, and control and arbitration lines. Because of these many lines, both 8-bit and 16-bit masters can be intermixed in a system.

MULTIBUS® maintains its own clock which is independent of the clocks of the modules it links together. This clock allows masters of different speeds to share the

Bus Arbiter

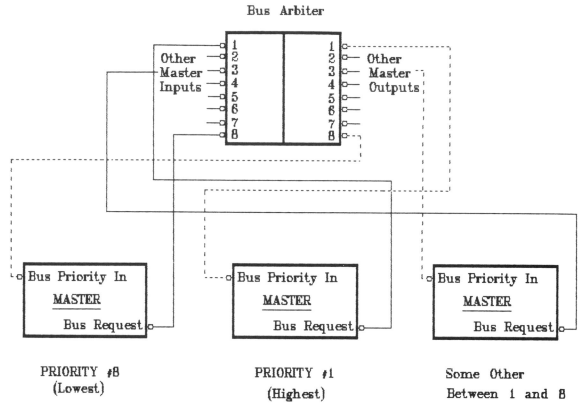

PRIORITY #8
(Lowest)

PRIORITY #1

(Highest)

Some Other

Between 1 and 8

Fig. 12-7. Parallel priority technique.

bus and allows the masters to operate asynchronously with respect to each other. MULTIBUS® arbitration logic permits slow masters to compete equitably for use of the bus. However, once a module has obtained the bus, transfer speeds depend on the capabilities of the transmitting and receiving modules.

The primary MULTIBUS® function is to provide a data transfer path between modules on the bus. It allows systems to be constructed with boards of varying capability and allows for variations in data path width, I/O address path width, and interrupt attributes.

MULTIBUS® II is designed to increase performance and multiprocessing capability of the 80386-based system. The new architecture includes message passing that makes higher multiprocessing performance possible. Message passing allows all transfers over the bus to occur at the fastest 32-bit data and burst-transfer rates available.

In addition to message passing, the MULTIBUS® II board modules support virtual interrupts, geographic addressing, and distributed arbitration. Virtual interrupt allows one processor to write into a special memory location of another processor, which gives nearly unlimited interrupt signaling flexibility.

Geographic addressing provides interconnect space for software configuration of OEM systems by incorporating on-board interconnect registers. Distributed arbitration gives MULTIBUS® II board products as many discrete arbitration levels as there are boards or slots in a system. This gives each board in a system the same priority for access time to the bus, which keeps high-performance master boards from locking out lower-priority boards. Discrete arbitration also allows multiprocessing with many potential bus masters.

The key concept when constructing a MULTIBUS® system is that of *required* versus *supplied* capability. Each product provides some individual, basic set of capabilities. A transaction between two such products is restricted to that capability which is the intersection of the sets of capabilities of the two products. In some cases, the intersection could be null, implying fundamental incapability.

POWER SUPPLY

The requirements of modern devices are for closely regulated direct current (DC) power. The regulation of the power may be done at the power supply or, as is the case in S-100 systems, on the individual circuit boards.

Most computer systems required a +5 volt DC power supply that delivers one to five amps. Typical requirements are 1, 3, 4, and 5 amps, depending on the system. Some systems require a current level of 10 amps at 5V. Power supplies often have a +12V supply at 2A to support diskette drives or hard disk drives.

SUMMARY

Interfacing means connecting the microprocessor with the external world and its own internal units. The more intelligent the device, the more important it is to pay close attention to the interconnecting capabilities.

Interfacing is one of the more difficult aspects of hardware development. It is here that more savings and tradeoffs can be made. In most applications, the signals that must be detected by the processor are seldom, if ever, compatible. In the simplest case, this may be just voltage conversion to compatible 5V transistor-to-transistor logic (TTL). Incompatible voltages can easily corrupt the processing signals. In other instances, analog-to-digital converters may be required.

13

Memory
Organization Overview

Memory transfers information through time. That transfer is always in the same direction: forward. The information can be saved in various ways in a computer system but think of memory as the channel that allows data to be retained for future use.

The smallest unit of information that a digital system stores is the binary digit or "bit": a binary one (1) or zero (0). This bit is first stored in a 1-bit *flip-flop* register. Flip-flop is a general term for a memory cell that has only two stable *states* in which it can remain, as long as its power supply is not interrupted. Inputs to that memory cell can change its state. Figure 13-1 shows a general description of a static MOS flip-flop, or single register circuit.

Thousands of such 1-bit registers can be incorporated into a single integrated circuit, an IC, and share common sets of inputs and outputs, and a single clock line. This entity is referred to as a *memory* chip. Memory capacity is usually specified in terms of the maximum number of bytes the memory stores.

A microcomputer is a system of modules that include a processor along with memory and I/O units. The processor can be broken down further into subunits in order to achieve greater flexibility. One such approach involves separating the processor's data-handling portion from that which handles instructions and their sequencing. The data-handling portion consists of the arithmetic-logic unit (ALU) and various data registers. This data handling is formed by cascading several identical data units. Each of these units is referred to as a *microprocessor slice* and consists of as an Arithmetic-Logic Unit and registers.

To form a complete microprocessor from microprocessor slices, additional components (such as a program counter, an instruction register, an instruction decoder, and a timing and control unit) are needed to handle instruction sequencing and decoding. These components fetch instructions from main memory according to the program counter and transfer them to the instruction register.

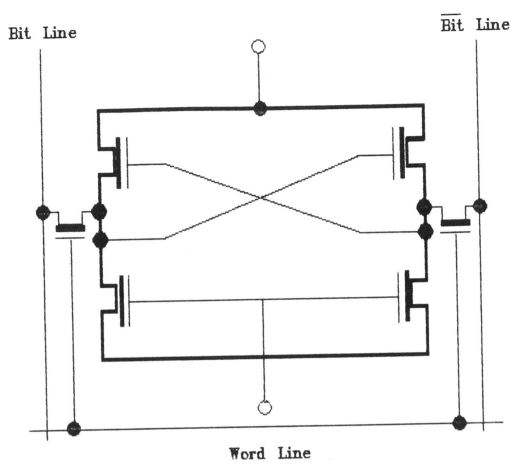

Fig. 13-1. Static MOS flip-flop circuit diagram.

REAL MEMORY

Memory is now normally implemented in CMOS, VLSI technology (see Chapter 11 for more information on the physical composition of CMOS). Some manufacturers include a limited amount of memory directly on the CPU chip itself. Most, however, don't waste the CPU "real estate" and keep memory (other than cache memory) on separate chips.

ROM and RAM

Semiconductor memories come in two fundamentally different types: program changeable (Random-Access Memory or RAM) and unchangeable (Read-Only Memory or ROM).

Random Access Memory (RAM). RAMs are memory cells that can be changed under program control. There are two types of RAM: *Static* (SRAM) and *Dynamic* (DRAM). SRAMs use a flip-flop for each memory element. Each flip-flop can be set or reset to store a binary one (1) or zero (0). The state of the flip-flop does not change unless new data is stored in it or power to the RAM is interrupted.

Dynamic RAMS (DRAMs) on the other hand, use an on-chip capacitor for each storage element. A charge on the capacitor indicates a 1; no charge indicates a 0. While this technique simplifies the storage cell and permits denser memory chips, there is a problem: the charge leaks off the capacitor in a few milliseconds (thousandths of a second). To correct this, the charge on the DRAMs must be *refreshed*.

DRAM refreshing consists of reading a sequence of memory locations within a specified time. While reading data, the RAM chip automatically rewrites the data back into the location just read. As a result, all the 1 bits are restored to full charge, and the 0 bits to a no-charge. DRAMs are typically refreshed at least every 2 milliseconds.

Read-Only Memory (ROM). ROMs provide a means of permanently storing programs and data, since ROMs retain their contents even when power is off. MOS tech-

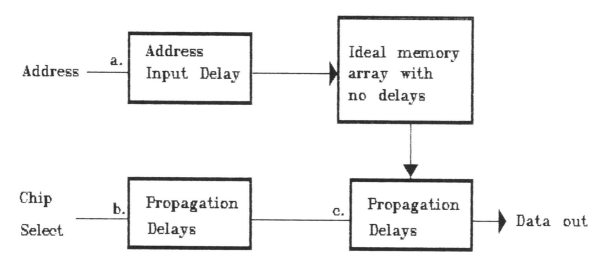

a. Includes all propagation delays associated with address input buffers, row and column decoders, and the memory array.

b. Includes all propagation delays associated with chip select logic.

c. Includes all delays associated with the output buffers.

Fig. 13-2. Simplified model of a ROM.

nology is ideal for the fabrication of ROMs, because of the very dense geometrical layouts that are possible in ROM. Figure 13-2 shows a simplified model of a ROM.

There are four types of ROMs: Mask-programmed, Programmable (PROM), Erasable-Programmable (EPROM), and Electrically Erasable (EEPROM).

Mask-programmable ROMs are programmed by the manufacturer who customizes the chip, based either on the manufacturer's or the customer's specifications. These ROMs are often used in high-volume products because they are the least expensive and the highest in bit density.

The user programs the PROM by electrically using a special device called a PROM programmer. Once the ROM is programmed, it cannot be changed. These ROMs are useful for special purposes when users require alterable environments that, once set, will continue.

The EPROM is similar to the PROM except that it can be erased and reprogrammed. Programmed bits are stored as a charge on a near-zero-leakage capacitor. Erasing is done by shining ultraviolet light through a clear window in the IC package. EPROMs are useful for prototypes or small-volume production runs.

The fourth type, the EEPROM, can be erased electrically while it is still in the circuit. A major advantage of the EEPROM over EPROM is that small sections of the EEPROM can be erased, while EPROMs must be completely erased. Typical applications include calibrated transducers, automatic telephone dialers, and digital TV tuners.

MEMORY SYSTEMS

Memory requirements of a typical system cannot be met with a single memory device; several devices must be interconnected to form a system. Capacity is expanded by increasing the number of words and/or by increasing the word length above that attainable by a single device.

Word length is increased by placing the outputs of two or more memory devices in parallel. The number of words in a memory system is increased by multiplexing outputs from two or more memory devices. Most memory devices have features that aid this multiplexing.

A memory system requires a way to expand addresses. That is, it needs a method to expand the number of memory address bits to which the memory system responds. The number of address bits that a processor provides dictates its physical *memory address space*.

Memory Organization

Memory is designed so that a single device meets all the fundamental component requirements: (1) an array of memory cells, each of which can store a single bit, (2) logic to address any location in memory, (3) circuitry to allow the reading of the contents of any memory location, and (4) for writeable memory, circuitry to allow any memory location to be written.

Memories contain input drivers, output buffers, and circuitry for address expansion, for easy interconnection between that device and other memory or logic circuits. The memory is organized internally several ways in an effort to obtain high speed, a large bit capacity, and low peripheral circuit and memory array costs.

Word Organized and Linear Selection. The simplest organization is a *word organized* array with *linear selection*. That is, the memory array has a column length equal to the number of words and a row length equal to the number of bits per word. Word selection requires a decoder with a mutually exclusive output for each word in memory. The address inputs to this decoder select one and only one word in the memory array. Although conceptually simple, the linear selection method requires a large decoder for a large number of words.

Two-Level Decoding. The address decoder size is reduced by organizing the memory array and word selection logic to allow *two-level* decoding. In a memory array using this method, one level corresponds to a physical word and one to a logical word. A physical word consists of the number of bits in a row of the array. A logical word is the number of bits of a physical word which are sensed and gated to the output device at one time.

Two-level decoding requires a row decoder that selects a physical word and a column decoder that selects one logical word from the selected physical word.

Bit Organized. A common method of memory organization is when the number of segments in a physical word is equal to the number of bits in the physical word. That is, each logical word is a single bit in length. The bit organized memory has a single output, a square memory array, and row and column decoders of equal complexity.

Memory Protection

A major problem in any system which has overlapping uses for memory is protecting the contents of that memory from unauthorized access or modification. It is generally left to the operating system to devise some scheme to keep each process from interfering from another, while at the same time protecting itself.

In a simple system, the user application is placed in one particular location and the operating system in another, each able to access its own space. Generally, in this type of system, it is assumed that any addresses issued by the operating system will be "good" ones and thus not checked. Any addresses issued by any other application must be assumed to be "suspect" and checked to be certain that those addresses fall within the allowed area. Often, it is the hardware that does the checking.

In order for the hardware to do this checking, it must know where the operating system starts and stops, and whether the user program or the operating system is running at any instant in time. The most common way to implement these requirements is by providing two modes of execution: a *user mode* and a *privilege mode*.

In the user mode, only a limited range of addresses are allowed—the addresses limited to the user area. In the privileged mode, all addresses in the memory area are valid. Transition between the two modes occurs when an interrupt occurs or when a special "enter operating system" instruction is issued.

Memory Addressing

In a random access memory system, any word location is directly accessible. Each word location is assigned an identifier and consists of a fixed number of memory elements. The word identifier is known as the *address* of the word location. This address allows each word location to be distinguished from others for the purpose of either a read or a write operation.

Direct addressing combines the instruction code and the effective address into one word which permits a memory reference instruction to be executed in two machine phases: fetch and execute. The location of the instruction's operand (which specifies the operation to be performed) indicates the source or destination register. For direct addressing, generally only two memory pages (zero and one) of static or dynamic RAM are allocated.

Quite often, applications and operating systems must use the same real memory and must be protected from each other. The use of a limit register is one method of protection. However, this has limitations when there are several applications that share and re-use space. The most satisfactory solution is to provide some relocation mechanism within the store accessing hardware itself. Each application or internal process now sees a *virtual store* that extends from a base address up to some limit.

The translation between real addresses and virtual addresses has to be done for every store access in user mode. This translation can be done well only if the design provides suitable hardware between the CPU and memory. The most effective hardware has a base and limit register that does the translation and limit checking. Figure 13-3 shows a generic arrangement.

Before doing a memory access, the base register is set to the start of the memory allocated to this process and the limit register is set to its size. These registers are set as part of the register reloading normally done when starting a process. In the user mode, all addresses are translated by adding the base register to the virtual address generated by the program. This produces a real address which is used for the memory access.

Memory Management Unit

Most computer systems have some kind of memory management unit (MMU)

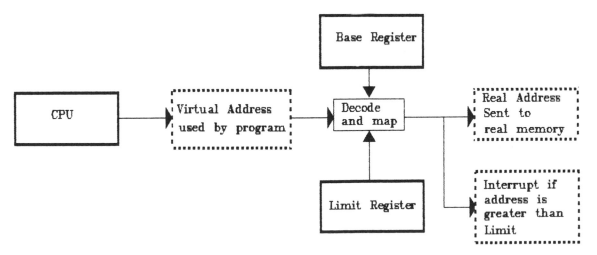

Fig. 13-3. Base and limit registers.

that helps the multitasking operating system allocate memory for each task and provide protection from user programs. For example, a common problem is when an application program makes an error in computing an address, perhaps using an array subscript which is too large or too small. If the system is not protected, this kind of problem can change operating system code, modify device tables, or actually cause a device to perform an undesired and unrequested function such as overwriting a data file.

Besides protecting the operating system from inadvertent tampering, the MMU provides automatic program relocation. Through the MMU, memory accesses by user programs are translated from a logical or program address to a physical or hardware address. These physical addresses may be located at a completely different place in memory than the logical address would imply. By doing the translating, the operating system and protected I/O are removed completely from the user address. Any attempt to read or write to memory outside the user's assigned address space causes the processor to abort the user's program.

Information generally is transferred in units of a fixed number of bits; the 80386 uses 32 bits when not specifically having been signaled to use 16 bits. These fixed bits are called words. When it goes into the memory system, the process is called a *memory write*. When the word is obtained from a memory position, the process is called a *memory read*.

There are two types of memory access methods: random and sequential. *Sequential access* refers to a type of memory system in which the word positions become available for access in some predefined order. *Random access,* on the other hand, refers to a type of memory system in which every word position may be directly selected and accessed in any order, and in approximately the same time.

No matter how good the memory, there will be propagation delays when the signal travels between devices. Propagation delay is the time required for a logic pulse signal to travel through a device or series of devices forming a logic string. This delay also includes all the interconnecting signal pulse lead paths between the IC chips.

Direct Memory Access (DMA)

Direct memory access (DMA) is the ability to transfer data directly between memory and external devices without the intervention of a program. DMA facilitates maximum I/O data rate and maximum concurrency. While interrupt I/O and programmed I/O route data through the processor, DMA directly transfers data between the I/O device and memory.

To keep the number of data pathways to a minimum, a special provision is made that allows the normal bus system to be used for DMA. To do this, the processor must release control of the buses so that the external device can then use and control them.

During the DMA process, program execution usually is suspended. The buses are released whenever a special DMA request control line is activated. The processor finishes the current execution, releases the Address and Data bus, and keeps one line on the Control bus so that unintentional events do not arise from undefined control signals.

The I/O interface transfers data directly to the memory unit by means of a special register. When there is a transfer to be made, the interface requests a memory cycle-time from the processor. After acknowledgment, the interface causes data to be transferred directly to memory as the processor halts for the cycle-time. The logic that does this transfer is called a *channel*.

The channel contains a memory address register to control the location in the memory to and from which the data is transferred. In most cases, it also contains a word counter that keeps track of the number of direct memory-transfers made. Additional circuitry must be provided for all the related operations in this transfer, such as control signals and timing. Figure 13-4 shows the logical connections between a CPU and a DMA controller.

DMA Components. The major components in a DMA are a request flip-flop, an address register, a counter, and a data register for the use of the peripheral device. DMA transfers involve (1) initializing the DMA logic to start the DMA during repeated cycle-stealing steps, (2) DMA occurs asynchronous to program operations, (3) signals end (the counter runs out or the device status changes), (4) a routine "cleans up" the end of transfer, and (5) DMA terminates through a program interrupt routine which switches back to the main program.

Data Block Transfer. DMA schemes for high-speed data devices involve the

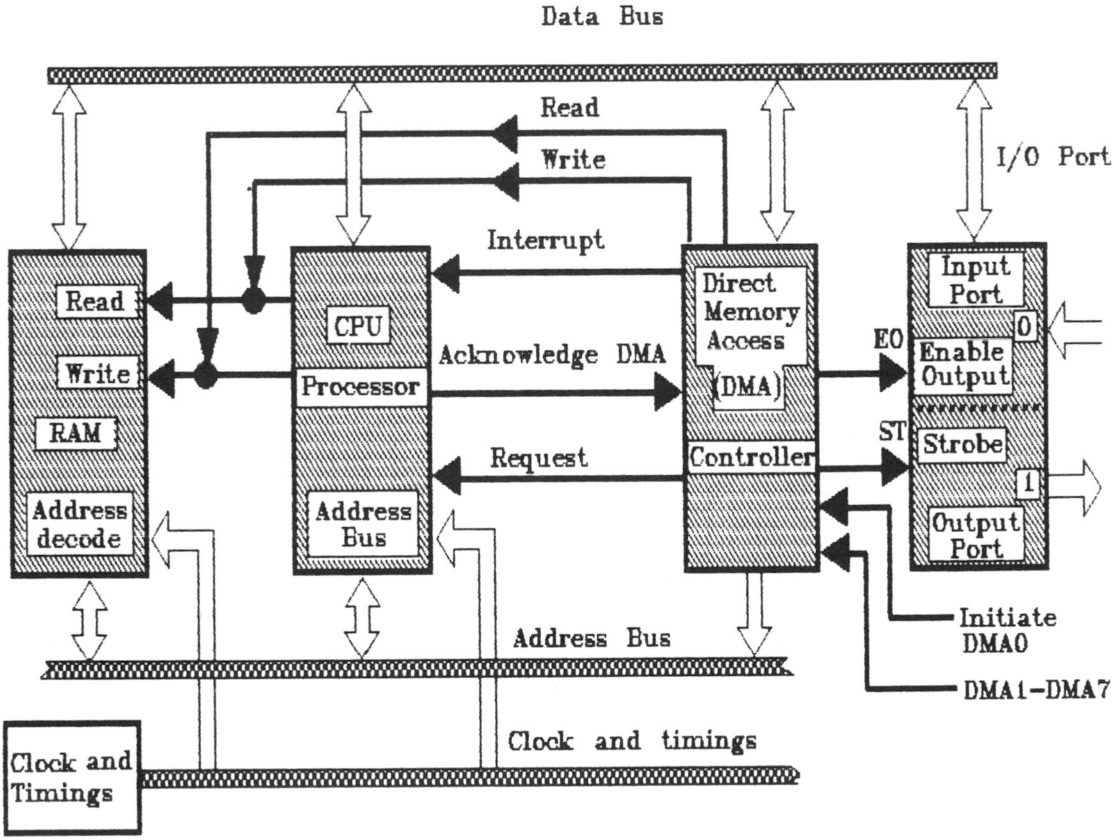

Fig. 13-4. Logical connections between a DMA controller and CPU.

transfer of data words in blocks. Under program control, the processor often initiates the transfer of a block of data and might specify the number of words that comprises the block. Actual transfer of the individual data words is, however, controlled by separate circuitry: the DMA Controller. The maximum rate of a DMA block transfer is limited only by the read or write cycle time of the memory and the speed of the DMA Controller.

Cycle Stealing DMA. A program initiates a block transfer by outputting the starting address to the address counters, then it outputs a count of words to the word counter and, finally, a start command. This type of DMA is often referred to as *cycle stealing* since it suspends the execution of a program for about one machine cycle at a time.

In cycle-stealing DMA, data is transferred concurrently with other processes being carried out by the processor. The steps in executing a cycle-stealing DMA are similar to those for the block transfer, except that the DMA Controller steals cycles from the processor during which it transfers data and thereby slows it.

Memory Segmentation

A segment is simply one small piece of a larger whole. Segmentation is the act of dividing memory into segments. To software designers, segmentation offers a convenient way of sharing information between processes. Individual segments can be shared without reducing the protection that each segment requires.

Segmentation also suggests the natural separation of code and data, and module from module.

To hardware designers, segmentation can also mean a specific division of memory by the physical units called ROM and RAM. For example, if each RAM is 64K, then each segment is a 64K segment. The allied circuitry, the physical registers, latches, and so on, all are built around that specific division.

In the Intel world, when the 8080 came out and addresses could be built up to the 65,536 bytes (64K), that number became the maximum memory size. For a relatively long time, 64K became the design base of the microcomputer world. The 8086 expanded this by implementing programmable segmentation which mapped 64K segments over a 1 megabyte address space.

Today with the 80386, physical address segments can vary from 1 byte to 4 gigabytes (4 billion). In virtual memory, the 80386 can address up to 64 terabytes (64 trillion bytes), with each segment given a different protection or priority level.

Virtual Memory

A simple memory system is one where the logical and physical address space are the same. Little memory management is needed for individual programs in this scheme. For a virtual memory system, on the other hand, the logical address space (the total needed for all programs and processes) is mapped onto the primary physical memory (that memory physically present in a system).

For instance, at any instant in time and using 4096 bytes of memory for this example, all 4096 bytes can be physically and directly addressed. However, those 4096 bytes need not relate on a one-to-one basis with physical memory. The operating system can tell the physical system that from now on, whenever the address 4096 is referenced, memory word 0 is used, and so on. In other words, the operating system defined a mapping from the address space onto the actual memory addresses. Figure 13-5 shows a mapping of 4K of memory onto memory addresses.

At each point in time, the entire logical address space may or may not reside entirely in the primary physical memory. Those portions that are not in main memory usually are stored in a memory hierarchy made up of auxiliary devices such as disk space. When a logical address not in the primary area is needed, it is brought into primary memory from the stored area and some mapping between physical and logical addresses is done.

Virtual Memory Management. Memory management is the application of strategy and algorithms to the problems of allocating the memory resource among competing processes. Virtual memory management involves a relocation technique, mapping an address space used by a process onto a physical address space. The major allocation technique, *dynamic relocation,* is that mapping: taking a program's logical information onto physical memory. This occurs immediately before any instruction of the program is executed.

In a *segmented virtual memory* system, the entire logical address space is divided into smaller logical segments which can be of any size. To point to a particular element within a segment, the segment name as well as a symbolic element name or its address within the segment must be addressed.

When any segment is brought into primary memory, it is placed into a space equal to or greater than the segment size. Since a segment and its physical location are unrelated, a segment table is built which contains the base address of each segment in memory. A reference to a segment name is then mapped by the system into a segment number which represents an offset into the segment table. Additional mapping in-

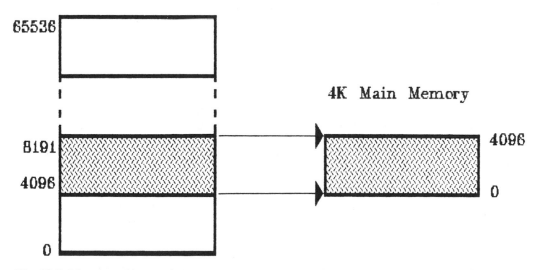

Fig. 13-5. Mapping addresses into memory.

dexes into the segment for references to a particular element.

Paged Virtual Memory. In a *paged virtual memory* system, the primary address space is divided into equal-sized blocks, each known as a *page*. The page represents a block of code and/or data with consecutive addresses. Since the logical address space is also divided into the same size pages, when information is transferred into physical memory, the basic unit of transfer is the page and fills the page frame.

If memory is not allocated well or is allocated in variable size units, it can fragment into pieces too small to be easily used. Then throughput slows because the CPU is forced to delay dispatching and reorganize physical memory by moving or swapping other tasks until a large enough place opens to continue processing.

To solve this fragmentation, the concept arose of allocating memory in fixed size units and then automatically overlaying the units into real memory. The process is called paging and the chunks of program read in from secondary memory are called pages, much the same as in the virtual paging system described above. The main memory into which the pages go are called *page frames*.

Paging is a practical division of the virtual space within a system and intended primarily to avoid the many problems of memory fragmentation. The main disadvantage of paging is that space may be wasted if only very small areas are required, as the smallest unit that can be allocated is a page.

Programs are written as though there were enough space in real memory for the entire required space. The hardware's internal logic devices and the operating system interact so that the programmer ignores the fact that pages will be loaded over previously used pages. This is contrasted to segmentation where the programmer must remember how each segment is used and how to address it.

To find which page is required for the next instruction, there is generally a word table called the *page table*. The table holds the beginning addresses for each page along with bits that show if the page is currently in memory. If so, hardware points to the page and continues. If not, the hardware interrupts so the operating system can find the page in auxiliary storage, load it into real memory, and then continue.

When a reference is made to a page that is not in main memory, an error called a *page fault* occurs. After a page fault, the operating system reads in the required page from secondary memory, enters its new physical memory location in the page table, then repeats the instruction that caused the fault.

Cache Memory

A cache is a buffer type of high-speed memory that is filled at medium speed from main memory, often with instructions and programs. In a computer system that uses cache memory, instructions and data are stored in main memory and some selected pieces of the instructions and data is copied in the cache. Figure 13-6 shows a block diagram of the 80386 cache memory.

Cache was designed when processors became much faster than RAM and had to wait because data items were not ready for processing. Information flows from secondary storage to main memory to cache memory. To get to cache, the following process occurs.

When a program tries to reference its address space, it presents a virtual address to the hardware or the microprogram. If the page or segment containing that address

Cache Memory System

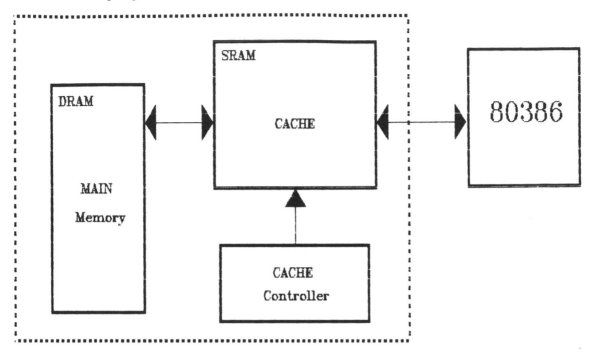

Fig. 13-6. Block diagram of a cache memory system.

is in main memory, the virtual address is translated into a main memory address. Otherwise, a fault occurs and the page/segment is brought into main memory.

The cache hardware then checks to see if the block is already in cache memory. If so, the contents of the addressed location are fetched from cache or the result is stored in cache. If not there, a cache block fault occurs (similar to a page fault) and the information is copied from main memory to the cache. After the block is loaded into cache, the instruction is executed again. Due to the short time involved, the cache-main memory paging system is handled by the logic external to the CPU without assistance from the operating system.

Cache Information Selection. The selection process is the key to making best use of the processor. Predicting the address of the next memory location to be accessed is highly uncertain if all memory accesses were truly random. They rarely are. Most programs access memory in the neighborhood of the location accessed most recently. This is called *program locality.* It is this locality that makes cache systems as efficient as they are.

For instance, in reading data variables, they are generally organized in some (often ascending) logical sequence which makes the next read immediately after the previous one. Character strings are most often scanned in sequence. Stacks change from one end so that the next few accesses are all near the top of the stack.

When the processor needs the next instruction or the next piece of data, it is programmed to search the cache first before requesting it from more distant and slower memory. If the requested data is found in the cache, the memory access is called a *cache hit*. If it is not, it is called a *cache miss*. The hit rate is the percentage of accesses that are hits. This percentage is affected by the size and the physical organization of the cache, the cache algorithm, and the program being run.

Block Fetch. A cache memory has a controller whose purpose is to maximize its efficiency and to manage its resources. The controller partitions the main memory into blocks of typically 2, 4, 8 or 16 bytes. A 32-bit processor usually uses two or four words per block. When there is a cache miss, the cache controller moves both the needed word from the main memory into the cache along with the entire block that contains the needed word.

The block fetch can get the data in one of three ways: (1) lookbehind—retrieving the data located before the requested byte, (2) lookahead—retrieving the data that follows the requested byte, or (3) both. Blocks are generally aligned on doubleword boundaries. An access to any byte in the block copies the entire block into cache.

Block size is a key parameter in a cache memory system. If the lookahead and lookbehind are too small, the hit rate is reduced. Too large a block size reduce the number of blocks that fit into a cache. In addition, as the block becomes larger, each new word is further from the requested word and less likely (because of program locality) to be needed by the processor. Finally, too large a block size requires a wider bus between main memory and the cache memory which results in increased cost.

Cache Organizations. Cache is high-speed memory that is used similar to a scratch pad. If a telephone number is needed soon, the digits are jotted down. They are then crossed out and the space used for something else as soon as the need is satisfied. It is in how this scratch pad is organized that determines how a system will use it. There are three general types of cache organization: fully associative, direct mapped, and set associative.

Fully Associative Cache. In a fully associative cache, the cache holds the blocks most likely to be used by the processor (normal process). However, there would be no single relationship between all the addresses of these blocks, so the cache would also have to store the entire address of each block as well as the block itself.

When the processor asks for data, the cache controller compares the address of the requested data with *each* of the addresses in the cache. If a match is found, the data for that address is sent to the processor. Either a hit or a miss occurs. If a miss, since the addresses have no relationship to each other, there is a tradeoff: sequential search, which is slow, or hardware to do a parallel search, which is expensive in its need for comparators and controllers.

Direct Mapped Cache. The direct mapped cache allows each block from main memory only one possible location in cache. This reduces the number of searches and compares to one, before a hit or miss is determined.

Each direct mapped address has two parts. The first is the cache index field. It contains enough bits to specify a block location within the cache. The second, the tag field, contains bits to distinguish a block from other blocks that may be stored at a particular cache location.

The major limitation of a direct mapped cache is that the cache controller allows only one location in the cache from a particular piece of main memory. If the program makes frequent requests from two conflicting locations, the cache must be swapped each time. This sort of program behavior is infrequent, so the direct mapped cache organization offers acceptable performance at a lower cost than fully associative.

Set Associative Cache. The set associative organization is a compromise between the fully associative and direct memory mapping cache. This type of cache has several sets of direct mapped blocks that operate as several direct mapped caches in parallel. For each cache index, there are several block locations allowed, one in each set. When a block of data arrives from main memory, it goes into a particular block location of any set.

For the same amount of memory, the set associative cache contains half as many mapping blocks, but each block can take two addresses which would have conflicted in a 1-way cache. Two- and 4-way caches appear to be most efficient in terms of the speed and cost performance tradeoffs.

The cache controller must decide which block of the cache to overwrite when a block fetch is executed. The controller has three choices, any of which is adequate depending on the program behavior. Those choices are: (1) overwrite at random, (2) overwrite in sequential order, or (3) overwrite the least recently accessed block. This last choice requires the controller to maintain an aging counter that indicates the block to overwrite. This counter must be updated on each cache transaction.

Cache Updating. An important point to remember when using cache is that two copies of the data and information exist, one in main memory and one in cache. If one of the copies is updated and the other is not, two different sets of information become associated with one memory address, resulting in erroneous data being saved if the wrong set is saved.

The two copies require that the cache contain an updating method which prevents old data (often called stale data) from being used. There are several ways that have been developed to store only "good" data: write-through, buffered write-through, write-back, and cache coherency.

In a *write-through* system, the cache controller writes data to the main memory immediately after it is written to the cache, thus making two writes for each updated piece of data. The results are that main memory always contains valid data and any block of cache can be overwritten without data loss. The major problem with this method is that there is performance loss due to the time required to write main memory. In addition, there is increased bus traffic, which is a significant problem in multiprocessing systems.

In a *buffered write-through* system, write accesses to main memory are buffered. This allows the processor to begin a new cycle before the write cycle to the main memory is completed. A speed up occurs when the next read finds a cache hit so that the processor can continue. This allows a simultaneous write and read. In this system, only a single write to main memory is buffered. Therefore, if the processor needs a second write, the processor must go to a wait state until the first write completes. Additionally, a write followed by a cache miss also requires a wait for new data to be brought from main memory.

The next design is called a *write-back* system. The tag field of each block in the cache includes a bit that shows if the block has been altered. Before overwriting any block in cache, the cache controller checks the altered bit. If it's set, the controller writes the block to main memory before reading new data into the cache block. Write-back is faster than either the first two methods because the number of altered bits written to main memory is generally much smaller than the number read into cache.

There are a few drawbacks to the write-back system. Once the majority of block of cache have been altered, *all* the block must be written to memory before processing can go on. Second, this write-back controller logic is more complex than the first two cache updating methods. Finally, if there is a catastrophic error such as a power failure, cache data is lost so there is no way to tell if main memory contains stale data.

The above three methods minimize stale data in main memory caused by cache write operations. However, another problem arises: *cache coherency*. This occurs when cache is used in a system where main memory is updated by more than one device. When memory can be updated from various devices, it's difficult to tell if data in cache is more stale than data in main memory. Three methods have been found to attack this problem.

The first is *cache flushing*. In the case of altered data, the data is written to main memory (most often through a write-through method) and then the contents of cache is flushed. If all the caches are flushed before a device writes to shared memory, stale data is eliminated from the caches.

The second approach to maintain cache coherency is through *hardware transparency*. In this case, the hardware guarantees non-stale data by ensuring that all accesses to memory mapped by a cache are seen by the cache. This is done one of two ways. The first is by copying all cache writes both to main memory and to all other caches that share the same memory; this technique is called broadcasting. The second way hardware guarantees non-stale data is by routing the accesses of all devices to main memory through the same cache.

Finally, cache coherency can be maintained by designating shared memory as *non-cacheable*. All accesses to the shared memory are cache misses because shared memory is never copied to cache. Software can help offset the reduction in hit rate by copying data between non-cacheable memory and cacheable memory and mapping shared memory accesses to the cacheable locations.

BUFFERS

Buffering is the process of storing results (outputs) of a process temporarily before forwarding them to the next process. Buffers are essential in smoothing out the flow of a system when the timing for each processing module involved is not fixed, and when that timing is vastly different (even in terms of milliseconds). For instance, the computer may have an extremely fast processor and much slower memory.

In addition to the memory array and decoding logic which make up a memory device structure, output buffers are used to buffer data from memory before it is output to the pins of the memory package. These buffers are useful in that they provide the desired output voltage levels and drive current, and allow easy multiplexing of the outputs of several IC packages.

Buffers are controlled by one or more chip selects, chip enables, or output enable inputs.

TIMING

A programmable counter/timer is a useful device that monitors external events.

The counter/timer can be addressed and accessed either as a memory location or an input/output port. The initial value of the counter can be set under program control. With each clock pulse, the contents of the counter can be either decremented or incremented.

Instructions have a different length of execution times, generally between one and six clock pulses. Total time is determined by how many clock pulses it takes for the instruction to do each step. In some cases, one or two clock pulses are automatically added to allow external logic to complete the requested operation. During this time, the CPU may go into wait state.

Timing Constraints

There are timing constraints on the sequencing of data, address, and control signals to a RAM device. These constraints ensure proper operation. The processor supplies the address and chip select signals to memory and must wait a period of time equal to the access time before it can use the output from memory.

SUMMARY

In a professional or business environment, many programs are being executed all the time and any one program may fill all the available microcomputer memory. Thus has grown the need for faster memory and multi-leaving of tasks.

Direct Memory Access allows the parallel transfer of data and continuation of CPU processing. DMA is a specialized transfer that temporarily isolates the CPU from the buses and manages the required transfer between memory and an I/O device.

14

Improving
System Performance

Early microcomputer design philosophy was based on the premise that, at any one time, only one person used one computer and ran one program. The typical user waited (perhaps) patiently for the program to complete before starting a second job. Today, users want to do several jobs (such as printing, editing, and sorting data) at the same time and expect the computer to perform efficiently while doing them. Users want "fast" computers.

Computer speeds are determined by three basic limitations. One concerns hardware; that is, how fast do gates switch and how many inches of wire or board must a signal traverse. The second limitation concerns the logic of the interaction of machine design and organization. The third looks at how effectively the operating system uses the hardware design. This chapter addresses these last two.

Early microcomputers executed one operation at a time. For example, they either computed, handled I/O or scheduled interrupts. However, the designers always knew that if more than one operation could be performed then program speedups would occur. As early as October 1842, Charles Babbage said in a lecture that ". . . when a long series of . . . computations is to be performed, such as those required for the formation of numerical tables, the machine can be brought into play so as to give several results at the same time, which will greatly abridge the whole amount of the processes."

CONTROL UNITS

In the 1950's, machine designs incorporated the concept of simultaneously executing several operations for solving differential equations. Today, many microcomputer manufacturers provide two-processor systems (for example, using a numeric coprocessor) and some have as many as four special-purpose processors. The processing speedups are due to parallelism between operations, as well as parallelism between memory and processor activities. To reach speed goals, many systems use some sort of control unit.

Control units for high-speed computers handle the traditional functions, including instruction fetch, I/O and interrupt handling, instruction sequencing, address mapping, and memory indexing. A well-designed control unit is one which does not get in the way of either the processor(s) or memory. It operates fast enough to supply instructions whenever they are needed by the processor.

An essential part of any computer system is the mechanism that allocates the system processor(s) among the various competitors for their services. This allocation is done automatically in today's systems with methods such as the use of interrupts and interval timers.

PROCESSOR INDEPENDENCE

At the base of any system performance improvement is the independence of each process. The basis for this idea is that certain sequences of actions follow naturally and are more or less independent of other sequences. For example, a disk-to-printer routine and a memory-to-memory move sequence are two very distinct processes which logically can execute independently of each other. In reality, it's realized that each may require one of the buses, but conceptually they're not otherwise interdependent.

One primary aim of an operating system is to share the computer's resources as effectively as possible among many programs making unpredictable (asynchronous) demands on those resources. An efficient operating system that uses the hardware in an optimum manner speeds throughput enormously.

Now, let's look at some concepts whose efficient use improves total computer throughput: (1) prefetching data before it's required, (2) pipelining instructions to get them into higher-speed work areas, (3) the use of coprocessors to achieve parallel work, (4) concurrent operation, and (5) multitasking and multiprogramming.

PREFETCHING

As processor effective speeds increased, memory tried to keep up. It failed to do so for three major reasons: propagation delays, gate density, and slower technological advances. Those issues are under attack by today's designers. In the meantime, other approaches had to be taken.

To avoid the processor spending too much time waiting for memory to produce requested data, some parallel or pipeline process became mandatory. The general approach taken is this: when the processor calls for the first pieces of information, a fetch goes out to memory for more. This fetching of information before it is required is called *prefetching*. The hardest task for prefetching is to determine which piece of memory is required next.

Prefetch Effectiveness

Prefetch effectiveness is based on the idea of locality. That is, it has been observed that the locus of reference of most programs varies (relatively) slowly over time and space. During certain periods of execution, the program accesses a subset of locations that lie in close spatial proximity. This subset changes over time. Simple prefetch algorithms then fetch information "next in line" from the previously fetched data.

Prefetching Algorithms

In general, prefetch algorithms are divided into two classes: demand and anticipatory.

Demand algorithms are based on the concept that a processor runs through the information already in the system and then page faults. That is, it sends a demand for the next portion of information.

Anticipatory algorithms, on the other hand, do not necessarily prefetch at the time of a fault; they do so at the first reference to a new page. Anticipatory prefetching generally saves transfer time because of the overlap between the time a page is requested and when the page is actually needed.

One Page Lookahead (OPLA)

One page lookahead (OPLA) assumes some behavior on the part of the program and prefetches accordingly. It assumes that the next sequential page will be the one required for continued execution.

PIPELINING

Pipelining is where several distinct tasks are compacted in any certain time-frame for simultaneous processing. Pipelining is one form of embedding parallelism or concurrency in a computer system. It refers to dividing a computer's processes into several subprocesses which are executed by dedicated autonomous units. Successive processes can be carried out in an overlapped mode.

For instance, the CPU may be engaged in decoding and executing one instruction while additional registers on the data bus could be prefetching or looking ahead for the next instruction. Figure 14-1 shows the difference in instruction processing in a non-pipelined system versus a pipelined one.

Methods

There are three steps in executing an instruction: fetching an instruction, decoding its operations, and fetching its operands. In Figure 14-1, four successive and independent instructions may be executed in parallel.

As you see, while the EXEC module executes the first instruction, the Operand Fetch (OF) module fetches the operand needed for the second instruction, the Instruction Decode (ID) module prepares the different operations for the third instruction, and the Instruction Fetch (IF) module fetches the fourth instruction. The overlapped execution among the four modules is shown in the space-time diagram.

Pipelining can be applied at more than one level. The first level usually chosen is at the processor, for instruction decoding as shown below. The next level is at the subsystem level. A typical example is the pipelined arithmetic units. Pipelined add, multiply, divide, and square-root functions are in existence in a number of contemporary computers.

One Instruction

Instruction Processing

Non-Pipelined Processor

Pieces of Four Instructions

Pipelined Processor

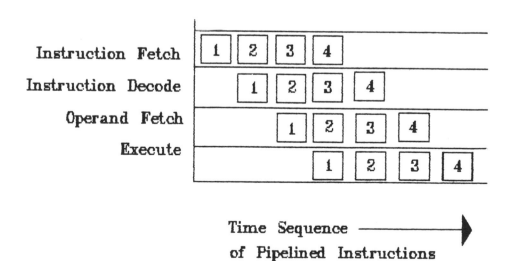

Instruction Fetch

Instruction Decode

Operand Fetch

Execute

Time Sequence ⟶
of Pipelined Instructions

Fig. 14-1. Pipelined versus nonpipelined instructions.

Problems

Program branching is extremely damaging to pipeline performance. When a conditional branch is found, the system cannot tell which instruction sequence will follow until the deciding result is available at the output. Therefore, a conditional branch not only delays further execution but also affects the entire pipe, starting from the instruction fetch. An incorrect branch of instruction fetched must be flushed from the pipeline before the correct branch can be loaded.

One way to minimize branching effects is to have a branch target buffer or a lookahead mechanism. The fetching process actually gets *both* possibilities and decodes the operands. This way, whichever way is finally determined as correct, the next set of instructions is at hand.

An interrupt can disrupt the continuity of the instruction stream. To offset this, a recovery mechanism can be used to save the pipelined instructions and recover them after the interrupt has been serviced. This can be costly, so it is seldom implemented.

Control Structure

Two major control structures are used in a pipelined system. The simpler one involves a streamlined (synchronized) flow of instructions through the system. One instruction or task follows another so they begin and end in the same order. There are simple interlocks in the system to make sure that there is a simultaneous flow through modules of different speeds. When a bottleneck appears at any segment, input is halted until the segment is once again free.

The second control structure is somewhat more complex. In this more flexible and powerful method, flow through the system is totally asynchronous. That is, each piece is allowed to go at its own speed. If a bottleneck occurs, the next instruction is allowed to go ahead. This scheme is useful whenever the system has multiple (either physical or virtual) execution units or facilities which run in parallel.

COPROCESSOR

Four system characteristics motivate the continued development of parallel processing subsystems: throughput, flexibility, availability, and reliability. These characteristics aim toward improving system performance. To do this, many manufacturers have designed coprocessors, such as the 80387 numeric coprocessor. A *coprocessor* is defined as a processor that operates under integrated control with the central processing unit.

One of the most fruitful uses of overlapped processing is the execution of arithmetic operations. Most often, a numeric coprocessor is used where the main processor ships arithmetic operations "sideways" and continues on. The results of the arithmetic are then shipped back, ready for when the processor needs them. This process is transparent to the systems programmer.

At the base of coprocessing are the concepts of interaction and transparency. The coprocessor's work must be transparent to the programmer and user, and solidly apparent to the hardware designer.

MULTITASKING AND MULTIPROGRAMMING

Performing two or more processing tasks by a single CPU is called *multiprogram-*

ming or multitasking. The CPU rapidly switches back and forth between two or more programs, executing the instructions for each one in turn. This switching became practical when the CPU became faster than I/O processes.

Most operating system (OS) environments schedule applications programs using a time-slicing algorithm for program tasks which are not currently waiting on I/O. The OS uses the system clock to time just how long each application is allowed to use the major system resources. Each application receives equal time slices of execution time, on a round-robin basis.

The time-slice approach is simpler than many other and more complex scheduling algorithms. The conventional approach is that while one program waits for an I/O request to complete, another program runs. Since some I/O operations are massive and time-consuming to the CPU, some operating systems break large I/O requests into smaller requests so that scheduling can occur more often.

Memory management is a complex aspect of concurrency. Some operating systems require memory to be fixed-size partitions and that operating characteristics be assigned to each partition. Other operating systems allocate memory dynamically using PIFs (Program Information Files) to describe the characteristics and needs of an application package. PIFs describe the amount of memory required, which peripherals are directly accessed, which interrupts are processed, and so on.

Defining foreground and background tasks is one method for managing access to displays and keyboards. The foreground task is given control of the keyboard and the entire screen; all others are background tasks.

Windowing allows multiple applications to share the screen. The screen is divided into tiled or overlapped segments called *windows,* where each window displays a portion of an application's output. In some cases, one application can own multiple windows; for other applications, the user is responsible for sizing, moving, or hiding windows and that user scrolls within the windows.

A significant problem in multiprocessing is the proper execution of applications that perform direct video I/O. These applications write directly to the screen and bypass the operating system. When they do this, they can interfere with the operating system and are called *ill-behaved* applications.

If a system supports multitasking, mechanisms must be provided for the synchronization transfers of information to shared resources, i.e., a video buffer.

Ordering of Events

The concept of time is fundamental in any ordering of system processes and events within those processes. Each computer system is composed of a collection of processes. Each process is subdivided into various events that occur in some sequence. The choice of what constitutes an event affects the ordering of the events within that process.

In a very basic sense, clock timing is just a way of assigning a number to an event, where the number is thought of as the time at which the event occurred.

Multitasking is a technique used to achieve concurrency by separating a single program or several programs into two or more interrelated tasks that share code, buffers, and files.

Multitasking involves providing a means for a program to interrelate referenced procedures and data manipulation, and to do this independently of their physical location in memory. In addition, multitasking provides a way for programs to use common procedures and data formatting. It expedites switching the actual computation hardware from one program/task to another.

Multiprogramming allows several users or programs to use the system at the same time. It does this by allowing a second program to use the processor while the first program is waiting for some external process (such as a request for data) to complete. Instead of the processor going to a *wait* state, it's busy processing. A wait state is that internal pause the processor takes when a synchronizing signal is not present or when it has been halted under program control to await input from another device. As soon as the second user needs an external process or finishes its task, the first program is brought back to continue running. This multi-use increases the productivity of the system by handling the processes effectively simultaneously instead of one at a time.

An increasing percentage of computation activity is carried out by multiprogrammed systems. Such systems are characterized by the application of computer resources (such as the processor, main memory, and peripherals) to many separate but interleaved operating computations. A *computation* is a set of processes that work together harmoniously on the same program or job.

Multiprogramming Properties

Four important properties of multiprogrammed systems are: (1) computation processes may be concurrent operation for more than one user, (2) many computations share pools of resources, such as memory, in a flexible way, (3) individual computations vary widely in their demands for computing resources at any point in time, and (4) the multiprogrammed system evolves to meet the changing user requirements. Concurrency in the micro world is normally confined to hardware-controlled concurrent processing of a main processor and a numeric coprocessor. Intel, with the 80386 and the LOCK/XCHG instruction, provides the potential of multiprocessing on a mainframe scale.

SUMMARY

One of the most important performance measures of a system is its throughput rate. *Throughput* is defined as the number of outputs or instructions processed per unit of time. It directly reflects the processing power of a system: the higher the throughput rate, the more powerful the system is.

The basic concept of parallelism in machine organization came into being as early as Charles Babbage's computing engines. It continues to be exploited, along with hardware speed improvements, to build and operate faster computers. It is expected that hardware costs will decrease faster than hardware speeds increase, thus forcing the increased use of parallelism and include the concepts discussed above.

Appendix 1

Integrated Circuits and Intel

The semiconductor industry really began in New Jersey at the Bell Telephone Laboratories. It soon transplanted to the intellectually fertile region of California just south of San Francisco. The Santa Clara Valley, soon dubbed "Silicon Valley," now holds hundreds of companies whose products are descendants of the early days.

In the mid-1950s, a small group of scientists left Bell Labs to start a venture, backed by Fairchild Camera and Instrument Company. The scientists formed the Fairchild Semiconductor Company and settled in Santa Clara Valley, CA. Two of those scientists, Robert Noyce and Gordon Moore, left Fairchild Semiconductor in 1968 to form another company in Sunnyvale, CA; they named it Intel—for *Int*egrated *Elec*tronics. Three years later, Intel introduced the first microprocessor with both high success and general industry acceptance.

The first IC calculators were limited in function and cost hundreds of dollars. Only slowly did engineers and manufacturers realize the potential of these first clunky machines. As more uses became apparent, engineers began to design chips for those special needs. Eventually the market for cheap pocket calculators became available and technology was ready.

In mid-1969, Busicom, a Japanese calculator manufacturer, asked Intel Corporation to develop a set of chips for a new line of programmable calculators. Busicom's engineers had a design which required twelve logic and memory chips with three to five thousand transistors each. Intel had recently developed a technique for manufacturing and fabricating 2,000-transistor chips. Busicom hoped that this technology would transfer easily into the calculator market.

NEW DESIGN CONCEPT

The industry-wide design strategy up until the early 1970's was for each chip to be designed to a particular customer's specifications. The processors were not powerful and were actually quite inadequate for general purpose computing.

345

While working on the Busicom project, an Intel engineer came up with a revolutionary design concept: why not have a general-purpose chip that could perform *any* logical task? The chip would have to be programmable, taking its instructions from some ROM and/or RAM chips. If customers wanted to have a specific product, they could program it and Intel would install that program into ROM. This meant that Intel would not design a new set of logic chips for each customer. The burden of design shifted from the manufacturer to the OEM people. That concept formed the basis for Intel's now-popular family of chips.

Designed by three people in less than a year, the first multipurpose chip, the 4004, rolled off the production line in late 1970. Industry experts were divided. Some felt that a general-purpose chip was too general to find a useful home. Others wondered why the concept hadn't been used before.

The 4004 Chip

The 4004 is a 4-bit (half-byte) microprocessor. Instead of distributing the arithmetic and logic functions of the calculator among several hardwired ICs, the 4004 included these functions on the chip itself.

The 4004 has 2,250 MOS transistors and can execute about 60,000 operations a second. It addresses 1,280 half-bytes of data and 4K (4096) bytes of programmed instructions. It isn't powerful enough to serve as a processor, but certainly enough as a base for a calculator.

This chip can add two 4-bit numbers in about eleven millionths of a second (eleven microseconds), but can multiply only by repeated additions. It contains a 4-bit adder, an accumulator, and sixteen registers for temporary storage. The ROM contained the inner program and stored 2K bits of data, while the RAM which provided temporary storage held only 320 bits. Its size is 0.110 inches by 0.150 inches.

The 4004 contains a great deal of logic associated with computer central processing unit (CPU) implementation. One large-scale integration (LSI) chip replaced hundreds of circuits that were found in conventional minicomputers at that time. The 46 instruction set is not large by today's standard, but it is adequate for control applications which require decision making that cannot easily be implemented in programmable-logic arrays.

The 8008 Chip

In April 1972, Intel introduced their first 8-bit microprocessor, the 8008. The 8008 has about 3,300 MOS transistors, a thousand more than the 4004. The 8008 executes over 30,000 operations a second and addresses 16K bytes of memory. The 8008 executes a single operation in 12.5 microseconds. It also multiplies by repeated addition, a time-consuming process. Its size is 0.125 inches by 0.170 inches.

The 8008 retains the PMOS fabrication techniques of the 4004, but offers an 8-bit wide *data bus* (the electronic pathway along which data flows) and a larger instruction set of 48 instructions. However, the 8008 instruction set is not compatible with the 4004 set.

The 8008 has a faster instruction execution time than the 4004, as data for both instruction execution and decoding and for operands could be handled in 8-bit slices.

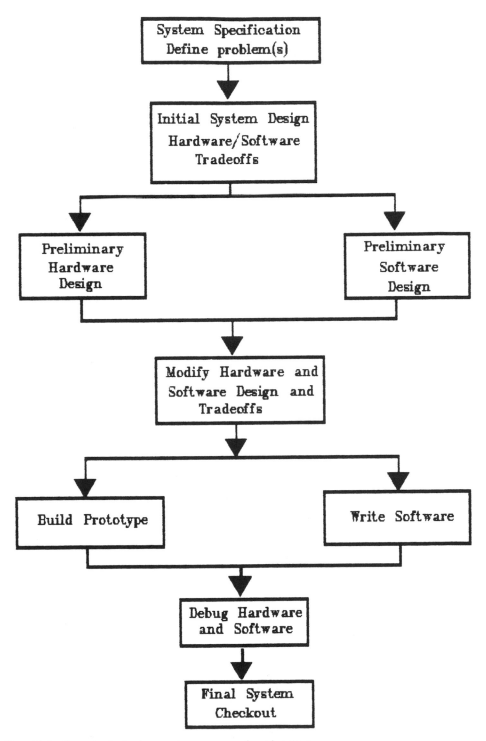

Fig. A1-1. Steps in designing a microprocessor-based system.

	4004	8008	8080
Chip Class	4 bit	8 bit	8 bit
Technology	PMOS	PMOS	NMOS
Word Size:			
Data	4 bits	8 bits	8 bits
Instruction	8 bits	8 bits	8 bits
Address capacity	4K	16K	64K
Clock kHz	740	800	2,083
Add time in microseconds	10.8	20	2
Package size	16 pin	18 pin	40 pin
Instruction set size	45	48	72 (includes 8008 inst.)

Fig. A1-2. Comparison of early chips.

In addition, the 8008 addresses 16,384 memory locations of 8 bits each, contains seven 8-bit registers, has memory stack capability, and has a single-level interrupt capability.

The 8080 Chip

In 1974, Intel brought out the 8080, designed to be useful in a great variety of applications. The 8080 chip is powerful enough to run a microcomputer, but had some drawbacks that Intel wanted to overcome, mainly processing speed. With more than 4,500 transistors, the 8080 executes about 200,000 operations a second.

To achieve compatibility with the 8008 instruction set, the 8080 instruction set included the 8008 set and added 30 more instructions. The 79 instructions of the 8080 had decidedly moved away from one for primarily control applications to one that had more general purposes. For the first time, Intel chips were upwardly compatible. The 8008 users could now change to a faster, more versatile microprocessor while not discarding their current software.

The 8080 is an NMOS microprocessor that allows faster clock rates than its predecessors. Additions of two 8-bit operands could now be carried out at rates of 500,000 per second. In addition, all other instruction times were shorter because the 8080 was built around a 40-pin chip, requiring the CPU to do much less time-sharing of the data bus between data transfers and instruction implementation.

Like its precursors, the 4004 and 8008, the 8080 has no multiply instruction and so must multiply by adding. The 8080 supplemented hardware features of the 8008. Instead of 16K, memory addresses went to 64K. Rather than a limited 7-level memory stack, the 8080 offers a memory stack in external memory itself instead of in the CPU. Its size is 0.165 inches by 0.191 inches.

The 8080 placed Intel as one of the largest IC companies in the United States, with 21,500 employees and over $1 billion in annual sales.

The 8080A Chip

In 1976, Intel brought out a variation on the 8080, the 8080A. The 8080A is an 8-bit microprocessor on a single chip, an NMOS device. It has about 4,000 transistors on a chip that is about 0.165 inches by 0.191 inches in size. It is a 40-pin, *dual in-line package* (DIP). Sixteen of the pins (A0 - A15) provide three-state outputs for addressing memory and input/output (I/O). Eight of the pins (D0 - D7) provide bi-directional three-state data for data transfer and internal state information. Finally, ten of the pins provide timing and control signals.

The 8080A instruction set consists of 72 instructions, which are supported by the next chip in the family, the 8085A.

The 8085A Chip

The 8085A is an enhanced, upward-compatible version of the 8080A and the two are nearly functionally equivalent. Basically, the 8085A is a single-chip version of the three-chip combination of the 8080A microprocessor, the 8224 clock driver, and the 8228 system controller.

The 8085A is an 8-bit microprocessor, NMOS device implemented with about 6,200 transistors. The chip is 0.164 inches by 0.222 inches, contained in a 40-pin DIP. The pins and their configuration is shown in Fig. A1-5.

The 8085A operates on a single 5V power supply. This chip is capable of directly addressing up to 64K memory locations with its 16-bit address. The I/O ports are treated as external registers. They can be treated as memory and written to and read from by any instruction that references memory.

Also, the 8085A directly addresses up to 256 input and 256 output ports, using special I/O instructions with an 8-bit address. The 8085A's internal data bus is 8 bits wide and transfers instructions and data among various internal registers or to external devices through the multiplexed address/data bus buffer latch.

Only two new instructions were added to the basic 8080 instruction set, to read and write serial and interrupt data. Since the 74 instructions of the 8085A set include those of the 8080A, programs written for the 8080A run on the 8085A. The execution times for those programs are different, even when clock frequencies are chosen which provide identical state times for the two microprocessors. This difference is

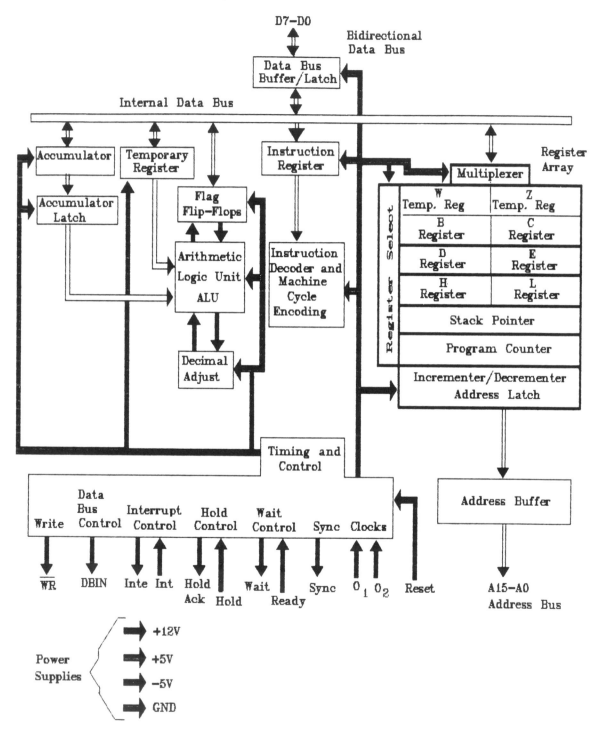

Fig. A1-3. Functional block diagram of the 8080A.

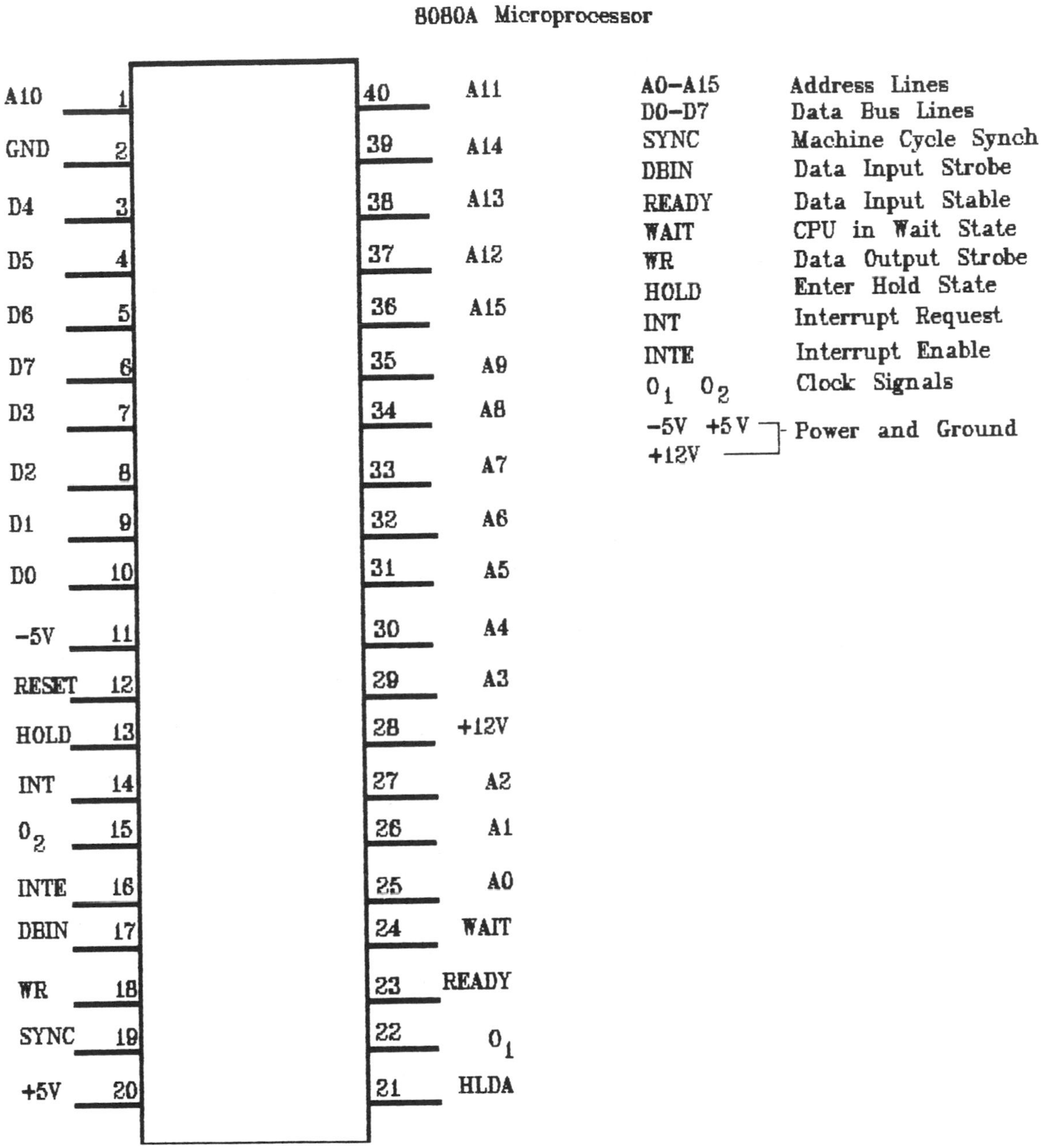

8080A Microprocessor

Pin	Left		Pin	Right
A10	1		40	A11
GND	2		39	A14
D4	3		38	A13
D5	4		37	A12
D6	5		36	A15
D7	6		35	A9
D3	7		34	A8
D2	8		33	A7
D1	9		32	A6
D0	10		31	A5
−5V	11		30	A4
RESET	12		29	A3
HOLD	13		28	+12V
INT	14		27	A2
0_2	15		26	A1
INTE	16		25	A0
DBIN	17		24	WAIT
WR	18		23	READY
SYNC	19		22	0_1
+5V	20		21	HLDA

A0–A15	Address Lines
D0–D7	Data Bus Lines
SYNC	Machine Cycle Synch
DBIN	Data Input Strobe
READY	Data Input Stable
WAIT	CPU in Wait State
WR	Data Output Strobe
HOLD	Enter Hold State
INT	Interrupt Request
INTE	Interrupt Enable
0_1 0_2	Clock Signals
−5V +5 V +12V	Power and Ground

Fig. A1-4. Pin assignments of the 8080A.

the result of the differing number of states in the instruction cycles of identical instructions on the two machines.

The 8086 Chip

Appearing in 1978, the 8086 was the first microprocessor capable of working

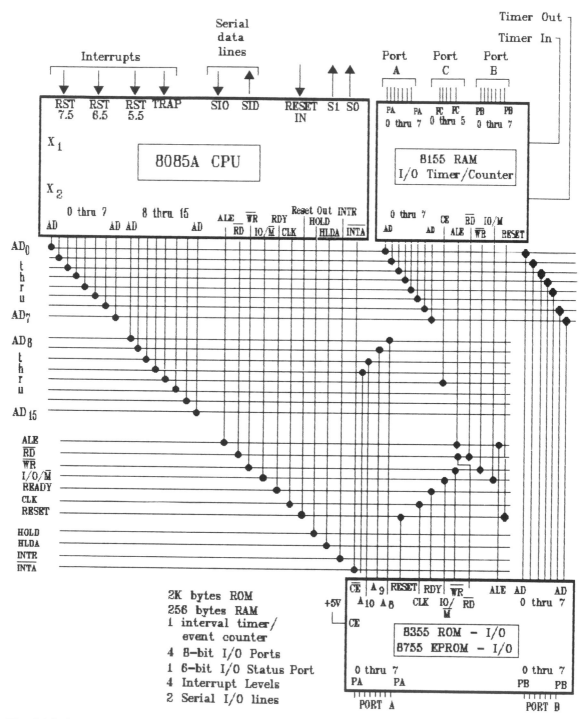

Fig. A1-5. 8085A microprocessor pin assignments.

with 16 bits of data at one time. Two key architectural concepts shaped the microprocessor designs, beginning with the 8086. These concepts are: memory segmentation and an instruction encoding scheme.

The 8086 processor is divided into two separate units. The first is the *bus interface unit* (BIU) and the second is the *execution unit* (EU).

The BIU has two main functions. They are (1) to fetch instructions from memory and (2) to pass data to and from the execution hardware and the outside world (outside from the view of the processor). The BIU contains the *instruction pointer* (IP)

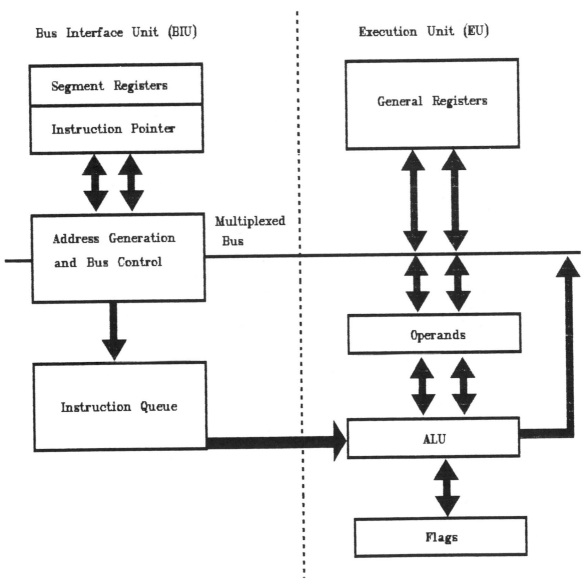

Fig. A1-6. Execution and bus interface units.

which holds the address of the next instruction to be fetched. The BIU also contains an instruction stream byte queue and the *segment registers.*

The 8086 segment registers are 16-bit registers and are called CS (Code Segment), DS (Data Segment), SS (Stack Segment), and ES (Extra Segment).

The BIU is independent from the Execution Unit (EU). While the BIU fetches additional instructions, the EU executes a previously fetched instruction. This is made possible by the instruction pipeline (or queue) between the BIU and the EU. The BIU fills this pipeline with instructions awaiting execution. Whenever the EU finishes a given instruction, the next instruction is usually ready for immediate execution without delays caused by instruction fetching. The 8086 BIU queue stores up to six bytes of the instruction stream.

The EU has no connection to the system bus, which it considers the outside world. The EU obtains instructions from the queue maintained by the BIU. When an instruction requires access to memory or to a peripheral bus, the EU requests the BIU to fetch or store the data. All addresses manipulated by the EU are 16 bits wide, but the address relocation facility provided by the BIU provides the EU with access to a full megabyte (one million bytes) of memory.

The EU contains the 16-bit *arithmetic logic unit* (ALU), the Operand and Flag File, and the General Register File containing registers AH, AL, BH, BL, CH, CL, DH, DL, BP, SP, SI, and DI. All register and data paths in the EU are 16 bits wide. The 8-bit registers combine to form 16-bit registers. For instance, AH and AL combine to form AX, the accumulator register. BH and BL form BX, the base register. CH and CL form CX, the count register. Finally, DH and DL form DX, the data register.

The general registers can be addressed either as 8-bit or 16-bit registers. This enables the 8086 to run 8080 instructions with only a code translation.

Depending on the number and complexity of the peripheral devices, the system designer can choose either a maximum and minimum system configuration mode. The two modes are defined by a pin (MN/MX) that is strapped either to ground (for maximum mode) or to the VCC potential (for minimum mode).

In the maximum mode configuration, a bus controller is used for generating the control signals to memory and I/O. This frees the minimum control signal pins to take on other functions such as bus-locking capability and extra direct memory access (DMA) control. In the minimum mode configuration, the 8086 generates the control signals used by the memory and I/O devices.

The instruction set of the 8086 is divided into six categories: Data transfer, Arithmetic, Logic, String manipulation, Control transfer, and Processor control.

Memory in the 8086 is made up of 8-bit bytes with any two consecutive bytes forming a 16-bit word. For the first time, more than 64K of memory could be addressed. Memory itself is composed of an arbitrary number of segments, each consisting of 64K successive bytes. The concept of *segments* is important since it is through such segments that memory addressing takes place.

Each memory segment begins at an address that is evenly divisible by 16. The method of specifying the segment of interest is through the four segment registers. At any specific moment, the 8086 can directly address the contents of the four seg-

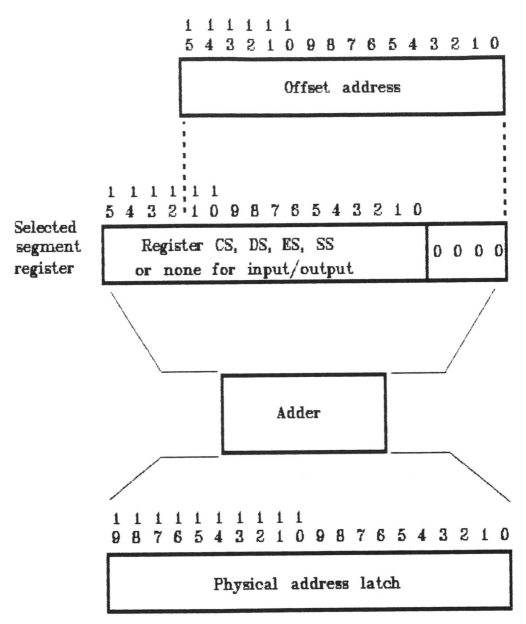

Fig. A1-7. Memory addressing in the 8086.

ments: code segment, data segment, stack segment, and extra data segment. Segments may overlap each other.

To address bytes or words inside a segment, a 16-bit offset address, often called the *effective address* (EA) is used with the contents of any of the segment registers. The programmer specifies which segment register is to be used and the designation of that segment register is incorporated within the instruction itself.

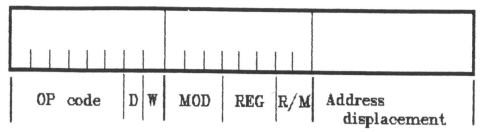

Fig. A1-8. 8086 instruction format.

The 8086 can address up to one megabyte of memory (actually 1,048,576 bytes). The physical address is constructed by using both the offset address and the content of the designated segment register. This begins by shifting the segment address left four places and appending four zeros (0000) to the low-order bit positions. The effective address is then added to this 20-bit number to form the actual physical address.

The basic form of the 8086 instruction is shown in Fig. A1-8. The first byte comprises an op code, a 1-bit D field and a 1-bit W field. The D means direction and the W is width. If D=0, it is a direction "to." If D=1, it is "from." The width field distinguishes between byte instructions, where W=0, and word instructions, where W=1.

The mode field, MOD, makes up the next two bits of the instruction format. MOD refers to the addressing mode being used. It specifies how the data in the R/M (register/memory) field is to be used in finding the operand. If MOD=11, the R/M field is treated as a register field.

The register field, REG, specifies either an 8-bit or 16-bit register, which is the location of the operand. The register fields are defined in Fig. A1-9.

Instruction Prefix	Address–Size Prefix	Operand–Size Prefix	Segment Override
0 or 1	0 or 1	0 or 1	0 or 1

Number of Bytes

Opcode	MOD R/M	SIB	Displacement	Immediate
1 or 2	0 or 1	0 or 1	0, 1, 2, or 4	0, 1, 2 or 4

Number of Bytes

Fig. A1-9. General instruction format.

The register/memory field specifies either the location in memory where the operand can be found or the location of the operand. One of two bytes can follow. They are the address displacement, if the R/M field requires it. Finally, the DISP is the displacement byte that follows the R/M field.

Certain memory locations in the 8086 (and later in the 8088 and the 80186) are reserved by Intel for use by future hardware and software products. The various locations are shown in Fig. A1-10.

8087 Coprocessors. During the evolution of Intel's processors, a parallel evolution occurred: coprocessors. A *coprocessor* is a subordinate processor that performs a specialized function for a general-purpose processor. The first popular coprocessor was the 8087, which performs floating-point computations for both the 8086 and the 8088. It also served as the coprocessor for the 80186 when that processor was developed.

The 8088 Chip

The 8088 is an 8-bit version of the 8086 and appeared in 1979. Memory handling in the 8088 is sequenced up to a million bytes, the same as with the 8086. The 8088 accesses memory in bytes, however. Word operands are accessed in two bus cycles regardless of their alignment. Instructions are also fetched one byte at a time.

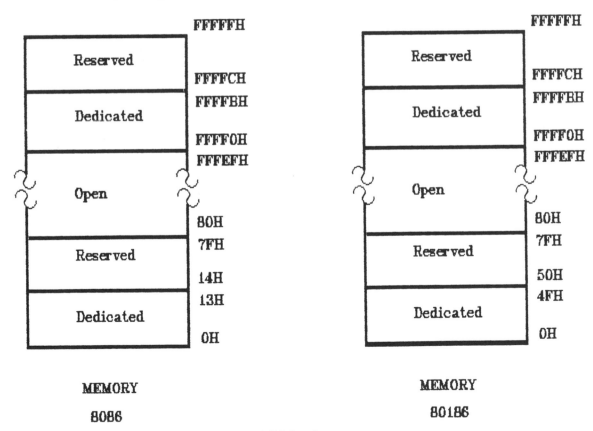

Fig. A1-10. Reserved and dedicated memory and I/O locations.

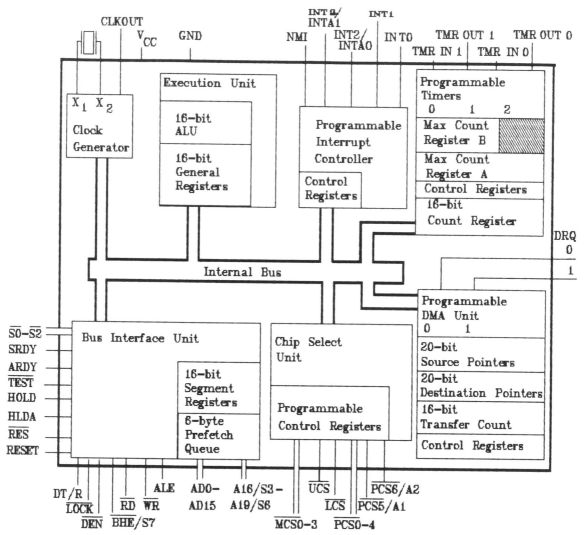

Fig. A1-11. 80186 block diagram.

As with the 8086, memory is made up of an arbitrary number of segments, each containing a maximum of 64K bytes. The calculation of the address is done the same way, to result in the 20-bit word address automatically by adding the 16-bit offset address (also called the logical address) to the contents of a 16-bit segment register, with the four low-order zero appended. See the more complete description under the 8086 chip. IBM used the 8088 as the processor for their popular IBM PC.

The 80186 Chip

In addition to the features of the 8086 and 8088 CPUs, the 80186 integrates a chip-select logic unit, two independent high-speed *direct memory address* (DMA) channels, three programmable timers, a programmable interrupt controller and a clock generator.

The register set of the 80186 is identical to that of the 8086 and the 8088, with the minor exception that the 8086 and 8088 Flags Register is referred to as the Status Word Register in the 80186. The contents of the two registers are the same. The 80186 is object code compatible with the 8086 and 8088, but adds ten additional instructions to the basic 8086/8088 instruction set.

The chip-select logic provides programmable chip-select generation for both memories and peripherals. Six memory chip-select outputs are provided for three address areas: (1) upper memory, (2) midrange memory, and (3) lower memory. The range of each chip-select is user programmable. The 80186 can also generate chip-selects for up to seven peripheral devices.

The 80186 DMA controller provides two independent high-speed DMA channels. This controller transfers data between memory and I/O, between memory and memory, or between I/O and I/O. Data can be transferred in bytes or words and may be transferred to or from even or odd addresses. The channels maintain both a 20-bit source and destination pointer which optionally can be incremented or decremented after each data transfer.

There are three 16-bit internal programmable timers. Two of them are flexible and connected to external pins. They can be used to count external events, time external events, generate nonrepetitive waveforms, and so on. Not connected to external pins, the third timer is useful for real-time coding and time delays.

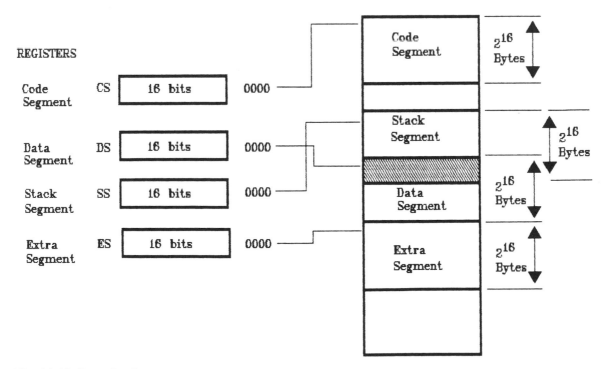

Fig. A1-12. Example of memory segments.

The on-chip clock generator provides both internal and external clock generation. It includes a crystal oscillator, a divide-by-two counter, synchronous and asynchronous ready inputs, and reset circuitry.

The interrupt controller on the 80186 receives interrupts from a number of sources, both internal and external. The internal interrupt controller merges these two requests on a priority basis for individual service by the CPU. This controller has its own control registers which it uses to set the mode of operation for the controller.

The BIU (bus interface unit) of the 80186 is functionally identical with the 8088, but is implemented differently to match the data path size which is 16 bits wide. Where the 8088 instruction queue held four bytes of the instruction stream, the 80186 stores up to six bytes. This queue size keeps the EU (execution unit) supplied with prefetched instructions under most conditions without monopolizing the system bus.

The 8086 and the 80186 access either 8 or 16 bits of memory at a time. If an instruction refers to a word variable, and that variable is located at an even-numbered address, both the 8086 and the 80186 access the complete word in one bus cycle. If the word is located at an odd-numbered address, it is accessed one byte at a time in two consecutive bus cycles.

The 80186 instruction set includes all the instructions from as early as the 8080 chip. Ten new instruction types were added to streamline the existing code or to produce optimum 80186 code.

The 80286 Chip

In 1983, Intel came out with the 80286, a big leap beyond the 80186. A year later, IBM announced that the 80286 would be the processor for their IBM PC/AT (AT stands for Advanced Technology.)

The 80286 has two modes of operation: *real* and *virtual*. In real mode, the 80286 operates much like a fast 8086. In *real mode*, think of the memory as a number of segments, each containing a maximum of 2^{16} bytes. Each segment begins at a byte address evenly divisible by 16. At any moment in time, the processor can access the contents of four segments. Those segments are the current code segment (CS), the current data segment (DS), the current stack segment (SS), and the current extra segment (ES). These segments may overlap and need not be unique. The addresses of these segments are stored in the segment registers.

Full addresses are computed by placing the 16 most significant bits of the address into the register. Four zeros are appended to the end. This scheme is the same as for the 8086.

Bytes within the segments are referred to by using a 16-bit offset within the segment. See Fig. A1-12 for an example of how segments are established. Note that the stack segment and the data segment overlap in the example.

In *virtual mode*, there are still segments and offsets. Virtual is different from real in that the segment start addresses are not computed by appending four zeros to the contents of segment registers but are obtained from tables indexed by the segment registers. Additional information on address calculations is given in Chapter 8.

The 80286 is first brought up in real mode and various necessary registers and flags are set. Then the processor switches from real to virtual mode by use of the LMSW (Load Machine Status Word) instruction. This instruction loads the Status

Word with a word in which the protection enable bit is set. Once the 80286 is in virtual mode, only a hardware reset signal can return it to real mode.

This processor addresses up to two megabytes (mega = million) of real memory or four gigabytes (giga = billion) of virtual memory. However, since it was designed to perform 16-bit arithmetic, the addresses it manipulates can only be 16 bits in length. The virtual mode was the answer.

The 80286 took the DMA controller off-chip. The purpose of a DMA channel is to produce a steady stream of memory references without involving the CPU. The off-chip controller allows overlap of execution with input or output to memory. The DMA controller contains four DMA channels, so up to four devices may be empowered to perform DMA.

The 80286 instruction set incorporates all the instructions sets, beginning with the 8086. In addition, there are new instructions for virtual and real modes. In real mode, the advanced 80286 features are suppressed. In virtual mode, they are enabled.

80287 Coprocessor. The popular 8087 floating-point processor that was used with the 8086 and 8088 was modified for the 80286 to handle the new coprocessor interface that Intel developed for the 80286. The new coprocessor was named 80287.

The 80287 provides additional registers for the floating point computation. The floating point operands of the 80287 instructions reside either in memory or in one

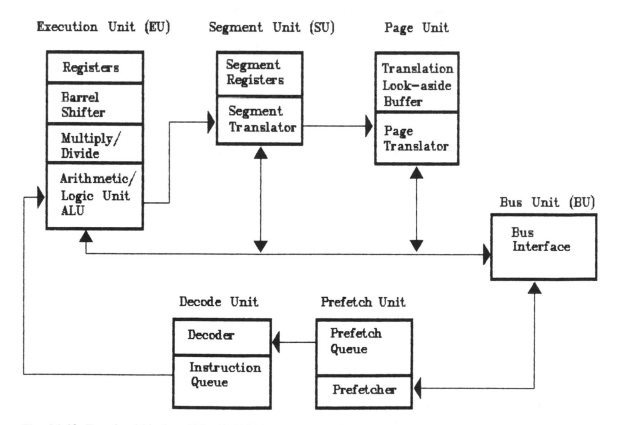

Fig. A1-13. Functional blocks within the 80386.

of the eight numeric registers. These registers hold numbers in extended precision format only.

It's possible for the 80286 and 80287 to both execute instructions simultaneously. When the 80286 finds an 80287 instruction (the first five bits are "11011"), it waits until the 80287 is idle then allows the 80287 to begin that instruction. In the meantime, the 80286 doesn't remain in wait state. It moves to the next instruction in the queue. If the 80286 finds another 80287 instruction *before* the 80287 has finished with its first one, then the processor does go into a wait state. Otherwise, it executes that next instruction.

Privilege Levels. The 80286 initiated a scheme for protecting various parts of memory for its virtual mode. The smaller level number, the more privileged the level. These privilege levels are stored in three different places. The first is the *Descriptor Privilege Level* (DPL), which is the segment classification. The second is the *Requested Privilege Level* (RPL). The third is the *Current Privilege Level* (CPL). These are automatically maintained by the 80286.

In order to access a segment for reading or writing, a program must load a selector for that segment into a segment register. To keep the program from simply accessing any segment simply by creating a selector for it and loading that selector into a segment register, the 80286 produces a protection exception if the currently executing program has a level less than that associated with the segment.

Multitasking. Another new feature the 80286 offers is the ability to support multiple tasks by switching from one task to another. With the task, the 80286 associates a memory segment containing all the information needed to start and stop the task. This special segment is called a *Task State Segment* (TSS). The main use for the TSS is to hold the contents of that task's registers when the 80286 is not executing the task.

The 80386 Chip

This section covers only a brief overview of the 80386, as it grew from previous chip designs. Chapters 1 through 7 contain the detailed 80386 architecture and design.

The 8086/8088 processors are the foundation of industry-standard personal computing. They provided the base from which the Intel processor family continued to evolve in both function and performance. However, hardware innovation outgrew the 8086/8088 architecture. Table A1-1 shows the growth in functional aspects of the Intel microprocessor chips.

The 80386 is a high-performance, 32-bit microprocessor that processes instructions as quickly as 3 to 4 million per second. It has a complete 32-bit architecture with a 4 gigabyte physical address space and on-chip support for paged virtual memory. The 80386 can address up to 2^{64} bytes of virtual memory—or 64 terabytes (tera = trillion). Shown in Fig. A1-13 is a block diagram of the functional blocks of the 80386.

The 80386 package is a 132-pin ceramic *pin grid array* (PGA). Pins in this package are arranged 0.100 inch (2.54 mm) center-to-center in a 14 x 14 matrix, three rows around. From the pin side of the package, pin number one is in the upper left corner. See Fig. A1-14.

With this processor, for the first time, true virtual machine capability is offered. Virtual memory allows very large programs, or groups of programs, to run in much

Table A1-1. Comparison of Intel Microprocessor Chips.

FEATURES	8086/8088	80286	80386
Maximum Physical Memory	1 MB	16 MB	4 GB
Maximum Virtual Memory	1 MB	1 GB	64 TB
Maximum Segment Size	64 KB	64 KB	64 KB/4 GB
Prefetch Queue in Bytes	4/6	6	12
Operand Sizes in Bits	8, 16	8, 16	8, 16, 32
Register Sizes in Bits	8, 16	8, 16	8, 16, 32
Paging Hardware	No	No	Yes
Memory-I/O Protection	No	Yes	Yes
Coprocessor Support	8087	80287	80287/80387

smaller amounts of physical memory without overlays. A virtual memory operating system stores all segments or pages in a large disk area, often called the *swap area*. The much smaller real memory holds only the most frequently used segments or pages.

The 80386 can switch between programs running under different operating systems such as MS-DOS and UNIX. This allows software designers to incorporate standard 16-bit applications software directly onto the new 32-bit system.

The 80386 instruction set is divided into nine categories of operations: Data transfer, Arithmetic, Shift/Rotate, String Manipulation, Bit Manipulation, Control Transfer, High Level Language Support, Operating System Support and Processor Control. The average instruction is 3.2 bytes long. Since the 80386 has a 16-byte instruction queue, that means an average of 5 instructions will be prefetched.

Operands in the 80386 instruction set can be 8, 16, or 32 bits long. When executing existing 80286 or 8086 code (both 16-bit codes), operands are 8 or 16 bits.

The two generations of processors (8086 and 80286) are compatible with the 80386 at the binary level. The 80386's most innovative step is its compatibility feature of Virtual 8086 capability. This capability establishes a protected 8086 environment within the 80386 multitasking framework.

Segments. The 80386 logical address space can be defined as one or more segments any size from 1 byte to 4 gigabytes. The segments can be individually protected by privilege level and thus selectively shared between tasks.

An 80386 program can potentially refer to multiple segments. Therefore, the logical address must identify the segment. The logical address consists of 16-bit *segment selector* and a 32-bit *offset* into the selected segment. The 80386 determines the segment's address by using the selector as an index into a *descriptor table* which it maintains. The processor then adds the offset part of the logical address to the base address it just obtained from the segment's descriptor to produce the operand address.

Coprocessor. The 80386 can use either the 80287 numeric coprocessor or a newly designed 80387 coprocessor. Both numeric coprocessors contain registers that improve the 80386's performance. By connecting either the 80287 or the 80387 to an 80386, the coprocessor's registers are effectively added to the 80386's.

Privilege Levels. The 80386 provides an array of protection mechanisms that operating systems can employ selectively to fit their needs. Many of the 80386 pro-

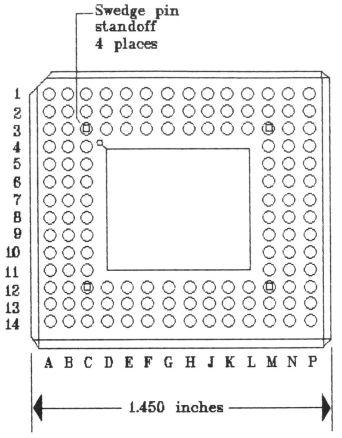
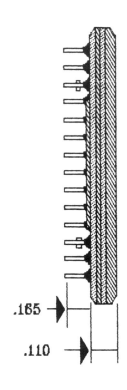

Fig. A1-14. 132-pin ceramic PGA package.

tection facilities are based on the notion of a *privilege hierarchy*. That is, various tasks or programs can be assigned various levels that are used on an exclusive basis to other tasks operating within the system.

An unprotected system can be implemented by simply placing all procedures in a segment (or segments) where the privilege level is 0 (zero). In a slightly more protected environment, the operating system can be placed in level zero while application programs can run in level 1 (one). And so on.

In a protected system, a task's privilege level determines what instructions it may execute and what subset of segments in its address space it may reference. An attempt by a task to use a more restricted segment results in a general protection exception.

In addition to defining which segments it can use, a task's privilege level defines the instructions it can execute. The 80386 was designed with a number of instructions whose execution must be tightly controlled to prevent serious system disruption. Those instructions are called *privileged instructions*.

Multitasking. Multitasking is the technique that manages the system's work when that work consists of multiple activities. Three examples of that work are: editing one file, compiling another, and transmitting a third to another computer system. In the multitasking system, each activity that can proceed in parallel with other activities is called a *task* or process.

The operating system simulates multiple processors by providing each task with a *virtual processor.* At any point in time, the operating system assigns the real processor to one of the virtual processors which runs its associated task. The operating system frequently switches the real processor to a different virtual processor, thus maintaining the illusion of one processor per task.

The operating system interleaves task execution according to a scheduling policy that sets the order in which tasks run. The 80386 keeps a selector and a descriptor for the running task's TSS in its *task register.*

Each task can have a system-wide logical address space which it stores in a *Global Descriptor Table* (GDT) and a logical address space which it stores in the *Local Descriptor Table* (LDT). These descriptor tables can contain up to 8,192 descriptors each. Together, they define the task's logical address space.

Appendix 2

Register, Bits, and Flags Listings

The following is an alphabetic list of all the registers used with the 80386 processor.

AH	High-order byte of AX Register
AL	Low-order byte of AX Register
AX	16-bit Register, part of EAX
BH	High-order byte of BX Register
BL	Low-order byte of BX Register
BP	16-bit Register, part of EBP
BX	16-bit Register, part of EBX
CH	High-order byte of CX Register
CL	Low-order byte of CX Register
CR0	Control Register, low order 16 bits is MSW
CR1	Control Register, Reserved
CR2	Page Fault Linear Address Register
CR3	Page Directory Base Address
CX	16-bit Register, part of ECX
DH	High-order byte of DX Register
DI	16-bit Register, part of EDI
DL	Low-order byte of DX Register
DR0	Debug Register, Linear Breakpoint Address 0
DR1	Debug Register, Linear Breakpoint Address 1
DR2	Debug Register, Linear Breakpoint Address 2
DR3	Debug Register, Linear Breakpoint Address 3
DR4	Debug Register, Intel Reserved
DR5	Debug Register, Intel Reserved
DR6	Debug Register, Breakpoint Status
DR7	Debug Register, Breakpoint Control

DS	Data Segment Register
DX	16-bit Register, part of EDX
EAX	General 32-bit Register
EBP	General 32-bit Register, Stack-Frame Base Pointer
EBX	General 32-bit Register
ECX	General 32-bit Register
EDI	General 32-bit Register
EDX	General 32-bit Register
EFLAGS	Flags Register
EIP	Instruction Pointer
ES	Data Segment Register
ESI	General 32-bit Register
ESP	Stack Pointer Register
FLAGS	The low-order 16 bits of EFLAGS
FS	Data Segment Register
GDT	Global Descriptor Table
GS	Data Segment Register
IDT	Interrupt Descriptor Table
IP	Instruction Pointer, low-order 16 bits of EIP
LDT	Local Descriptor Table
SI	16-bit Register, part of ESI
SP	16-bit Register, part of ESP
SS	Stack Segment Register
TR6	Test Register for Page Cache, Test Control
TR7	Test Register for Page Cache, Test Status
TSS	Task State Segment

The following is a list of the flags used in the 80386 and its environs, along with which register they're in. Note that if the bit is in the EFLAGS register, it is commonly called a 'flag'; otherwise it's called a 'bit.'

Bit/Flag	Location	Description
A	Bit 5 of Page Table Entry	Accessed
AF	Bit 4 of EFLAGS	Auxiliary Carry
CF	Bit 0 of EFLAGS	Carry Flag
D	Bit 6 of Page Table Entry	Dirty
DF	Bit 10 of EFLAGS	Direction Flag
EM	Bit 2 of CR0	Emulate Coprocessor
ET	Bit 4 of CR0	Processor Extension Type
IF	Bit 9 of EFLAGS	Interrupt Enable
IOPL	Bit 13/12 of EFLAGS	I/O Privilege Level
MP	Bit 1 of CR0	Monitor Coprocessor
NT	Bit 14 of EFLAGS	Nested Task Flag
OF	Bit 11 of EFLAGS	Overflow
P	Bit 0 of Page Table Entry	Present

PE	Bit 0 of CR0	Protection Enable
PF	Bit 2 of EFLAGS	Parity Flag
PG	Bit 31 of CR0	Paging Enable
R/W	Bit 1 of Page Table Entry	Read/Write
RF	Bit 16 of EFLAGS	Resume Flag
SF	Bit 7 of EFLAGS	Sign Flag
TF	Bit 8 of EFLAGS	Trap Flag
TS	Bit 3 of CR0	Task Switched
U/S	Bit 2 of Page Table Entry	User/Supervisor
VM	Bit 17 of EFLAGS	Virtual 8086 Mode
ZF	Bit 6 of EFLAGS	Zero Flag

Appendix 3

Acronyms
and Letter Groups

AC	Alternating Current
ACC	Accumulator
ACK	Acknowledge
ADMA	Advanced Direct Memory Access
ADS#	Address Status Pin on 80386
ALU	Arithmetic/Logic Unit
ASCII	American Standard Code for Information Interchange
ASR	Automatic Send and Receive
A0-Ann	Address pins from A0 to a number, usually 32
BCD	Binary Coded Decimal
BCR	Byte Count Register
BEn#	Byte Enable Pins on 80386, n=0 to 3
BIU	Bus Interface Unit
BPS	Bits Per Second
BS16#	Bus Size Pin of 80386
BSC	Binary Synchronous Communication
CAD	Computer-Aided Design
CAM	Computer-Aided Manufacturing, also Content-Addressable Memory
CAS	Column Address Select
CCD	Charge-Coupled Device
CE	Chip Enable
CLK	Clock
CML	Current Mode Logic
CMOS	Complementary Metal Oxide Semiconductor
CPG	Clock Pulse Generator
CPL	Current Privilege Level

CPS	Characters Per Second
CPU	Central Processing Unit
CRn	Control Registers, 0 to 3
CRT	Cathode Ray Tube
CRTC	CRT Controller
CS	Chip Select, also Code Segment Register
CU	Control Unit
DC	Direct Current
DCD	Data Carrier Detect
DIP	Dual In-Line Pins or Package
DMA	Direct Memory Access (or Address)
DMAC	Direct Memory Access/Address Controller
DOS	Disk Operating System
DPL	Descriptor Privilege Level
DRAM	Dynamic Random Access Memory
DS	Data Segment Register
DTL	Diode Transistor Logic
DO-Dnn	Data Lines zero through a number
E	Enable
EA	Effective Address
EAROM	Electrically Alterable Read Only Memory
EBCDIC	Extended Binary-Coded-Decimal Information Code
ECL	Emitter Coupled Logic
EIP	Instruction Pointer, 32-bit implementation
EMI	Electromagnetic Interface
EOF	End of File
EOR	Exclusive OR
EOT	End of Tape, or End of Text
EPL	Effective Privilege Level
EPROM	Erasable Programmable Read Only Memory
ES	Extra Segment Register
ESI	Electrostatic Interface
ESP	Extended Stack Pointer
EU	Execution Unit
FDC	Floppy Disk Controller
FDM	Frequency-Division Multiplexing
FET	Field Effect Transistor
FF	Flip-Flop
FIFO	First-In-First-Out
FPLA	Field Programmable Logic Array
FSK	Frequency Shift Keying
GDT	Global Descriptor Table
GDTR	Global Descriptor Table Register
GP	General Purpose
GPIB	General Purpose Interface Bus
GR	General Registers

HDLC	High-Level Data Link Control
HEX	Hexadecimal
HMOS	High-Density Metal Oxide Semiconductor
I	Interrupt, also Interrupt Mask
IC	Integrated Circuit
IDT	Interrupt Descriptor Table
IDTR	Interrupt Descriptor Table Register
INT	Interrupt
INTR	Maskable Interrupt
I/O	Input/Output
IOCS	Input/Output Control System
IOPL	Input/Output Privilege Level
IP	Instruction Pointer, 16-bit implementation
IRET	Interrupt Return
IRQ	Interrupt Request
JP	Jump
K	Kilo, Also 1024
KSR	Keyboard Send Receive
LAN	Local Area Network
LCD	Liquid Crystal Display
LED	Light-Emitting Diode
LDT	Local Descriptor Table
LDTR	Local Descriptor Table Register
LIFO	Last-In-First-Out
LP	Line Printer
LPM	Lines Per Minute
LSB	Least Significant Bit
LSI	Large Scale Integration
M/IO	Memory and Input/Output
MHz	Mega-Hertz, millions of cycles per second
MMU	Memory Management Unit
MOFFS	Memory Offset
MOS	Metal Oxide Semiconductor
MOSFET	Metal Oxide Semiconductor Field Effect Transistor
MPSC	Multi-Protocol Serial Controller
MPU	Microprocessor Unit
MSB	Most Significant Bit
MSI	Medium Scale Integration
MSW	Machine Status Word (used on 80286)
MUX	Multiplexer
N	Negative
NDRO	Non-Destructive Read Out
NMI	Non-Maskable Interrupt
NMOS	N-Channel Metal Oxide Semiconductor
OEM	Original Equipment Manufacturer
OP	Operation

OPLA	One-Page Lookahead
OS	Operating System
P	Positive
PAL	Programmable Array Logic
PC	Printed Circuit, also Personal Computer
PCI/O	Program Controlled Input/Output
PCM	Pulse Code Modulation
PDBR	Page Directory Base Register
PEREQ	Coprocessor Request
PFR	Power Fail Restart
PGA	Pin Grid Array
PIC	Priority Interrupt Control
PIO	Programmable Input/Output Chip (Interface)
PIT	Programmable Interval-Timer
PL	Privilege Level
PLA	Programmable Logic-Array
PLL	Phase-Locked Loop
PMOS	P-channel Metal Oxide Semiconductor
PROM	Programmable Read Only Memory
PSW	Programmable Status Word
R	Read
R/W	Read/Write
RALU	Register Arithmetic Logic Unit
RAM	Random Access Memory
RAS	Row Address Select
RDSR	Receiver Data Service Request
RDY	Ready
RES	Reset
ROM	Read Only Memory
RPL	Requestor's Privilege Level
RPT	Repeat
RS	Register Select
RST	Restart
RTC	Real-Time Clock
RTS	Request To Send
SDLC	Synchronous Data Link Control
Si	Silicon (element)
SIB	Scale Index Base
SIP	Single In-Line Package
SLSI	Super Large Scale Integration
SOS	Silicon-On-Saphire
SP	Stack Pointer
SR	Service Request
SRAM	Static Random Access Memory
SS	Stack Segment Register
SSI	Small Scale Integration

STB	Strobe
STEN	Status Enable
SUB	Subroutine
TDM	Time Division Multiplexing
TSS	Task State Segment
TLB	Translation Lookaside Buffer
TOS	Top Of Stack
TTL	Transistor-Transistor Logic
U/S	User/Supervisor
USART	Universal Synchronous/Asynchronous Receiver Transmitter
V_{ss}	Ground
VLSI	Very Large Scale Integration
VM	Virtual Mode, also Virtual Machine
W	Write
WPM	Words Per Minute
X	Index
XOR	Exclusive OR
Z	Zero Bit

Appendix 4

Multibus® I/II and the 80386

The system bus structure that supplies the interface for all the hardware connections is one of the most important elements in a computer system. This structure permits various system components to interact with each other and to share resources. Resource sharing results in a significant increase in throughput over a single-bus system. Among other actions, the system bus allows memory and I/O data transfers, direct memory accesses, and the generation of interruptions.

System buses are usually isolated from failures occurring in other parts of the system, which enhances the system's overall reliability. As samples of a general bus, the Intel MULTIBUS® I and II architectures provide a communications channel that can be used to coordinate a wide variety of computing modules.

MULTIBUS® I and II were introduced in Chapter 12. Some background is included here but this appendix primarily addresses the bus and its relationship with the 80386.

Both MULTIBUS® I and II are built on the master-slave concept. A *master* is any module that has the ability to control the bus. The master does this by acquiring the bus through bus exchange logic and then generating command signals, address signals, and I/O or memory addresses. To do these tasks, the master is equipped with either a central processing unit or logic dedicated to transferring data over to the bus to and from other destinations. A *slave* is a module that decodes the address lines and acts upon the command signals from the masters; a slave is *not* capable of controlling the bus. This handshake between the master and slave allows modules of different speeds to be interfaced via the bus. The bus master can override the bus control logic when it is necessary to guarantee itself back-to-back bus cycles. This is called "locking" the bus, which temporarily prevents other masters from using the bus.

Another important feature is the bus' ability to connect multiple master modules for multiprocessing systems.

MULTIBUS® I allows for both 8- and 16-bit data paths, and up to a 24-bit address path. MULTIBUS® II can accept 8-, 16-, and 32-bit data and up to 32-bit addresses. MULTIBUS® I and II protocols are described in detail in the Intel documentation, which should be studied in detail before implementing either MULTIBUS® I or II on a system.

MULTIBUS® I

Intel's MULTIBUS® I is a 16-bit multiprocessing system bus that conforms to the IEEE 796 standard. Figure A4-1 shows a block diagram of the MULTIBUS® I interface. The figure does not include the 80386 local bus interface and local resources.

MULTIBUS® I Interface Sample

One way to construct an interface between the 80386 and MULTIBUS® I is to generate all the MULTIBUS® I signals using only PAL and TTL devices. A simpler way is to use the 80286-compatible interface, outlines of which are shown below.

This MULTIBUS® I interface consists of the 80286-compatible 82289 Bus Arbiter and the 82288 Bus Controller. The 82288 operates in either local-bus mode or MULTIBUS® I mode; a pullup resistor on the 82288 MB input activates the MULTIBUS® I mode. The MBEN output of the address decoder PAL selects both the 82288 and the 82289. The AEN# signal from the 82289 enables the 82288 outputs.

Communication between the 80386 processor and these two devices is done with PALs that are programmed to do the necessary signal generation and translation. Along with the bus arbiters of other processing subsystems, the 82289 coordinates control of MULTIBUS® I by providing the control signals to perform MULTIBUS® I accesses.

In a MULTIBUS® I system, each processing subsystem contends for the use of shared resources. If a subsystem requests access to the bus while another is already using it, the second must wait. Bus arbitration logic controls all accesses to the bus by the subsystems. Each of the processing subsystems has its own 82289 Bus Arbiter. The 82289 directs its processor onto the bus and allows higher and lower priority bus masters to access the bus, based on pre-established priorities.

Two common techniques for resolving priority are serial priority and parallel priority. Serial priority is implemented by daisy-chaining the Bus Priority In (BPRN#) and Bus Priority Out (BPRO#) signals of all the bus arbiters in the system. There is some built-in delay in this scheme, which limits the number of bus arbiters that can be attached. Parallel priority requires external logic to recognize the BPRN# inputs from all bus arbiters and to return the BPRO# signal active to whichever requesting bus arbiter that has the highest priority. The number of arbiters that can be attached with parallel priority is limited by the complexity of the decoding logic.

After a MULTIBUS® I cycle, the controlling bus arbiter can either keep control or release it to another bus arbiter. To release control, the bus arbiter can release the bus at the end of each cycle, retain control of the bus until a higher priority bus master requests control, or retain control until another bus master of any priority requests control.

MULTIBUS® I allows up to 24 address lines and 16 data lines. Its addresses are located in a 256-kilobyte range (between F00000H and F3FFFFH) and all 24 lines are used. The 16 data lines consist of the lower half (least significant 16 bits) of the

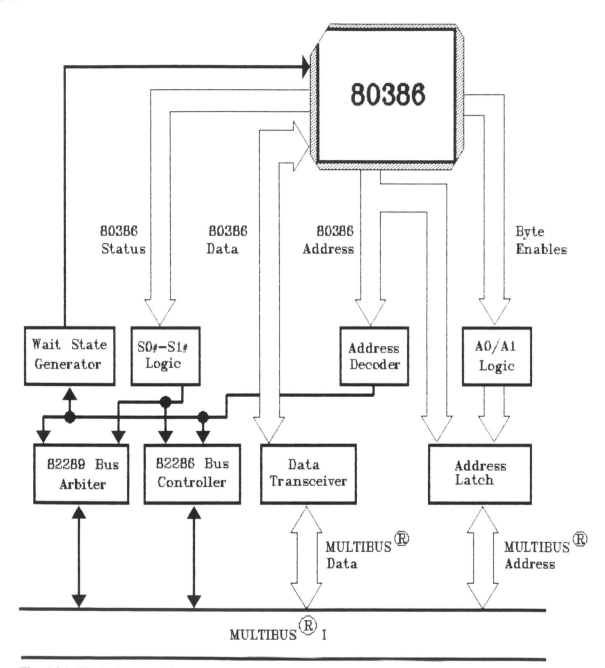

Fig. A4-1. Block diagram of 80386-MULTIBUS® I interface.

32-bit 80386 data bus. MULTIBUS® I address bits are numbered in hexadecimal; A23-A0 on the 80386 bus becomes ADR17#-ADR0# on MULTIBUS® I. Inverting addresses latches convert the 80386 address outputs to the active-low MULTIBUS® I address bits.

Address Decoder. A MULTIBUS® I system generally has both shared and local memory. In addition, I/O devices can also be located on either a local bus or on MULTIBUS® I. That means that (1) the address space of the 80386 must be allocated between MULTIBUS® I and the local bus and (2) address decoding logic must be used to select one bus or the other. Two signals are needed for MULTIBUS® I selection:

   1. MULTIBUS® Enable (MBEN) selects the 82288 Bus Controller and the 82289 Bus Arbiter on the MULTIBUS® I interface. The decoder PAL has other outputs that are programmed to select memory and I/O devices on the local bus.
   2. Bus Size 16 (BS16#) must be returned active to the 80386 to ensure the 16-bit bus cycle. Other terms for other devices that require a 16-bit bus can be added to the BS16# PAL equation. (For a sample PAL equation, see Chapter 7. Contact Intel for suggested PAL equations.)

   I/O resources residing on MULTIBUS® I can be either I/O-mapped into the I/O address space independent of the physical location of the devices on MULTIBUS® I or memory-mapped into the memory space of the 80386. The addresses of memory-mapped I/O devices must be decoded to generate the correct I/O read or I/O write commands for all the memory references that lie within the I/O-mapped region of the memory space.

Address Latches/Data Transceivers. The address on all bus cycles is latched because MULTIBUS® I requires address outputs to be valid for at least 50 nanoseconds after the MULTIBUS® I command goes inactive. The 82289 Bus Arbiter Address Enable (AEN#) output goes active when the 82289 has control of MULTIBUS® I. AEN# is an output enable for the MULTIBUS® I latches. As shown in Figure A4-2, the 82288 Bus Controller ALE# output latches the 80386 address.

   MULTIBUS® I data bits are numbered in hexadecimal, so that D15-D0 converts to DATF#-DAT0#. Inverting latch/transceivers provide active-low MULTIBUS® I

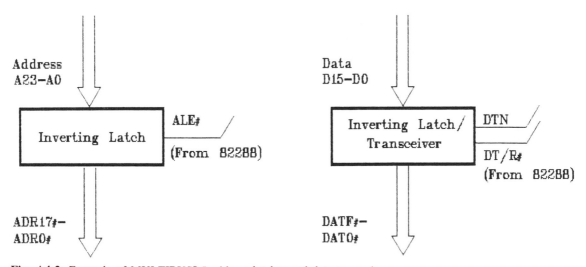

Fig. A4-2. Example of MULTIBUS® I address latches and data transceivers.

data bits. Data is latched only on write cycles. During *write* cycles, the 82288 ALE#, DEN, and DT/R# inputs control the address latches and the data latch/transceivers. For *read* cycles, the local bus RD# signal controls the latch/transceivers because, if DEN were used, data contention on the 80386 local bus would occur when a MULTIBUS® I read cycle immediately followed a local write cycle.

iSBX Expansion I/O Bus

The iSBX Bus is independent of processor or board type. Each expansion interface supports up to 16 8-bit I/O ports directly. Enhanced addressing capability is available using slave processors or FIFO devices. Also, each expansion interface can optionally support a DMA channel capable of data rates up to 2 Mwords/second.

There are two basic elements of the iSBX: the baseboard and the expansion module. The *baseboard* is any board that provides one or more I/O expansion interfaces (connectors) that meet the electrical and mechanical requirements of the Intel specification. Logically, the baseboard is always the master device. This makes it responsible for generating all addresses, chip selects and commands.

The iSBX *expansion module* is a small, specialized I/O board that attaches to a baseboard. Each module can be single wide and double wide. The purpose of an expansion module is to convert the general bus interface into a specific I/O interface.

Increasing the number of functions residing on each system board attached to the MULTIBUS® I interface increases system performance. The improved performance results because the resident functions are accessed without bus arbitration.

Multi-Channel Bus

The Multi-Channel Bus is a specialized electrical and mechanical interfacing protocol operating within the overall MULTIBUS® I interfacing system. This bus is designed for high speed block data transfers between the MULTIBUS® I system and the interconnected peripheral devices. Where a series of bytes or words are moved to or from consecutive locations, the block data transfer protocol minimizes that transfer overhead. The transfers are asynchronous and use a positive handshake protocol along with transfer parity verification to assure accurate data transfer.

Reducing the impact of burst-type peripherals on MULTIBUS® I provides a means of increasing system performance. The data transfers from a burst type peripheral can saturate a general purpose interface. The Multi-Channel bus protocol specifically accommodates burst-type data transfers. The full performance improvement requires use of dual port memory accessed over both the Multi-Channel Bus and the MULTIBUS® I interface.

iLBX Execution Bus

The iLBX bus is designed for direct high-speed Master-Slave data transfers and provides: (1) two (maximum) masters that can share the bus, limiting the need for complex bus arbitration, (2) bus arbitration that is asynchronous to the data transfers, (3) a minimum of two and maximum of five devices that can be connected over the iLBX bus, (4) slave devices that are defined as byte-addressed memory resources, and (5) slave devices whose functions are directly controlled from iLBX bus signal lines.

Increasing the local (on-board) memory resources of a high performance processor provides a means of increasing system performance. As with other special functions, memory residing on the processor board improves performance because the processor directly addresses the memory without waiting for bus arbitration. However, because of physical limits, there is a restricted amount of memory that can reside on the processor board. The iLBX bus helps to reduce that physical space limitation.

Using the iLBX bus, additional memory no longer needs to be located on the processor board. The full number of megabytes of memory addressable by the processor can be accessed over the iLBX bus and appears to the processor as though it were resident on the processor's board. Dual porting the memory between the iLBX bus and the MULTIBUS® I interface makes the same memory available to other system components.

Up to five devices can be attached to the iLBX bus. This set must include a *primary master* and one *slave* device. The remaining three devices are optional and may include additional slave devices and one *secondary master*. The primary master controls the iLBX bus and manages the secondary master access to the slave memory resources. The optional secondary master provides alternate access over the iLBX board to the slave resources.

MULTIBUS® I Design Considerations

There are design considerations that must be kept in mind when using MULTIBUS® I with the 80386. Those include interrupt handling, 8-bit transfers, timeout protection, and power failure handling. For complete details, a designer should obtain Intel's latest manuals on the MULTIBUS® I architecture. A summary of those items follows.

Interrupt Handling. When the 80386 receives an interrupt, it generates an interrupt-acknowledge cycle to fetch an 8-bit interrupt vector from a device such as the 8259A Programmable Interrupt Controller which can be located on either MULTIBUS® I or on a local bus. Multiple 8259As can be cascaded (one master and up to eight slaves) to process up to 64 interrupts.

The 80386 responds to an active INTR input by performing two bus cycles. During the first cycle, the master interrupt controller determines which of its slave controllers should return the interrupt vector. During the second cycle, the 80386 reads the vector from the selected interrupt controller and uses this vector to service the interrupt.

8-Bit Transfers. All byte transfers on a MULTIBUS® I must be performed on the lower eight data lines, regardless of the address of the data. An 80386 system must swap data from eight of its upper 24 lines (D8-D15, D16-D23 or D24-D31) to its lower eight data lines (D0-D7) before transferring data to MULTIBUS® I. It also must swap data from its lower data lines to the appropriate upper data lines when reading a byte from MULTIBUS® I. This byte-swapping maintains compatibility between 8-bit, 16-bit, and 32-bit systems sharing the same MULTIBUS® I.

BS16# is generated and returned to the 80386 for all MULTIBUS® I cycles. The 80386 automatically swaps the data on its data bus and adds an extra bus cycle as necessary to complete the data transfer. Thus only logic to swap from D8-D15 to D0-D7 needs to be added.

Bus Timeouts. The MULTIBUS® I XACK# (transfer acknowledgment) signal ends an 80386 bus cycle by driving the wait-state generator logic. If the 80386 addresses a nonexistent device on MULTIBUS® I, the XACK# signal is never generated. If the system does not have a bus-timeout protection circuit, the 80386 could wait indefinitely for a never-arriving active READY# signal which would prevent other processors from using MULTIBUS® I.

Power Failure Handling. MULTIBUS® I includes a Power Fail Interrupt (PFIN#) signal that indicates an imminent system power failure. PFIN# is typically connected to the nonmaskable interrupt (NMI) request input of each 80386. The NMI service routine should direct the 80386 to save its environment immediately, before falling voltages and the MULTIBUS® I Memory Protect (MPRO#) signal prevent further memory activity. In a system with memory backup power or nonvolatile memory, this saved environment can be recovered on power-up.

The 80386 power-up sequence should check the state of the MULTIBUS® I Power Fail Sense Latch (PFSN#). If a previous power failure occurred, the 80386 can branch to a routine that resets the latch using the Power Fail Sense Reset signal (PFSR#) and then restore the previous 80386 environment to resume execution.

MULTIBUS® II

The MULTIBUS® II is a processor-independent bus architecture. It features a 32-bit parallel system bus with a maximum throughput of 40 megabytes per second, a low-cost serial system bus, and high-speed local bus access to off-board memory. MULTIBUS® II does this through five Intel buses: (1) Local Bus Extension (iLBX II), (2) Multi-Channel DMA I/O Bus, (3) Parallel System Bus (iPSB), (4) Serial System Bus (iSSB) and (5) System Expansion I/O Bus (iSBX).

The multiple bus structure provides advantages over a single, generalized bus. For instance, each bus is optimized for a special function and performs operations in parallel. Also buses that are not needed for a particular system can be omitted, which avoids unnecessary cost. Three of those buses are described in summary below. For full details, it is recommended that the user/designer obtain Intel's latest MULTIBUS® II architecture manuals.

iPSB Parallel System Bus

The iPSB Parallel System Bus is used for interprocessor data transfers and communication. It has a burst transfer capability that provides a maximum sustained bandwidth of 40 megabytes per second.

A *bus agent* is a board that encompasses a functional subsystem. Each bus agent must provide a means of transferring data between its 80386, its interconnect registers, and the iPSB bus. The iPSB supports four address spaces per bus agent. Those four spaces are: (1) conventional I/O, (2) conventional memory address space, (3) a 255 address message space that supports message passing, and (4) an interconnect space that allows geographic addressing, which is the identification of any bus agent (board) by slot number. Since the 80386 accesses only memory space or I/O space, the message space and interconnect space can be mapped into either memory space or the I/O space.

Three types of bus cycles define the activity that passes over the iPSB. The first is an *arbitration cycle* that determines the next owner of the bus. This cycle is made up of decision phase, which determines priority for bus control, and an acquisition phase, where the agent with the highest priority starts a transfer cycle.

The second iPSB bus cycle is a *transfer cycle* which performs a data transfer between the bus owner and another bus agent. The third iPSB bus cycle is the *exception cycle* which indicates that an exception has occurred during a transfer cycle.

iLBX II Local Bus Extension

The iLBX II Local Bus Extension is a high-speed execution bus designed for quick access to off-board memory. One iLBX II bus extension can support either two processing subsystems plus four memory subsystems, or a single processing subsystem plus five memory subsystems. A MULTIBUS® II system can contain more than one iLBX II to meet its memory requirements. For a 16 MHz 80386-based system, a typical iLBX access cycle requires six wait states.

The iLBX features a 32-bit data bus and a separate 26-bit address bus. Since these are separate paths, the iLBX allows transfer cycle pipelining. Three additional iLBX features are (1) a unidirectional handshake for fast data transfers, (2) interconnect space (for each bus agent) through which the primary requesting agent initializes and configures all other bus agents, and (3) mutual exclusion capability to control multiported memory.

iSSB Serial Bus

The iSSB Serial System Bus provides a low-cost alternative to the iPSB Parallel System Bus where high performance of the iPSB bus is not required. The iSSB bus can contain up to 32 bus agents, distributed over a maximum of 10 meters. Bus control is determined through an industry-standard access protocol, the Carrier Sense Multiple Access with Collision Detection (CSMA/CD). Bus agents use this protocol to transmit data whenever they are ready. In case of simultaneous transmission by two or more agents, the iSSB invokes collision resolution algorithms to grant fair access to all the requesting agents.

Appendix 5

Instructions Used
in Protected Mode
and a Sample Program

The program listed in this appendix first sets up an 80386 environment and then task switches to a virtual 8086 (V86) task. From the V86 task, a return and stay-resident exit is made to MS-DOS. Input/Output and I/O interrupt masking is left up to MS-DOS. Figure A5-1 shows the overview flow chart. Following the chart is a word description of the logic flow to the program.

The program is included as a demonstration of use of 80386 instructions and is *not* meant as a model to learn the most effective or efficient way to program. It tries to use most of the instructions a ''working'' program would. It has thorough internal documentation which programmers can easily follow.

The major pieces of program documentation have been extracted and expanded slightly in the *Logic Flow* section of this appendix. We wrote this program using the Microsoft Macro Assembler, version 4.0, which is widely available from Microsoft Corporation. There is not (yet) an 80386 assembler, so the program uses 16-bit operands and addresses.

The computer system on which the program was developed was built around an 80286 chip, using 125-ns memory. The 80286 chip was removed, and an adapter board with an 80386 chip was plugged into the 80286 slot.

LOGIC FLOW

Most of the program interrupts are reflected to the MS-DOS interrupt handlers. IRET and INT nn instructions cause an interrupt 13. IRET is emulated. INT nn interrupts are also, with the exception of INT 00 which is used to test instructions.

STEP 1: Define the macros for the 80386 instructions, prefixes, and so on, which are used in the instruction examples.

- Convert an 8086 segment register value to a linear address.
- Set TSS linear address into a descriptor.
- Convert an 8086 segment into a linear address in a segment descriptor.

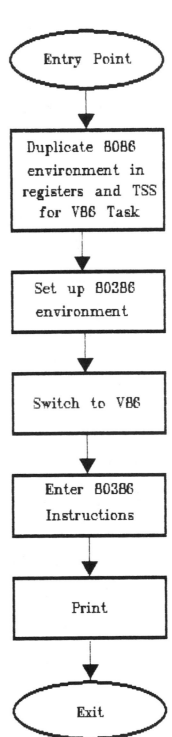

Fig. A5-1. Overview flow chart.

Step 2: Describe the data structures used by the program. The TSS is described within the body of the data in order to allow use of data references for its initialization. This descriptor is "generic" since descriptors define segments, such as code segments, data segments, stacks, and so on.

Description	Structure	Explanation
LIMIT	Word	Offset of last byte of TSS or (if not a TSS), the low 16 bits that limit the descriptor
BASE_L	Word	Bits 0-15 of 32-bit address
BASE_M	Byte	Bits 16-23 of address
ACCESS	Byte	Access Privilege
GRAN	Byte	Granularity and LIMIT
BASE_H	Byte	Bits 24-31 of BASE

• Describe the stack of the Level 0 interrupt handler for the V86 (Virtual 8086) mode task. Note that, in the program, the description is "upside down" because it is used as a data area which addresses from low to high, not a stack.

Step 3: Define the segmented structure of the program. A simple model with a single real segment was chosen because it is easily converted to a ".COM" file.

Step 4: Declare the Stack Segments and the Data Segments.

Step 5: Define the Global Descriptor Table (GDT) space.

• Level 3 empty LDT
• Level 0 empty LDT
• Dynamic data reference used in Interrupt Handler
• Reference to real location zero for MS-DOS interrupt vectors
• Descriptors for use by Interrupt Handlers
• Descriptors for use by instruction execution task

Step 6: Define the Interrupt Descriptor Table (IDT) space. The addresses are initialized as part of the setup. The selector is that of the supervisor code descriptor.

Step 7: This section describes a Task State Segment (TSS). On some of the field names, a "t" is prefixed to keep from using the standard 80386 system name.

Step 8: This section defines various TSSs and Work Areas.

TSS Definitions:

• The first TSS gets control on an INT 00 from the V86 mode task. It runs as a Level 0 protected mode task.

• The second TSS is an 80386 task switched out of, to start the V86 task.

• V86 Task, under which MS-DOS will execute. All 8K of the I/O Bit Map bits are set to zero, to allow I/O to devices 0000-FFFF. A byte of all "1's" ends the I/O map.

Local data and work areas

• Debug dump controls
    "1" in a byte enables trace entries
    "2" causes a normal dump to be taken

''3'' causes a disaster dump to be taken

''0'' means no output

- Define displacement into stack for Interrupt Handler
- Set segment descriptors

STEP 9: Build and set up Segment Descriptors for use by 80386 task.

- Convert the real mode segment registers into linear addresses in 80386 descriptors
- Set interrupt handler displacements in their descriptors. We count on the fact that the descriptors and handlers are each generated in a group so they are adjacent within their group.
- Convert linear address of data areas for segment descriptors, such as TSS descriptors and LDT descriptors.

STEP 10: Convert the segment selectors in the 80386 TSS for Interrupt Handlers

STEP 11: Set the Code, Stack, and EFLAGS Registers

- An EFLAGS register of 0002 is fine, so it's left as it is initialized in the TSS.

STEP 12: Set up the V86 TSS. Set descriptor values into the V86 TSS. In this ease, we duplicate the environment of the real mode 8086 that would be actually running.

- Set the Level 0 interrupt handler stack segment selector and pointer. We really only need Level 0 but set Level 1 and Level 2 for completeness. We also set only the low 16 bits of ESP because we know that the upper 16 bits will always be zero.
- Set register values needed to continue in 8086 mode (IP and SP).
- Set the EFLAGS in the TSS so it will execute in the V86 mode.
- VM = 1, IOPL = 3, and Interrupts are enabled.
- Set the LDT value in the V86 TSS

STEP 13: Set up the 80386 registers to run in protected mode.

- Set the GDT and IDT registers in the 80386 CPU.
- We compute the linear address for the descriptor table and store it in memory. We store the size of the table and then load the Descriptor Table Register with these values.

STEP 14: The 80386 environment is set. Now transfer into protected mode. Set the protected mode bit in CR0 and do an intrasegment jump to flush the instruction pipeline.

- Now executing in protected mode
- Debug aid will optionally dump the data areas just built

STEP 15: Set the 80386-form descriptor, the Task Register, and do an intersegment jump to load CS. At this point, all descriptors are of 80386 form, even CS.

- Now set the Nested Task (NT) flag and go to the V86 task.
- We transfer to the V86 mode using an IRET. The back chain in the current TSS and the NT flag cause the transfer. The end result is that, from here on, MS-DOS runs as a virtual 8086 task. Entry to protected mode can be done by an INT 00.

NOTE: This transfer to MS-DOS leaves the user in memory. This is both fortuitous and planned because real control of the CPU is in the hands of the rest of the program. The code to this point could be overlaid; its purpose is complete.

Additional Support Code for Protected Mode:

- Generate the initial entry points for the interrupt handlers. These entries have a correspondence with the 8086 interrupt vector table. They are the same length (4 bytes) and the return address from the call is used to generate the proper displacement into that table.
- Handle all interrupts and traps. The handler here reflects the interrupt to MS-DOS. This initial code provides a known stack format for later use. We also have saved the interrupt error code, if any, and have the vector number in an easily computable form. The five steps are followed for other than an interrupt 13.

The action taken is:

If an "error code" was stacked, POP it off.

1. Save the interrupt task's registers
2. Set descriptor selectors for use
3. Move IP, CS, and Flags to the interrupted task's stack and adjust its SP.
4. Move the MS-DOS vector to the interrupt handler's (the current) stack.
5. Restore registers saved and IRET.

If the interrupt is a "13," it will normally be either an INT nn or an IRET, which require that step 3 above be varied.

Check the value at CS:IP or IRET op codes. If neither, do a disaster dump. No device or 8086 interrupt occurs at this number.

If an INT nn—Fetch the nn value. Step IP by 2 on the stack. If nn is other than 00, we set nn*4 as the vector pointer and join the "normal" steps at step 3. If nn is 00, copy the V86 CS, AX and DX to the CX, AX, and DX in the Supervisor TSS. Then CALL the Supervisor task and on return continue at Step 5.

If an IRET—Move the flags, CS and IP from the V86 stack to this stack, adjust the V86 SP, and go to Step 5.

- We need to check if it's an INT or IRET so we must get V86 CS as a descriptor so we can check.
- The 00 Supervisor Task operates as a protected mode task in 80386 mode. The interrupt handler for the V86 task CALLs this task when it detects an INT 00. This task (which is included primarily for illustrative purposes) then executes the instructions pointed to by the V86 task's DS:DX. The instructions must be followed by a RET FAR instruction.

DEBUG SUPPORT

The choice of printed output for debug rather than display output is based on the fact that errors in this level of code often causes the system to re-boot. This causes one's debug information to be overprinted on the screen. The following are various procedures used in debug.

- The first is a procedure to set both a descriptor in the GDT to the segment's linear address (segment value is in BX), and to load BP with the descriptor value. The caller will move it (usually) into DS, which forces the linear address to be loaded from the GDT, overriding any previously cached value.

- Put out on printer the byte in AL. Note: AL is destroyed, but only AL.
- Convert a hex digit on printable form and print it.
- Print the byte in AL as an ordered pair of hex digits.
- Convert the word in AX to hex and print it.
- Convert the doubleword in EAX to hex and print it.
- Put out a carriage return and line feed.
- Dump the memory at DS:AX for 16 bytes. Follow with a display and CR/LF. AX is returned pointing to the next address to dump. ES is set to the standard DS for execution.
- Get the linear address for the DS, either as an 8086 or 80386 value. Note that this decision depends on the DS value being above GDT-size for 8086, which is normally the case for this program.
- Print AX in hex, followed by a space.
- Dump all registers
- Dump a TSS and its stack (64 bytes of it). At procedure entry, CX has the TSS displacement.
- Dump the contents of the task's stack. First, we need to build a DS to map the task's SS, which can be either 80386-style or V86-style. Then dump the data.
- Dump the GDT, IDT, and all TSS's. The displacement to the TSS of interest is in CX.
- Minimum dump for trace.

80386 SOFTWARE

The following software is available from TAB BOOKS Inc., P.O. Box 40, Blue Ridge Summit, PA 17214.

System Requirements:

1. A computer based on an 80386 processor.
2. MS-DOS (or compatible), with at least version 3.1.
3. Any standard Video Display Unit.
4. To assemble source: Microsoft *Macro Assembler*, or compatible software.
5. Memory: much less than 256K.
6. Printer, hooked up to the "normal" IBM printer address.

Diskette Contents:

VIRT86L.ASM	The source for the 80386 virtual 8086 monitor.
VIRT86L.EXE	The executable link edited object of the ASM file.
VIRT86L.LST	The assembly listing of the ASM file.
VIRT86L.CRF	The cross reference of the above assembly.
DOINST.ASM	The source for an example of a program which uses the VIRT86L monitor to execute instructions.

DOINST.EXE   The executable link edited object of the DOINST.ASM file.
DOINST.LST   The assembly listing of the DOINST.ASM file.
DOINST.CRF   The cross reference of the above assembly.

Program Listing

The following are the assembly listings and the cross reference listings for the VIRT86L and DOINST programs. These listings will print on a printer with either (1) a 132 character width or (2) one with the ability to ''condense'' and print on an 8 1/2 by 11 inch paper. We used a C. Itoh Prowriter which condensed for the smaller sized paper.

```
1
2                               PAGE    59,132          ;Set page depth and width
3                                       .286P
4                       ; c.1987 Don Brumm and Penn Brumm
5                       ;     P.O. Box 9888, San Jose, CA  95157
6                       ;       .XLIST
7                       ;  V86L.ASM
8                       ; This program sets up an 80386 task and then does a task switch
9                       ; to a virtual 8086 (V86) task.  From the V86 a return and stay resident
10                      ; exit is made to MS-DOS.  I/O and I/O interrupt masking is left up to
11                      ; MS-DOS.
12                      ;
13                      ; Most interrupts are reflected to the MS-DOS interrupt handlers.
14                      ; IRET and INT nn instructions cause an interrupt 13.  IRET is emulated.
15                      ; INT nn interrupts are also, with the exception of INT 00 which is used
16                      ; to test instructions.
17                      ;
18                      ; The demonstration program is written using the Microsoft (r)
19                      ; Macro Assembler version 4.0 which is widely available from
20                      ; Microsoft Corporation.  This is not (yet) an 80386 assembler so
21                      ; the program was written using 16 bit operands and addresses.
22                      ;
23                      ; The "steps" below are further discussed and refered to by the overview
24                      ; logic in the book "80386 Architecture" by Penn Brumm and Don Brumm.
25                      ;
26                      ;
27                      ;
28                      ; Step 1:
29                      ;   Define macros for the 80386 instruction prefixes, data areas, and
30                      ;   repetative instructions used in the program.
31                      ;
32                      ;
33                      opsize  MACRO                   ;;Override the operand size
34                              db      66h
35                              ENDM
36
37
38                      ;
39                      ; Convert an 8086 segment register value to a linear address
40                      ;
```

```
41                      segadr    MACRO     segr
42                                db        66H
43                                sub       AX,AX          ; Clear Whole register
44                                mov       AX,&segr       ; Get segment register
45                                db        66H
46                                shl       AX,4           ; Get as an address
47                                ENDM
48                      ;
49                      ; Set TSS linear address into a descriptor
50                      ;
51                      settssa   MACRO     reg,tss,seg
52                                db        66h
53                                lea       reg&X,&tss     ; Get displacement to TSS
54                                db        66h
55                                add       reg&X,AX       ; Get a linear address in register
56                                mov       seg&.base_l,reg&X ; Set low 16 bits of linear address
57                                db        66h
58                                SHR       reg&X,8        ; Shift bits 16-23 to H
59                                mov       seg&.base_m,reg&H ; and set mid range.
60                                ENDM
61                      ;
62                      ; Convert an 8086 segment to a linear address in a segment descriptor
63                      ;
64                      segcvt    MACRO     segr,segm
65                                segadr    segr
66                                mov       segm&.base_l,AX ; Set supv base of data
67                                db        66H
68                                shr       AX,8           ; Get it in AH
69                                mov       segm&.base_m,AH ; Put it in midrange byte
70                                ENDM
71                      ;
72                      ; Step 2:
73                      ;   Describe data structures used by the program.  (The TSS is
74                      ;   described within the body of the data in order to allow use
75                      ;   of data references for its initializations.)
76                      ;
77                      ;   Define the descriptor.  The fields and their sizes are described.
78                      ;
79                      desc      struc
80 0000  0000           limit     dw        0              ; Offset of last byte
81 0002  0000           base_l    dw        0              ; Low 16 bits of 32 bit addr
82 0004  00             base_m    db        0              ; Bits 16-23
83 0005  00             access    db        0              ; Access priv
84 0006  00             gran      db        0              ; Granularity and Limit
85 0007  00             base_h    db        0              ; Bits 24-31 of the Base
86 0008                 desc      ends
87
88                      ;
89                      ; Describe the stack of the L0 interrupt handler for the V86 mode task.
90                      ;   (note that the description is 'upside down' because it is used
91                      ;   as a data area which addresses from low to high not a stack.)
92                      ;
```

```
 93                              stkdef    struc
 94 0000  0000                   oldip     dw      0              ; Low 16 bits of EIP
 95 0002  0000                             dw      0              ;
 96 0004  0000                   oldcs     dw      0              ; CS value
 97 0006  0000                             dw      0              ;
 98 0008  0000                   oldfl     dw      0              ; Low 16 bits of EFLAGS
 99 000A  0000                             dw      0              ;
100 000C  0000                   oldsp     dw      0              ; Low 16 bits of ESP
101 000E  0000                             dw      0              ;
102 0010  0000                   oldss     dw      0              ; SS value
103 0012  0000                             dw      0              ;
104 0014  0000                   oldes     dw      0              ; ES value
105 0016  0000                             dw      0              ;
106 0018  0000                   oldds     dw      0              ; DS value
107 001A  0000                             dw      0              ;
108 001C  0000                   oldfs     dw      0              ; FS value
109 001E  0000                             dw      0              ;
110 0020  0000                   oldgs     dw      0              ; GS value
111 0022  0000                             dw      0              ;
112 0024                         stkdef    ends
113
114                                        PAGE
115                              ;
116                              ; Step 3.
117                              ;  Define the segmented structure of the program.
118                              ;
119                              ; A simple model with a single real segment was chosen because it
120                              ; is easily converted to a .COM file.
121                              ;
122                              ; The program operates by establishing a protected mode environment
123                              ; and a virtual 8086 task segment then returning to MS-DOS in the
124                              ; virtual 8086 task.  The continued execution of MS-DOS is monitored
125                              ; by the protected mode interrupt handler.  An interface to execute
126                              ; instructions in protected mode is provided using INT 00.
127                              ;
128 0000                        code      SEGMENT para public 'CODE'
129                                        ASSUME  cs:code, ds:code, ss:code
130 0100                                   org     100h           ; Leave space for prefix
131                              ;
132                              ; On entry just skip over the stack and data areas.
133                              ;
134 0100                        begin     PROC    far
135 0100  E9 4B25 R                        jmp     segsetup       ; Jump to code area
136 0110                                   org     begin+16       ; provide para alignment
137                              ;
138                              ; Step 4:
139                              ;  Declare the Stack and Data space
140                              ;
141 0110  2000[                            DB      2000h DUP(?)   ; Provide stack space
142           ??
143                     ]
144
```

```
145
146
147                          ;
148                          ; Step 5:
149                          ;   Define the Global Descriptor Table's (GDT) space
150                          ;
151 2110  0000      gdt_def    desc    <>                    ; The first one is a dummy.
152 2112  0000
153 2114  00
154 2115  00
155 2116  00
156 2117  00
157                                                           It can be used as a null.
158                          ;
159                          ;
160                          ;   Level 3 empty LDT
161                          ;
162 2118  0007      ref_l3     desc    <7,0,0,11100010b,0,0> ; p,3,type 2 limit=7
163 211A  0000
164 211C  00
165 211D  E2
166 211E  00
167 211F  00
168
169 = 000B          refl3      equ     ref_l3-gdt_def+3
170                          ;
171                          ;   Level 0 empty LDT
172                          ;
173 2120  0007      ref_l0     desc    <7,0,0,10000010b,0,0> ; p,0,type 2 limit=7
174 2122  0000
175 2124  00
176 2125  82
177 2126  00
178 2127  00
179
180 = 0010          refl0      equ     ref_l0-gdt_def
181                          ;
182                          ;   Dynamic data reference used in Interrupt Handler
183                          ;
184 2128  FFFF      ref_d      desc    <0FFFFh,0,0,10010010b,00001111b,0>   ; Data
185 212A  0000
186 212C  00
187 212D  92
188 212E  0F
189 212F  00
190
191 = 0018          ref_dta    equ     ref_d-gdt_def
192                          ;
193                          ;   Dynamic data reference used in Dump TSS
194                          ;
195 2130  FFFF      ref_dd     desc    <0FFFFh,0,0,10010010b,00001111b,0>   ; Data
196 2132  0000
197 2134  00
```

```
198 2135  92
199 2136  0F
200 2137  00
201
202 = 0020                    ref_dtad   equ    ref_dd-gdt_def
203                           ;
204                           ;   Reference to real location zero for MS-DOS interrupt vectors.
205                           ;
206 2138  FFFF                ref_zer    desc   <0FFFFh,0,0,10010010b,00001111b,0>   ; Loc zero
207 213A  0000
208 213C  00
209 213D  92
210 213E  0F
211 213F  00
212
213 = 0028                    ihzero     equ    ref_zer-gdt_def
214 2140  FFFF                stk_data   desc   <0FFFFh,0,0,10010010b,00001111b,0>    ; Stack as data
215 2142  0000
216 2144  00
217 2145  92
218 2146  0F
219 2147  00
220
221 = 0030                    stkdata    equ    stk_data-gdt_def
222 2148  0000                           desc   <0,0,0,10010110b,0,0>  ;stack
223 214A  0000
224 214C  00
225 214D  96
226 214E  00
227 214F  00
228
229 2150  0067                ref_0      desc   <sz386t-1,0,0,10001001b,00000000b,0> ; 80386 Task
230 2152  0000
231 2154  00
232 2155  89
233 2156  00
234 2157  00
235
236 = 0040                    ref0d      equ    ref_0-gdt_def
237 2158  0067                ref_1      desc   <sz386t-1,0,0,10001001b,00000000b,0> ; 80386 Task
238 215A  0000
239 215C  00
240 215D  89
241 215E  00
242 215F  00
243
244 = 0048                    ref1d      equ    ref_1-gdt_def
245 2160  2068                v86_0      desc   <szv86t,0,0,11101011b,00000000b,0>   ; V86 Task
246 2162  0000
247 2164  00
248 2165  EB
249 2166  00
250 2167  00
```

```
251
252 = 0053                    v860d    equ     v86_0-gdt_def+3
253                           ;
254                           ;
255                           ;    Descriptors for use by Interrupt Handlers
256                           ;
257 2168  FFFF                sup_c    desc    <0FFFFh,0,0,10011010b,00001111b,0>   ; Code
258 216A  0000
259 216C  00
260 216D  9A
261 216E  0F
262 216F  00
263
264 = 0058                    supcd    equ     sup_c-gdt_def                        ; DPL=0, nonconforming
265                                                                                 ; Readable
266                           ;
267 2170  FFFF                sup_d    desc    <0FFFFh,0,0,10010010b,00001111b,0>   ; Data
268 2172  0000
269 2174  00
270 2175  92
271 2176  0F
272 2177  00
273
274 = 0060                    supdd    equ     sup_d-gdt_def                        ; DPL=0, writeable
275                           ;
276 2178  0000                sup_s    desc    <0,0,0,10010110b,00000000b,0>        ; Stack
277 217A  0000
278 217C  00
279 217D  96
280 217E  00
281 217F  00
282
283 = 0068                    supsd    equ     sup_s-gdt_def                        ; Expand down
284                                                                                 ; Writeable
285                           ;
286                           ;
287                           ;    Descriptors for use by Instruction execution task
288                           ;
289 2180  FFFF                exe_c    desc    <0FFFFh,0,0,10011010b,00001111b,0>   ; Code
290 2182  0000
291 2184  00
292 2185  9A
293 2186  0F
294 2187  00
295
296 = 0070                    execd    equ     exe_c-gdt_def                        ; DPL=0, nonconforming
297                                                                                 ; Readable
298                           ;
299 2188  FFFF                exe_d    desc    <0FFFFh,0,0,10010010b,00001111b,0>   ; Data
300 218A  0000
301 218C  00
302 218D  92
303 218E  0F
```

```
304 218F  00
305
306 = 0078                         exedd     equ     exe_d-gdt_def                    ; DPL=0, writeable
307                                ;
308 2190  0000                     exe_s     desc    <0,0,0,10010110b,00000000b,0>    ; Stack
309 2192  0000
310 2194  00
311 2195  96
312 2196  00
313 2197  00
314
315 = 0080                         exesd     equ     exe_s-gdt_def                    ; Expand down
316                                                                                   ; Writeable
317                                ;
318                                ;    End of the GDT
319                                ;
320 = 0088                         gdt_size  equ     $-gdt_def
321                                ;
322                                ; Step 7:
323                                ;    Define the Interrupt Descriptor Table's (IDT) space.
324                                ;    The addresses are initialized as part of the setup.
325                                ;    The selector is that of the supervisor code descriptor.
326                                ;
327                                          .SALL
328 = 2198                         idt_def   equ     $
329                                          REPT    256
330                                          desc    <0,supcd,0,8Eh,0,0>
331                                          ENDM
332 = 0800                         idt_size  equ     $-idt_def
333
334
335                                ;
336                                ; Step 2A:
337                                ;    This section describes a Task State Segment (TSS).  On some
338                                ;    of the field names, a "t" is prefixed to keep from using the
339                                ;    standard 80386 system name.  (This description is here because
340                                ;    it contains references to the descriptors just defined.)
341                                ;
342                                tss_d     struc
343 0000  0000                     back      dw      0                   ; Back link to any previous TSS
344 0002  0000                               dw      0                   ; Reserved
345 0004  00 04 00 00              esp0      dd      400h                ; SP for level 0 interrupt
346 0008  0068                     ss0       dw      supsd               ; and SS.
347 000A  0000                               dw      0                   ; Reserved
348 000C  00 04 00 00              esp1      dd      400h                ; Level 1 interrupt handler's stack
349 0010  0068                     ss1       dw      supsd
350 0012  0000                               dw      0                   ; Reserved
351 0014  00 04 00 00              esp2      dd      400h                ; Level 2 interrupt handler's stack
352 0018  0068                     ss2       dw      supsd
353 001A  0000                               dw      0                   ; Reserved
354 001C  00 00 00 00              tcr3      dd      0
355 0020  0000                     teip      dw      0                   ; Instruction Pointer
356 0022  0000                               dw      0
```

```
357 0024  0002              teflags  dw      2                   ; EFLAGS
358 0026  0000                       dw      0
359 0028  0000              teax     dw      0                   ; AX for init
360 002A  0000                       dw      0
361 002C  0000              tecx     dw      0                   ; CX for init
362 002E  0000                       dw      0
363 0030  00 00 00 00       tedx     dd      0
364 0034  00 00 00 00       tebx     dd      0
365 0038  1000 0000         tesp     dw      1000h,0
366 003C  00 00 00 00       tebp     dd      0
367 0040  00 00 00 00       tesi     dd      0
368 0044  00 00 00 00       tedi     dd      0
369 0048  0060              tes      dw      supdd               ; Extended Segment selector
370 004A  0000                       dw      0                   ; Reserved
371 004C  0058              tcs      dw      supcd               ; Code Segment selector
372 004E  0000                       dw      0                   ; Reserved
373 0050  0068              tss      dw      supsd               ; Stack Segment selector
374 0052  0000                       dw      0                   ; Reserved
375 0054  0060              tds      dw      supdd               ; Data Segment selector
376 0056  0000                       dw      0                   ; Reserved
377 0058  0000              tfs      dw      0                   ; F segment selector
378 005A  0000                       dw      0                   ; Reserved
379 005C  0000              tgs      dw      0                   ; G segment selector
380 005E  0000                       dw      0                   ; Reserved
381 0060  0010              tldt     dw      refl0               ; Local Descriptor Table (LDT)
382 0062  0000                       dw      0                   ; Reserved
383 0064  0000                       dw      0                   ; Reserved
384 0066  0068              iomap    dw      104                 ; Displacement to I/O Map base
385 0068              tss_d    ends
386                         ;
387                         ; Step 8:
388                         ;   Define the Task State Segments (TSS)
389                         ;
390                         ;   This task gets control on an INT 00 from the virtual 8086 mode task.
391                         ;   It runs as a level 0 protected mode task.
392                         ;
393 2998  0000         supv     tss_d  ()                       ; Space for supv task
394 299A  0000
395 299C  00 04 00 00
396 29A0  0068
397 29A2  0000
398 29A4  00 04 00 00
399 29A8  0068
400 29AA  0000
401 29AC  00 04 00 00
402 29B0  0068
403 29B2  0000
404 29B4  00 00 00 00
405 29B8  0000
406 29BA  0000
407 29BC  0002
408 29BE  0000
409 29C0  0000
```

```
410 29C2  0000
411 29C4  0000
412 29C6  0000
413 29C8  00 00 00 00
414 29CC  00 00 00 00
415 29D0  0001[
416            1000
417            0000
418                              ]
419 29D4  00 00 00 00
420 29D8  00 00 00 00
421 29DC  00 00 00 00
422 29E0  0060
423 29E2  0000
424 29E4  0058
425 29E6  0000
426 29E8  0068
427 29EA  0000
428 29EC  0060
429 29EE  0000
430 29F0  0000
431 29F2  0000
432 29F4  0000
433 29F6  0000
434 29F8  0010
435 29FA  0000
436 29FC  0000
437 29FE  0068
438
439 = 0068                          sz386t    equ    $-supv
440                                 ;
441                                 ;  This task is swiched out of to start the virtual 8086 task.
442                                 ;
443 2A00  0053                      supv2     tss_d  <v860d>              ; Task switched out of
444 2A02  0000
445 2A04  00 04 00 00
446 2A08  0068
447 2A0A  0000
448 2A0C  00 04 00 00
449 2A10  0068
450 2A12  0000
451 2A14  00 04 00 00
452 2A18  0068
453 2A1A  0000
454 2A1C  00 00 00 00
455 2A20  0000
456 2A22  0000
457 2A24  0002
458 2A26  0000
459 2A28  0000
460 2A2A  0000
461 2A2C  0000
462 2A2E  0000
```

```
463 2A30   00 00 00 00
464 2A34   00 00 00 00
465 2A38   0001[
466           1000
467           0000
468                              ]
469 2A3C   00 00 00 00
470 2A40   00 00 00 00
471 2A44   00 00 00 00
472 2A48   0060
473 2A4A   0000
474 2A4C   0058
475 2A4E   0000
476 2A50   0068
477 2A52   0000
478 2A54   0060
479 2A56   0000
480 2A58   0000
481 2A5A   0000
482 2A5C   0000
483 2A5E   0000
484 2A60   0010
485 2A62   0000
486 2A64   0000
487 2A66   0068
488
489                          ;
490                          ;
491                          ;   This is the TSS for the virtual 8086 task - under which
492                          ;   MS-DOS will execute.
493                          ;
494 2A68   0000             v86      tss_d  ()                      ; Define v86 task state segment
495 2A6A   0000
496 2A6C   00 04 00 00
497 2A70   0068
498 2A72   0000
499 2A74   00 04 00 00
500 2A78   0068
501 2A7A   0000
502 2A7C   00 04 00 00
503 2A80   0068
504 2A82   0000
505 2A84   00 00 00 00
506 2A88   0000
507 2A8A   0000
508 2A8C   0002
509 2A8E   0000
510 2A90   0000
511 2A92   0000
512 2A94   0000
513 2A96   0000
514 2A98   00 00 00 00
515 2A9C   00 00 00 00
```

```
516 2AA0  0001[
517          1000
518          0000
519                              ]
520 2AA4  00 00 00 00
521 2AA8  00 00 00 00
522 2AAC  00 00 00 00
523 2AB0  0060
524 2AB2  0000
525 2AB4  0058
526 2AB6  0000
527 2AB8  0068
528 2ABA  0000
529 2ABC  0060
530 2ABE  0000
531 2AC0  0000
532 2AC2  0000
533 2AC4  0000
534 2AC6  0000
535 2AC8  0010
536 2ACA  0000
537 2ACC  0000
538 2ACE  0068
539
540 2AD0  1000[                          dw      4096 dup (0)      ; I/O bit map of 8K, all bits=0
541          0000
542                              ]
543
544                                                                ; allow I/O to devices 0000 - FFFF.
545 = 2068                       szv86t  equ     $-v86
546 4AD0  FFFF                            dw      -1                ; A byte of all 1s ends the I/O map
547                                      PAGE
548                              ;
549                              ;
550                              ; Some local data and work areas.
551                              ;
552 4AD2  0000                   dtsize  dw      0                 ; Size of descriptor table
553 4AD4  00 00 00 00            dtload  dd      0                 ; Address of descriptor table
554 4AD8  0000                   intcd1  dw      0                 ; Pop1 if int code stored
555 4ADA  0000                   intcd2  dw      0                 ; Pop2
556                              ;
557                              ; debug dump controls: A 1 in a byte enables trace entries,
558                              ;                      2 causes a normal dump to be taken,
559                              ;                      3 causes a disaster dump to be taken, and
560                              ;                      0 enters the quiet zone of no output.
561                              ;
562 4ADC  00                     debugf  db      0                 ; Prior to entry of protected mode
563 4ADD  00                     debugf0 db      0                 ; Ihcommon entry point
564 4ADE  00                     debugf0a db     0                 ; and exit
565 4ADF  02                     debugf1 db      02                ; Int 13 entry
566 4AE0  00                     debugf1a db     0                 ; and INT nn exit,
567 4AE1  00                     debugf1b db     0                 ; IRET exit as well as all others.
568 4AE2  0000                   retdisp dw      0                 ; Address of interrupt handler call
```

```
569                                          ;                           (See int_hand0 and its write up.)
570 4AE4   0000 0000                          dsaddr    dw      0,0          ; Address of data area
571 4AE8   0000                               dumpcal   dw      0            ; Address of call to dump for debug
572 4AEA   56 69 72 74 75 61 6C               success   db      'Virtual 8086 mode is established! Enter G (go) or D - $'
573        20 38 30 38 36 20 6D
574        6F 64 65 20 69 73 20
575        65 73 74 61 62 6C 69
576        73 68 65 64 21 20 45
577        6E 74 65 72 20 47 20
578        28 67 6F 29 20 6F 72
579        20 44 20 2D 20 24
580 4B21   0D 0A 24                            newline   db      0dh,0ah,'$'
581 4B24   00                                  endad     db      0
582 = 2A24                                      datasiz   equ     $-gdt_def+15    ; size of data area
583                                             ;
584                                             ; define displacement into stack for interrupt handler
585                                             ;
586 = 1800                                      ihspv     equ     1800h           ; initial value of SP
587 = 17DC                                      ihspn1    equ     ihspv-size stkdef ; no interrupt code on stack
588 = 17D8                                      ihspn2    equ     ihspn1-4          ; interrupt code stored
589                                             PAGE
590                                             ;
591                                             ;   Set segment descriptors (we're in real mode).
592                                             ;
593 4B25                                        segsetup:
594 4B25   8C C8                                          mov     AX,CS          ; Set segment address into AX
595 4B27   8E D0                                          mov     SS,AX          ; Set SP to 2000h
596 4B29   BC 2000                                        mov     SP,2000h
597 4B2C   8E D8                                          mov     DS,AX          ; Set DS
598 4B2E   0E C0                                          mov     ES,AX          ; and ES
599
600                                             ;
601                                             ; Step 9:
602                                             ;   Build and set segment descriptors for use by 80386 task.
603                                             ;
604 4B30   FC                                            cld                    ; Force direction of strings from low to high
605 4B31   FA                                            cli                    ; Set interrupts off
606                                             ;
607                                             ; Step 9A:
608                                             ;   Convert various segment registers into linear addresses in
609                                             ;   80386 descriptors
610                                             ;
611                                                       segcvt  DS,sup_d       ; Set Data Segment
612                                                       segcvt  CS,sup_c       ; Set Code Segment
613                                                       segcvt  SS,sup_s       ; Set Stack Segment
614                                                       segcvt  SS,stk_data    ; As a Data segment too.
615                                                       segadr  DS             ; Get DS as a linear in EAX
616                                                       opsize
617 4B8C   A3 4AE4 R                                      mov     dsaddr,AX      ; Save it for later uses
618                                             ;
619                                             ; step 9B:
620                                             ;   Set interrupt handler displacements in their descriptors.
621                                             ;   We count on the fact that the descriptors and handlers are
```

```
622                                       ; each generated in a group so they are adjacent within their group.
623                                       ;
624 4B8F  2B DB                                    sub     BX,BX                  ; Clear index,
625 4B91  8D 06 4D7B R                             lea     AX,int_hand0           ; get first displacement,
626 4B95  B9 0100                                  mov     CX,256                 ; and set count.
627
628 4B98                          fillihd1:
629 4B98  89 87 2198 R                             mov     idt_def.limit[BX],AX ; Set the displacement
630 4B9C  05 0004                                  add     AX,4                   ; then step it by its size.
631 4B9F  83 C3 08                                 add     BX,8                   ; Step the descriptor index too.
632 4BA2  E2 F4                                    loop    fillihd1               ; Do it 256 times.
633
634                                                segadr  DS                     ; Get DS as a linear in EAX
635                                       ;
636                                       ; Step 9C:
637                                       ;    Convert linear address of data areas for segment descriptors
638                                       ;    such as TSS descriptors and LDT descriptors.
639                                       ;
640                                                settssa D,supv,ref_0           ; Point selector to supv
641                                                settssa D,supv2,ref_1          ; Point to supv 2
642                                                settssa D,v86,v86_0            ; Point to V86 TSS
643
644                                                settssa D,gdt_def,ref_13       ; Point 13 ldt at null of gdt
645                                                settssa D,gdt_def,ref_10       ; 10 ldt too
646
647                                       ;
648                                       ; Step 10:
649                                       ;    Set the segment selectors in the 80386 TSS for Interrupt Handlers
650                                       ;
651 4C11  C7 06 29E4 R 0058                         mov     supv.tcs,supcd        ; Set code descriptor
652 4C17  B8 0060                                   mov     AX,supdd              ; Get the data segment selector
653 4C1A  A3 29EC R                                 mov     supv.tds,AX           ; and set in the TSS data
654 4C1D  A3 29E0 R                                 mov     supv.tes,AX           ; and set in the TSS extra
655 4C20  A3 29F0 R                                 mov     supv.tfs,AX           ; and set in the TSS FS
656 4C23  A3 29F4 R                                 mov     supv.tgs,AX           ; and set in the TSS GS
657 4C26  C7 06 29E8 R 0068                         mov     supv.tss,supsd        ; Set stack selector in the TSS
658 4C2C  B8 0010                                   mov     AX,ref10              ; Get LDT pointer
659 4C2F  A3 29F8 R                                 mov     supv.tldt,AX          ; and set the LDT pointer
660 4C32  A3 2A60 R                                 mov     supv2.tldt,AX         ; in both supervisor TSSs
661                                       ;
662                                       ; Step 11:
663                                       ;    Set the Code, Stack, and EFLAGS Registers
664                                       ;
665                                                opsize
666 4C36  2B C0                                    sub     AX,AX                  ; Clear EAX
667 4C38  B8 1200                                  mov     AX,01200h              ; Get SP value (SS has 2000h)
668                                       ;                                         80386 gets lower 1800h
669                                                opsize                         ; Override for double word
670 4C3C  A3 29D0 R                                mov     supv.tesp,AX           ; and set in the TSS
671 4C3F  B8 5386 R                                mov     AX,offset instexe      ; Get the code to exec
672                                                opsize                         ; Override for double word
673 4C43  A3 29B8 R                                mov     supv.teip,AX           ; Set in the TSS
674                                       ;
```

```
675                                        ; An EFLAGS register of 0002 is fine, so we leave it as is.
676                                        ;
677 4C46  C7 06 29A0 R 0068                   mov    supv.ss0,supsd         ; Set lev 0 SS for interrupt
678 4C4C  C7 06 299C R 0800                   mov    word ptr supv.esp0,800h ; Set an SP value too
679                                        ;
680 4C52  C7 06 29A8 R 0068                   mov    supv.ss1,supsd         ; Set lev 1 SS
681 4C58  C7 06 29A4 R 0800                   mov    word ptr supv.esp1,800h ; Set an SP value too
682
683 4C5E  C7 06 29B0 R 0068                   mov    supv.ss2,supsd         ; Set lev 2 SS
684 4C64  C7 06 29AC R 0800                   mov    word ptr supv.esp2,800h ; Set an SP value too
685                                        ;
686                                        ; Step 12:
687                                        ; Set up the virtual 8086 TSS.
688                                        ;    Set descriptor values into the Virtual 8086 task state segment (TSS).
689                                        ;    In this case, we duplicate the environment of the real mode 8086 that
690                                        ;    is now running into the V86 TSS.
691
692 4C6A  8C D8                               mov    AX,DS                  ; Get DS in AX
693 4C6C  A3 2AB0 R                           mov    v86.tes,AX             ; Set for V86 execution
694 4C6F  A3 2ABC R                           mov    v86.tds,AX             ; in all data segment pointers.
695 4C72  A3 2AC0 R                           mov    v86.tfs,AX
696 4C75  A3 2AC4 R                           mov    v86.tgs,AX
697 4C78  8C D0                               mov    AX,SS                  ; Get SS value of current stack
698 4C7A  A3 2AB8 R                           mov    v86.tss,AX             ; and set it.
699 4C7D  8C C8                               mov    AX,CS                  ; Get CS value
700 4C7F  A3 2AB4 R                           mov    v86.tcs,AX             ; and set it too.
701                                        ;
702                                        ; Set the level 0 interrupt handler stack segment selector and pointer.
703                                        ;    We really only need Level 0 but set L1 and L2 for completeness.
704                                        ;    We also set only the low 16 bits of ESP because we know that the
705                                        ;    upper 16 bits will allways be zero.
706                                        ;
707 4C82  C7 06 2A70 R 0068                   mov    v86.ss0,supsd          ; Set lev 0 SS
708 4C88  C7 06 2A6C R 1800                   mov    word ptr v86.esp0,ihspv ; Set an SP value too
709                                        ;
710 4C8E  C7 06 2A78 R 0068                   mov    v86.ss1,supsd          ; Set lev 1 SS
711 4C94  C7 06 2A74 R 1600                   mov    word ptr v86.esp1,1600h ; Set an SP value too
712
713 4C9A  C7 06 2A80 R 0068                   mov    v86.ss2,supsd          ; Set lev 2 SS
714 4CA0  C7 06 2A7C R 1400                   mov    word ptr v86.esp2,1400h ; Set an SP value too
715                                        ;
716                                        ; Set register values needed to continue in 8086 mode (IP and SP)
717                                        ;
718                                           opsize
719 4CA7  2B C0                               sub    AX,AX                  ; Ensure top is clear
720 4CA9  B8 4D4A R                           mov    AX, offset resume      ; Get the resume address
721                                           opsize
722 4CAD  A3 2A88 R                           mov    v86.teip,AX            ; and set it
723 4CB0  8B C4                               mov    AX,SP                  ; Get the SP value
724                                           opsize
725 4CB3  A3 2AA0 R                           mov    v86.tesp,AX            ; and set it
726                                        ;
727                                        ; Set the EFLAGS in the TSS so it will execute in V86 mode.
```

```
728                                      ;
729 4CB6  C7 06 2A8C R 3202                      mov     v86.teflags,0011001000000010b ; Set low 16 bits
730                                      ;               Flag Names ===) NIOODITSZ A P C
731                                      ;                                   PL
732                                      ;
733 4CBC  C7 06 2A8E R 0002                      mov     v86.teflags+2,0000000000000010b ; and the high 16
734                                      ;               Flag Names =====)            VR
735                                      ;                                            M
736                                      ; VM is on, IOPL = 3 and Interrupts are enabled.
737                                      ;
738 4CC2  C7 06 2ACE R 0068                      mov     v86.iomap,sz386t  ; Set displacement to I/O table
739                                      ;
740                                      ; Set the LDT value in the V86 TSS
741                                      ;
742 4CC8  C7 06 2AC8 R 000B                      mov     v86.tldt,refl3    ; set level 3 ldt
743                                      ;
744                                      ; Step 13:
745                                      ; Set up 80386 registers to run in protected mode.
746                                      ;
747                                      ; Set the GDT and IDT Registers in the 80386 CPU
748                                      ;
749                                              opsize
750 4CCF  A1 4AE4 R                              mov     AX,dsaddr         ; Load 32 bit address
751                                      ;
752                                      ; Use the DS linear address to get both the GDT and IDT register values
753                                      ; Set the GDT value into memory first
754                                      ;
755                                              opsize
756 4CD3  2B DB                                  sub     BX,BX             ; Clear EBX
757 4CD5  8D 1E 2110 R                           lea     BX,gdt_def        ; Get displacement to GDT
758                                              opsize
759 4CDA  03 D8                                  add     BX,AX             ; Then linear address of GDT
760                                              opsize
761 4CDD  89 1E 4AD4 R                           mov     word ptr dtload,BX ; Plug that value in
762 4CE1  C7 06 4AD2 R 0087                      mov     dtsize,gdt_size-1 ; and the size of table.
763
764 4CE7  0F 01 16 4AD2 R                        LGDT    qword ptr dtsize  ; Load the table parms
765
766                                      ;
767                                      ; Then load the IDT value into memory.
768                                      ;
769                                              opsize
770 4CED  2B DB                                  sub     BX,BX             ; Clear EBX
771 4CEF  8D 1E 2198 R                           lea     BX,idt_def        ; Get displacement to IDT
772                                              opsize
773 4CF4  03 D8                                  add     BX,AX             ; then linear address of IDT.
774                                              opsize
775 4CF7  89 1E 4AD4 R                           mov     word ptr dtload,BX ; Plug that value in
776 4CFB  C7 06 4AD2 R 07FF                      mov     dtsize,idt_size-1 ; and the size of table.
777
778 4D01  0F 01 1E 4AD2 R                        LIDT    qword ptr dtsize  ; Load the table parms
779
780                                      ;
```

```
781                                 ; Step 14:
782                                 ;   The 80386 environment is set.
783                                 ;   Now transfer into Protected Mode.
784                                 ;
785                                 ;         mov     EAX,CR0
786 4D06  0F 20 C0                            db      0fh,20h,0c0h        ; Move CR0 into AX
787 4D09  0C 01                               or      AL,1                ; Set protected mode
788                                 ;         mov     CR0,EAX
789 4D0B  0F 22 C0                            db      0fh,22h,0c0h        ; Move CR0 from AX
790 4D0E  7A 00                               jp      local               ; Clear pipelined decode queue
791 4D10                           local:
792                                 ;
793                                 ;   We are now executing in protected mode
794                                 ;
795
796
797 4D10  B8 0010                             mov     AX,ref10            ; Point to empty LDT desc
798 4D13  0F 00 D0                            lldt    AX                  ; and set LDT
799
800                                 ;
801                                 ; Debug aid
802 4D16  80 3E 4ADC R 00                     cmp     debugf,0            ; is dump wanted
803 4D1B  74 06                               je      skip01              ; no - skip it
804
805 4D1D  E8 55D2 R                           call    edump               ; Get what is necessary
806 4D20  E8 5464 R                           call    newln               ; do cr/lf
807 4D23                           skip01:
808
809 4D23  B8 0060                             mov     AX,supdd            ; Get 386 data descriptor
810 4D26  8E D8                               mov     DS,AX
811 4D28  8E C0                               mov     ES,AX
812                                 ;         mov     FS,AX
813 4D2A  8E E0                               db      8eh,0e0h
814                                 ;         mov     GS,AX
815 4D2C  8E E8                               db      8eh,0e8h            ; into all data descriptors
816 4D2E  B8 0068                             mov     AX,supsd            ; get 386 stack descriptor
817 4D31  8E D0                               mov     SS,AX
818 4D33  EA                                  db      0eah                ; do a far jump to set CS
819 4D34  4D38 0058                           dw      godoit-begin+100h,supcd
820
821                                 ;
822                                 ; Step 15:
823                                 ;   At this point all descriptors are of 80386 form, even CS.
824                                 ;
825                                 ;   Now set the Nested Task (NT) flag and go to the V86 task
826                                 ;
827 4D38                           godoit:
828 4D38  B9 0048                             mov     CX,ref1d            ; Get value for task register
829 4D3B  0F 00 D9                            ltr     CX                  ; and set it.
830                                           opsize
831 4D3F  9C                                  pushf                       ; Push EFLAGS
832                                           opsize
833 4D41  58                                  pop     AX                  ; Get them into EAX
```

```
834 4D42  80 CC 40                   or      AH,40h          ; Set the nested task flag
835                                  opsize
836 4D46  50                         push    AX              ; Push EFLAGS again
837                                  opsize
838 4D48  9D                         popf                    ; then get them into flags reg
839                          ;
840                          ;   Now transfer to the Virtual 8086 (V86) mode using an IRET.  The
841                          ;   back chain in our TSS and the nested task flag cause the transfer.
842                          ;
843 4D49  CF                         iret                    ; and transfer to V86
844
845                          ;
846                          ; Step 16:
847                          ;  We are now executing in virtual 8086 mode. The code issues a message
848                          ;  and wait for a capitol G (for go) from the keyboard.  When received,
849                          ;  the code continues by executing the DOS exit-but-remain-resident
850                          ;  call.
851                          ;
852                          ;  The end result is that from entry here, MS-DOS runs as a virtual
853                          ;  8086 task.  Entry to protected mode can be effected by an INT 00.
854                          ;
855 4D4A            resume:
856 = 4D4A          resumed   equ  resume-begin+100h
857 4D4A  FC                         cld                     ; Normal direction
858 4D4B              resloop:
859 4D4B  8D 16 4AEA R               lea     DX,success      ; Point to the message
860 4D4F  B4 09                      mov     AH,9            ; Set write code
861 4D51  CD 21                      int     21h             ; Let DOS put it out.
862 4D53  B4 01                      mov     AH,1            ; get a keyboard char
863 4D55  CD 21                      int     21h
864 4D57  50                         push    AX              ; save the character
865 4D58  8D 16 4B21 R               lea     DX,newline      ; point to new line string
866 4D5C  B4 09                      mov     AH,9            ; set write code
867 4D5E  CD 21                      int     21h             ; call DOS
868 4D60  58                         pop     AX              ; Get char back
869 4D61  3C 47                      cmp     AL,'G'          ; have a go?
870 4D63  74 0B                      je      todos           ; yes - off to DOS
871 4D65  3C 44                      cmp     AL,'D'          ; want a dump
872 4D67  75 E2                      jne     resloop         ; no try again
873 4D69  C6 06 4ADD R 03            mov     debugf0,3       ; force a dump next int
874 4D6E  EB DB                      jmp     resloop         ; go try again
875
876 4D70              todos:
877 4D70  8D 16 5853 R               lea     DX,totalsize+20fh ; Point to top address
878 4D74  C1 EA 04                   shr     DX,4            ; convert to paragraphs
879 4D77  B4 31                      mov     AH,31h          ; Set stay resident
880 4D79  CD 21                      int     21h             ; Assume we are done
881                          ;
882                          ; The above transfer to MS-DOS leaves us in memory.  (This is both
883                          ; fortuitous and planned because real control of the CPU is in the
884                          ; hands of the rest of this program!)
885                          ;
886                          ; The code to this point could now be overlayed - its purpose is now
```

```
887                     ; completed.
888
889                             PAGE
890                     ;
891                     ; SUPPORT CODE
892                     ; 1.
893                     ;
894                     ; Generate the initial entry points for the interrupt handlers.
895                     ; These entries have a correspondence with the 8086 interrupt
896                     ; vector table.  They are the same length (4 bytes) and the
897                     ; return address from the call is used to generate the proper
898                     ; displacement into the table.  (At this point we have CS and
899                     ; our SP/SS to work with.)
900                     ;
901 4D7B               int_hand0:                      ; Initial displacement
902                             REPT    256             ; Interrupts 0-255
903                             call    ih_common       ; A 3 byte call
904                             iret                    ; A 1 byte iret
905                             ENDM
906                     ; 2.
907                     ;
908                     ; Handle all interrupts and traps.
909                     ; The handler here reflects the interrupt to MS-DOS.  The action
910                     ; taken is simply:
911                     ;                       0) If an 'error code' was stacked, pop it off.
912                     ;                          (If we were handling interrupts here we would
913                     ;                          examine and use the error code.)
914                     ;                       1) Save the interrupted task's registers and
915                     ;                       2) set descriptor selectors for use here.
916                     ;       For other than interrupt 13
917                     ;                       3) Move IP, CS, and Flags to the interrupted task's
918                     ;                          stack and adjust its SP.
919                     ;                       4) Move the MS-DOS vector to the interrupt handler's
920                     ;                          (our current) stack.
921                     ;                       5) Restore registers saved and IRET.
922                     ;
923                     ; Interrupt 13 will normally be either an INT nn or an IRET which
924                     ; require that step 3 above be varied.
925                     ;                       3) Check the value at CS,IP for INT or IRET op codes
926                     ;                          if neither, do a disaster dump - No device or 8086
927                     ;                          interrupt occurs at this number.
928                     ;
929                     ;                       3-INT) Fetch the nn value, step IP by 2 on my stack.
930                     ;                          If nn is other than 00 we set nn*4 as the vector
931                     ;                          pointer and join at step 3.
932                     ;                          If nn is 00 we copy the v86 CS, AX, and DX to
933                     ;                          CX, AX, and DX in the supv TSS.  We then call
934                     ;                          the supv task and on return continue at step 5.
935                     ;
936                     ;                       3-IRET) Move the flags, CS and IP from the v86 stack
937                     ;                          to our stack, adjust the v86 SP and take step 5.
938
939 517B               ih_common:
```

```
940 517B  50                      push    AX              ; Save one register
941 517C  B8 0060                 mov     AX,supdd        ; Get data addressability
942 517F  8E D8                   mov     DS,AX
943 5181  58                      pop     AX              ; SP now points to return of the
944                          ;                                interrupt entry's call here.
945 5182  8F 06 4AE2 R            pop     retdisp         ; Get it off the stack into a save area.
946 5186  81 FC 17D8              cmp     SP,ihspn2       ; Is there an int code on the stack?
947 518A  75 08                   jne     ihcommn         ; No - don't mess with it.
948 518C  8F 06 4AD8 R            pop     intcd1          ; Get the interrupt code's word 1
949 5190  8F 06 4ADA R            pop     intcd2          ; and 2 off stack.
950                          ;
951                          ; The above provides us with a known stack format.  We also have saved
952                          ; the interrupt error code if any, and have the vector number in easily
953                          ; computable form.  (Not bad for 11 instructions.)
954                          ;
955 5194                  ihcommn:
956 5194  60                      pusha                   ; Save registers
957
958 5195  B8 0030                 mov     AX,stkdata      ; Get the stack as data desc
959 5198  8E C0                   mov     ES,AX           ; into ES
960 519A  8B DC                   mov     BX,SP           ; Get SP into BX
961 519C  26: 8B 47 1A            mov     AX,ES:[BX+26]   ; Load high word of EFLAGs
962 51A0  24 02                   and     AL,2            ; Isolate the VM bit
963 51A2  75 0A                   jnz     stillok         ; If there - normal
964                          ;
965                          ; An interrupt from other than virtual 8086 mode is treated as an
966                          ; error in this code.  If this were a general purpose interrupt
967                          ; handler we would process the interrupt as a normal 80386 event.
968                          ; However, we dump and ignore the encounter.
969                          ;
970 51A4  C6 06 4ADD R 03         mov     debugf0,3       ; Force dump of disaster
971 51A9  C6 06 4ADE R 03         mov     debugf0a,3
972 51AE                  stillok:
973 51AE  8C DA                   mov     DX,DS           ; Set normal descriptor selector
974 51B0  8E C2                   mov     ES,DX           ; into ES.
975 51B2  80 3E 4ADD R 00         cmp     debugf0,0       ; Want a dump?
976 51B7  74 42                   je      skip02          ; No - skip it
977 51B9  80 3E 4ADD R 01         cmp     debugf0,1       ; Just trace type?
978 51BE  75 09                   jne     fulld02         ; No - do full
979 51C0  A1 4AE2 R               mov     AX,retdisp      ; Get the int number
980 51C3  E8 5633 R               call    mindump         ; and trace it
981 51C6  EB 33 90                jmp     skip02          ; Done
982 51C9                  fulld02:
983 51C9  80 3E 4ADD R 02         cmp     debugf0,2       ; Normal dump desired?
984 51CE  74 20                   je      fulld02e        ; Yes - go dump
985 51D0  C6 06 4ADD R 00         mov     debugf0,0       ; Do disaster dump once
986                          ; make sure we get extra stack for disaster
987 51D5  B8 0030                 mov     AX,stkdata      ; Get stack area again
988 51D8  8E D8                   mov     DS,AX           ; Dump stack info
989 51DA  B8 0780                 mov     AX,780h         ; Low part first -
990 51DD  B9 0008                 mov     CX,8            ; for 128 bytes
991 51E0                  badstk0:
992 51E0  E8 5471 R               call    dumpln
```

```
 993 51E3  E2 FB                            loop    badstk0             ; Get it all
 994
 995 51E5  E8 5464 R                        call    newln               ; Space between
 996 51E8  B8 1780                          mov     AX,1780h            ; Then high part -
 997 51EB  B9 0008                          mov     CX,8                ; for 128 bytes
 998 51EE                    badstk1:
 999 51EE  E8 5471 R                        call    dumpln
1000 51F1  E2 FB                            loop    badstk1             ; Get it all
1001 51F3  E8 5464 R                        call    newln               ; and a space
1002 51F6  8E DA                            mov     DS,DX               ; Set normal descriptor selector
1003
1004 51F8                    fulld02e:
1005 51F8  E8 55D2 R                        call    edump
1006 51FB                    skip02:
1007 51FB  8B 36 4AE2 R                     mov     SI,retdisp          ; Get return displacement
1008 51FF  81 EE 4D7B                       sub     SI,int_hand0-begin+100h ; As a displacement
1009 5203  81 E6 FFFC                       and     SI,0fffch           ; into MS-DOS interrupt vectors.
1010 5207  89 36 4AE2 R                     mov     retdisp,SI          ; Clear it for debug
1011
1012 520B  B8 0030                          mov     AX,stkdata          ; Get stack as data selector
1013 520E  8E C0                            mov     ES,AX               ; into ES
1014 5210  8B DC                            mov     BX,SP               ; Get SP into BX
1015 5212  83 C3 10                         add     BX,16               ; Point to IP location
1016 5215  83 FE 34                         cmp     SI,13*4             ; Is this int 13
1017 5218  75 03                            jne     notint13            ; Nope - just muddle along
1018 521A  E9 52DC R                        jmp     isint13             ; yes - go process special
1019
1020 521D                    notint13:
1021 521D  26: 8B 47 10                     mov     AX,ES:[BX].oldss    ; Get SS of V86 task
1022 5221  8A CC                            mov     CL,AH               ; Set high byte in CL
1023 5223  C1 E0 04                         shl     AX,4                ; Convert desc to linear address
1024 5226  C0 E9 04                         shr     CL,4                ; in AX and CL
1025 5229  A3 212A R                        mov     ref_d.base_l,AX     ; Set bits 0-15 in the descriptor
1026 522C  88 0E 212C R                     mov     ref_d.base_m,CL     ; Then bits 16-23 (we ignore 24-31 heh)
1027
1028 5230  26: 8B 4F 0C                     mov     CX,ES:[BX].oldsp    ; Get SP of V86 task,
1029 5234  83 E9 06                         sub     CX,6                ; adjust it for fake interrupt,
1030 5237  26: 89 4F 0C                     mov     ES:[BX].oldsp,CX    ; and put it back.
1031
1032 523B  26: 8B 2F                        mov     BP,ES:[BX].oldip    ; Get interrupted IP,
1033 523E  26: 8B 7F 04                     mov     DI,ES:[BX].oldcs    ; CS,
1034 5242  26: 8B 47 08                     mov     AX,ES:[BX].oldfl    ; and flags.
1035
1036 5246  BA 0018                          mov     DX,ref_dta          ; Get descriptor
1037 5249  8E DA                            mov     DS,DX               ; into DS
1038 524B  87 D9                            xchg    BX,CX               ; Put v86 SP into BX & save stack disp
1039
1040 524D  89 2F                            mov     [BX],BP             ; Stack IP,
1041 524F  89 7F 02                         mov     [BX]+2,DI           ; CS, and
1042 5252  89 47 04                         mov     [BX]+4,AX           ; flags on v86 stack.
1043
1044 5255  25 FCFF                          and     AX,0fcffh           ; Clear interrupt and trap flags
1045 5258  BB 0028                          mov     BX,ihzero           ; Get zero base descriptor selector
```

```
1046 525B  8E DB              mov    DS,BX                ; as DS
1047 525D  8B DE              mov    BX,SI                ; Index into the vector table
1048 525F  8B 2F              mov    BP,[BX]              ; Get vector's IP
1049 5261  8B 7F 02           mov    DI,[BX]+2            ; and CS.
1050
1051 5264  8B D9              mov    BX,CX                ; Get stack displ back
1052 5266  26: 89 47 08       mov    ES:[BX].oldfl,AX     ; Set flags,
1053 526A  26: 89 2F          mov    ES:[BX].oldip,BP     ; IP, and
1054 526D  26: 89 7F 04       mov    ES:[BX].oldcs,DI     ; CS on my stack.
1055
1056 5271           rejoin:
1057 5271  BA 0060            mov    DX,supdd             ; Get data addressability
1058 5274  8E DA              mov    DS,DX
1059 5276  8E C2              mov    ES,DX
1060 5278  80 3E 4ADE R 00    cmp    debugf0a,0           ; Is an exit dump wanted?
1061 527D  74 54              je     skip03               ; No - bypass it
1062 527F  80 3E 4ADE R 01    cmp    debugf0a,1           ; Just a trace?
1063 5284  75 08              jne    fulld02a             ; No - do full
1064 5286  8B C5              mov    AX,BP                ; Get the to address
1065 5288  E8 5633 R          call   mindump              ; Trace it
1066 528B  EB 46 90           jmp    skip03               ; Done
1067 528E           fulld02a:
1068 528E  E8 55D2 R          call   edump
1069
1070 5291  B8 0030            mov    AX,stkdata           ; Get stack as data selector
1071 5294  8E D8              mov    DS,AX                ; into DS.
1072 5296  BB 17DC            mov    BX,ihspn1            ; Set offset to PL0 stack area
1073 5299  8B 47 10           mov    AX,[BX].oldss        ; Get SS of V86 task,
1074 529C  8B 5F 0C           mov    BX,[BX].oldsp        ; and SP.
1075 529F  8E DA              mov    DS,DX                ; Restore DS
1076 52A1  8A CC              mov    CL,AH                ; Prepare to set
1077 52A3  C0 E9 04           shr    CL,4
1078 52A6  88 0E 212C R       mov    ref_d.base_m,CL      ; bits 16-23
1079 52AA  C1 E0 04           shl    AX,4                 ; then
1080 52AD  A3 212A R          mov    ref_d.base_l,AX      ; bits 0-15 of address in descriptor.
1081 52B0  B8 0018            mov    AX,ref_dta           ; Get descriptor's selector
1082 52B3  8E D8              mov    DS,AX                ; into DS.
1083 52B5  8B C3              mov    AX,BX                ; Set SP as displacement
1084 52B7  B9 0004            mov    CX,4                 ; Prepare to dump
1085 52BA           dumpit380:
1086 52BA  E8 5471 R          call   dumpln               ; Put it out 16 at a time
1087 52BD  E2 FB              loop   dumpit380
1088
1089 52BF  B8 0060            mov    AX,supdd             ; Get normal DS value back
1090 52C2  8E D8              mov    DS,AX                ; into DS
1091
1092 52C4  E8 5464 R          call   newln                ; Do cr/lf
1093 52C7  80 3E 4ADE R 03    cmp    debugf0a,3           ; Doing a disaster dump?
1094 52CC  75 05              jne    skip03               ; No - leave as is
1095 52CE  C6 06 4ADE R 00    mov    debugf0a,0           ; Shut it off
1096 52D3           skip03:
1097 52D3  2B C0              sub    AX,AX                ; Get a zero
1098 52D5  8E D8              mov    DS,AX                ; for DS and
```

```
1099 52D7  8E C0                 mov     ES,AX            ; ES.
1100 52D9  61                    popa                     ; Restore all regs
1101                         ;
1102                         ; Because we choose to use 16 byte operand sizes we
1103                             opsize                   ; need a 32 bit IRET size to recognize
1104 52DB  CF                    iret                     ; a switch back to virtual 8086 mode.
1105
1106                         ;
1107                         ; 3.
1108                         ;
1109                         ; int 13 - we need to check if INT or IRET so we must get v86 CS as
1110                         ;          a descriptor so we can check.
1111                         ;
1112 52DC               isint13:
1113 52DC  26: 8B 47 04         mov     AX,ES:[BX].oldcs ; Get CS in AX
1114 52E0  26: 8B 37            mov     SI,ES:[BX].oldip ; Put IP in SI (for LODSB index)
1115 52E3  8A CC                mov     CL,AH            ; Prepare to compute mid
1116 52E5  C1 E0 04             shl     AX,4             ; Get descriptor as low 16
1117 52E8  C0 E9 04             shr     CL,4             ; and get mid 8 bits
1118 52EB  A3 212A R            mov     ref_d.base_l,AX  ; Set low 16
1119 52EE  88 0E 212C R         mov     ref_d.base_m,CL  ; and mid 8 bits of linear for CS
1120 52F2  B8 0018              mov     AX,ref_dta       ; get just built descriptor' selector
1121 52F5  8E D8                mov     DS,AX            ; into DS
1122 52F7  FC                   cld                      ; Ensure that SI will increment
1123 52F8  AC                   lodsb                    ; Get faulting op code
1124 52F9  3C CF                cmp     AL,0cfh          ; Is it an IRET?
1125 52FB  74 4A                je      prociret         ; Yes - go emulate it
1126 52FD  3C CD                cmp     AL,0cdh          ; Is it INT nn?
1127 52FF  74 10                je      procint          ; Yes - emulate it
1128                         ;
1129                         ; This is unexpected - force dump
1130                         ;
1131 5301  8E DA                mov     DS,DX            ; Set normal data desc
1132 5303  E8 55D2 R            call    edump            ; Take a dump now
1133 5306  C6 06 4ADE R 03      mov     debugf0a,3       ; Force dump on way out
1134 530B  BE 0034              mov     SI,13*4          ; Set normal displacement
1135 530E  E9 521D R            jmp     notint13         ; and join normal interrupt
1136
1137                         ;
1138                         ; 4.
1139                         ;
1140                         ; INT nn processing
1141                         ;
1142 5311               procint:
1143 5311  AC                   lodsb                    ; Get nn
1144 5312  26: 89 37            mov     ES:[BX].oldip,SI ; Set new IP on stack
1145 5315  8E DA                mov     DS,DX            ; Set normal DS
1146 5317  B4 00                mov     AH,0             ; Clear high byte of AX
1147 5319  03 C0                add     AX,AX            ; Get nn*2
1148 531B  03 C0                add     AX,AX            ; and nn*4
1149 531D  8B F0                mov     SI,AX            ; as interrupt vector
1150 531F  75 23                jnz     notint00         ; normal if it isn't int 00
1151                         ;
```

```
1152                                    ; A request to execute an instruction has been issued -
1153                                    ;   copy the caller's DS, AX and DX to the supv TSS as param pointers.
1154                                    ;
1155 5321   26: 8B 47 18                        mov     AX,ES:[BX].oldds   ; Set DS into supv's CX
1156 5325   A3 29C4 R                            mov     supv.tecx,AX
1157 5328   8B CB                                mov     CX,BX              ; Save pointer into stack
1158 532A   8B DC                                mov     BX,SP              ; Get pointer to registers
1159 532C   26: 8B 47 0E                         mov     AX,ES:[BX+14]      ; Get caller's AX to supv's AX
1160 5330   A3 29C0 R                            mov     supv.teax,AX
1161 5333   26: 8B 47 0A                         mov     AX,ES:[BX+10]      ; and DX too.
1162 5337   A3 29C8 R                            mov     word ptr supv.tedx,AX
1163 533A   8B D9                                mov     BX,CX              ; Restore normal index
1164                                    ;       call    ref0d:0            ; Call 80386 task for handling
1165 533C   9A                                   db      09ah
1166 533D   0000 0040                            dw      0,ref0d
1167 5341   E9 5271 R                            jmp     rejoin             ; We just return in line for int 00
1168 5344                               notint00:
1169 5344   E9 521D R                            jmp     notint13           ; join normal interrupt
1170                                    ;
1171                                    ; 5.
1172                                    ;
1173                                    ; IRET processing -
1174                                    ;
1175 5347                               prociret:
1176 5347   8E DA                                mov     DS,DX              ; The V86 CS is no longer interesting
1177 5349   26: 8B 47 10                         mov     AX,ES:[BX].oldss   ; We need to get ret from v86 stack
1178 534D   8A CC                                mov     CL,AH              ; So - compute the descriptor
1179 534F   C0 E9 04                             shr     CL,4
1180 5352   C1 E0 04                             shl     AX,4
1181 5355   A3 212A R                            mov     ref_d.base_l,AX    ; Bits 0-15
1182 5358   88 0E 212C R                         mov     ref_d.base_m,CL    ; and bits 16-23
1183 535C   26: 8B 4F 0C                         mov     CX,ES:[BX].oldsp   ; Get V86 SP
1184 5360   B8 0018                              mov     AX,ref_dta         ; Get v86 SS
1185 5363   8E D8                                mov     DS,AX              ; as my DS
1186 5365   87 D9                                xchg    BX,CX              ; Set v86 SP into BX
1187 5367   8B 07                                mov     AX,[BX]            ; Get ret IP,
1188 5369   8B 77 02                             mov     SI,[BX+2]          ; CS, and
1189 536C   8B 7F 04                             mov     DI,[BX+4]          ; flags.
1190 536F   83 C3 06                             add     BX,6               ; Adjust the SP
1191 5372   87 D9                                xchg    BX,CX              ; and put it into CX.
1192 5374   26: 89 4F 0C                         mov     ES:[BX].oldsp,CX   ; Now put the values on my stack
1193 5378   26: 89 07                            mov     ES:[BX].oldip,AX
1194 537B   26: 89 77 04                         mov     ES:[BX].oldcs,SI
1195 537F   26: 89 7F 08                         mov     ES:[BX].oldfl,DI
1196 5383   E9 5271 R                            jmp     rejoin             ; Join exit/return
1197
1198                                    ;
1199                                    ; 6.
1200                                    ;
1201                                    ;       This code operates as a protected mode task in 80386 mode.  The
1202                                    ;       interrupt handler for the v86 task calls this task when it detects
1203                                    ;       an INT 00.  This task (which is a task primarily for illustrative
1204                                    ;       purposes) then executes the instructions pointed to by the v86 task's
```

```
1205                                    ;    DS:DX. The instructions must be followed by a RET FAR instruction.
1206                                    ;
1207                                    ;    The interrupt handler stores the DS and DX values into the tss
1208                                    ;    prior to calling the task.
1209                                    ;
1210 5386                      instexe  PROC
1211 5386                      instexb:
1212 5386  80 3E 4ADF R 00              cmp     debugf1,0           ; Is a dump wanted
1213 538B  74 12                        je      skip04              ; No - bypass it
1214 538D  80 3E 4ADF R 01              cmp     debugf1,1           ; Just trace
1215 5392  75 08                        jne     fulld04             ; No - do full
1216 5394  B8 0E0D                      mov     AX,0e0dh            ; Get the int number
1217 5397  E8 5633 R                    call    mindump             ; Trace it
1218 539A  EB 03                        jmp     short skip04        ; - done
1219 539C                      fulld04:
1220 539C  E8 55D2 R                    call    edump               ; Get the data
1221 539F                      skip04:
1222 539F  50                           push    AX                  ; Save control info
1223                                    opsize
1224 53A1  2B C0                        sub     AX,AX               ; Get a clear register and
1225 53A3  8B C1                        mov     AX,CX               ; copy the descriptor to it.
1226                                    opsize
1227 53A6  2B C9                        sub     CX,CX               ; Clear ECX too
1228 53A8  8B CA                        mov     CX,DX               ; Get displacement to code in ECX
1229                                    opsize
1230 53AB  C1 E0 04                     shl     AX,4                ; Get descriptor as a linear
1231                                    opsize
1232 53AF  03 C1                        add     AX,CX               ; and the linear address of the code.
1233 53B1  A3 2182 R                    mov     exe_c.base_l,AX     ; Set low 16 bits into the code,
1234 53B4  A3 218A R                    mov     exe_d.base_l,AX     ; data and
1235 53B7  A3 2192 R                    mov     exe_s.base_l,AX     ; stack descriptors.
1236                                    opsize
1237 53BB  C1 E8 08                     shr     AX,8                ; get bits 16-24 in AH
1238 53BE  88 26 2184 R                 mov     exe_c.base_m,AH     ; Set mid 8 bits into the code,
1239 53C2  88 26 218C R                 mov     exe_d.base_m,AH     ; data and
1240 53C6  88 26 2194 R                 mov     exe_s.base_m,AH     ; stack descriptors.
1241 53CA  BB 0078                      mov     BX,exedd            ; Set data selector in BX
1242 53CD  B9 0080                      mov     CX,exesd            ; and stack into CX.
1243 53D0  58                           pop     AX                  ; Restore caller's AX
1244                             ;       call    execs:0             ; and call the code
1245 53D1  9A                           db      09ah
1246 53D2  0000 0070                    dw      0,execd
1247 53D6  75 03                        jnz     skipdmp             ; If non zero is returned - skip
1248 53D8  E8 55D2 R                    call    edump               ; else dump my environment
1249 53DB                      skipdmp:
1250 53DB  B8 0060                      mov     AX,supdd            ; Get my data selector
1251 53DE  8E D8                        mov     DS,AX               ; and ensure next entry is ok
1252 53E0  8E C0                        mov     ES,AX
1253 53E2  CF                           iret                        ; return to v86 caller
1254 53E3  EB A1                        jmp     instexb             ; to the start
1255                          instexe  ENDP
1256                                   PAGE
1257
```

```
1258                         ;
1259                         ; DEBUG SUPPORT
1260                         ;
1261                         ;    The choice of printed output for debug rather than display output
1262                         ;    is based on the fact that errors in this level of code often cause
1263                         ;    the system to re-boot.  This causes one's debug information to be
1264                         ;    visable only as an after-image on the retina.  I need more lasting
1265                         ;    data (as do most of us).
1266                         ;
1267
1268 53E5            getdsv   PROC
1269                         ;
1270                         ;    Proc to set both a descriptor in the GDT to the segment's linear
1271                         ;    address (segment value is in BX), and to load BP with the
1272                         ;    descriptor value.  The caller will move it into (usually) DS
1273                         ;    which will force the linear address to be loaded from the
1274                         ;    GDT (overriding any previously cached value).
1275                         ;
1276                                  opsize
1277 53E6  50                        push     AX
1278                                  opsize
1279 53E8  2B C0                      sub     AX,AX             ; Clear EAX
1280 53EA  8B C3                      mov     AX,BX             ; Get segment register
1281                                  opsize
1282 53ED  C1 E0 04                   shl     AX,4              ; Get linear address of segment
1283 53F0  A3 2132 R                  mov     ref_dd.base_l,AX  ; Set low 16 bytes
1284                                  opsize
1285 53F4  C1 E8 08                   shr     AX,8              ; and get bits 16-23 in AH
1286 53F7  88 26 2134 R               mov     ref_dd.base_m,AH  ; into descriptor.
1287 53FB  BD 0020                    mov     BP,ref_dtad       ; Get value of the selector
1288                                  opsize
1289 53FF  58                         pop     AX
1290 5400  C3                         ret
1291             getdsv   ENDP
1292
1293 5401            printc   PROC
1294                         ;
1295                         ;    Put out on printer the byte in AL
1296                         ;    Note: AL is destroyed but only AL
1297                         ;
1298 5401  51                         push     CX              ; Save regs used
1299 5402  53                         push     BX
1300 5403  52                         push     DX
1301 5404  BA 03BC                     mov     DX,03bch        ; Get port address (data)
1302 5407  EE                          out     DX,AL           ; Print the byte
1303 5408  B3 10                       mov     BL,10h          ; Set delay outer count
1304 540A  2B C9                       sub     CX,CX           ; and loop count
1305 540C  42                          inc     DX              ; Point to status port
1306 540D            busyl:
1307 540D  EC                          in      AL,DX           ; Get status
1308 540E  A8 80                       test    AL,80h          ; Check busy bit
1309 5410  75 06                       jnz     strobe          ; Not now - signal data ready
1310 5412  E2 F9                       loop    busyl           ; 64K times
```

```
1311 5414  FE CB                    dec     BL              ; 16 we check
1312 5416  75 F5                    jnz     busy1           ; for busy
1313 5418                  strobe:
1314 5418  B0 0D                    mov     AL,0dh          ; Signal printer we have data
1315 541A  42                       inc     DX              ; Use the strobe port
1316 541B  EE                       out     DX,AL           ; Send that signal
1317 541C  B9 00FF                  mov     CX,255          ; Short delay
1318 541F                  sign1:
1319 541F  E2 FE                    loop    sign1
1320 5421  FE C8                    dec     al              ; Set strobe bit off
1321 5423  EE                       out     DX,AL
1322 5424  5A                       pop     DX              ; Restore registers
1323 5425  5B                       pop     BX
1324 5426  59                       pop     CX
1325 5427  C3                       ret
1326
1327                       printc   ENDP
1328
1329
1330 5428                 hexit     PROC
1331                       ;
1332                       ; convert a hex digit to printable form and print it
1333                       ;
1334 5428  0C 30                    or      AL,30h          ; Make it a number?
1335 542A  3C 3A                    cmp     AL,3ah          ; Did we?
1336 542C  7C 02                    jl      yes1            ; If low - it is one
1337 542E  04 07                    add     AL,7            ; Convert to A-F
1338 5430                 yes1:
1339 5430  E8 5401 R              Call      printc          ; Print the char
1340 5433  C3                       ret
1341                       hexit    ENDP
1342
1343 5434                 prtalx    PROC
1344                       ;
1345                       ;     Print the byte in AL as an ordered pair of hex digits
1346                       ;
1347 5434  50                       push    AX              ; Save register
1348 5435  C0 E8 04                 shr     AL,4            ; Get high nibble
1349 5438  E8 5428 R                call    hexit           ; Put it out as hex digit
1350 543B  58                       pop     AX              ; Get the character back
1351 543C  50                       push    AX              ; but save the register
1352 543D  24 0F                    and     AL,0fh          ; Try the low nibble
1353 543F  E8 5428 R                call    hexit           ; Print the hex digit
1354 5442  58                       pop     AX
1355 5443  C3                       ret
1356                       prtalx   ENDP
1357
1358 5444                 prtaxx    PROC
1359                       ;
1360                       ;     Convert the word in AX to hex and print it
1361                       ;
1362 5444  50                       push    AX              ; Save it
1363 5445  50                       push    AX              ; twice
```

```
1364 5446  8A C4                        mov     AL,AH           ; Do upper byte first
1365 5448  E8 5434 R                     call    prtalx          ; Print it
1366 544B  58                            pop     AX
1367 544C  E8 5434 R                     call    prtalx          ; Then the lower byte
1368 544F  58                            pop     AX
1369 5450  C3                            ret
1370                       prtaxx         ENDP
1371
1372 5451                 prteaxx        PROC
1373                                      ;
1374                                      ;     Convert the double word in EAX to hex and print it
1375                                      ;
1376                                              opsize
1377 5452  50                            push    AX              ; Save it
1378                                              opsize
1379 5454  50                            push    AX              ; twice
1380                                              opsize
1381 5456  C1 E8 10                      shr     AX,16           ; Get the high word first
1382 5459  E8 5444 R                     call    prtaxx          ; Print it
1383                                              opsize
1384 545D  58                            pop     AX
1385 545E  E8 54E3 R                     call    prt16           ; Then the lower word
1386                                              opsize
1387 5462  58                            pop     AX
1388 5463  C3                            ret
1389                       prteaxx        ENDP
1390
1391
1392 5464                 newln          PROC
1393                                      ;
1394                                      ;     Put out a c/r and l/f
1395                                      ;
1396 5464  50                            push    AX
1397 5465  B0 0D                         mov     AL,0dh          ; Put out C/R
1398 5467  E8 5401 R                     call    printc
1399 546A  B0 0A                         mov     AL,0ah          ; and line feed
1400 546C  E8 5401 R                     call    printc
1401 546F  58                            pop     AX
1402 5470  C3                            ret
1403                       newln          ENDP
1404
1405 5471                 dumpln         PROC
1406                                      ;
1407                                      ;     Dump the memory at DS:AX for 16 bytes - Follow with display and C/R LF
1408                                      ]     AX is returned pointing to the next address to dump.
1409                                      ;     ES is set to our standard DS for execution.
1410                                      ;
1411 5471  53                            push    BX              ; Save registers
1412 5472  51                            push    CX
1413 5473  50                            push    AX
1414                                      ;
1415                                      ;     Get the linear address for the DS either as a 8086 or 80386 value
1416                                      ;     Note this decision depends on the DS value being above gdtsize
```

```
1417                            ;     for 8086. (normally the case for this program)
1418                            ;
1419                                  opsize
1420 5475  2B C8                      sub     AX,AX              ; Clear EAX
1421                                  opsize
1422 5478  2B DB                      sub     BX,BX              ; and EBX
1423 547A  8C DB                      mov     BX,DS              ; Get the segment selector
1424 547C  B8 0088                    mov     AX,gdt_size        ; Get max 80386 style
1425                                  opsize
1426 5480  3B D8                      cmp     BX,AX              ; Check form
1427 5482  7F 17                      jg      do8086             ; Must be 8086 form
1428                            ;
1429                            ; We could be wrong and make a garbage value here but normally we're ok
1430                            ;
1431 5484  06                         push    ES                 ; Save current ES
1432 5485  B8 0060                    mov     AX,supdd           ; Get standard data selector
1433 5488  8E C8                      mov     ES,AX              ; into ES
1434 548A  26: 8A A7 2114 R           mov     AH,ES:gdt_def.base_m[BX] ; Get high byte
1435                                  opsize
1436 5490  C1 E0 08                   shl     AX,8               ; into the high half
1437 5493  26: 8B 87 2112 R           mov     AX,ES:gdt_def.base_l[BX] ; Then the low 16 bits
1438 5498  07                         pop     ES                 ; Restore ES
1439 5499  EB 06                      jmp     short dolinear     ; Combine the segment
1440 549B               do8086:
1441 549B  8B C3                      mov     AX,BX              ; Get descriptor in AX
1442                                  opsize
1443 549E  C1 E0 04                   shl     AX,4               ; Times 16 in EAX
1444 54A1               dolinear:
1445                                  opsize
1446 54A2  2B DB                      sub     BX,BX              ; Clear EBX
1447 54A4  5B                         pop     BX                 ; Get displacement
1448 54A5  53                         push    BX                 ; (save for the text)
1449                                  opsize
1450 54A7  03 C3                      add     AX,BX              ; Now we have the linear address
1451
1452 54A9  E8 5451 R                  call    prteaxx            ; Put out address
1453 54AC  B0 20                      mov     AL,' '             ; and 2 spaces
1454 54AE  E8 5401 R                  call    printc
1455 54B1  B9 0008                    mov     CX,8               ; Do 8 words
1456 54B4               nxtword:
1457 54B4  8B 07                      mov     AX,[BX]            ; Get with bytes reversed
1458 54B6  83 C3 02                   add     BX,2               ; Step pointer
1459 54B9  86 C4                      xchg    AL,AH              ; Re-reverse them
1460 54BB  E8 54E3 R                  call    prt16              ; Print as hex
1461 54BE  E2 F4                      loop    nxtword            ; for all 8
1462 54C0  B0 20                      mov     AL,' '             ; Get another space
1463 54C2  E8 5401 R                  call    printc             ; and print byte
1464 54C5  5B                         pop     BX                 ; Get pointer back
1465 54C6  B9 0010                    mov     CX,16              ; Get byte count
1466 54C9               nxtbyte:
1467 54C9  8A 07                      mov     AL,[BX]            ; Get a byte
1468 54CB  43                         inc     BX                 ; and step pointer
1469 54CC  3C 20                      cmp     AL,' '             ; Check to a space
```

```
1470 54CE  7C 04                          jl     isactl        ; If less - go make a dot
1471 54D0  3C 7E                          cmp    AL,07eh       ; Is it too high to print?
1472 54D2  7E 02                          jng    nothigh       ; If not - use as is
1473 54D4                 isactl:
1474 54D4  B0 2E                          mov    AL,'.'        ; If so - replace with dot
1475 54D6                 nothigh:
1476 54D6  E8 5401 R                      call   printc        ; Print the char
1477 54D9  E2 EE                          loop   nxtbyte       ; and loop for 16
1478
1479 54DB  E8 5464 R                      call   newln         ; Do cr/lf
1480
1481 54DE  8B C3                          mov    AX,BX         ; Set return value for AX
1482 54E0  59                             pop    CX
1483 54E1  5B                             pop    BX
1484 54E2  C3                             ret
1485                      dumpln ENDP
1486
1487 54E3                 prt16  PROC
1488                      ;
1489                      ; proc to print AX in hex followed by a space
1490                      ;
1491 54E3  E8 5444 R                      call   prtaxx        ; Print the AX value
1492 54E6  B0 20                          mov    AL,' '        ; Follow it with a space
1493 54E8  E8 5401 R                      call   printc        ; (put it out)
1494 54EB  C3                             ret
1495                      prt16  ENDP
1496
1497 54EC                 dumprg PROC
1498                      ;
1499                      ;    Dump all the registers
1500                      ;
1501                                      opsize
1502 54ED  50                             PUSH   AX
1503
1504 54EE  E8 5464 R                      call   newln         ; Do cr/lf
1505
1506                                      opsize
1507 54F2  9C                             pushf                ; Save EFLAGS
1508 54F3  E8 5451 R                      Call   prteaxx       ; Put out AX,
1509                                      opsize
1510 54F7  8B C3                          mov    AX,BX
1511 54F9  E8 5451 R                      call   prteaxx       ; then BX,
1512                                      opsize
1513 54FD  8B C1                          mov    AX,CX
1514 54FF  E8 5451 R                      call   prteaxx       ; then CX,
1515                                      opsize
1516 5503  8B C2                          mov    AX,DX
1517 5505  E8 5451 R                      call   prteaxx       ; then DX,
1518                                      opsize
1519 5509  8B C5                          mov    AX,BP
1520 550B  E8 5451 R                      call   prteaxx       ; then BP,
1521                                      opsize
1522 550F  8B C4                          mov    AX,SP
```

```
1523 5511  E8 5451 R            call    prteaxx         ; then SP,
1524                            opsize
1525 5515  8B C6                mov     AX,SI
1526 5517  E8 5451 R            call    prteaxx         ; then SI,
1527                            opsize
1528 551B  8B C7                mov     AX,DI
1529 551D  E8 5451 R            call    prteaxx         ; and then DI.
1530
1531 5520  E8 5464 R            call    newln           ; Do cr/lf
1532
1533 5523  8C C8                mov     AX,CS
1534 5525  E8 54E3 R            call    prt16           ; and then CS,
1535 5528  8C D8                mov     AX,DS
1536 552A  E8 54E3 R            call    prt16           ; then DS,
1537 552D  8C C0                mov     AX,ES
1538 552F  E8 54E3 R            call    prt16           ; then ES,
1539 5532  8C D0                mov     AX,SS
1540 5534  E8 54E3 R            call    prt16           ; then SS,
1541 5537  8C E0                db      8ch,0e0h
1542 5539  E8 54E3 R            call    prt16           ; then FS,
1543 553C  8C E8                db      8ch,0e8h
1544 553E  E8 54E3 R            call    prt16           ; then GS,
1545 5541  0F 00 C0             sldt    AX
1546 5544  E8 54E3 R            call    prt16           ; then LDT,
1547 5547  0F 00 C8             str     AX
1548 554A  E8 54E3 R            call    prt16           ; and task register.
1549
1550 554D  E8 5464 R            call    newln           ; Do cr/lf
1551
1552                    ;       mov     AX,CR0
1553 5550  0F 20 C0             db      0fh,20h,0c0h    ; Get CR0 and
1554 5553  E8 5451 R            call    prteaxx         ; print it.
1555 5556  0F 20 D0             db      0fh,20h,0d0h    ; Get CR2 and
1556 5559  E8 5451 R            call    prteaxx         ; print it.
1557 555C  0F 20 D8             db      0fh,20h,0d8h    ; Get CR3 and
1558 555F  E8 5451 R            call    prteaxx         ; print it.
1559 5562  0F 01 06 4AD2 R      sgdt    qword ptr dtsize ; Store the GDT register,
1560                            opsize
1561 5568  A1 4AD4 R            mov     AX, word ptr dtload ; get the address
1562 556B  E8 5451 R            call    prteaxx         ;and put it out.
1563 556E  0F 01 0E 4AD2 R      sidt    qword ptr dtsize ; Store the IDT register,
1564                            opsize
1565 5574  A1 4AD4 R            mov     AX, word ptr dtload ; get the address,
1566 5577  E8 5451 R            call    prteaxx         ;and put it out.
1567                            opsize
1568 557B  58                   pop     AX              ; Get EFLAGS register and
1569 557C  E8 5451 R            call    prteaxx         ; put it out.
1570
1571 557F  E8 5464 R            call    newln           ; Do cr/lf
1572
1573                            opsize
1574 5583  58                   pop     AX
1575 5584  C3                   ret
```

```
1576                               dumprg    ENDP
1577
1578 5585                          dmptss    PROC
1579                               ;
1580                               ; Dump a TSS and its stack (64 bytes of it).
1581                               ;    At entry CX has the tss displacement
1582                               ;
1583 5585  50                                push    AX              ; Save registers used
1584 5586  53                                push    BX
1585 5587  51                                push    CX              ; Save TSS displacement
1586 5588  8B C1                             mov     AX,CX           ; Set displacement of TSS
1587 558A  B9 0007                           mov     CX,7            ; Prepare to dump 70 hex
1588 558D                          dumpit2:
1589 558D  E8 5471 R                         call    dumpln          ; Put it out 16 at a time
1590 5590  E2 FB                             loop    dumpit2
1591
1592 5592  E8 5464 R                         call    newln           ; Do cr/lf
1593
1594                               ;
1595                               ; Now we dump the contents of the stack of the task.
1596                               ;    First we need to build a DS to map the task's SS
1597                               ;       which can be either 80386 style or V8086 style.
1598                               ;    Then we can dump the data.
1599                               ;
1600 5595  5B                                pop     BX              ; Get displ to this TSS
1601 5596  53                                push    BX              ; and save it again
1602 5597  8B 4F 50                          mov     CX,[BX].tss     ; Get task's SS value and the
1603 559A  8B 57 38                          mov     DX,[BX].tesp    ; task's SP (16 bit).
1604 559D  8B 47 26                          mov     AX,[BX].teflags+2 ; Get the upper 16 bits of EFLAGS and
1605 55A0  24 02                             and     AL,2            ; isolate the v86 mode flag.
1606 55A2  75 11                             jnz     short gotss     ; If we have it in v86 form ok.
1607 55A4  80 E1 F8                          and     CL,0f8h         ; Don't allow for local stacks.
1608 55A7  8D 1E 2110 R                      lea     BX,gdt_def      ; Get locaction of the GDT.
1609 55AB  03 D9                             add     BX,CX           ; Sset displacement
1610                                         opsize
1611 55AE  8B 4F 02                          mov     CX,[BX].base_l  ; Get the low 24 bits in ECX
1612                                         opsize
1613 55B2  C1 E9 04                          shr     CX,4            ; and an 8086 style desc in CX
1614 55B5                          gotss:
1615 55B5  8B D9                             mov     BX,CX           ; Put in reg for proc
1616 55B7  E8 53E5 R                         call    getdsv          ; BP has descriptor just built
1617 55BA  8E DD                             mov     DS,BP           ; Set as DS
1618 55BC  8B C2                             mov     AX,DX           ; Set the SP value
1619 55BE  B9 0004                           mov     CX,4            ; Set count
1620 55C1                          dumpiSS:
1621 55C1  E8 5471 R                         call    dumpln          ; Put it out 16 at a time
1622 55C4  E2 FB                             loop    dumpiSS
1623
1624 55C6  BB 0060                           mov     BX,supdd        ; Get std DS back
1625 55C9  8E DB                             mov     DS,BX           ; into DS
1626
1627 55CB  E8 5464 R                         call    newln           ; Do cr/lf
1628
```

```
1629 55CE  59                              pop    CX              ; Restore registers saved
1630 55CF  5B                              pop    BX
1631 55D0  58                              pop    AX
1632 55D1  C3                              ret
1633                          dmptss       ENDP
1634
1635 55D2                     edump        PROC
1636                          ;
1637                          ;
1638                          ;      Dump the GDT, IDT, and all tss's
1639                          ;      The displacement to the tss of interest is in CX.
1640                          ;
1641 55D2  8F 06 4AE8 R                     pop    dumpcal         ; Set call addr in mem
1642 55D6  FF 36 4AE8 R                     push   dumpcal         ; Get it back on stack
1643 55DA  50                               push   AX              ; Save AX
1644 55DB  53                               push   BX              ; BX
1645 55DC  51                               push   CX              ; CX
1646 55DD  52                               push   DX              ; and DX
1647
1648 55DE  E8 54EC R                        call   dumprg          ; Print Registers first
1649
1650 55E1  E8 5464 R                        call   newln           ; Do cr/lf
1651 55E4  8D 06 4AD2 R                     lea    AX,dtsize       ; Point to debug data and dump it.
1652 55E8  E8 5471 R                        call   dumpln
1653 55EB  E8 5471 R                        call   dumpln
1654 55EE  E8 5464 R                        call   newln
1655
1656 55F1  8D 06 2110 R                     lea    AX,gdt_def      ; Set displacement of GDT
1657 55F5  B9 000A                          mov    CX,(idt_def-gdt_def+31)/16 ; Prepare to dump all
1658 55F8                     dumpitg:
1659 55F8  E8 5471 R                        call   dumpln          ; Put it out 16 at a time
1660 55FB  E2 FB                            loop   dumpitg
1661
1662 55FD  E8 5464 R                        call   newln           ; Do cr/lf
1663 5600  8D 0E 2998 R                     lea    CX,supv         ; Point to supv TSS
1664 5604  E8 5585 R                        call   dmptss
1665 5607  8D 0E 2A00 R                     lea    CX,supv2        ; Point to supv2 TSS
1666 560B  E8 5585 R                        call   dmptss
1667 560E  8D 0E 2A68 R                     lea    CX,v86          ; Point to v86 TSS
1668 5612  E8 5585 R                        call   dmptss
1669
1670 5615  E8 5464 R                        call   newln           ; Do cr/lf
1671
1672 5618  B9 0006                          mov    CX,6            ; Prepare to dump
1673 561B  8B C4                            mov    AX,SP           ; from SP and
1674 561D  8C D3                            mov    BX,SS           ; SS
1675 561F  8E DB                            mov    DS,BX
1676 5621                     dumpit30:
1677 5621  E8 5471 R                        call   dumpln          ; Put it out 16 at a time
1678 5624  E2 FB                            loop   dumpit30
1679
1680 5626  B8 0060                          mov    AX,supdd        ; Get normal DS value back
1681 5629  8E D8                            mov    DS,AX           ; into DS
```

```
1682
1683 562B  E8 5464 R                          call   newln          ; Do cr/lf
1684
1685 562E  5A                                 pop    DX             ; Restore registers
1686 562F  59                                 pop    CX
1687 5630  5B                                 pop    BX
1688 5631  58                                 pop    AX
1689 5632  C3                                 ret                   ; Return
1690                          edump   ENDP
1691
1692 5633                     mindump PROC
1693                          ;
1694                          ; Minimum dump for trace without too much inteferance
1695                          ;
1696                                           opsize
1697 5634  C1 E0 10                            shl    AX,16          ; Move AX to high EAX
1698 5637  58                                 pop    AX             ; Get return addr
1699 5638  50                                 push   AX             ; Back on stack
1700 5639  E8 5451 R                           call   prteaxx        ; Put it out
1701 563C  E8 5464 R                           call   newln          ; Space a line
1702                                           opsize
1703 5640  C1 E8 10                            shr    AX,16          ; Get AX back
1704 5643  C3                                 ret
1705                          mindump ENDP
1706 5644                     totalsize:
1707                          begin   ENDP
1708 5644                     code    ENDS
1709                                           END    begin
```

Macros:

N a m eLines

```
OPSIZE . . . . . . . . . . . . .    1
SEGADR . . . . . . . . . . . . .    5
SEGCVT . . . . . . . . . . . . .    5
SETTSSA . . . . . . . . . . . .     8
```

Structures and Records:

```
            N a m e          Width   # fields
                             Shift   Width   Mask   Initial

DESC . . . . . . . . . . . . .   00080006
   LIMIT . . . . . . . . . . .     0000
   BASE_L . . . . . . . . . .      0002
   BASE_M . . . . . . . . . .      0004
   ACCESS . . . . . . . . . .      0005
   GRAN . . . . . . . . . . .      0006
   BASE_H . . . . . . . . . .      0007
STKDEF . . . . . . . . . . . .   00240012
   OLDIP . . . . . . . . . . .      0000
   OLDCS . . . . . . . . . . .      0004
```

```
  OLDFL   . . . . . . . . . . . . 0008
  OLDSP   . . . . . . . . . . . . 000C
  OLDSS   . . . . . . . . . . . . 0010
  OLDES   . . . . . . . . . . . . 0014
  OLDDS   . . . . . . . . . . . . 0018
  OLDFS   . . . . . . . . . . . . 001C
  OLDGS   . . . . . . . . . . . . 0020
TSS_D   . . . . . . . . . . . . 0068002A
  BACK  . . . . . . . . . . . . 0000
  ESP0  . . . . . . . . . . . . 0004
  SS0   . . . . . . . . . . . . 0008
  ESP1  . . . . . . . . . . . . 000C
  SS1   . . . . . . . . . . . . 0010
  ESP2  . . . . . . . . . . . . 0014
  SS2   . . . . . . . . . . . . 0018
  TCR3  . . . . . . . . . . . . 001C
  TEIP  . . . . . . . . . . . . 0020
  TEFLAGS . . . . . . . . . . . 0024
  TEAX  . . . . . . . . . . . . 0028
  TECX  . . . . . . . . . . . . 002C
  TEDX  . . . . . . . . . . . . 0030
  TEBX  . . . . . . . . . . . . 0034
  TESP  . . . . . . . . . . . . 0038
  TEBP  . . . . . . . . . . . . 003C
  TESI  . . . . . . . . . . . . 0040
  TEDI  . . . . . . . . . . . . 0044
  TES   . . . . . . . . . . . . 0048
  TCS   . . . . . . . . . . . . 004C
  TSS   . . . . . . . . . . . . 0050
  TDS   . . . . . . . . . . . . 0054
  TFS   . . . . . . . . . . . . 0058
  TGS   . . . . . . . . . . . . 005C
  TLDT  . . . . . . . . . . . . 0060
  IOMAP . . . . . . . . . . . . 0066
```

Segments and Groups:

N a m e	Size	Align	Combine	Class
CODE	5644	PARA	PUBLIC	'CODE'

Symbols:

N a m e	Type	Value	Attr
BADSTK0	L NEAR	51E0	CODE
BADSTK1	L NEAR	51EE	CODE
BEGIN	F PROC	0100	CODE Length = 5544
BUSYL	L NEAR	540D	CODE
DATASIZ	Number	2A24	
DEBUGF	L BYTE	4ADC	CODE
DEBUGF0	L BYTE	4ADD	CODE

```
DEBUGF0A . . . . . . . . . . . L BYTE 4ADECODE
DEBUGF1 . . . . . . . . . . . . L BYTE 4ADFCODE
DEBUGF1A . . . . . . . . . . . L BYTE 4AE0CODE
DEBUGF1B . . . . . . . . . . . L BYTE 4AE1CODE
DMPTSS . . . . . . . . . . . . N PROC5585CODELength = 004D
DO8086 . . . . . . . . . . . . L NEAR549BCODE
DOLINEAR . . . . . . . . . . . L NEAR54A1CODE
DSADDR . . . . . . . . . . . . L WORD 4AE4CODE
DTLOAD . . . . . . . . . . . . L DWORD4AD4CODE
DTSIZE . . . . . . . . . . . . L WORD 4AD2CODE
DUMPCAL . . . . . . . . . . . L WORD 4AE8CODE
DUMPISS . . . . . . . . . . . L NEAR55C1CODE
DUMPIT2 . . . . . . . . . . . L NEAR558DCODE
DUMPIT30 . . . . . . . . . . . L NEAR5621CODE
DUMPIT380 . . . . . . . . . . L NEAR52BACODE
DUMPITG . . . . . . . . . . . L NEAR55F8CODE
DUMPLN . . . . . . . . . . . . N PROC5471CODELength = 0072
DUMPRG . . . . . . . . . . . . N PROC54ECCODELength = 0099

EDUMP  . . . . . . . . . . . . N PROC55D2CODELength = 0061
ENDAD  . . . . . . . . . . . . L BYTE 4B24CODE
EXECD  . . . . . . . . . . . . Number0070
EXEDD  . . . . . . . . . . . . Number0078
EXESD  . . . . . . . . . . . . Number0080
EXE_C  . . . . . . . . . . . . L 00082180CODE
EXE_D  . . . . . . . . . . . . L 00082188CODE
EXE_S  . . . . . . . . . . . . L 00082190CODE

FILLIHD1 . . . . . . . . . . . L NEAR4B98CODE
FULLD02 . . . . . . . . . . . L NEAR51C9CODE
FULLD02A . . . . . . . . . . . L NEAR528ECODE
FULLD02E . . . . . . . . . . . L NEAR51F8CODE
FULLD04 . . . . . . . . . . . L NEAR539CCODE

GDT_DEF . . . . . . . . . . . L 00082110CODE
GDT_SIZE . . . . . . . . . . . Number0088
GETDSV . . . . . . . . . . . . N PROC53E5CODELength = 001C
GODOIT . . . . . . . . . . . . L NEAR4D38CODE
GOTSS  . . . . . . . . . . . . L NEAR55B5CODE

HEXIT  . . . . . . . . . . . . N PROC5428CODELength = 000C

IDT_DEF . . . . . . . . . . . NEAR 2198CODE
IDT_SIZE . . . . . . . . . . . Number0800
IHCOMMN . . . . . . . . . . . L NEAR5194CODE
IHSPN1 . . . . . . . . . . . . Number17DC
IHSPN2 . . . . . . . . . . . . Number17D8
IHSPV  . . . . . . . . . . . . Number1800
IHZERO . . . . . . . . . . . . Number0028
IH_COMMON . . . . . . . . . . L NEAR517BCODE
INSTEXB . . . . . . . . . . . L NEAR5386CODE
INSTEXE . . . . . . . . . . . N PROC5386CODELength = 005F
INTCD1 . . . . . . . . . . . . L WORD 4AD8CODE
```

```
INTCD2 . . . . . . . . . . . . . .   L WORD 4ADACODE
INT_HAND0 . . . . . . . . . .         L NEAR4D7BCODE
ISACTL . . . . . . . . . . . .        L NEAR54D4CODE
ISINT13 . . . . . . . . . . .         L NEAR52DCCODE

LOCAL . . . . . . . . . . . .         L NEAR4D10CODE

MINDUMP . . . . . . . . . . .         N PROC5633CODELength = 0011

NEWLINE . . . . . . . . . . .         L BYTE 4B21CODE
NEWLN . . . . . . . . . . . .         N PROC5464CODELength = 000D
NOTHIGH . . . . . . . . . . .         L NEAR54D6CODE
NOTINT00 . . . . . . . . . . .        L NEAR5344CODE
NOTINT13 . . . . . . . . . . .        L NEAR521DCODE
NXTBYTE . . . . . . . . . . .         L NEAR54C9CODE
NXTWORD . . . . . . . . . . .         L NEAR54B4CODE

PRINTC . . . . . . . . . . . .        N PROC5401CODELength = 0027
PROCINT . . . . . . . . . . .         L NEAR5311CODE
PROCIRET . . . . . . . . . . .        L NEAR5347CODE
PRT16 . . . . . . . . . . . .         N PROC54E3CODELength = 0009
PRTALX . . . . . . . . . . . .        N PROC5434CODELength = 0010
PRTAXX . . . . . . . . . . . .        N PROC5444CODELength = 000D
PRTEAXX . . . . . . . . . . .         N PROC5451CODELength = 0013

REF0D . . . . . . . . . . . .         Number0040
REF1D . . . . . . . . . . . .         Number0048
REFL0 . . . . . . . . . . . .         Number0010
REFL3 . . . . . . . . . . . .         Number000B
REF_0 . . . . . . . . . . . .         L 00082150CODE
REF_1 . . . . . . . . . . . .         L 00082158CODE
REF_D . . . . . . . . . . . .         L 00082128CODE
REF_DD . . . . . . . . . . . .        L 00082130CODE
REF_DTA . . . . . . . . . . .         Number0018
REF_DTAD . . . . . . . . . . .        Number0020
REF_L0 . . . . . . . . . . . .        L 00082120CODE
REF_L3 . . . . . . . . . . . .        L 00082118CODE
REF_ZER . . . . . . . . . . .         L 00082138CODE
REJOIN . . . . . . . . . . . .        L NEAR5271CODE
RESLOOP . . . . . . . . . . .         L NEAR4D4BCODE
RESUME . . . . . . . . . . . .        L NEAR4D4ACODE
RESUMED . . . . . . . . . . .         Number4D4A
RETDISP . . . . . . . . . . .         L WORD 4AE2CODE

SEGSETUP . . . . . . . . . . .        L NEAR4B25CODE
SIGNL . . . . . . . . . . . .         L NEAR541FCODE
SKIP01 . . . . . . . . . . . .        L NEAR4D23CODE
SKIP02 . . . . . . . . . . . .        L NEAR51FBCODE
SKIP03 . . . . . . . . . . . .        L NEAR52D3CODE
SKIP04 . . . . . . . . . . . .        L NEAR539FCODE
SKIPDMP . . . . . . . . . . .         L NEAR53DBCODE
STILLOK . . . . . . . . . . . .       L NEAR51AECODE
STKDATA . . . . . . . . . . .         Number0030
```

```
STK_DATA . . . . . . . . . . . . L 00082140CODE
STROBE . . . . . . . . . . . . . L NEAR5418CODE
SUCCESS . . . . . . . . . . . . L BYTE 4AEACODE
SUPCD . . . . . . . . . . . . . Number0058
SUPDD . . . . . . . . . . . . . Number0060
SUPSD . . . . . . . . . . . . . Number0068
SUPV . . . . . . . . . . . . . L 00682998CODE
SUPV2 . . . . . . . . . . . . . L 00682A00CODE
SUP_C . . . . . . . . . . . . . L 00082168CODE
SUP_D . . . . . . . . . . . . . L 00082170CODE
SUP_S . . . . . . . . . . . . . L 00082178CODE
SZ386T . . . . . . . . . . . . Number0068
SZV86T . . . . . . . . . . . . Number2068

TODOS . . . . . . . . . . . . . L NEAR4D70CODE
TOTALSIZE . . . . . . . . . . . L NEAR5644CODE

V86 . . . . . . . . . . . . . . L 00682A68CODE
V868D . . . . . . . . . . . . . Number0053
V86_0 . . . . . . . . . . . . . L 00082160CODE

YES1 . . . . . . . . . . . . . L NEAR5430CODE


    1459 Source  Lines
    2375 Total   Lines
     191 Symbols

    39670 Bytes symbol space free

        0 Warning Errors
        0 Severe  Errors

    Symbol Cross-Reference        (# is definition)              Cref-1

ACCESS . . . . . .   83    83#

BACK . . . . . . .  343   343#
BADSTK0. . . . . .  991   991#  993
BADSTK1. . . . . .  998   998#  1000
BASE_H . . . . . .   85    85#
BASE_L . . . . . .   81    81#   612   613   614   615   641   642   643   645   646   1025   1080   1118
                   1181  1233  1234  1235  1283  1437  1611

BASE_M . . . . . .   82    82#   612   613   614   615   641   642   643   645   646   1026   1078   1119
                   1182  1238  1239  1240  1286  1434

BEGIN. . . . . . .  134   134#   136   819   856   1008  1709
BUSYL. . . . . . . 1306  1306#  1310  1312

CODE . . . . . . .  128   128#   128   129   129   129   1708

DATASIZ. . . . . .  582   582#
```

170 Symbols

```
 1                              PAGE    59,132
 2                              .286P
 3
 4                      ;
 5                      ;  Test bed program for code to be executed in 80386 protected
 6                      ;  mode.  The VIRT86L program is assumed to be running the MS-DOS
 7                      ;  system as a virtual 8086 task.  The INT 00 escape is used to
 8                      ;  to gain linkage in protected mode at 'goback'.
 9                      ;
10 0000          code      SEGMENT para 'CODE'
11                         ASSUME  CS:code, DS:code, SS:code
12 0100                    org     100h
13 0100          begin     PROC    far
14 0100  E9 0210 R         jmp     startex
15 0110                    org     begin+16        ; Align on paragraph boundry.
16 0110  0100[             db      256 dup (0)
17         00
18                 ]
19
20 = 0210         stkwork   equ     $
21 0210           startex:
22 0210  BC 0210            mov     SP,100h+stkwork-begin ; Set an SP value.
23 0213  8D 16 0230 R       lea     DX,goback       ; Set displacement to code.
24 0217  8C C9              mov     CX,CS           ; Get a value
25 0219  8E D9              mov     DS,CX           ; for our DS (we use CS).
26 021B  CD 00              int     0               ; Invoke protected mode call.
27                      ;
28                      ;  A real program might have other things to do here.  Feel free to
29                      ;  do whatever is necessary or desirable.
30                      ;
31 021D  B4 4C             mov     AH,4ch          ; Set 'terminate' code
32 021F  CD 21             int     21h             ; and end via MS-DOS call.
33 = 0020        orgpt     equ     $-startex+15 and 0fff0h
34 0230                    org     startex+orgpt   ; Align on a para boundry
```

```
35                                        ;
36                                        ; Define the protected mode routine. (Again this is expandable to
37                                        ; suit whatever is needed.)
38                                        ;
39 = 0230                                 goback   equ     $
40                                        ;
41                                        ; At entry, the code segment points here. The value in BX is a
42                                        ; selector for a data descriptor which points here. The value in
43                                        ; CX is a selector for a stack segment which also points here.
44                                        ;
45                                        ; On return from the code here, we want the original DS, SS, and SP
46                                        ; values in effect. If we set a zero flag the code takes a dump
47                                        ; as it exits.
48                                        ;
49 0230  8C D6                            mov      SI,SS          ; Save SS of monitor
50 0232  8B FC                            mov      DI,SP          ; and the SP also.
51 0234  BA 0200                          mov      DX,200h        ; Set an SP for myself
52 0237  8E D1                            mov      SS,CX          ; Set our passed SS
53 0239  8B E2                            mov      SP,DX          ; and our new SP.
54 023B  60                              pusha                   ; Save all the registers
55 023C  1E                              push     DS             ; now save DS
56 023D  8E DB                            mov      DS,BX          ; and set our DS value
57 023F  90                              nop
58 0240  90                              nop
59                                        ;
60                                        ; Execute whatever instructions are desired here
61                                        ;
62 0241  66                              db       66h            ; Override size
63 0242  60                              pusha                   ; Save the extended registers
64 0243  66                              db       66h
65 0244  9C                              pushf                   ; And the EFLAGS
66 0245  E8 0257 R                        call     instspec       ; Go do the  instruction
67 0248  66                              db       66h
68 0249  9D                              popf
69 024A  66                              db       66h
70 024B  61                              popa                    ; Our stack is now back to
71
72                                        ;
73                                        ; Reverse the entry code to restore the proper environment for our
74                                        ; return.
75                                        ;
76 024C  1F                              pop      DS             ; Restore DS
77 024D  61                              popa                    ; Get registers back
78 024E  8E D6                            mov      SS,SI          ; Restore SS
79 0250  8B E7                            mov      SP,DI          ; and SP
80                                        ;
81                                        ; Set a zero condition code to get a dump. Set non-zero to avoid one.
82                                        ;
83 0252  B0 01                            mov      AL,1           ; set a proper value in AL
84 0254  0A C0                            or       AL,AL          ; and set the condition code
85 0256  CB                              ret
86                                        ;
87                                        ; provide a routine for the issuance of an instruction
```

```
88                                      ;
89 0257                      instspec   PROC
90 0257  90                             nop
91 0258  90                             nop
92 0259  90                             nop
93 025A  90                             nop
94 025B  90                             nop
95 025C  90                             nop
96 025D  90                             nop
97 025E  90                             nop
98 025F  90                             nop
99 0260  90                             nop
100 0261 90                             nop
101 0262 90                             nop
102 0263 C3                             ret
103                          instspec   ENDP
104 0264 0100[                          dw      256 dup(0)         ; Ensure space for stack et al
105      0000
106                  ]
107
108                          begin      ENDP
109 0464                     code       ENDS
110                                     END     begin
```

Segments and Groups:

```
             N a m e         SizeAlignCombine Class

CODE . . . . . . . . . . . . 0464PARANONE'CODE'
```

Symbols:

```
             N a m e         TypeValueAttr

BEGIN  . . . . . . . . . . . F PROC0100CODELength = 0364

GOBACK . . . . . . . . . . . NEAR 0230CODE

INSTSPEC . . . . . . . . . . N PROC0257CODELength = 000D

ORGPT  . . . . . . . . . . . Number0020

STARTEX  . . . . . . . . . . L NEAR0210CODE
STKWORK  . . . . . . . . . . NEAR 0210CODE

    104 Source  Lines
    104 Total   Lines
     28 Symbols

  49746 Bytes symbol space free

      0 Warning Errors
      0 Severe  Errors
```

```
Symbol Cross-Reference        (# is definition)              Cref-1

BEGIN. . . . . . . . . . . . .   13    13#    15    22   110

CODE . . . . . . . . . . . . .   10    10#    10    11   11    11   109

GOBACK . . . . . . . . . . . .   23    39     39#

INSTSPEC . . . . . . . . . . .   66    89     89#

ORGPT. . . . . . . . . . . . .   33    33#    34

STARTEX. . . . . . . . . . . .   14    21     21#   33   34
STKWORK. . . . . . . . . . . .   20    20#    22


7 Symbols
```

SAMPLE RUNS:

Load your system. When you get the system prompt, place the diskette into your floppy drive. In our system, we only have one floppy drive; however, we have the programs on Drive C, the hard disk, so all the prompts in the following will be "C>"

The system prompts will be shown. Your responses are italicized.

RUN #1—Running the 80386 program.

C> *VIRT86L*

Virtual 8086 mode is established! Enter G(go) or D − *G*

C>

NOTE: Now you are in Virtual 8086 mode. MS-DOS is under control of the 80386 program VIRT86L. You can do whatever MS-DOS commands you wish. To get out of this mode, you must re-IPL your system, generally with the CNTL-ALT-DEL keys.

RUN #2—In this sample, answer "D" at the prompt and get a dump.

C> *VIRT86L*

Virtual 8086 mode is established! Enter G(go) or D − *D*

NOTE: The dump you get prints a block of hexadecimal characters, divided by blank lines. Prior to dumping, verify the port addresses for your parallel printer. The sections are:

1. The stack used for the INT00 interrupt handler.
2. The normal stack for the program.
3. Registers.
4. Dump Control Segment.
5. Global Descriptor Table and elements of the Interrupt Descriptor Table.

6. The TSS for the V86 INT00 Interrupt Handler.
7. The stack for the TSS of #6, above.
8. The TSS switched out of to enter V86 mode.
9. The stack for #8, above.
10. The TSS for the Virtual 8086 mode.
11. The stack for #10, above.
12. The stack being used by the caller of the dump.

RUN #3—The next is if you go into VIRT86L and run the DOINST program while under V86 mode.

C> *VIRT86L*

Virtual 8086 mode is established! Enter G(go) or D − *G*

C> *DOINST*

NOTE: This gives you a dump. The sections are:

1. The registers.
2. The dump control segment.
3. The Global Descriptor Table and elements of the Interrupt Descriptor Table.
4. Dump Control Segment.
5. Global Descriptor Table and elements of the Interrupt Descriptor Table.
6. The TSS for the V86 INT00 Interrupt Handler.
7. The stack for the TSS of #6, above.
8. The TSS switched out of to enter V86 mode.
9. The stack for #8, above.
10. The TSS for the Virtual 8086 mode.
11. The stack for #10, above.
12. The stack being used by the caller of the dump.

If you type ''DOINST'' at the ''C>'' while outside of control of the VIRT86L program, you will get a ''Divide Overflow'' error.

Glossary

absolute address—The fully defined address by a memory address number.

access time—The interval between a request for data or information from the memory unit and its actual availability to the processing unit.

accumulator—One or more registers for the storage of immediate results and operands in the Arithmetic Logic Unit (ALU).

active elements—Those components in a circuit that provide gain, or control direct current flow, such as transistors and diodes.

adder—Switching circuits that combine binary bits to generate the sum and carry of those bits.

address—Information used to identify individual storage locations or words in a memory unit.

address decoder—A circuit that converts the 80386 address into chip-select signals which are sent to the bus control logic.

address decoding—Condensing an address on the bus into a single signal, which either selects or disables a particular device and sets the current number of wait states for that device.

address latch—A circuit that maintains its contents for a specified period of time. Latches are used to maintain the I/O address for the duration of a bus cycle.

address space—The total area accessible to a program.

address translation—Converting a selector and offset into a physical address.

addressing mode—The specification of an operand in an instruction.

alphameric—Alphabetic, numeric, and special characters.

ALU—See Arithmetic Logic Unit.

American Standard Code for Information Interchange (ASCII)—A binary encoding scheme using seven bits to represent alphabetic characters, numbers, and special symbols.

analog—An item that represents something else. For example, a meter movement that indicates a voltage value on a scale.

AND gate—A circuit that forms a logic gate whose output is a 1 only when all its inputs are 1. The gate output for all other conditions is a 0.

anode—The lead on a diode or other device that receives positive voltage. This is opposed to the other lead, the cathode, that receives negative voltage.

architecture—An orderly organization of subsystems to satisfy overall system objectives.

Arithmetic Logic Unit (ALU)—A unit that performs all the arithmetic and logic operations in a microprocessor.

ASCII—See *American Standard Code for Information Interchange*.

assembler—A software program that translates assembly language into binary machine language.

assembly language—A symbolic notation for writing machine instructions.

asynchronous operations—A mode of operation for interacting systems in which each system is independent of the internal timing constraints of every other system.

bar—A sign that denotes the inverse, or complement, of a function. It is written as a line over the function or value.

base address—The physical address of the start of a segment.

BCD—See *binary coded decimal*.

benchmark—A program used to test and evaluate the performance characteristics of different systems.

bi-directional—A term used to describe signal-transmission lines that can transmit signals in either direction.

binary—A term used to describe the base-two number system.

binary coded decimal—BCD. A coding scheme in which every decimal digit from 0 to 9 is represented by its equivalent four-bit binary number.

bistable multivibrator—A flip-flop.

bit—A digit in the binary number system. It is a "made up" word, taking the "b" from binary and the "it" from digit.

bit field—A contiguous sequence of bits. A bit field may begin at any bit location of any byte and may contain up to 32 bits in the 80386.

bits per second (BPS)—A common measure of the rate of flow of information between digital systems.

bit string—A contiguous sequence of bits. A bit string may begin at any bit position of any byte and may contain up to $2^{32}-1$ bits, in the 80386.

Boolean approach—To impose the condition that all logic statements, reasons, facts, and so on, are either true or false.

bootstrap—A technique for starting up the operations of a computer system from a very small program in its memory.

BPS—See *bits per second*.

buffer—Storage elements such as registers or memory locations for the temporary storage of information prior to its use by the intended system, such as a peripheral device.

bus—A collection of signal transmission lines.

bus command—A signal directing that a particular operation be performed on the bus.

bus cycle—A single transfer of information on the bus.

bus driver—A source of electrical current used to maintain or transmit signals along a bus.

byte—A collection of eight adjacent bits.

cache—A buffer type of high-speed memory that is filled at medium speed from main memory. Cache memory is the fastest portion of the overall memory that stores only the data that the processor may need in the immediate future.

cancel—To remove a binary 1 from a flip-flop. Also, the process of removing a binary number from a register.

cathode—The lead on a diode or other device that receives negative voltage. See also *anode*.

central processing unit (CPU)—This consists of the microprocessor, the Arithmetic Logic Unit, various registers, and control and timing circuits.

character—This general term refers to all alphameric punctuation marks, mathematical operators, alphabetic characters, and the coded representation of such symbols.

chip—A small piece of semiconductor material containing miniaturized electronic circuits; an integrated circuit.

clear/reset—This process sets all relevant data to binary zero.

clock—A generator of periodic electrical pulses that control the timing of electronic switching circuits in computers. Clock speed is limited by the response time of the ICs used in the system. All other things being equal, the faster the clock frequency the more functions that can be performed in the same amount of real time.

CMOS—See *complementary metal oxide semiconductor*.

code—A means of representing information in digital form by assigning a specific pattern of bits to each item of information.

comparator—A component which compares two binary numbers.

compile—To translate a high-level language program to the desired machine-level set of program steps. A compile is done via the required language compiler.

compiler—A program that translates high-level language source code into machine language.

complementary metal oxide semiconductor (CMOS)—A combination of a p-channel and an n-channel transistor that creates a fast, low-power electronic switch. CMOS is a technology for fabricating electronic components.

conforming—A property of a segment that indicates that each procedure in that segment will move outward to the ring of its caller when it is called.

control bus—That part of a bus used to transmit control and status signals among support chips and a processor.

control register—In the 80386, these registers hold data of machine states of a global nature. They are called CR0, CR1, CR2, and CR3. The low-order 15 bits of CR0 are called the Machine Status Word, for compatibility with the 80286.

control transfers—In the 80386, transfer of control is done by use of exceptions, interrupts and by the instructions CALL, JMP, INT, IRET, and RET. A "near" transfer goes to a place within the current code segment. "Far" transfers go to other segments.

controller—That element or group of elements in a computer system that directs a series of operations and sends the proper signals to other computer circuits to carry out.

coprocessor—An auxiliary processor that operates in coordination with the CPU, allowing architectural capabilities which, in view of the limitations of contemporary technology, could not otherwise be provided. Coprocessors furnish the hardware to perform functions that would otherwise be performed in software. In addition, they extend the instruction set of the main processor.

counter—A device capable of changing state in a specified sequence on receiving appropriate input signals.

CPL—See *current privilege level*.

CPU—See *central processing unit*.

Current Privilege Level (CPL)—The privilege level of the program which currently is executing. In general, CPL can be determined by examining the lowest 2 bits of the Code Segment (CS) register.

cycle time—A fixed time interval.

cycle stealing—A channel controller or multiplexer of the interface system may "steal" a memory cycle-time to transmit a word from the external data storage medium into main memory or vice versa.

data—Facts, symbols, numbers, letters, anything that can be represented as binary bits on a computer.

data bus—That part of a bus used to transfer data among the support chips and a processor.

debug registers—In the 80386, there are six programmer-accessible registers: DR0-DR3 and DR6 and DR7. DR0-DR3 specify the four linear breakpoints. DR4 and DR5 are reserved by Intel. DR6 displays the current state of the breakpoints and DR7 is used to set the breakpoints.

decoder, binary—A combination of logic gates that converts any binary number into a decimal number.

delay—The slowing up of the propagation of a pulse, either deliberately to prevent inputs from changing while clock pulses are present, or unintentionally as caused by transistor rise-and-fall time, pulse-response characteristics.

descriptor—An 8-byte quantity specifying an independently protected object.

descriptor cache—See *shadow register*.

descriptor privilege level (DPL)—A field in a descriptor indicating how protected the descriptor is. The DPL is the least privileged level at which a task may access a particular descriptor and access the segment associated with that descriptor.

digit—A single decimal number, 0 through 9.

digit, binary—A single binary number, 0 or 1.

digital circuit—A semiconductor configuration that operates as a switch. Also called a binary circuit.

DIP—See *dual in-line package*.

direct addressing—Specifying a memory location by an address embedded in an instruction.

direct memory addressing (DMA)—This is a technique for transferring data in or out of memory without disturbing the program being executed by the processing unit.

discrete circuit—An electronic circuit comprising separate individually manufactured and assembled transistors, diodes, resistors, capacitors, and other components.

displacement—A 16-bit value specified in an instruction and used for computing address offsets.

display—A list of pointers to the stack frames of the procedure in which the currently executing procedure is enclosed.

DMA—See *direct memory addressing*.

DPL—See *descriptor privilege level*.

DRAM—See *dynamic random access memory*.

DRAM controller—A component which handles the details of interfacing to dynamic random access memory.

driver—An element coupled to the output stage of a circuit to increase its power capability or fanout.

dual in-line package (DIP)—The container in which a chip resides. This refers to the double, parallel rows of pins that connect the resident chip to the circuit board.

dump—Recording the system's memory contents on an external medium, such as magnetic tape.

dynamic random access memory (DRAM)—Random access memory which must be periodically refreshed in order not to lose data.

editor—A program used to manipulate a source program in an interactive manner.

effective privilege level (EPL)—The EPL is the least privileged of the RPL and DPL.

emulate—To create the machine language instructions of one processor for another, by means of microprogramming.

error correcting codes (ECC)—A parity-bit check which allows the detection of erroneous bits in a code word.

error value—See *exception value*.

exception—A condition occurring when an instruction violates the rules of normal operation.

exception value—A special value that is produced by an instruction if it causes a masked exception.

execution time—Time required by a microprocessor to execute a machine-language instruction. Execution time varies from one instruction to another.

expand down—A property of a segment that causes the processor to check that in all accesses to that segment, offsets are greater than the segment's limits. This is used for stack segments.

expand up—A property of a segment that causes the processor to check that all accesses to that segment offsets are no greater than the segment's limit. Generally, all segments other than stack segments have this property.

explicit cache—See *shadow register*.

fall time—The decay time of the trailing edge in a pulse waveform.

fan-in—The total number of inputs to a particular gate or function.

fan-out—The total number of loads connected to a particular gate or function.

far pointer—In the 80386, a 48-bit logical address of two components: a 16-bit segment selector and a 32-bit offset.

fetch—To obtain or secure information from a memory unit.

flag bit—A single bit that indicates one of two mutually exclusive conditions or states.

flat memory organization—An address space, in the 80386, that consists of a single array of up to 4 gigabytes. The 80386 maps the 4 gigabyte flat space onto the physical address space by address translation mechanisms.

flip-flop—A circuit with two and only two stable states.

gate—The simplest logic circuit. Its output voltage will be high or low depending on the states of the inputs and the type of gate that is employed. There are generally four types of gates: a call gate, a trap gate, an interrupt gate, and a task gate.

GDT—See *global descriptor table.*

general register—One of the 16-bit registers: AX, BX, CX, or DX.

glitch—A false digital pulse.

global descriptor table (GDT)—A table in memory containing descriptors for segments that are shared by all tasks.

global descriptor table register (GDTR)—In the 80386, this register holds the 32-bit linear base address and the 16-bit limit of the Global Descriptor Table.

graphics—Pictorial display of data.

handshaking—A colloquial term that describes a method of data transfer among asynchronous devices.

hang-up—The inability of a flip-flop to be triggered from a pulse command.

hard-wired logic—Logic design that uses a number of nonprogrammable chips as the logic elements.

hertz (Hz)—Cycles per second.

IC—See *integrated circuit.*

IDT—See *interrupt descriptor table.*

immediate operand—A constant contained in an instruction and used as an operand.

index register—One of the 16-bit registers: SI or DI. Generally, an index register holds an offset into the current data or extra segment.

indirect addressing—Accessing a memory location by first fetching the desired address from some other memory location or register.

initialization—The step that sets certain counters and clears certain registers in preparation for a following task.

instruction—A single step in a program, a single line of code.

instruction pointer (IP)—A register containing the offset of the instruction currently being executed. A selector for the segment containing this instruction is stored in the CS register. In the 80386, the instruction pointer (EIP) is a 32-bit register that contains the offset address of the next sequential instruction to be executed. The low-order 16 bits of EIP are the IP.

instruction register—A register in the microprocessor that stores the current instruction being executed.

instruction set—The set of all machine-language instructions which can be executed by a processor.

integer—A signed binary numeric value contained, in the 80386, in a 32-bit doubleword, a 16-bit word, or an 8-bit byte. The sign bit is located in bit 31 of the doubleword, in byte 15 of the word, and in bit 7 of the byte.

integrated circuit (IC)—A complex electronic circuit that is fabricated on a single piece of semiconductor material.

interface—A common boundary between two systems, across which information is exchanged.

interleaving—A technique for improving the performance of computer memories. Successive memory locations are assigned to different banks, cycling through the available banks. Then the concurrency offered by multiple banks is fully exploited when accessing memory locations in sequence.

interrupt—To suspend execution of the current program on a processor in order to service one or more peripheral devices. Also, a forced call, not appearing explicitly in a program which is triggered by an exception, by a signal from a device external to the processor, or by a special interrupt instruction.

interrupt controller—A component which prioritizes multiple interrupt requests.

interrupt descriptor table (IDT)—A table in memory which is indexed by interrupt number and which contains gates to the corresponding interrupt handlers.

interrupt descriptor table register (IDTR)—This register points to a table of entry points for interrupt handlers. In the 80386, the register holds the 32-bit linear base address and the 16-bit limit of the Interrupt Descriptor Table.

interrupt distributor—An interrupt handler provided by the operating system which transfers to a different user-supplied interrupt handler, depending on which task is interrupted.

interrupt handler—A procedure or task which is called in response to an interrupt.

interrupt latency—That elapsed time before an interrupt request is serviced.

interrupt procedure—A procedure that is called in response to an interrupt.

interrupt task—A task that is activated in response to an interrupt.

interval timer—A component that interrupts the processor after a period of time elapses. Software can set the time period and specify whether the timer should interrupt repetitively or stop after the first instance.

I/O permissions bit map—The mechanism that allows the 80386 to selectively trap references to specific I/O addresses. The Permissions Bit Map resides in the Task State Segment (TSS). The map is a bit vector and its size and location in the TSS are variable. The 80386 locates the map by means of the I/O Map Base field in the fixed portion of the TSS.

IP—See *instruction pointer*.

jump—An instruction that causes a transfer of control from one part of the program to another.

labels—Identifying statements or numbers used to describe flip-flop or logic-gate positions.

large-scale integration (LSI)—A technique for fabricating a large number of integrated electronic circuits on a small piece of semiconductor.

last-in-first-out (LIFO)—A method by which the last item placed in a stack or unit is the first one to be processed.

latch—A component that memorizes its current input on command. Also, a feedback loop in a symmetrical digital circuit, such as a flip-flop, for retaining a state.

LDT—See *local descriptor table*.

LIFO—See *last-in-first-out*.

linear address space—Address space that runs from 0 bytes to the maximum physical address that a processor can address. In the case of the 80386, the linear address space runs up to 4 gigabytes.

local address space—The collection of segments accessible through a task's LDT.

local descriptor table (LDT)—A table in memory containing descriptors for segments which are private to a task.

local descriptor table register (LDTR)—This register holds the 16-bit selector for the Local Descriptor Table.

lock—In a multiple processor system, this is a signal from one processor which prevents the others from accessing memory. The processor has exclusive use of the memory until it stops sending the signal.

logic diagrams—Drawings that show how flip-flops and gates must be connected to perform specific computer functions.

logic gates—An electronic circuit that performs a logic operation, such as OR.

logic levels—One of two possible: 0 or 1.

logical address—A logical address, in the 80386, consists of a selector and offset. The selector points to some segment's descriptor, which includes a segment's linear base address. The offset tells how far into the segment the required byte is.

looping—Executing a fixed set of instructions over and over.

LSI—See *large-scale integration*.

machine language—A format for coding instructions as binary codes that can be directly interpreted by a processor.

machine status word (MSW)—A register that contains a bit for controlling the mode (real versus virtual) and bits which control the processor's execution of WAIT and ESC instructions.

mask bit—A bit used to cover up or disable some condition.

masked exception—An exception which produces an exception value rather than an interrupt.

masking—A means of examining only certain bits in a word. This is usually done by ANDing the word with a mask containing 1's in the desired bit locations.

memory—A medium for storing programs and data.

memory management—The facilities for mapping the address space of a task into the available memory.

memory-mapped input/output—A technique whereby a peripheral device masquerades as a memory location.

memory unit—The part of a computer that stores information such as instructions and operands.

memory passing—A technique for inter-task communication in which data is transmitted from one task to another.

metal oxide semiconductor (MOS)—A technique for manufacturing field-effect transistors in which the flow of charge inside a semiconductor material is controlled by means of the electrical potentials of metal electrodes attached to the surface.

microprocessor—Central Processing Units (CPUs) built into chips by means of VLSI technology.

microprogram—A sequence of micro-instructions that can be directly related to the very basic operations of a processor.

mnemonic—A symbolic name, particularly used for opcodes.

MOS—See *metal oxide semiconductor*.

MSW—See *machine status word*.

multiplexing—Distributing and sharing a common resource among several users.

multitasking—The creation and use of multiple tasks on a computer.

NAND—Logic function that produces the inverted AND (*not*-AND) function.

n-channel MOS (NMOS)—The same as MOS, except that the majority of carriers in the semiconductor material are negatively charged.

near pointer—In the 80386 a 32-bit logical address. A near pointer is an offset within a segment.

negative edge gating—A circuit response as the control signal goes from high to low.

NMI—See *nonmaskable interrupt*.

NMOS—See *n-channel MOS*.

nonmaskable interrupt (NMI)—A signal to the processor from an external device indicating that a problem has arisen or is imminent.

NOR—The logical negation of the OR function.

NOR gate—An electronic circuit that forms a logic gate and whose output is a 1 only when all inputs are 0.

NOT—A Boolean logic operation that denotes negation.

Not-a-Number (NaN)—An exception value produced by the numeric processor in response to a masked invalid operation exception.

not present—In a virtual-memory, this describes a segment which is on disk but not in main memory.

null selector—A selector in which all bits are zero (0).

object program—The numeric, machine language output of an assembler.

offset—A quantity specifying the position of a byte within a segment.

opcode—The part of an instruction that specifies the operation to be performed, as opposed to the items upon which the operation is performed.

operand—Data operated on arithmetically or logically by a processor.

OR—A logic operation that produces a 1 at the output if at least one input is a 1.

ordinal—An unsigned binary numeric value contained in a byte, a 16-bit word, or a 32-bit doubleword.

p-channel MOS (PMOS)—Same as MOS except that the majority of the carriers in the semiconductor material are positively charged.

packed BCD—A packed byte representation of two decimal digits, each in the range of 0 through 9. One digit is stored in each half-byte. The digit in the high-order half-byte is the most significant.

page—A set of consecutive bytes. Pages begin on 4K byte boundaries. Paging divides programs into multiple uniform sized pages which have no direct relationship to the logical structure of a program.

page fault—In the 80386, if the processor finds one of the two following conditions, it issues an Interrupt 14: (1) if the current procedure does not have enough privilege to access the indicated page; or (2) if the page-table entry or page-directory that is needed for the address translation has a zero in its present bit. That is, the page is not currently loaded from auxiliary storage.

page frame—A 4K byte unit of contiguous addresses of a physical memory. The page frame address specifies the physical starting address of a page; the low-order 12 bits are always zero.

page table—An array of 32-bit page specifiers. The table itself is a page and contains 4 kilobytes of memory, or up to 1K 32-bit entries.

parallel—A technique for processing binary data in which all bits are acted upon simultaneously.

parameter—An item transmitted to a procedure by its caller.

parity—An indication of whether a number of 1's in a number is even or odd.

passive elements—Elements without gain, such as resistors, inductors, or capacitors.

peripheral device—An electronic device connected to the processor. Peripheral devices communicate to the processor by means of input and output instructions, interrupts, or memory-mapped input/output.

physical address—A number transmitted to the memory hardware in order to specify the location of a memory access.

PICU—See *priority interrupt control unit.*

PIO—See *programmable parallel input/output.*

PMOS—See *p-channel MOS.*

physical address—The mechanism which actually selects the memory where a required byte is located. Physical address differs from linear address only when paging is in effect.

pointer—An address which is used by software and consists of a selector and offset. In real mode, pointers are real addresses; in virtual mode, they are virtual addresses.

pointer register—One of the BP or BX registers. Generally, a pointer register holds an offset into the current stack segment.

polling—A technique for identifying the source of an interrupt signal, by periodically interrogating each external device.

port—A chip through which peripheral devices are connected to a microprocessor.

position-independent code—Code that will execute properly regardless of whether it is placed in memory.

positive-edge gating—A circuit that responds as control signals go from low to high.

positive logic—Logic operations in which the more positive voltage represents the 1 state.

precharge—A period of dormancy required between accesses to a dynamic random access memory (DRAM) chip.

prefix—A byte preceding the opcode of an instruction. It specifies that the instruction should be repeated or locked or that an alternate segment should be used.

priority—Refers to a precedence relationship applied to simultaneous occurrences.

priority interrupt control unit (PICU)—A device that arbitrates the priority of simultaneous interrupt requests.

privilege level—A number in a predetermined range which indicates the degree of protection or degree of privilege.

procedure—A portion of a program performing a particular function which may be used at several points in the program.

process—See *task*.

processor cycle—A unit for measuring instruction execution time.

program counter—A register in a processor that stores the address of the next instruction to be executed.

program locality—The principle that explains that programs tend to access memory near the most previous access. It is program locality that enables a cache memory to be as effective as it is.

program status word (PSW)—A special register used to keep track of the address of the next instruction to be executed, also often other status flags are stored in the PSW.

programmable array logic (PAL)—PALs are integrated circuits that can be programmed to perform specific logic functions. A PAL device consists logically of a programmable AND array whose output terms feed a fixed OR array.

programmable parallel input/output (PIO)—Interface circuitry.

programmable read-only memory (PROM)—A read-only memory whose contents are generally set just after fabrication and then not changed.

protected virtual address mode—A mode of operation in which the processor offers multitasking, advanced protection facilities, and virtual memory.

RAM—See *random access memory*.

random access memory (RAM)—Read/write memory.

read-only memory (ROM)—Memory in which information is stored during or immediately after fabrication and not changed later.

ready list—A list of tasks waiting to use the processor.

real address—An address consisting of selector and offset in real address mode.

real address mode—A mode of operation in which the processor closely mimics the behavior of a ''lower level'' chip in the chip family. For example, an 80386 mimic of an 8086.

real time operation—An operation in which a processor, interacting with an external process, executes its program concurrently with the evolution of the external process.

re-entrant code—Code which allows the program to be interrupted during execution.

refresh—The process of reading and then writing back a cell of a dynamic random access memory (DRAM).

register—Fast, temporary-storage locations, usually in the processor itself.

ROM—See *read-only memory*.

rendezvous—A method for synchronizing two tasks. The first to reach the synchronization point waits for the other.

requested privilege level (RPL)—A field in a selector which indicates the degree of ''trust'' or privilege a program has in the selector. RPL is determined by the least two significant bits of a selector.

reset—A signal which causes computer hardware to reinitialize itself, a part of system initialization.

restartable—An instruction is restartable after suffering a partial exception if, after removing the cause of the exception, the program may be correctly continued by re-executing the instruction.

rise time—The time required for the leading edge of a waveform to proceed from 10 percent to 90 percent of maximum amplitude points.

RPL—See *requested privilege level.*

scatter read—Reading a block of data into noncontiguous locations in memory.

segment—A region of memory, in a range of 1 byte to the maximum that can be handled by the processor. Also units of contiguous address space.

segment descriptor table—A memory array of 8-byte entries that contain descriptors. An 80386 descriptor table may contain up to 8192 descriptors.

segment register—One of the registers: CS, DS, ES or SS.

segmented memory organization—An address space that consists of up to 16,383 linear address spaces up to 4 gigabytes each. The total space, as viewed by a program in the 80386, can be as large as up to 2^{46} bytes (64 terabytes).

selector—A quantity that specifies a segment.

semaphore—A variable shared between tasks or processors and used for synchronization. A zero means proceed and a non-zero means wait.

serial data—The data that are available as a series of bits occurring one after the other in a single file.

shadow register—A hidden register associated with a visible register. A shadow register holds the descriptor corresponding to the selector in the associated visible register.

shift—The process of moving data from one place to another.

shutdown—The quiescent state from which the processor may be awakened by a reset or nonmaskable interrupt.

signature—The particular reference signal of a given circuit.

simulator—A program that simulates a processor on a different computer or processor.

single stepping—Executing a program one instruction at a time and pausing after each instruction. This is generally a means by which programmers determine the effect of a line of code.

software—A comprehensive set of computer programs and associated documentation.

SRAM—See *static random access memory.*

stack—A buffer whose information is generally accessed in a LIFO manner. See also *LIFO.*

stack frame—Storage for the values of a procedure's local variables. This corresponds to a particular invocation of the procedure.

stack pointer—A register that stores the memory address of the top (last-in) element of a stack in memory.

state—The condition of an input or output of a circuit concerning whether it is a logical 1 or logical 0.

static random access memory (SRAM)—Random access memory in which data is retained indefinitely except if the power is turned off.

string—A contiguous sequence of bytes, words, or double words. A string may contain from zero bytes through $2^{32} - 1$ bytes (or 4 gigabytes in the 80386).

strobe—A signal to a latch to memorize its current input. The output of the latch will be the memorized value, even if the input changes until another strobe signal occurs.

swapping—Moving a segment from disk to memory (swapping in) or from memory to disk (swapping out).

synchronous—Operation of a switching network by a clock- pulse generator. All circuits in the network switch simultaneously. All actions take place synchronously with the clock.

system clock—The fundamental time signal in a system.

system initialization—A series of operations performed by a combination of software and hardware when power is first applied to a computer system, or if the reset switch is used.

task—A defined function that is unique within the computer. Tasks are also referred to as processes.

task dispatching—Selecting a task and running it.

task force—A group of related tasks which share the same Logical Descriptor Table (LDT).

task register—(TR) This register points to the information needed by the processor to define the current task.

task state segment—(TSS) A segment which holds the contents of a task's registers when the processor is executing another task.

task switch—Changing from one task to another.

test card—A troubleshooting aid for comprehensive check-out of all input/output functions.

test registers—Registers TR6 and TR7 are used to control testing of the CAM (content addressable memory) in the Translation Lookaside Buffer.

time-slicing—A technique that allows several tasks to share a computer. The computer switches from one task to another, never staying with a single task for longer than a very small, fixed time.

toggle—To change a binary storage element to its opposite value.

translation lookaside buffer (TLB)—The TLB is a cache used for translating linear addresses to physical addresses. The TLB is a four-way, set-associative memory. The TLB testing mechanism is unique to the 80386, and may not be implemented in the same way in future Intel processors.

transfer of control—The condition brought about when instructions are executed in sequence starting at some new location instead of executing the instruction stored after the current instruction in memory.

trigger—A timing pulse used to initiate the transmission of logic signals through the appropriate signal paths. Also, the input pin on a flip-flop.

true—A true condition is the statement for a logic 1 in Boolean algebra.

TSS—See *task state segment*.

unload—To remove information in massive quantities.

universal synchronous/asynchronous receiver transmitter (USART)—A mechanism used by a processor to communicate with a device that uses a serial data format.

vectored interrupt—A technique of interrupt processing in which each interrupt specifies the address of the first instruction of its service routine.

virtual address—An address consisting of selector and offset in protected virtual address mode.

virtual memory—A technique for running programs which are larger than the available physical memory. Pieces of the program area stored on disk and are moved into memory only as necessary. This movement is automatically performed by the operating system and is invisible to the program.

virtual mode—See *protected virtual address mode.*

very large-scale integration (VLSI)—An abbreviation for a chip which contains more than 1,000 gates.

wait state—An extra processor cycle added to the bus cycle in order to allow for slower devices on the bus to respond.

word—A machine-dependent unit of storage that is generally the width of the data bus or internal registers.

Bibliography

Ashborn, Jim, "Intel Microprocessors: A Tradition of Innovation," *Solutions,* page 8-9, November/December 1985.

——-, "MULTIBUS® II Adds Punch to 80386-Based Designs," *Solutions,* page 10, November/December 1985.

Augarten, Stan, *Bit by Bit,* Ticknor & Fields, New York, NY, 1984.

——-, *State of The Art,* Ticknor & Fields, New York, NY, 1983.

Carr, Joseph J., *Microprocessor Interfacing,* TAB Books Inc., Blue Ridge Summit, PA, 1982.

Chorafas, Dimitris N., *Microprocessors For Management,* Petrocelli Books, New York, NY, 1984.

Ciarcia, Steve, *Ciarcia's Circuit Cellar,* McGraw-Hill Book Company, New York, NY, 1984.

Cluley, J.C., *Computer Interfacing and On-Line Operation,* Crane Russak, New York, NY, 1975.

Coli, Vincent J., "Introduction to Programmable Array Logic," *Byte,* page 207-219, January 1987.

Crosswy, Caldwell and Mike Perez, "Upward to the 80386," *PC Tech Journal,* page 51-66, February 1987.

Fawcette, James E., "80386: The Megabyte Manager," *PC World,* page 238-243, February 1986.

Frederiksen, Thomas M., *Intuitive IC CMOS Evolution,* National Semiconductor Corporation, Sunnyvale, CA, 1984.

Freedman, Robert A., "Getting Started with PALs," *Byte,* page 223-230, January 1987.

Glorioso, Robert M. and Fernando C. Colon Osorio, *Engineering Intelligent Systems,* Digital Press, Bedford, MA, 1980.

Graham, Neill, *Introduction to Computer Science,* West Publishing Co., New York, NY, 1979.

Hayes, Norman M. "Chip Set Geared To Unix Simplifies High- End Designs," *Computer Design,* page 65-72, January 1, 1986.

Hindin, Harvey J., "32-bit Parts and Architectures Vie for Attention," *Computer Design,* page 49-61, January 1, 1986.

Intel Corporation, *Microprocessor and Peripherals Handbook,* Intel Corporation, 1983.

Intel Corporation, *80386 Hardware Reference Manual,* Intel Corporation, 1986.

Intel Corporation, *80386 Programmer's Reference Manual,* Intel Corporation, 1986.

Lau, Edwin J., *Performance Improvement of Virtual Memory Systems,* UMI Research Press, Ann Arbor, MI, 1982.

Lewis, Peter H., "32-bit Chip: Powerhouse in the Wings," *New York Times,* August 29, 1985.

Markhoff, Nicolas, "Complete Systems Now Possible with 32- bit Chip Sets," *Computer Designs,* page 77-89, July 1, 1985.

McGrievy, D.J. and K.A. Pickar, *VLSI Technologies Through the 80s and Beyond,* IEEE Computer Society Press, Silver City, MD, 1982.

Mead, C. and L. Conway, *Introduction to VLSI Systems,* Addison-Wesley, Reading, MA, 1980.

Middleton, Robert G., *New Handbook of Troubleshooting Techniques,* Prentice-Hall, Englewood Cliffs, NJ, 1984.

Monds, Fabian, *The Business of Electronic Product Development,* Peter Peregrinus Ltd. on behalf of the Institution of Electrical Engineers, London, UK, 1984.

Phillips, David, "Mainframe Tricks Raise Performance of 32-bit Micros," *Computer Designs,* page 95-103, July 1, 1985.

Pooch, Udo W. and Rahul Chattergy, *Designing Microcomputer Systems,* Hayden Book Company, Rochelle Park, NJ, 1979.

Rafiquzzaman, Mohamed, *Microprocessors and Microcomputer Development Systems,* Harper and Row, New York, NY, 1984.

Rant, Jon, "Extending the Legacy of Leadership: The 80386 Arrives," *Solutions,* page 2-7, November/December 1985.

Shires, Glen, "80386 Cache Design," *Solutions,* page 12-27, November/December 1985.

Short, Kenneth L., *Microprocessors and Programmed Logic,* Prentice Hall, Englewood Cliffs, NJ, 1981.

Theaker, Colin J. and Graham R. Brookes, *A Practical Course on Operating Systems,* Springer-Verlag, New York, NY, 1983.

Thomplait, Cliff, "Memory Management Boosts Efficiency of Powerful Micros," *Computer Design,* page 105-109, July 1, 1985.

Thompson, Roger and Anil Uberoi, "Processor Offers Code Compatibility, VAX-Like Architecture," *Computer Design,* page 76-80, January 1, 1986.

Tseng, Vincent, Ed., *Microprocessor Development and Development Systems,* McGraw-Hill Book Company, New York, NY, 1982.

Zaks, Rodnay, *From Chips To Systems,* Sybex, Berkeley, CA, 1981.

Index

80386—A Programming and Design Handbook

If you are intrigued with the possibilities of the programs included in *80386—A Programming and Design Handbook* (TAB Book No. 2937), you should definitely consider having the disk containing the software applications. This software is guaranteed free of manufacturer's defects. (If you have any problems, return the disk within 30 days, and we'll send you a new one.) Not only will you save the time and effort of typing the programs, the disk eliminates the possibility of errors that can prevent the programs from functioning. Interested?

Available on disk for systems having an 80386 CPU. (Also requires the Microsoft MACRO ASSEMBLER version 4.0) at $24.95 for each disk plus $1.00 each shipping and handling.